Dynamic Dreamweaver MX

Rachel Andrew

Omar Elbaga

Alan Foley

Bob Regan

Rob Turnbull

Published by glasshaus Ltd,
Arden House,
1102 Warwick Road,
Acocks Green,
Birmingham,
B27 6BH, UK

Printed in the United States
ISBN 1-904151-10-8

Dynamic Dreamweaver MX

glasshaus

web professional to web professional

© 2002 glasshaus

Trademark Acknowledgements

glasshaus has endeavored to provide trademark information about all the companies and products mentioned in this book by the appropriate use of capitals. However, glasshaus cannot guarantee the accuracy of this information.

Credits

Authors
Rachel Andrew
Omar Elbaga
Alan Foley
Bob Regan
Rob Turnbull

Technical Reviewers
Kapil Apshankar
Dave Gibbons
Nancy Gill
Allan Kent
Martina Kosloff
Aaron Richmond
Murray Summers

Proof Reader
Agnes Wiggers

Indexer
Adrian Axinte

Commissioning Editor
Simon Mackie

Lead Technical Editor
Chris Mills

Technical Editors
Alessandro Ansa
Matt Machell
Simon Mackie
Dan Walker

Managing Editor
Liz Toy

Project Manager
Sophie Edwards

Production Coordinator
Rachel Taylor
Pip Wonson

Cover
Dawn Chellingworth

The cover image for this book was created by Don Synstelien of http://www.synfonts.com, co-author of the glasshaus book, "Usability: The Site Speaks For Itself". You can find more of Don's illustration work online at http://www.synstelien.com.

About the Authors

Rachel Andrew

Rachel Andrew runs her own web solutions company in the UK, *edgeofmyseat.com*, the company web site also being home to various "web standards"-focused articles and Dreamweaver extensions. Rachel is a member of the Web Standards Project on the Dreamweaver Task Force, and hopes to encourage best practices in the support and use of W3C Standards in Dreamweaver.

When not writing code, or writing about writing code, Rachel spends time with her daughter, tries to encourage people to use Debian GNU/Linux, studies with the Open University, and enjoys a nice pint of beer.

Thanks must go to everyone at glasshaus for making the process of working on this book enjoyable; to Drew McLellan for his constant love and support; and to my daughter Bethany, who thinks that all mummies are permanently attached to a computer. Thank you.

Omar Elbaga

Starting out as a fine artist, Omar Elbaga (on the right!) gradually moved to computer graphic arts. He was particularly amazed by the power of the World Wide Web, so he embarked upon building small-scale sites for fun utilizing HTML and his art background. Falling in love with designing web pages and its potential, he began a career in web design. Omar has since been in the web development field for several years. With his head in computer books nearly 24 hours a day, Omar moved on to enhance his skills from web design to web programming.

Most of his work involves building database-driven web sites for small companies. Omar is currently a Tutorial Manager for udzone.com and runs a popular Dreamweaver MX resource site named *udnewbie.com*.

Having had the opportunity to study the Arabic language abroad for several months in an intensive course at the Fajr Center in Cairo, Omar is also a translator who translates mostly 12th century scholarly Arabic manuscripts into English. Omar is currently a senior at New Jersey City University completing a double major in English Literature and Secondary Education.

Alan Foley

Alan Foley is an assistant professor of Instructional Technology at North Carolina State University in Raleigh, North Carolina, where he teaches graduate classes in the College of Education. Alan holds a Ph.D. in Educational Technology from the University of Wisconsin – Madison. His current research interests include web accessibility and pedagogy, and accessible multimedia production.

Prior to completing his Ph.D., Alan was a high school English teacher. While teaching he was introduced to the world of instructional technology and web design. He has taught web design in a variety of educational and corporate settings and consults schools and universities on accessibility and usability issues.

Bob Regan

Bob Regan is the product manager for accessibility at Macromedia. In that role, he works with designers, developers, and engineers from around the world to communicate existing strategies for accessibility as well as develop new strategies. He works with engineers and designers within Macromedia to develop new techniques and improve the accessibility of Macromedia tools.

Bob has a Masters degree from Columbia University in Education. He is currently a doctoral student in Education at the University of Wisconsin – Madison. His dissertation research looks at accessibility policy implementation strategies.

Bob spent six years as a teacher and technology leader in Chicago and New York City. Working with teachers and students across a range of ages and subject matter, he has extensive knowledge of elementary and secondary education. Bob spent two years teaching web design and accessibility at the University of Wisconsin – Madison.

Rob Turnbull

Rob Turnbull is the senior developer for Lighthouse; an established new media Design Company based in Shrewsbury, UK. Clients across Europe from small businesses to blue chip companies provide an increasing workload, which includes the development of databases, web sites, multimedia presentations, interactive CD-ROMs, promotional videos and 3D artwork in both animated and still form.

His personal web site, *www.robgt.com*, is primarily focused on offering help and guidance to fellow Dreamweaver and UltraDev users including tutorials and links to helpful resources and some useful extensions.

My thanks go to the invisible team working just as hard behind the scenes that actually get a book like this published; you guys have been great to work with. Perhaps more importantly, my thanks, my gratitude, and my respect go to Sarah. Your care and support have been fantastic and I look forward to seeing you in the daylight hours again!

Table of Contents

Table of Contents

Table of Contents

Table of Contents

Introduction

The first version of Dreamweaver was released in 1997. It rapidly grew to be the most popular web site development tool around; with a reported 2 million users by January 2002 Dreamweaver 4 was released in 2000, and received critical acclaim.

However, Dreamweaver 4 was felt to be lacking in some areas – for example, it didn't have any native facility for generating dynamic web pages with server-side scripting languages (such as ASP) – this was provided via another package called UltraDev.

The end of May 2002 saw the release of the fantastic new version of Dreamweaver – Dreamweaver MX, which seems to have solved a lot of the problems associated with its predecessors, and provided us with some excellent new features to make web site development easier than ever before!

In this book, we will be concentrating on getting you up to speed with the new advanced features of Dreamweaver MX:

- Creating truly standards-compliant, usable web pages using XHTML and CSS

- Accessibility features that not only allow easy development of sites that are accessible to people with disabilities, but also allow people with disabilities to use Dreamweaver MX

- Moving over to the server-side – whereas previous versions of Dreamweaver only allowed creation of static sites, Dreamweaver MX allows you to easily create dynamic web sites using your choice of server-side language (**ASP**, **ASP.NET**, **JSP**, **Cold Fusion**, or **PHP**), via Server Behaviors – ready-written functions that you can just plug in to your site.

Who's This Book For?

This book is primarily for anyone who wants to learn how use the new advanced features of Dreamweaver MX – we won't be covering usage of all the basic Dreamweaver interfaces, as even though the interfaces have changed, the premise of how they are used has remained constant. Working knowledge of any of the previous versions of Dreamweaver (or another WYSIWYG tool) should be sufficient, in conjunction with the product manual.

This book assumes some knowledge of HTML and web development concepts.

What Do I Need to Begin?

To use this book you need a PC with the following installed:

- Windows 95/98, NT, 2000, or XP

- Dreamweaver MX

- A web browser or two, to test your web pages on

- A web server to serve your web sites (see *Chapter 5* for installation of web servers)

Style Conventions

We've used a number of styles in the book to help you understand what's going on.

We've used the **important words** style to flag up new or important subjects.

Screen Text is used to indicate anything you'd see on the screen, including URLs.

New blocks of code are in this code foreground style:

```
<html>
<body>
<script language="JavaScript">

  var myCalc = 1 + 2;
  document.write("The calculated number is " + myCalc);

</script>
</body>
</html>
```

If we're amending a script, perhaps adding in a new line or making changes to an existing one, then we use the code background style for the code that you've already seen together with the foreground style to highlight the new code:

```
<html>
<body>
<script language="JavaScript">

   var userEnteredNumber = prompt("Please enter a number","");
   var myCalc = 1 + userEnteredNumber;
   var myResponse = "The number you entered + 1 = " + myCalc;
   document.write( myResponse);

</script>
</body>
</html>
```

To talk about code within text we use this `code in text` style, which is also used for filenames like `myFirstJavaScript.htm`.

```
Essential not–to–be–missed information is in boxes like this.
```

Asides to the current discussion are presented like this.

A Note About Code Formatting

We've tried to make the code as easy to read as possible. This does mean that there is sometimes whitespace in the scripts that would break the code if you used it exactly as it is printed. For example, this JavaScript code:

```
output+="<a href=\""+getPageName(pages[i][j])+".html\" class=\"page\"
title=\""+pages[i][j]+"\">";
```

will look like this in the book:

```
output+="<a href=\""+getPageName(pages[i][j])+".html\" class=\"page\"
            title=\""+pages[i][j]+"\">";
```

The code in the download is without the whitespace.

Support/Feedback

Although we aim for perfection, the sad fact of book publication is that a few errors will slip through. We would like to apologize for any errors that have reached this book despite our efforts. If you spot such an error, please let us know about it using the e-mail address `support@glasshaus.com`. If it's something that will help other readers, then we'll put it up on the errata page at *http://www.glasshaus.com*.

This address can also be used to access our support network. If you have trouble running any of the code in this book, or have a related question that you feel that the book didn't answer, please mail your problem to the above address quoting the title of the book, the last 4 digits of its ISBN, and the chapter and page number of your query.

Web Support

Feel free to go and visit our web site, at *http://www.glasshaus.com*. It features:

- **Code Downloads**: The example code for this, and every other glasshaus book, can be downloaded from our site.

- **On-line Resource Center**: We will be building up a definitive reference on the Web, containing all the up-to-date reference material that you'll need. We've decided to put this reference material on the Web rather than weighing down our books with hefty appendices. It will be added to over time, so if there is anything you feel isn't up there but should be, please let us know.

1

- Overview of Dreamweaver MX

- The Dreamweaver MX interface

- Templates

- Library items

Author: Rob Turnbull

Introducing Dreamweaver MX

First released in 1997, Dreamweaver has become the industry standard web site production tool over the course of the last five years. A quick point release upgrade shortly after the initial release saw it gain momentum in the web development arena, and each year that followed brought a new full release with it. The release of Dreamweaver MX brings Dreamweaver right up-to-date after a longer break from the upgrade cycle.

There are several factors that make it such a great piece of software:

- A relatively shallow learning curve when coming from previous releases or competitive products

- Ease of use for visual designers through templates, library items, and tight integration with the whole family of Macromedia MX products for example Flash, Fireworks, and Freehand

- Ease of use for coders through added features in the code environment such as code hints, tag completion, and the integrated JavaScript debugger

- Extensible architecture

- Lots of available extensions (and extension developers), that add extra functionality to the base product, such as extended form validations, and XML feed integration

- Friendly and intuitive interface

- Increased page production speeds over traditional hand coding methods

It brings with it a huge array of very powerful tools that enable a novice user to create a dynamic web site with just a few clicks of the mouse.

Knowledge of HTML when creating a web site is an enormous benefit, especially as a project becomes more complex, but the fact still remains that Macromedia have created a product that allows anybody to create a professional web site in a very short amount of time with limited knowledge.

What Is Dreamweaver MX?

Dreamweaver 4 wasn't the only tool that Macromedia released in 2000 to compete in the web development arena; they also introduced us to **Dreamweaver UltraDev**, which was a merging of ideas from Drumbeat 2000 and Dreamweaver, that would prove to be a large step forward in the area of dynamic web site production – they took all the best ideas of Dreamweaver (by this time a well-established design tool for producing static web sites), and the data integration and server-side aspects of Drumbeat 2000 and meshed them together into one very neat dynamic web site production tool.

> *Drumbeat 2000 was a piece of software that Macromedia acquired in 1999. It was a visual design tool used for producing dynamic web sites, but it had its limitations in terms of scalability and it was also known to produce rather bulky code. Some elements of Drumbeat still haven't managed to make it to the shipping product of Dreamweaver MX, such as an integrated e-commerce system, although there are free and commercial extensions available to deal with these shortcomings. It was, however, a great starting point for Macromedia to begin building the new breed of web development software, which is exactly what they did.*

It stands to reason that over the course of time these two very closely related products, Dreamweaver and Dreamweaver UltraDev, would end up being merged into one product. Dreamweaver MX is that product.

The web development arena is a constantly evolving place and as such, the tools that we use need to evolve with it in order for us to remain competitive. With this in mind, Macromedia have released a new series of products under the MX banner, including Dreamweaver. They have upgraded ColdFusion to ColdFusion MX and included it in the package, along with an upgraded version of Homesite, called Homesite+.

This larger suite of MX-compatible products includes Flash, Fireworks, and Freehand, all designed with interoperability in mind. All MX products share a common workspace to enable easy switching from one program to another. As with previous versions, you can create files that can then be shared between the products – each product has the ability to launch the others for the editing of specific file types. The difference is in the seamlessness of the integration between the products.

> *For more information on any of these products, go to Macromedia's web site at http://www.macromedia.com.*

What Dreamweaver MX Can Do For You

Dreamweaver MX is an extremely capable tool that enables you to deliver your web site applications at a far greater speed than ever before. It comes with a large amount of pre-built content for you to utilize in your projects, such as snippets of code that can be as small as a single line of HTML or as large as an entire page, and that can be reused with a click of the mouse. Quick-start items include pre-built web designs, pre-built accessible web sites, sample site structures, sample CSS styles and sample JavaScript functions, to name a few.

Other features include:

- **Server Behaviors** that allow you to create dynamic applications that react to (or interact with) data to provide your users with content relevant to them, along with many other possibilities. **Application Objects** take this a step further by giving you a quick start in your development of form layout and data interaction – they create the tables and form elements on the page automatically and bind the database objects to them, often providing the functionality of multiple server behaviors at once.

- The ability to connect to third-party Web Services and utilize them in your own web applications. Alternatively, you can create your own web services using Dreamweaver MX.

- Validation of your web pages to ensure that the code you have produced will work as you intend it to in your target browsers. You can choose the level of compatibility you want to achieve with your web page and then validate it accordingly. A report shows you possible problems, enabling you to debug your pages quicker and easier than ever before.

- You can choose the standards that you want your pages to comply with and also the level of compliance you want to achieve in the code that Dreamweaver MX generates for you.

Templates have come a long way since their inception in Dreamweaver. It is now possible to create templates that comply with the logic you have defined to decide whether elements should be visible on the page or not. Logic, in this instance, includes the ability to define optional or repeating content, variable substitution, and evaluation of expressions. Although it may sound complex, it is a very powerful new feature that will greatly enhance the usage of templates in your everyday workflow.

For the ColdFusion developers among you, Dreamweaver MX makes development and use of ColdFusion Components, or CFCs, almost too easy. The inbuilt ability to introspect these components, along with Web Services, JavaBeans and COM objects, makes it very easy to link together your page elements with server logic.

The accessibility of your web pages is very important – accessibility standards are being adopted to ensure that people with disabilities are able to access the web pages that you build. You can set preferences in Dreamweaver MX to prompt you to add the relevant attributes for your page elements as you add them to your pages. The tools that create them are also targeted – Dreamweaver MX also contains options to allow people with disabilities to effectively use it to create web sites.

Static to Dynamic

Dreamweaver has always been a web production tool for producing static HTML pages. With the release of MX, everything went dynamic! Dynamic web site production is possibly the largest area of web development today and, as more and more web sites are hooked up to databases for their content, so the need grows for a tool to create this new breed of dynamic web application. Making the switch from static to dynamic web site production doesn't need to be a difficult experience; in fact, it can really be very easy thanks to Dreamweaver MX.

There are a growing number of server-side languages to choose from in the ever increasing and diversifying market of dynamic web site production. Fortunately, Dreamweaver MX is able to help you create your web pages in many of these languages, and because of its extensible architecture, if you have the knowledge to do so you could add even more to the list, which already includes:

- ASP/VBScript

- ASP/JavaScript

- VB.NET

- C#.NET

- JSP

- PHP

- ColdFusion

Dreamweaver MX is also clever enough to know which parts of the program you should be able to make use of depending upon which server-side language you are programming in. For example, if you are using ASP/ VBScript as your server-side language, then ColdFusion Components will not be available to your project.

Server-Side Technology in Dreamweaver MX

The creation of dynamic data-driven web sites relies on the ability to connect to a data source and to extract the required data. Dreamweaver MX makes it incredibly easy to do this. With the use of its server-side technologies you can:

- Create connections to data sources, which are then reusable throughout your site

- Build recordsets to hold the data you want to use on your web pages

- Create database interactions such as inserts, updates, and deletes

- Make use of basic server-side data objects such as data submitted from a form, or session variables

Through the use of an intelligent interface that only lets you build the objects that are permitted for your chosen server-side language, you can quickly create dynamic web applications that utilize the strengths of your chosen development platform.

If you are developing in ColdFusion you can:

- Automatically set up a ColdFusion site

- Create, edit, introspect, and utilize ColdFusion components

- Use internal trace and debug utilities through the *Live Server Debugging* panel

- Browse database structures and transfer files to and from ColdFusion servers through RDS

If you are developing in ASP.NET you can:

- Create `DataSet`, `DataGrid` and `DataList` objects to enable complex data display and manipulation

- Develop web form tags to allow for advanced visualization and editing

- Import custom tags and view their structure attributes

For the JSP developer there is support for JavaBeans introspection enabling you to integrate them with JSP applications.

Along with those feature-specific items, there are commonly shared abilities for each of the server-side development languages, such as recordset creation and data manipulation.

Why You Need Dreamweaver MX

Web site creation used to be the domain of single developers or small teams. They would create a site specification, design the visuals, and then implement the site and its server-side logic.

Teamwork is key to the structure of Dreamweaver MX. Whether you approach web design from a visual design perspective, from a coding perspective, or perhaps even a mix of both, Dreamweaver MX offers many advantages that will empower you to do more in a shorter amount of time and more cost-efficiently than previously possible with a single tool.

With Dreamweaver MX, the design elements are in place to enable the easy visual creation of web pages and the code elements are in place to enable the coding teams to take a visual concept and make it a reality. It packs an impressive punch in terms of its capabilities but perhaps most importantly, it is a single piece of software that every member of a web development team can use to build the application.

Designing

The integrated workspace is a familiar environment in which to work and is the same across all Macromedia MX products, making the transition between Flash MX and Fireworks MX to Dreamweaver MX much easier, and in doing so enhancing productivity. The content and visuals that you create in these Macromedia products are easily brought into the Dreamweaver environment through tight integration.

There are many elements for designers to use to quickly visualize sites in Dreamweaver MX, including the quick start elements that can help you to lay out single pages or entire sites.

You can utilize the new template features to keep the visual style of a set of pages consistent, as they are developed through the creation of sophisticated rules, enabling you to manage and update page content without losing control of the design.

An integrated file explorer gives you quick and easy access to any files on your desktop, file system, or network, meaning that no matter what the location of the media you need to incorporate into your page, it can be utilized in your page as long as it is accessible on your network. Any media brought to the site from outside of your site structure will automatically be added to the default images location defined when you set up your site.

Coding

Dreamweaver MX affords you complete control over your code and offers greatly increased editing support through code hints and customizable syntax with coloring for tags, attributes, and more:

- You have an editable, customizable **Tag Library** into which you can add custom tags

- Tag editors enable you to edit the relevant attributes of specific tags in HTML, CFML, and ASP.NET

- Code libraries are available to help you visually create your web sites using the leading server-side technologies, including ASP, PHP, ASP.NET, ColdFusion, and JSP

- The database panel enables you to view the structure of your databases prior to building queries that will draw on their content

- You have instant access to a large quantity of code snippets that come with the product and are as easy as point-and-click to use. You can store your own code snippets for later reuse too

- You can validate documents in many markup languages, including HTML, XHTML, XML, WML, SMIL, and CFML. The creation and editing of documents utilizing these languages (and many more) is also catered for including support for Flash ActionScript coding

- You can see the page structure of XML, HTML, and ColdFusion documents in a collapsible tree-view with a listing of all the relevant attributes

In addition to all this, the integrated JavaScript debugger is a powerful feature that has many useful options. It allows you to find and fix errors in your JavaScript syntax or logic. You can set breakpoints to check on variable values as the script is running and step through code and execute statements line by line to ensure that the results you are after from your script are achieved. You can also watch and edit variable values, changing them as the script runs to see the effect different values have on your code.

ColdFusion Studio 5 and Homesite 5 have been merged into a new single product, Homesite+, which is included with Dreamweaver MX, so if you feel the need to switch from the extended capabilities of Dreamweaver MX's coding environment, the option is there.

Moving Around in Dreamweaver MX

There has been a lot of work put in to the Dreamweaver MX workspace by the engineers at Macromedia. If you're a Windows user, there are now two workspaces for you to choose from. Macintosh users only have access to the standard floating panels workspace.

The New MDI

The new **MDI**, or **Multiple Document Interface** brings everything together in a very intuitive way from a development standpoint, so no matter what you need, it is only a mouse-click away:

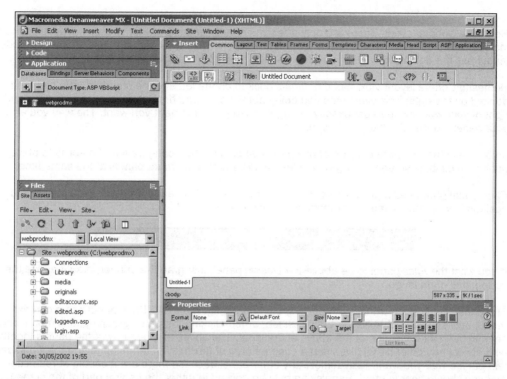

When you first launch Dreamweaver MX on the Windows platform, you are asked to select which workspace you would like to use (as seen below). You have the choice of the old floating panels workspace, or the new MDI workspace. You can change this selection in the *Preferences* panel later if you need to.

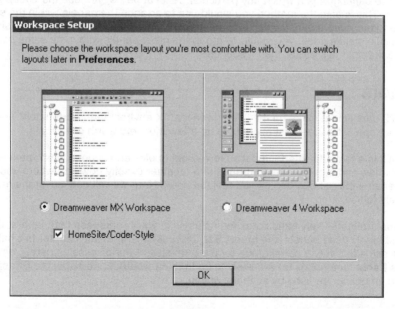

If you choose the new MDI layout, you then have the choice of using the standard layout or the Homesite/Coders layout. There are only a few minor differences between these two layouts, which includes the side on which your panel groups will be shown in the interface. Also, Homesite/Coders layout has the default view as Code View and the property inspector is collapsed.

Homesite/Coders layout view has the panels docked on the left and the standard view has them docked on the right. This won't stop you being able to drag and drop panel groups to the left and right of your workspace to get exactly the right working environment you want. The way you arrange your panel groups is entirely up to you.

If you are in the fortunate position of having a multiple monitor configuration, the ability to place panels on multiple screens can give you instant access to even more panels at the same time.

Each panel group has a gripper in its top left corner, which is used to drag and drop panels into position in your environment. The gripper is shown here:

If you want the *Files* panel to be above the *Design* panel, just grab the gripper, drag it above the code panel, then let go.

The panels that reside within each panel group are configurable too. Each panel has a context menu, accessed by right-clicking the panel tab, or left-clicking the panel group options menu icon, as seen in the right-hand side of the above screenshot. The ability to group any of the panels together with almost any other panel gives you a huge amount of flexibility in terms of getting the workspace laid out the way you want. I say almost any other panel because there are a couple of restrictions that you should bear in mind. Panels can only be docked in either the central part of the screen above or below the main document, or to the left or right of the main document window. For instance, the *Insert* bar can only be docked in the central part of the screen.

To change the panel group in which any particular panel appears, you use the *Group [panel] with* menu option. This is also the method you would use to arrange the panels within the same panel group. When you group a panel within a panel group it gets added to the right-hand side of that panel group. To shuffle it left, you would re-group the other panels within the same panel group to add them to the right. It's easier than it sounds!

The Panels

There are 22 panels that make up the Dreamweaver MX environment. Fortunately, you don't have to have them all open at once – that might take up a few monitors worth of space!

The new MDI is a fantastic interface because you get to pick and choose which panels are important to your work flow and then you get to group them together exactly how and where you want – you can even rename the panel groups if you feel the need! Here we will only cover the main panels that you are likely to use often.

Some panels are more likely candidates for inclusion in your workspace than others. Of the more obvious and highly used panels, the **Insert Bar**, discussed later in this chapter (it's called the *Insert* bar, but it's still effectively a panel group for the purposes of our discussion here!), and the **Properties Panel** (see opposite) are likely to be in there whereas, perhaps, the **Sitespring Panel**, for instance, might not be used by so many of you.

Hopefully, you will have started using CSS in your work rather than HTML font styles. That being the case, you will be able to close and forget about the HTML styles panel. If you haven't, then now is the time to start. In the previous screenshot you can see the little "s" icon between the Format drop-down list and the CSS styles list. This icon allows you to switch the text **Property Inspector** between the old font mode and the much better CSS mode. It is currently in CSS mode and so the icon is a "stylesheet S" but if you switch back to font mode, the icon becomes an A.

Chapter 3 is devoted entirely to CSS and will take you through what CSS is and how to use it along with Dreamweaver MX's many CSS capabilities. The CSS design panel is seen here:

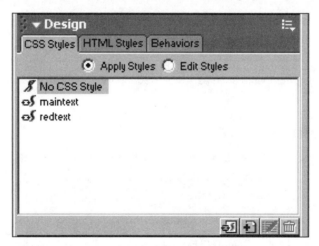

One of the easiest ways to hide unwanted panels is to create a new panel group, put all your unwanted panels in that group and then simply close it.

The Application Panel Group

For the development of dynamic web applications, the **Application Panel Group** (see overleaf) is very important. It contains a panel to show your data sources and their structure (*Databases*), the bindings that each page has made to that data source (*Bindings*) and the server-side logic you have applied to each page (*Server Behaviors*):

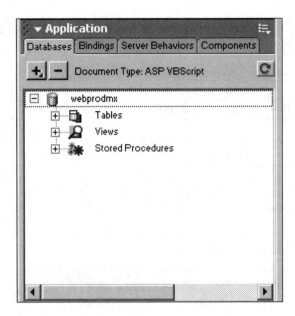

You also have the components panel grouped here but, if you code in a server-side language that doesn't make use of components such as ASP/VBScript, then you can close it to make room for something else.

The Code Panel Group

The **Code Panel Group** contains panels to help you with the coding side of your development:

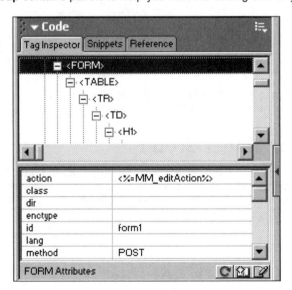

The **Tag Inspector Panel** displays the whole of your page as a collapsible tree structure of HTML tags. This greatly helps the debugging process in cases where your tags are incorrectly nested. Another use might be to select a tag in a page that contains, for example, deeply nested tables. The tag selector at the foot of the document displays tags from the start of the page to the point in which your cursor is placed and you might have too many tags for the tag selector to display them all (they would bleed off the right-hand side of the page) and so access would be found through the Tag Inspector.

The **Snippets Panel** comes filled with an abundance of useful content in ten categories and can make a good starting point to a page in some cases. Also included are highly functional and frequently requested snippets of JavaScript that you can add to your pages with a click of the mouse.

You can use and reuse elements from this panel wherever your need arises and, perhaps more importantly, you can create your own snippets for later reuse. If you write a piece of code that you think might be useful to you later, make a snippet out of it! Snippets may be new to most Dreamweaver users and possibly a lot of UltraDev users but users of Homesite will be very likely to recognize the *Snippets* panel and know its usefulness in a production environment.

The **Reference Panel** is the place to look if you need to quickly find the relevant information on any markup languages, JavaScript objects, and CSS styles and their attributes.

There are eight reference titles included with Dreamweaver MX – some coming directly from Macromedia and some coming from other renowned third party publishers, such as Wrox.

The titles include:

- Macromedia CFML Reference

- O'Reilly CSS Reference

- O'Reilly HTML Reference

- O'Reilly JavaScript Reference

- Sitespring Project Site Tag Reference

- UsableNet Accessibility Reference

- Wrox ASP 3.0 Reference

- Wrox JSP Reference

The *Reference* panel displays context-relevant information for the specific tags, objects, or styles that you are working with at the time you open the panel. For example, if you are in Code View of a page with a form on it and you need to know what METHODS are available to you for posting the form, or indeed, what posting METHODS are and what they do in relation to a form, then by selecting the word METHOD in Code View and pressing *Shift + F1* you will see the relevant information in the reference panel.

The Files Panel Group

Your site can now be viewed in the traditional separate full screen mode, or as a panel in your workspace environment (see below), giving you access to all your sites documents and constituent elements as you work on the pages.

This new panel has all the functionality of the full screen version with the added bonus of making the drag and drop features of Dreamweaver MX work even more to your advantage. You can browse your images folder (we've called it *media* above) to find an image and then just drag it onto the page, or onto the property inspector, or into Code View! It is a much more comfortable way of working when you have multiple files open at the same time.

Not only that, but it has an integrated file browser that enables you to gather content from anywhere on your local computer or network for incorporation into the site. Dreamweaver MX is also smart enough to put any media you find outside of the defined site into your default images folder, bringing that new content into an easily found place within your site. The link tracking features will also help you to keep your documents up-to-date, if you decide to move any item to a new location, be that a page or a piece of media.

You can use the site panel for all the standard file maintenance operations, including:

- Creating new documents

- Moving files or opening them with their native applications

- Creating, editing, and deleting items such as folders and files

- Transferring files between your local site, your remote site, and your testing server

The Tag Selector

The **Tag Selector** is located in the status bar at the bottom of the document window:

```
<body> <form#form1> <table.maintext> <tr> <td> <h1>                    587 x 456 ▾  17K / 5 sec
```

It displays a hierarchy of tags that starts from the opening <body> tag and finishes with the current selection in the Design View. In the above illustration, my cursor is currently in the middle of a heading located in a row of a table that has a CSS style called .maintext applied to it; that table is in a form called form1.

Left-clicking any of the tags listed will highlight the content of that tag, while right-clicking on the tags will pop up a context menu that enables you to edit the contents of the selected tag, remove the selected tag (and its contents), or set the ID or class (CSS style) of the selected tag.

There is another menu available from the status bar; the window size pop-up menu. You can use this to resize the current document window to any of the listed sizes. You can also add your own sizes to this list, should you need to. This design-time-only tool is useful for visualising your pages at different screen sizes but it does not affect your code in any way.

To the right of that menu are two figures that represent the estimated document size and the estimated download time based on your preferences. You select a modem speed to use in this calculation, by going to *Edit* > *Preferences* > *Status Bar* > *Connection Speed* (a drop-down list). The estimated document size is calculated by including all files that make up the document, including but not limited to images, JavaScript, and CSS. The download speeds are estimated on theoretical speeds rather than actual speeds, which can bias the result slightly. Bearing that in mind, it does give you a reasonable indication as to the time your page will take to load.

The Insert Bar

The **Insert Bar** is the old objects panel on steroids!

There are several tabs contained within the *Insert Bar*.

- Common

- Layout

- Text

- Tables

- Frames

- Forms

- Templates

- Characters

- Media

- Head

- Script

- Application

If you have used Dreamweaver before, then some of these names will be familiar to you and some have been renamed to make them more applicable to their content. However, there are some added extras within some of these familiar headings that you won't have seen before. Things like the *Image Placeholder* for adding a placeholder for an image to your page. You might use this for visual layout purposes until an actual piece of artwork is finished and ready to use or for attaching dynamic data to for creating data-driven images.

The extra tabs that you see may include some options that are only available to the server-side language you are using. There may even be extra tabs that only appear for your chosen server-side language and no others – for instance, the ASP tab will not appear on the *Insert* bar if you are developing ColdFusion applications, but you will see three extra tabs in the ColdFusion development environment that are not available to you when developing ASP pages.

The Document Toolbar

The **Document Toolbar** gives instant access to many development tools quickly and easily:

The three leftmost buttons on the toolbar allow you to switch between the three views: Code View, split view, and Design View. Now let's go through the remaining buttons in order, from left to right:

- The *Live Data View* button is a very powerful feature that allows you to view actual data from your database on the page you are creating, while you are creating it. You can make design changes (or code changes) to your page and see, in real time, what presentational effect they will have on the data being displayed.

- The *File Management* button is used for quick access to file actions such as `Get`, `Put`, and `Locate` in site.

- The *Preview/Debug in Browser* button allows you to launch one of the browsers listed for preview/debugging purposes. You can also edit the browser list from this menu.

- The *Refresh Design View* button is there for you to bring the Design View into line with any changes you may have made in Code View. Most of the changes you make will be reflected in Design View but for those times that they are not, this button does the trick.

- The *Reference* button will display the reference panel in a context sensitive manner. For instance, selecting an input field on your page and then clicking the *Reference* button will open up the reference panel to show the details for the `<input>` HTML tag.

- The *Code Navigation* button helps you to navigate through your JavaScript code. If you have many functions on the page you are working on and need to find a specific function quickly, selecting it in the drop down list from this button will locate it for you. You can also utilize the debugging features to help you find and fix errors in your code.

- The *View Options* button lets you decide how you want certain visual elements to be displayed – you can use any or all of the visual aids that Dreamweaver MX has to offer and you use this menu to specify which. If you work in split view, you also have the option of setting the Design View to be above or below the code window.

The Standard Toolbar

The **Standard Toolbar** is another useful addition that includes often-used file, clipboard and page based commands:

From left to right the first four buttons are: *New*, *Open*, *Save* and *Save-All*. Next we have the clipboard section with *Cut*, *Copy* and *Paste*. Finally, we have the page commands *Undo* and *Redo*. One that is missing is a *Save-As* button – this command can only be accessed from the file menu, or by right-clicking the document tab at the foot of every maximised document and selecting it from the menu that appears.

The quickest way to activate the *Standard* toolbar is to right-click on the *Document* toolbar, where a pop-up menu will display a tick next to the name of any visible toolbars – make sure the relevant selection is ticked.

The Results Panel Group

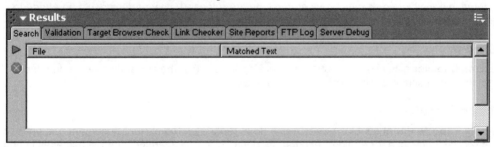

When you run a validation check or a report on your documents or your entire site, the details of these are output to the relevant panel of the **Results Panel Group**. When results are displayed in the display area, you can double-click a line of the report to go directly to that part of the specified document. If that document isn't open yet, it will be opened for you, usually in split view so you can see the exact part of the code referenced.

As the screenshot shows, there are seven panels in the panel group, which we'll discuss now.

Search Panel

The **Search Panel** will report every match from *Find* and *Replace* actions. The green "play" button just below the tab will launch the *Find* and *Replace* dialog only if you have a document open. You can also launch that dialog from the context menu (right-click) in Code View or the code portion of the split view. Just below the green "play" button is a stop button that is only active when a results panel task is running. These buttons, and more, are available on all except the *FTP log* panel and the *Server Debug* panel. Other buttons you might see in this area are a "*More info*" button, which is a white speech bubble with an "i" in it, a "*Save report*" button that uses a disk icon, and a "*Browse report*" button which uses a globe icon.

Validation Panel

The **Validation Panel** gives you quick access to the validation options in Dreamweaver MX. The green "play" button on this panel has a small black "down" arrow signifying a submenu is available to you. Clicking the Green "play" button displays a submenu that gives you the following 5 options.

- **Validate Current Document** – this will validate the document that currently has the focus

- **Validate Current Document as XML** – this will validate the document that currently has the focus as an XML document

- **Validate Entire Site** – this will validate the entire site

- **Validate Selected Files in Site** – this will validate all the currently selected files in the site window

- **Settings...** – This launches the Validator section of the preferences palette, allowing you to modify your validation settings as you choose

Target Browser Check Panel

The **Target Browser Check Panel** helps you to check for browser-specific issues with your pages before other people can find them for you. The default installation of Dreamweaver MX will check your documents against the browser profiles of Internet Explorer versions 2 to 6, Netscape Navigator versions 2 to 6, and Opera versions 2.1 to 6. These browser profiles are stored in text files and are, of course, extensible, so as new browser versions are released, new profiles could be added to enable you to validate your documents against them.

Link Checker

The **Link Checker** gives you the option of checking links within the currently open document or within the entire site and will report any broken ones.

Site Reports Panel

The **Site Reports Panel** enables you to run various reports on the current document, the entire site, selected files in the site, or a folder, and can help you to quickly identify common mistakes in your HTML files. Once the report has run, clicking the *More Info* button after selecting a row with a grey question mark icon in it will open up the reference panel and display the relevant usability reference material that corresponds with your report selection. Double-clicking a row will display the section of offending code.

FTP Log Panel

The **FTP Log Panel** is a useful tool if you make use of Dreamweaver MX's FTP tools. Every FTP command issued through Dreamweaver MX is recorded in a log file and this panel can help you to find the cause of any problems that may occur during FTP.

Server Debug Panel

The **Server Debug Panel** is only for ColdFusion pages and helps you in your debugging efforts by presenting you with several pieces of useful information, such as a list of all the pages the server had to process in order to render the page, all the SQL queries that were executed, and all the server variables and their values.

Templates

Templates are very useful in helping to insure a consistent look and feel throughout your web site, the idea being that you create a single page to base all others within the site on. If you update any part of a template that has been used to create other pages in your site with, when saving you will be asked, if you want to update those pages to reflect the changes you made to the templates. You can skip it if you like and update them all at a more convenient time from the _Modify > Templates_ menu.

Templates were fairly basic prior to Dreamweaver MX in that you could define an editable region of a template that would allow its content to be modified on a page-by-page basis. All other parts of a template were locked, meaning that you could only modify that content on the template itself and in doing so: you changed the content in every page that used the template. Effective, but at the same time, a little limiting in terms of usability in a large dynamic web site that may have some strict design rules and also some diverse page content.

The new templates in Dreamweaver MX have taken evolutionary steps from this original idea and as such, they cater for far more variation by including new capabilities.

The ability to create nested templates opens up whole new ways of creating and maintaining the look and feel of a site. This would involve creating a base template with defined editable regions and then creating a new template, based on the original template, to further define how a selected editable region should look. That could include adding editable regions within existing editable regions.

An example where you might use this technique is to define the base visual of a page for the entire site and then create a nested template from the base page for a search results page layout. This would include specific design features for part of the page whilst still retaining the overall base visual. The same could be done for a details page layout where, once again, specific design elements need to be in place over and above the base page.

As well as the editable regions mentioned above, you have further template capabilities that enable a site designer to maintain the visual style throughout the site while still allowing content contributors to add dynamic content to the page.

These come under the following three headings:

Repeating Regions

You will regularly come across the need to display a dynamic list of data on a page; to insure the consistent look of these parts of the web page, you can create **Repeating Regions** on a template that will take into account the need to show multiple rows of data while still maintaining visual style.

You can create two types of repeating regions in Dreamweaver MX:

- A **Repeating Region** is part of a template that can be duplicated multiple times but is not, by default, editable. To make it editable, you need to create an editable region within your repeating region

- A **Repeating Table** is a repeating region that includes editable regions in a table – you can define which table cells are editable

Optional Regions

An **Optional Region** is an area of a template-based page that may or may not be used on a page based on the template. This optional region uses variables to decide whether or not to show this region on the page.

For example, there might be a need to display extra images or text on some pages, but not others and you might like to maintain a visual style over all of those elements but not necessarily included them on every page. Optional regions cater for these situations.

Going a step further, **Template Expressions** evaluate a value for an optional region and show or hide it based on the value. They are created from a subset of JavaScript, but you still have enormous power with them. Things such as single or multiple IF statements can be created to test for values before displaying your optional regions. These expressions are written in Code View and are represented in Design View by an expression marker on the page. To edit the expression in Design View, select the expression marker and the code is displayed in the property inspector.

Editable Tag Attributes

If you want to have certain attributes of tags in a page based on a template editable by the content providers, such as text justification or image size, you can now make those chosen specific tag attributes editable on your template.

Library Items

Library items can be images, text, or any other object, such as a piece of script, that you want to use and reuse in your web site. You create a library to hold these library items in and you can then reuse them throughout your site.

The idea of library items is to keep items of page content consistent. If you want to reuse the same image on many pages, you can turn it into a library item and then use it throughout your site. When the time comes to change that image, you only need to change it once, in the library, and all pages that use it can be updated automatically.

You do have the option of not updating your pages immediately, or even at all, but if you should need to update later, you can use the _Modify > Library > Update Pages_ menu.

There are limitations in regard to the types of elements that you can turn into a library item; however, the main rule is simple – only elements that can be added to the body of a document can be turned into library items. So, for instance, CSS styles can't be library items as they are added to the head of a document. That said, you can include, for example, a rollover image as a library item. Then, when you apply that library item to a page, Dreamweaver MX is smart enough to know that the JavaScript code required to produce the rollover effect will be needed in order for this library item to work correctly and so it is added to the head of the document.

There are some similarities between library items and templates, but the distinction should be made that templates are for maintaining visual style of the overall page and library items are there to store reusable and updateable segments of page content.

Summary

We have seen many of the new and improved features of Dreamweaver MX here and you have hopefully gained some insight into the various new technologies that are being brought with this new release.

The design features and the code features that enable you to work faster and more efficiently, be that as a lone developer or as part of a development team, have all received attention, along with the new interface and many of the constituent panels.

The extensibility of the product means that a growing number of extension developers will be releasing extensions that increase the functionality of the base product – some will be free and some will be commercial but they will all bring added value to the product.

Standards compliance, accessibility and page validation are strongly featured in Dreamweaver MX along with capable tools that enable you to produce pages of code that can be seen by anyone on the Internet.

Speaking of validation, this leads us neatly into _Chapter 2_ where we'll cover the production of valid HTML and XHTML in Dreamweaver MX.

2

- Why should I move over to XHTML?

- Practices for authoring valid XHTML

- Working with XHTML in Dreamweaver MX

Author: Rachel Andrew

Valid (X)HTML in Dreamweaver MX

With the launch of Dreamweaver MX, Macromedia has introduced many features into Dreamweaver that will enable developers to quickly create markup that is valid, well-formed, and that follows best practices. Some of the new features include the ability to work in XHTML, much improved CSS support, and an inbuilt validator that allows you to validate your markup against W3C standards without needing to use an online tool. In this chapter we will not only explore these new features within Dreamweaver MX, but also discuss why they are useful, and why developing to the recommendations and standards set out by the World Wide Web Consortium (W3C) is a good idea.

The beginning of this chapter focuses on XHTML because it is the most recent recommendation from the W3C, and developers creating new web sites will begin to move towards it. If you have never considered moving to XHTML, or know very little about it, then this chapter will give you reasons why transitioning to XHTML is a move in the right direction. Using valid XHTML can make your site a lot more accessible to users with disabilities who depend on assistive technologies such as screen readers, and also to people viewing your pages on devices such as PDAs. Moving to XHTML means that you will be getting yourself up to speed with the requirements of authoring XML documents, while using a markup language that looks familiar to you and will also allow the integration of other XML applications. However, much of what we will be discussing here is relevant whether you are working in HTML or XHTML.

In the second half of this chapter we will walk through creating a simple page in HTML with Dreamweaver, and then again in XHTML. We will also validate this page against the various XHTML standards and look at how we can convert existing HTML sites to XHTML.

HTML

Hypertext Markup Language (HTML) was devised as a means of exchanging scientific and technical documents. It uses a subset of tags from the far more powerful language, Standard Generalized Markup Language (SGML), in order to allow the quick creation and distribution of documentation. SGML is a meta language designed for marking up text into structural units, the idea being that the language was independent of the device used to view it and could be implemented on any machine. HTML used some of the tags from SGML and the basic structure of the language. Tim Berners-Lee, the creator of HTML also added support for hypertext, allowing the linking of content, something that did not exist in SGML.

HTML was designed to be a language that was easy to use. This ease of use meant that almost anyone could create an HTML document, and as it grew in popularity, authors wanted more than just the simple, structured, hyper-linked documents required by scientists and researchers. The browser manufacturers took on HTML and developed their own propriety extensions and tags, sometimes these tags were standard across browsers, but by the time Microsoft and Netscape launched their version 4 browsers, many of those who were creating web sites were resigned to building two sites – one for each major browser – and hoping that their visitors weren't using something else entirely!

Alongside this development by browser manufacturers, the W3C was formed in order to formulate standards for HTML markup (*http://www.w3.org/*). These standards took the basic HTML markup as it was then, and added some of the new features that had become popular. When we talk about validating our pages, we are talking about making sure our document does not include things that are not in the particular specification we are writing to. In order that browsers (and the validator) know which version of HTML we are writing to, we add a line of code called a **DOCTYPE** to the top of each document which specifies which standard we are writing to.

To some extent the efforts of the W3C have been very successful. The web developer of 2002 will be aware of visitors using screen readers, Braille readers, PDAs and a variety of 'traditional' browsers on a myriad of platforms and operating systems, and the latest releases of the major browsers – Internet Explorer and Netscape – are touting standards compliancy as a main feature, instead of all the fun things that you can do if you code for their browser only.

What Is the Future for HTML?

Despite the fact that browser support and adoption of HTML standards is better than it ever has been, there will be no further version of HTML. The current version, HTML 4.01, will be the final HTML standard, and the current recommended markup language for use on the Web is XHTML. Although there will be no further versions of HTML it is unlikely to make a sudden disappearance from the Web, and validating to any DOCTYPE (even if that is HTML 3.2) is better than validating to none. However, as I shall explain as we go through this chapter, there are many benefits to, and very few problems with moving to XHTML, so new web site developers are encouraged to use XHTML.

XHTML

XHTML (Extensible HyperText Markup Language) is a subset of XML, which (like HTML) is a subset of SGML. XML and SGML are **meta languages**. A meta language is a language that allows you to create other languages using Document Type Definitions (DTDs) that define the structure of that document so that it can be interpreted. XHTML is one such language created from XML.

XHTML has been developed as a web language that reproduces all the features of HTML yet conforms to the stricter rules of XML. It is a logical progression from HTML 4.01 and certainly not something to be worried about, especially now that you can use your familiar visual development environment, Dreamweaver, to help you in making the transition.

> *"The XHTML family is the next step in the evolution of the Internet. By migrating to XHTML today, content developers can enter the XML world with all of its attendant benefits, while still remaining confident in their content's backward and future compatibility."*
>
> *– W3C XHTML Specification (*http://www.w3.org/TR/xhtml1/*)*

Why Should I Move to XHTML?

Knowing what XHTML is, is all very well but, as a web professional, why should you wake up one morning and decide to start working in XHTML as opposed to HTML? Why might you consider converting an existing site to XHTML? There are many real and definable benefits for moving to this new language.

Cleaner Markup

HTML allows developers to write HTML in a very flexible manner. Whilst web browsers are good at interpreting the markup and displaying it, it can be very difficult to manipulate the document in any other way, because the flexibility that current desktop browsers allow can lead to untidy, sloppy markup. A valid XHTML document can easily be read by traditional browsers as well as other devices, such as PDAs and other mobile devices that lack the processing power needed to interpret sloppy markup.

Greater Platform Independence

XHTML's insistence on clean, structured markup makes it far easier to port documents to different environments. Not all devices have the power of a traditional web browser to interpret incorrect or convoluted markup and display it correctly. XHTML's strict nature means it is far more likely to display in a well-structured manner on all devices.

Accessibility

XHTML documents must adhere to strict rules. This makes it easier for alternative devices such as Braille readers, screen readers, and other assistive technologies to interpret the content and present it to the user in a useful and navigable manner. A valid XHTML document leaves no room for non-standard markup, therefore eliminating the chance of anything in the document interfering with its accessibility.

Forwards Compatibility

As we have already seen, there will be no future version of HTML. Browser manufacturers will be looking towards the future with new releases, and while it is unlikely that we will see support for HTML dropped any time soon, it is always a good idea to work to the newest standards. By doing so your pages are far less likely to break when the next versions of the major browsers appear on the scene. As we shall see later in this chapter, working with the Transitional DOCTYPE enables you to create XHTML documents that will display properly in older browsers, whilst still creating a document that validates against an XHTML DOCTYPE.

Learning the Rules of XML

XML is here to stay – by writing XHTML documents you are adhering to the strict rules of XML markup, something that will stand you in good stead in the future. Getting into the habit of creating well-formed documents will make creating XML documents for different applications in the future second nature to you.

Integrating with Other XML Applications

XHTML allows the incorporation of tags from other XML definitions, such as MathML, SMIL (Synchronized Multimedia Integration Language), or SVG (Scalable Vector Graphics). This might not seem particularly useful to many designers and developers today, but is likely to become more important as uptake and use of other XML applications grows, and so learning XHTML at this relatively early stage will enable your résumé and skills to look very up to date.

Page Load Time

Valid XHTML documents load faster because the browser does not need to reinterpret bad markup. HTML, with its leniency in regard to unclosed tags and improperly nested markup, leaves more to the interpretation of the browser. Additionally, HTML's inherent flexibility encourages sloppy markup, which in turn can also add load time onto the page. As we move towards creating XHTML pages that follow the Strict DTD, we need to move style and presentation aspects into CSS, thus trimming our pages down further. Despite the increasing numbers of people with broadband, high-speed connections, load time of pages is still an important issue. Whilst writing valid, well-structured HTML will also enable faster loading pages, XHTML enforces that strictness and prevents sloppiness creeping in.

The 'Rules' of Writing XHTML

For anyone with a good understanding of HTML, XHTML is not difficult to learn and, of course, Dreamweaver MX will help you all the way. All you need to do is follow a few simple rules that are common to all XHTML (and therefore XML) documents.

XML Declaration

The XML Declaration, `<?xml version="1.0" encoding="iso-8859-1"?>`, that Dreamweaver adds before the `DOCTYPE` at the top of a new XHTML document is not strictly required in an XHTML document although the W3C states that "XHTML document authors are strongly encouraged to use XML declarations in all their documents."

The XML Declaration simply states that the document is an XML document, and can also (as in the case of the declaration that Dreamweaver inserts) provide information on character encoding for the document.

DOCTYPE

An XHTML document must validate against one of the three XHTML DTDs: XHTML strict, XHTML transitional, or XHTML frameset. As we will see later on in this chapter, XHTML strict doesn't allow any deprecated elements or framesets, XHTML transitional supports deprecated elements but not frames, and XHTML frameset supports framesets. There must be a `DOCTYPE` declaration in the document above the `<html>` tag, and it must reference one of these three DTDs we will discuss in greater depth later on in the chapter. Dreamweaver MX inserts the XHTML Transitional DTD as default when you create a document with the *Make Document XHTML Compliant* checkbox checked in the *New Document* dialog. However, if you are creating a frameset, it will insert the Frameset DTD. Opposite is a screenshot showing the HTML 4.01 Transitional DTD as inserted by Dreamweaver:

```
▼ Insert    Common  Layout  Text  Tables  Frames  Forms  Templates  Characters  Media  Head  Script  Application

<!DOCTYPE HTML PUBLIC "-//W3C//DTD HTML 4.01 Transitional//EN">
<html>
<head>
<title>Untitled Document</title>
<meta http-equiv="Content-Type" content="text/html; charset=iso-8859-1">
</head>
```

Quotation Marks

All attribute values must be enclosed in quotation marks. In the following `<img>` tag, the `height` and `width` attributes are incorrectly defined:

```
<img height=100 width=300 alt="my logo" src="logo.gif" />
```

This is the correct way to do it:

```
<img height="100" width="300" alt="my logo" src="logo.gif" />
```

Whilst previous versions of Dreamweaver have tended to quote attributes correctly, you may find that code snippets that you or other developers on your team use, may not be as careful. Selecting *Commands > Clean up XHTML* will quote any unquoted attributes within your document.

Case Sensitivity

Element and attribute names must be in lowercase.

Both of these lines are incorrect:

```
<IMG HEIGHT="100" WIDTH="300" ALT="my logo" SRC="logo.gif" />
<img HEIGHT="100" WIDTH="300" ALT="my logo" SRC="logo.gif" />
```

Here is the correct XHTML:

```
<img height="100" width="300" alt="my logo" src="logo.gif" />
```

If you have always written your HTML tags in uppercase to easily differentiate between tags and content, you may find this change difficult at first. JavaScript event handlers – such as `onclick` or `onmouseover` – must also be written in lowercase.

The following JavaScript is incorrect:

```
onMouseOver="MM_swapImage('img1','','i/button01b.gif',1)"
```

And this is the correct way to do it:

```
onmouseover="MM_swapImage('img1','','i/button01b.gif',1)"
```

Dreamweaver MX, when working on an XHTML document will generate lowercase code, including JavaScript. If you are working in HTML then you can choose whether to use upper-or lowercase for HTML tags in the *Preferences* dialog. However it is not a bad idea to begin to work in lowercase, even in HTML, as it will be necessary in the future.

Closing Tags for Non-Empty Elements

By a *non-empty* element we mean a tag that contains something between the start tag and the end tag. Some HTML elements can be written without the closing tag, for example the closing </p> tag of the paragraph element is optional and therefore omitted by many HTML authors. In XHTML however, all elements must be closed.

The following, while valid in HTML, is incorrect in XHTML:

```
<p>This is some text formatted in a paragraph.
<p> This is the second paragraph.
```

This is the XHTML way of marking up the same text:

```
<p>This is some text formatted in a paragraph.</p>
<p> This is the second paragraph.</p>
```

Dreamweaver MX closes all non-empty elements, whether you are working in HTML or XHTML, and will add closing tags when you run the *Clean Up HTML* command.

Empty Elements

Empty elements are those HTML tags that stand alone and do not include anything between the beginning and end tag such as <br> and <hr>. In XHTML these need to be closed:

The HTML empty elements such as <br> and <hr>, become <br /> and <hr /> in XHTML.

> Note the additional space after the tag and before the forward slash. Although it is also correct to close your tags without this additional space, the space will allow those browsers that do not recognize XHTML to display your content correctly.

Dreamweaver MX uses the correct syntax for empty tags such as <br /> when generating markup in an XHTML document and also when cleaning up XHTML.

Nesting

An XHTML document must be **well-formed**. This means that all tags must nest correctly – the first tag that you open should be the last to be closed. Incorrect nesting is illegal in SGML-based languages but was tolerated by browsers.

This is an example of badly formed markup:

```
<p><strong>This is bold text.</p></strong>
```

This is the proper way of nesting the tags:

```
<p><strong>This is bold text.</strong></p>
```

Dreamweaver MX nests elements correctly and will also correct nesting of elements when cleaning up XHTML.

Attribute Minimization

Attributes in valid XHTML documents cannot be minimized. Attribute minimization refers to the practice of writing only the attribute's name without specifying a value, which sets the attribute to its default value. All attributes should be written as name-value pairs even where this means that the value is the same as the name.

This is incorrect in XHTML:

```
<input type="checkbox" name="checkbox" id="checkbox" value="True" checked />
```

This is the corrected version:

```
<input type="checkbox" name="checkbox" id="checkbox" value="True"
    checked="checked" />
```

Dreamweaver MX will insert this correct markup and also will convert minimized attributes to name value pairs if you convert an HTML document into XHTML.

Here is an example of an XHTML document that complies with the above guidelines:

```
<?xml version="1.0" encoding="iso-8859-1"?>
<!DOCTYPE html PUBLIC "-//W3C//DTD XHTML 1.0 Transitional//EN"
"http://www.w3.org/TR/xhtml1/DTD/xhtml1-transitional.dtd">
<html xmlns="http://www.w3.org/1999/xhtml">
  <head>
    <title>My XHTML Document</title>
  </head>
  <body>
    <p><strong>Hello! World</strong></p>
  </body>
</html>
```

Authoring Valid XHTML and HTML

Now that you have some idea of what XHTML is, and can make an informed choice as to whether you would like to develop with XHTML or HTML, we need to look at the different implementations that are available for your documents to validate against and why you might even feel the need to validate your documents.

Why Does Writing Valid (X)HTML Matter?

Perhaps at this point you might be wondering why it is important to validate your HTML; after all, there are many sites that display perfectly well in all the common browsers despite throwing errors when run through a validator. Is validating just going to cause a load of extra work that can't be charged, or explained to your clients?

- If you do not validate your page to a standard DTD then you are throwing away control to the browser over the way your page is displayed. Compliant browsers tend to render valid (X)HTML as expected, and the things that do not render correctly tend to be well documented.

- Validating and correcting your markup is a good debugging process: often problems will disappear once errors thrown up by the validator have been corrected, and if they don't, at least you know that the problem isn't simply due to an unclosed or incorrectly nested tag.

- Even if you have used browser-specific tags, or have done something for visual effect that you know will cause your page to be invalid in the eyes of a validator, it is never a bad idea to validate the rest of your page regardless. You can then make an informed decision to include something that isn't within the specification, in full knowledge of any problems that it could possibly cause, but know that the rest of your site is valid and will display correctly.

- Good, valid markup is far more easily spidered and indexed by search engine robots than messy, bloated code filled with font tags and presentational HTML hacks.

- Finally, validating your markup will ensure that your document is viewable for the future. Browser manufacturers look to the W3C specifications as they design their next version web browsers, they may or may not retain support for their own special tags, or for widely used 'hacks' that just happen to create a certain effect. The precedent for this has already been set when Netscape 6 was launched, support for their propriety `<layer>` tag disappeared from the browser in order to make way for the standards compliancy and support for the W3C DOM that we see in Netscape 6x. This could easily happen again, and the best chance of avoiding your web sites being inaccessible when a new generation of browsers appears, is to use valid markup now.

Choosing a Document Type Declaration

A Document Type Declaration (DTD) tells the browser or device which version of XHTML or HTML you have used to create the document. It means that the browser doesn't need to do so much guesswork about what you are using and can get on with quickly rendering your page.

XHTML Strict

```
<!DOCTYPE html PUBLIC "-//W3C//DTD XHTML 1.0 Strict//EN"
          "http://www.w3.org/TR/xhtml1/DTD/xhtml1-strict.dtd">
```

Validating your documents against the XHTML Strict DTD is the toughest option. This DTD does not support any of the deprecated elements listed later in this chapter, or framesets.

XHTML Transitional

```
<!DOCTYPE html PUBLIC "-//W3C//DTD XHTML 1.0 Transitional//EN"
    "http://www.w3.org/TR/xhtml1/DTD/xhtml1-transitional.dtd">
```

The Transitional DTD is the choice of most designers and developers moving from HTML to XHTML and is the default DTD inserted by Dreamweaver when you create a new XHTML document. This DTD supports the deprecated elements that are not allowed in XHTML Strict, but does not allow framesets. Documents must still conform to the rules of XHTML.

XHTML Frameset

```
<!DOCTYPE html PUBLIC "-//W3C//DTD XHTML 1.0 Frameset//EN"
    "http://www.w3.org/TR/xhtml1/DTD/xhtml1-frameset.dtd">
```

You must use the Frameset DTD if you are using frames and wish to create valid XHTML documents. Dreamweaver will insert this DTD for you if you are working with a frameset and have requested XHTML compliance for your documents.

HTML 4.01 Strict

```
<!DOCTYPE HTML PUBLIC "-//W3C//DTD HTML 4.01//EN"
        "http://www.w3.org/TR/html4/strict.dtd">
```

The HTML 4.01 Strict DTD does not allow the use of any deprecated elements, or framesets.

HTML 4.01 Transitional

```
<!DOCTYPE HTML PUBLIC "-//W3C//DTD HTML 4.01 Transitional//EN"
        "http://www.w3.org/TR/html4/loose.dtd">
```

HTML 4.01 Transitional will allow the use of deprecated elements and attributes.

HTML 4.01 Frameset

```
<!DOCTYPE HTML PUBLIC "-//W3C//DTD HTML 4.01 Frameset//EN"
        "http://www.w3.org/TR/html4/frameset.dtd">
```

DOCTYPE Sniffing: Standards and Quirks

Today's Web contains a varied mix of web sites, some written to the new standards of HTML 4.01 or XHTML, and others that are a mixture of HTML versions and utilize browser-specific tags and quirks for specific effects. In order to cope with this, the latest browser releases use the DOCTYPE to decide whether the document author expects a standards-compliant browser to be rendering the page or whether the page was written for older, non standards compliant browsers and may be relying on quirky, non-standard behavior. DOCTYPE 'sniffing' as it has come to be described, relies on the fact that most of these quirky documents either have no DOCTYPE or use an old DOCTYPE.

Using any of the above examples will cause modern browsers to switch into standards-compliant mode, and render your pages relatively close to the W3C specifications. For new web sites this is a good thing. By developing to the standards and requesting that browsers display your site in accordance with them, you are far less likely to have disastrous differences between the rendering of one modern browser and another. If you use an incomplete DOCTYPE such as:

```
<!DOCTYPE HTML PUBLIC "-//W3C//DTD HTML 4.01 Transitional//EN">
```

or no DOCTYPE at all, IE 6, Mozilla and Netscape 6 will presume that you want your pages to look as they did in older versions of browsers and revert to their 'Quirks' mode. XHTML DOCTYPEs always force standards-compliance mode for browsers, and rightly so.

Dreamweaver MX adds the Transitional DOCTYPE without the URL to new HTML documents that it creates. So, by default, pages created with Dreamweaver MX will make modern, standards-compliant browsers operate in their quirks mode. If you are adding pages to an older site, you will possibly be very glad of this behavior. Changing DOCTYPES, or beginning to use a DOCTYPE on some pages of a site and not others, is a recipe for inconsistent design, and as previous versions of Dreamweaver did not insert a DOCTYPE there will be many people in that situation. For new web sites however, using the full DTDs, as shown above, will help to ensure that your site does not break in newer versions of browsers that may not include this ability to switch rendering modes.

Coping with Deprecated Tags

Moving to XHTML may not be simple if your site relies heavily on some of the deprecated tags, or elements that are browser-specific and therefore not included in the specification. Although there are some commonly used tags that the specification has deemed as deprecated (and that cannot be used in an XHTML Strict document), the tags are usually those that were being used for a specific visual effect that can be far better replicated with CSS.

Even if you are not validating to the strict DTD, it is worth remembering that these tags are deprecated, which means that they will be totally removed in a future version of XHTML. For the sake of forwards compatibility you will do well to move to the alternative where there is one.

Tags Deprecated in XHTML

Element	Description
`<applet>`	Java applets
`<basefont>`	Font properties defined as default
`<bgsound>`	Background sound tag
`<blink>`	Make text blink on and off
`<center>`	Align a block of text
`<embed>`/`<noembed>`	Embed an applet etc.
`<font>`	Assign font size or color
`<layer>`/`<ilayer>`/`<nolayer>`	Netscape positionable layer tags
`<marquee>`	Scrolling text
`<menu>`	A menu list
`<s>`	Strike-through text
`<strike>`	Struck-out text
`<u>`	Underlined text

Attributes Deprecated in XHTML

Attribute	Description/example
align	`<td align="right">`
	`<div align="right">`
alink, vlink, link	as applied to the `<body>` tag to color links within the document
background	as applied to the `<body>` tag to apply an image background to a document
bgcolor	`<body bgcolor="... >`
	`<td bgcolor="... >`
border	`<img border="0" ...`
clear	as applied to the ` ` tag
color	`<font color="...`
face	`<font face="...`
height	`<td height="...`
noshade	`<hr noshade>`
nowrap	`<td nowrap>`
size	`<hr size="...`
	`<font size="...`
width	`<td width="...`
	`<hr width="...`

In *Chapter 3* we will be looking at some of the above commonly used tags and seeing how the same effect can be achieved with CSS, at no cost to the structure and accessibility of your pages.

Best Practices for Markup

Whichever DTD you are validating against, there are many ways in which developers misuse some aspects of HTML for visual effects. The reason that the misused tags are being deprecated is all in line with the push to separate the presentation of your document from the content and structure.

In the future we will all need to think more about alternative devices that are accessing our web sites: not just devices to enable those with disabilities to access the web, but also the many PDAs, phones, and similar devices that are now being used. Using HTML tags inappropriately is likely to cause problems when the content is being accessed with traditional web browsers as a traditional web site, and even more problems when accessed with other devices.

Working in a visual development environment enables rapid development of documents and web sites. However, it can lead to our forgetting what is actually happening in the code as we move things around our document window, aiming for the right look and feel for our latest project. By structuring a document badly, or using tags inappropriately, your document may validate, but could still cause accessibility problems for those on alternative devices.

Avoiding Font Tags for Styling and Sizing Text

The browsers that are in wide use today can all cope with CSS for styling text. While you may be reluctant to move to CSS for positioning page elements, there is simply no need to ignore the huge benefits of using CSS instead of `<font>` tags for text styling. The cleaner markup that results from the removal of font tags leads to faster downloads, easier maintenance and redesign of a site. We will cover these advantages fully in *Chapter 3*.

Heading Tags for Structure

The levels of headings provided by (X)HTML are designed to give structure to the document; they are not an easy way to have different sized titles. Although you may use CSS to alter the visual appearance of these tags, make sure that you are using them logically within the document so that any browser or device that does not recognize the CSS can follow the structure of the document correctly.

Avoiding Blockquote for Indentation

For the same reasons that you should not use the heading tags simply for sizing, `<blockquote>` (or lists) should not be used to indent text. A non-traditional browser may well interpret `<blockquote>` as a quote; if you want to indent text for visual appearance only, then you can use CSS to create a custom class for indented text – and we'll discuss these issues more in the next chapter.

List Definitions

In HTML 4.01 and XHTML there are three, non-deprecated list definitions to choose from: Ordered list, Unordered list, and Definition list. It is important to use the correct type of list when entering your information and not simply choose one or another for visual effect; once again if you are going for a certain 'look' then use CSS to achieve that.

Ordered Lists

For a list of items numbered in sequential order, useful for a list of step-by-step instructions or ranked items.

```
<ol>
        <li>list item one</li>
        <li>list item two</li>
</ol>
```

This displays in most browsers like so:

Unordered Lists

For a list of unordered items, useful for lists of attributes:

```
<ul>
        <li>list item one</li>
        <li>list item two</li>
</ul>
```

This displays in most browsers like so:

Definition Lists

Use a definition list if you have a list of items and explanations. By using this type of list you make it clear to someone using an assistive technology such as a screen reader or other device that can only see the structure of the document, that the list contains items and their definitions. If you make this kind of list just by altering the presentational aspects of the page, your intentions may not be clear to someone who cannot see that presentation. The definition list includes tags for terms <dt> and definitions <dd>:

```
<dl>
        <dt>the term</dt>
        <dd>the definition</dd>
        <dt>another term</dt>
        <dd>another definition</dd>
</dl>
```

This markup displays in most browsers as show here:

Special Characters

When inserting special characters such as <, >, &, you should always use the correct Unicode Character Entities. If you enter common characters into the *Design View*, Dreamweaver MX will enter the correct character code for you, for example adding `&lt;` in place of < and `&amp;` in place of &. However, if you are working in Code View, or need to insert a character that is not on your keyboard, there are additional characters available from the *Characters* tab of the *Insert* Toolbar that you can insert into the document. The *Characters* tab is shown below:

The more unusual characters can be found by clicking the button on the right of the *Characters* tab, which will open up a panel of characters for you to choose from and insert into your document:

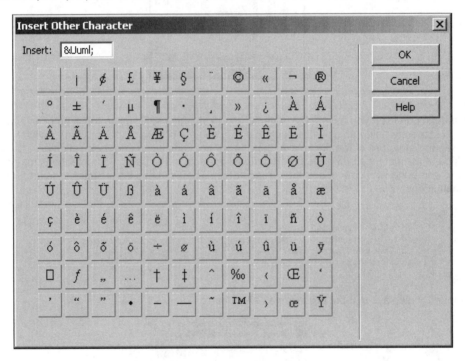

Working in Dreamweaver MX

After reading all of the above, you may feel that there is an awful lot to remember when migrating to XHTML, or even when coding to best practices, whether you are developing in HTML 4.01 or XHTML. Thankfully, Dreamweaver MX will remember most of these things for you, and assist you in your new way of working.

Setting Preferences

Setting your preferences will ensure that, right from the outset, Dreamweaver MX is working with you to create valid XHTML or HTML documents. To access the preferences dialog select *Edit > Preferences*.

General

In the *General* pane of the *Preferences* dialog make sure that the *Use <strong> and <em> instead of <b> and <i>* option is checked:

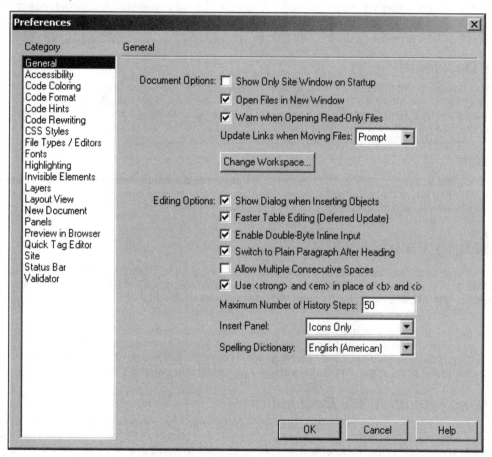

<b> and <i> won't cause your page to be invalid, but, from a best practices point of view, it is suggested that you use <strong> and <em> instead. Why? <b> for bold text and <i> for italic text are presentational tags designed to tell the browser how something should look. <strong> and <em> are logical tags that tell the browser, or device, that the document author wishes that word or statement to have particular emphasis. A screen reader, for example, may interpret these tags differently, with an inflection designed to give the person listening to the page the same understanding as someone seeing your bold or italic text. Your page should look exactly the same in a conventional browser whichever choice you make, so this is one place where making a small change can really lift the accessibility of your web site without you needing to do anything that might alter the look of the pages.

While in this pane, make sure that the checkbox *Allow Multiple Consecutive Spaces* is well and truly unchecked! If this is checked, then hitting the spacebar will insert multiple ` ` into your code, which is really annoying if you don't expect that to happen! From a best practices viewpoint, indentation of page elements should be created with CSS, and not by adding non-breaking spaces.

Accessibility

In the *Accessibility* pane, under *Show Attributes when inserting:* ensure that the *Images* checkbox is checked. For your documents to validate they must have `alt` text, and this dialog will remind you to add that text each time you insert an image. If you are keen to create valid and accessible code, you may want to check the other boxes for Form Objects, Frames, Media, and Tables too. These features will be discussed further in *Chapter 4*.

New Document

If you have decided that you will now work in XHTML for new work, you can set Dreamweaver MX to make its new document XHTML-compliant. To do that check the box labeled *Make document XHTML compliant* in this pane. Otherwise, you can request that documents are XHTML-compliant each time you create a new document in Dreamweaver MX, but the default will be HTML.

Validator

In this pane you can set which DTD you wish to validate against with the internal validator. Check the DTD that you will most often be using – you can always go back and change it if you are working on a site with a different DTD.

Creating Valid Markup

In this section of the chapter we will look at the tools available for creation of content, creating a valid HTML 4.01 document, an XHTML Transitional document, and looking at the changes needed to make an XHTML Transitional document validate against the Strict DTD.

> Note: The features that we will use and documents that I shall describe in this chapter will seem rather plain, as from a best practices viewpoint all presentation is taken away from the document and described in an external style sheet. Chapter 3 will also use these plain, structured documents and turn them into visual delights!

Working with an HTML Document

If you are planning to stick with tried and trusted HTML markup for the time being, validating your documents to an HTML DTD and working in a manner that enables accessibility is still a worthwhile aim. At some point in the future you may need to upgrade to XHTML, a process that will be far simpler if your HTML markup is valid, and many of the points in favor of using valid XHTML apply to any valid document.

All the preferences settings mentioned above apply from a best practices standpoint, apart from the *Make Document XHTML Compliant* option. With preferences ready to enable maximum assistance from Dreamweaver MX in our goal of valid HTML, let's create a document!

Selecting *File* > *New* from within Dreamweaver MX opens up the *New Document* dialog box:

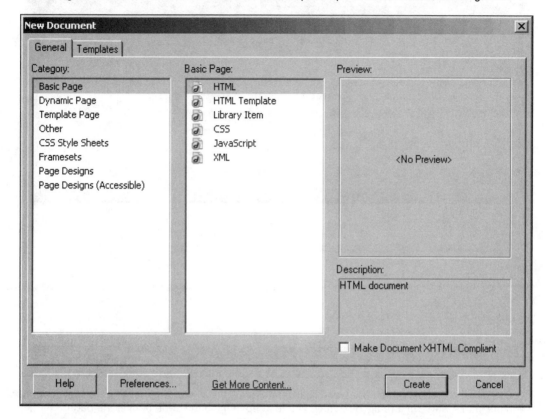

Dreamweaver MX allows you far more choice when creating your initial documents, and by selecting the different options in the first list you can see the choices that you have at this point. Today we are working in straightforward HTML so we simply need to select the first two options: *Basic Page* in the first category list and then *HTML* in the second list.

Clicking *Create* will create you a new document, switch into *Code View* and you will see that it has by default given you the HTML 4 Transitional DTD, without the URL:

```
<!DOCTYPE HTML PUBLIC "-//W3C//DTD HTML 4.01 Transitional//EN">
```

Switch back to *Design View*. As we already considered, one of the problems with working in a powerful visual editor such as Dreamweaver MX is the fact that you can very easily forget that you are working with a markup language and feel as if you are using a word processor or print page layout tool. If you want to keep an eye on the document's structure while designing its layout, you may find it helpful to switch to Spilt Screen mode, as shown here:

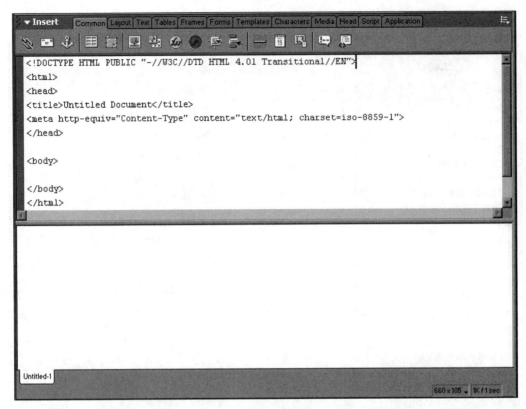

It does depend on the amount of screen real estate available to you whether you will feel comfortable working in this way, but it really does help you to keep in mind the code behind the page.

Additionally, the Properties Inspector has a new CSS mode that we will be discussing in more detail in *Chapter 3*. Switching to CSS mode means that the font tag attributes are no longer taking up prime real estate on your screen. To switch your Property Inspector just click on the 'A' symbol on the default View and it will switch from this:

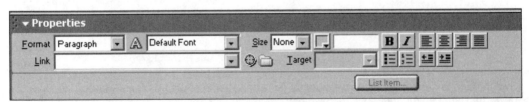

to this:

We will be using this new Properties Inspector in *Chapter 3* as we use CSS to style our pages.

Laying Out a Page

Working in *Design View*, insert a table setting the properties of that table to the following:

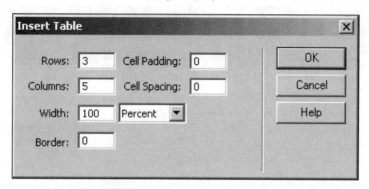

This should insert a five-column, three-row table into your document window. This table is for layout purposes. Although the W3C specify that CSS should be used for page layout rather than tables, because tables are designed for tabular data and not for laying out graphics, many designers find that the older browser's support for tableless design is not good enough for them to consider making this change yet. We will be learning how to use CSS to recreate this layout in the next chapter, but for now, we will do it using the layout tables.

> Note: When using tables for layout, bear in mind that a screen reader (accessibility device used by persons who are visually impaired) or other text-only browsing device will 'linearize' the content of your table cells. This means that they will display the content cell by cell in the sequence that they appear. Make sure that your information makes sense even when linearized and you will overcome one of the main problems of tabular layouts.

Into this table we can add some navigation buttons, which are small images alongside a spacer image to ensure that the background color of the rest of the cells matches perfectly.

As soon as the first image is inserted, the *Image Tag Accessibility Attributes* dialog appears; if you remember back when we set our Preferences we turned on the *Show Attributes when inserting: Images* option, this is the dialog that is opened for each inserted image when that preference is activated (see below). *Chapter 4* will discuss these accessibility attributes further.

After inserting the first navigation image, we can use the `width` attribute of the `<td>` tag to make the width of its surrounding cell the same as the width of the image (*Chapter 3* will describe how to do this with CSS). By using a spacer image, the same color as the background of my buttons to fill in the final cell, I can make this layout **liquid** – that is stretching to fit the browser window:

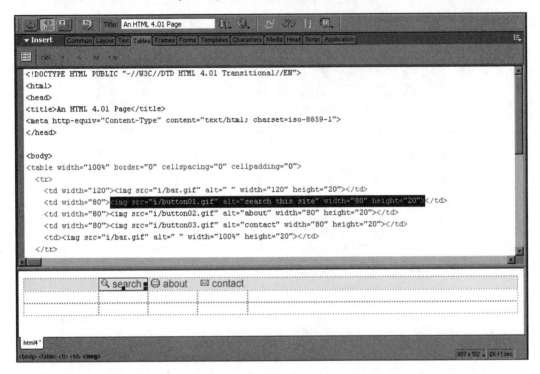

Note: When adding an image purely for layout purposes, such as this spacer, give the image an empty `alt` attribute: `<img src="myspacer" height="20" width="100" alt="">` this will cause browsers that cannot display images to skip over this image and not read out the image name.

The next step is to merge the four bottom cells of the table to create an area for content. Select the cells, then select *Modify > Table > Merge Cells*.

Inserting Rollover Images

To make our navigation more interesting, let's add some rollover buttons. Dreamweaver makes effects such as this simple and the process hasn't changed from Dreamweaver/UltraDev 4.

All you have to do is select the image and give it a unique name. Then, in the *Behaviors Panel*, expand the list of behaviors by clicking the + icon, and choose *Swap Image*. Next, browse to the image you want to appear upon mouse rollovers and click *OK*, making sure that *Preload Image* and *Restore Images onMouseOut* are both checked:

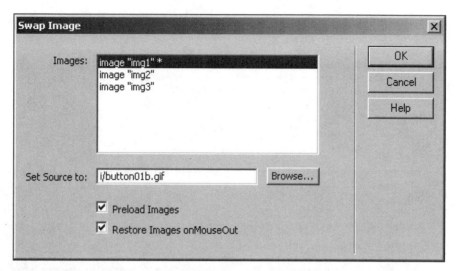

Repeating this for all images in the navigation bar should, when previewed in a browser, give you neat rollover buttons.

All that remains now is to add some content and we have the page, as shown here:

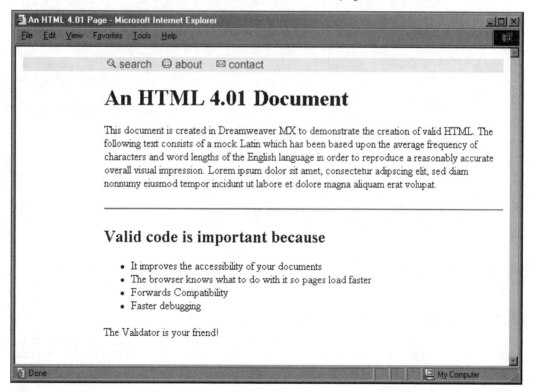

The HTML code behind this page looks like this (with JavaScript and content removed for brevity!):

```
<!DOCTYPE HTML PUBLIC "-//W3C//DTD HTML 4.01 Transitional//EN">
<html>
<head>
  <title>An HTML 4.01 Page</title>
  <meta http-equiv="Content-Type" content="text/html; charset=iso-8859-1">
  <script language="JavaScript" type="text/JavaScript">
    <!--
      Dreamweaver generated JavaScript here
    //-->
  </script>
</head>

<body
onLoad="MM_preloadImages('i/button01b.gif','i/button02b.gif','i/button03b.gif')">
<table width="100%" border="0" cellspacing="0" cellpadding="0">
  <tr>
    <td width="120"><img src="i/bar.gif" alt=" " width="120" height="20"></td>
    <td width="80"><a href="javascript:;"
onMouseOver="MM_swapImage('img1','','i/button01b.gif',1)"
onMouseOut="MM_swapImgRestore()"><img src="i/button01.gif" alt="search this site"
name="img1" width="80" height="20" border="0" id="img1"></a></td>
    <td width="80"><a href="javascript:;"
onMouseOver="MM_swapImage('img2','','i/button02b.gif',1)"
onMouseOut="MM_swapImgRestore()"><img src="i/button02.gif" alt="about" name="img2"
width="80" height="20" border="0" id="img2"></a></td>
    <td width="80"><a href="javascript:;"
onMouseOver="MM_swapImage('img3','','i/button03b.gif',1)"
onMouseOut="MM_swapImgRestore()"><img src="i/button03.gif" alt="contact"
name="img3" width="80" height="20" border="0" id="img3"></a></td>
    <td width="100%"><img src="i/bar.gif" alt=" " width="100%" height="20"></td>
  </tr>
  <tr>
    <td> </td>
    <td> </td>
    <td> </td>
    <td> </td>
    <td> </td>
  </tr>
  <tr>
    <td> </td>
    <td colspan="4"><h1>An HTML 4.01 Document</h1>
      <p>Content here! </p></td>
  </tr>
</table>
</body>
</html>
```

Validating HTML Documents in Dreamweaver

There only remains one final thing to do with our document, and that is to validate it. Before doing so make sure that in *Edit* > *Preferences* > *Validator* you have checked HTML 4.0 to validate against. To run the validator, open up the results panel and click the small, green arrow:

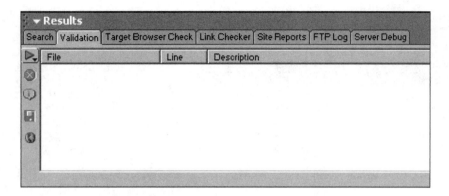

You can also validate your document by selecting File > Check Page > Validate Markup (for HTML) or File > Check Page > Validate as XML (for XHTML).

You can then choose to validate the current document, the entire site, or just selected files in the site. The validator preferences can also be set here.

Our document validates as HTML 4.0 without having to edit the code by hand.

Using the W3C HTML Validator

Although the internal validator is a useful tool when working on your documents within Dreamweaver, validating at the W3C makes a good final check. The URL for the W3C HTML Validator is *http://validator.w3.org/*.

The W3C tool allows you to validate by entering the URI of the page that requires validation, or by uploading the document. The easiest way to validate your pages is to FTP them to your web site and then point the validator to the URL. If you are using the Dreamweaver validator as you work on your site, you will probably only need to make a check with the W3C validator as part of your final testing anyhow to ensure that all documents, including those that contain dynamic data, are valid.

We will discuss the validators, and their often cryptic error messages, later on in this chapter but hopefully this has demonstrated how, with a little care and attention, Dreamweaver MX can assist you in creating valid HTML documents visually.

Working with an XHTML Document

Dreamweaver MX makes working in XHTML easy. To create a new XHTML document select *File > New* from within Dreamweaver MX to open up the *New Document* dialog box. Select the first two options – *Basic Page* in the first category list and then HTML in the second list. This time remember to check *'Make Document XHTML Compliant'* at the bottom of this dialog:

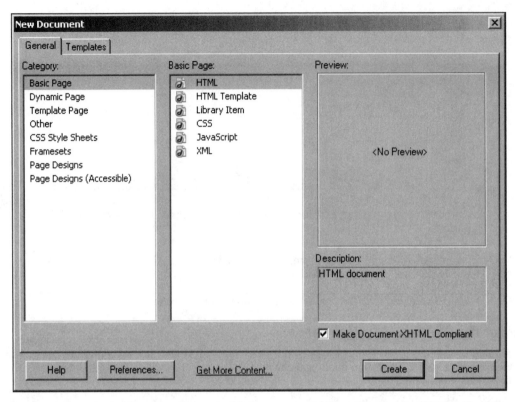

If you switch to *Code View* you will see that Dreamweaver MX has inserted the XHTML Transitional DTD. We are now going to create our page exactly as we did for the HTML page. If you are working in *Split View*, or switch to *Code View*, you will see that:

- when you add the images, Dreamweaver is adding the correct XHTML syntax with the closing / >

- the JavaScript event handlers onmouseover and onmouseout for the swap image behavior are lowercase

- <hr /> and <br /> tags are closed correctly

- when you add a name to an image, an id is added as well

The XHTML markup as generated by Dreamweaver is below, but once again, without content and JavaScript functions:

```
<?xml version="1.0" encoding="iso-8859-1"?>
<!DOCTYPE html PUBLIC "-//W3C//DTD XHTML 1.0 Transitional//EN"
"http://www.w3.org/TR/xhtml1/DTD/xhtml1-transitional.dtd">
<html xmlns="http://www.w3.org/1999/xhtml">
<head>
  <title>Untitled Document</title>
  <meta http-equiv="Content-Type" content="text/html; charset=iso-8859-1" />
  <script language="JavaScript" type="text/JavaScript">
```

```
    <!--
       Dreamweaver generated JavaScript here
    //-->
  </script>
</head>

<body
onload="MM_preloadImages('i/button01b.gif','i/button02b.gif','i/button03b.gif')">
<table width="100%" border="0" cellspacing="0" cellpadding="0">
  <tr>
    <td width="120"><img src="i/bar.gif" alt=" " width="120" height="20" /></td>
    <td width="80"><a href="javascript:;"
onmouseover="MM_swapImage('img1','','i/button01b.gif',1)"
onmouseout="MM_swapImgRestore()"><img src="i/button01.gif" alt="search this site"
name="img1" width="80" height="20" border="0" id="img1" /></a></td>
    <td width="80"><a href="javascript:;"
onmouseover="MM_swapImage('img2','','i/button02b.gif',1)"
onmouseout="MM_swapImgRestore()"><img src="i/button02.gif" alt="about" name="img2"
width="80" height="20" border="0" id="img2" /></a></td>
    <td width="80"><a href="javascript:;"
onmouseover="MM_swapImage('img3','','i/button03b.gif',1)"
onmouseout="MM_swapImgRestore()"><img src="i/button03.gif" alt="contact"
name="img3" width="80" height="20" border="0" id="img3" /></a></td>
    <td width="100%"><img src="i/bar.gif" alt=" " width="100%" height="20" /></td>
  </tr>
  <tr>
    <td> </td>
    <td> </td>
    <td> </td>
    <td> </td>
    <td> </td>
  </tr>
  <tr>
    <td> </td>
    <td colspan="4"><h1>An XHTML 1.0 Transitional Document</h1>
      <p>Content here! </p></td>
  </tr>
</table>
</body>
</html>
```

Validating Your XHTML Document in Dreamweaver

To validate an XHTML document in Dreamweaver, first make sure that you have set your validator preferences to the XHTML DTD that you are working to, in this case XHTML Transitional. To validate an XHTML document, either click the green arrow in the results pane and select *Validate Current Document as XML* or select *File > Check Page > Validate as XML*.

Converting an HTML Document To XHTML

If you have existing HTML sites and would like to convert them to XHTML, you will not need to make these changes by hand. Dreamweaver MX ships with a *Convert to XHTML* feature that will assist you in this conversion.

51

To convert an existing document select *File > Convert > XHTML*. (If your document contains frames you will need to do this to each frame individually.) The conversion utility will:

- Replace the HTML DOCTYPE with the correct XHTML Transitional DOCTYPE (or add a DOCTYPE if none existed)

- Turn uppercase tags into lowercase

- Make all JavaScript event handlers lowercase

- Add quotes to unquoted attributes

- Duplicate any name attributes of images with an id attribute

- close all non-empty tags

- close all empty tags with the correct / > closing

Converting the HTML page we created earlier gives us a page identical to the XHTML Transitional page that we created by hand. Obviously these are simple examples and there is much more for the converter to cope with on a real site, but by running the converter and then validating your page afterwards you will quickly be able to pinpoint any areas that still need some work to allow for valid XHTML markup.

Moving to XHTML Strict

As we discussed earlier in this chapter, the XHTML Transitional DTD allows the use of deprecated attributes that will be removed from future versions. The Strict DTD does not allow for the use of these deprecated attributes.

To convert our document from the Transitional DTD to the Strict we will need to work in *Code View*, Dreamweaver MX creates XHTML Transitional markup in recognition of the fact that most developers still need to create pages that are backwards compatible with older (pre-version 5) browsers, however the changes that we will need to make are relatively simple.

Change the DOCTYPE

In *Code View*, change the DOCTYPE at the top of the page to:

```
<?xml version="1.0" encoding="iso-8859-1"?>
<!DOCTYPE html PUBLIC "-//W3C//DTD XHTML 1.0 Strict//EN"
  "http://www.w3.org/TR/xhtml1/DTD/xhtml1-strict.dtd">
```

Revalidate Your Page in Dreamweaver

In *Edit > Preferences > Validator* check the checkbox to validate against XHTML Strict. Run *Validate as XML* again. This time you will get a list of errors, shown with a red exclamation mark – as shown opposite:

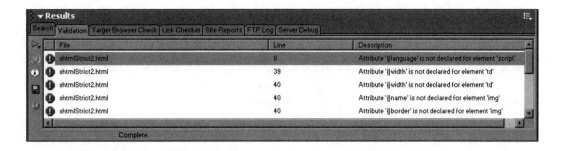

You can also save this list (on PC right-click and on Mac Command-Click, then Select *'Save Results'*) or open the list in a browser (select *'Open Results in Browser'*) which is useful if you are validating a large document or entire site as you can use the list as a checklist to ensure that you have caught all instances of invalid code.

The validator at the W3C site gives a similar list of errors:

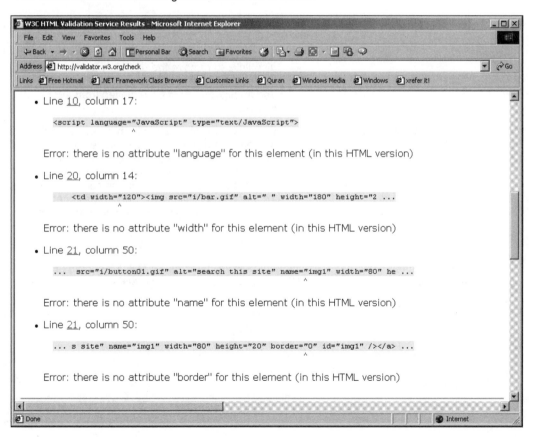

This list however, is very helpful in making our page validate against the XHTML Strict DTD as it gives us a quick way to see the deprecated elements (because we know that since our document validates as XHTML Transitional, it conforms to the rules of being well-formed).

The following table shows the errors that the validator flagged up, and how these are solved:

Error	Solution
Attribute '{}language' is not declared for element 'script'	This refers to `<script language="JavaScript" type="text/JavaScript">` ;the `language` attribute is deprecated and should be removed.
Attribute '{}width' is not declared for element 'td'	`<td width="80">` the `width` attribute of the `<td>` tag has been deprecated; as it can be replaced by CSS, all `width` attributes of table cells should be removed.
Attribute '{}border' is not declared for element 'img'	`<img border="0" [...] >` We have become used to using `border="0"` on images that are also links to remove the unsightly border around the image. It is possible to use CSS to do this and so `border` must be removed from all images.
Attribute '{}name' is not declared for element 'img'	Dreamweaver MX inserts both a `name` attribute and an `id` attribute when you name an image. The `name` attribute is still used by older browsers and ensures backwards compatibility, whilst the `id` attribute is the attribute in the specification. To use both is valid in XHTML Transitional, but in Strict the deprecated `name` attribute has to go.

After removing the above attributes the document now validates as XHTML Strict both in the Dreamweaver validator and online at the W3C. Below is the new, edited XHTML:

```
<?xml version="1.0" encoding="iso-8859-1"?>
<!DOCTYPE html PUBLIC "-//W3C//DTD XHTML 1.0 Strict//EN"
  "http://www.w3.org/TR/xhtml1/DTD/xhtml1-strict.dtd">
<html xmlns="http://www.w3.org/1999/xhtml">
  <head>
    <title>Untitled Document</title>
    <meta http-equiv="Content-Type" content="text/html; charset=iso-8859-1" />
    <script type="text/JavaScript">
      <!-
    Dreamweaver generated javascript here
```

```
         //-->
       </script>
     </head>

     <body
onload="MM_preloadImages('i/button01b.gif','i/button02b.gif','i/button03b.gif')">
       <table width="100%" border="0" cellspacing="0" cellpadding="0">
         <tr>
           <td><img src="i/bar.gif" alt=" " width="180" height="20" /></td>
           <td><a href="javascript:;"
onmouseover="MM_swapImage('img1','','i/button01b.gif',1)"
onmouseout="MM_swapImgRestore()"><img src="i/button01.gif" alt="search this site"
width="80" height="20" id="img1" /></a></td>
           <td><a href="javascript:;"
onmouseover="MM_swapImage('img2','','i/button02b.gif',1)"
onmouseout="MM_swapImgRestore()"><img src="i/button02.gif" alt="about" width="80"
height="20" id="img2" /></a></td>
           <td><a href="javascript:;"
onmouseover="MM_swapImage('img3','','i/button03b.gif',1)"
onmouseout="MM_swapImgRestore()"><img src="i/button03.gif" alt="contact"
width="80" height="20" id="img3" /></a></td>
           <td><img src="i/bar.gif" alt=" " width="100%" height="20" /></td>
         </tr>
         <tr>
           <td> </td>
           <td> </td>
           <td> </td>
           <td> </td>
           <td> </td>
         </tr>
         <tr>
           <td> </td>
           <td colspan="4"><h1>An XHTML 1.0 Strict Document</h1>
           <p>Content goes here</p></td>
         </tr>
       </table>
     </body>
   </html>
```

The preview of our page in a browser doesn't look so good now, as we can see overleaf. Without the width attributes on table cells the navigation bar falls apart, and the images now have a great big border around them:

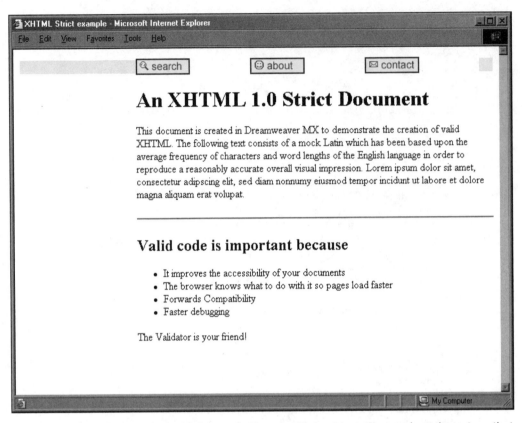

In *Chapter 3* we will take this design a step further and find out how to reproduce those tags that have been deprecated in XHTML with CSS.

Using External Files for JavaScript

Dreamweaver MX inserts all JavaScript required by its behaviors into the head of your document. This is not ideal. For instance, the JavaScript in the document we created in this chapter that enables the rollover effect is 23 lines long. That same block of script will need to be inserted into every page of the web site, and loaded each time.

Removing this JavaScript to a central file that is linked to all pages will trim down the load times of your pages, it also means that search engine spiders do not have to crawl through lines and lines of script to find your content, and generally make pages easier to maintain and keep consistent.

To do this, simply copy the JavaScript onto the clipboard and open up a JavaScript document in Dreamweaver by clicking *File > New* then select *Other*, then *JavaScript*. Once you have a JavaScript document save it, say as `functions.js`, and paste the contents of the clipboard into it. You can now return to the original XHTML document and delete everything between the `<script>` tags. You should just be left with:

```
<script language="JavaScript" type="text/javascript"></script>
```

if you are working in HTML or XHTML Transitional, or:

```
<script type="text/javascript"></script>
```

if you are working in XHTML Strict.

Now all we need to do is add a link within the `<script>` tags to the source of the JavaScript:

```
<script language="JavaScript" type="text/javascript" src="functions.js"></script>
```

If you add any other behaviors to other page elements, Dreamweaver will continue to add them to your document. However, you can add as many different functions to your external JavaScript file as you like. Just copy and paste them over to your file and remember to delete any additional `<script>` tags that Dreamweaver inserts. The only code inserted by Dreamweaver that you may not put into an external file is the timeline code.

When you want to create a new page with any or all of the functions used in your `functions.js` file, all you need do is paste the link to the functions file into the head of your document and the functions will be available to that page. When using templates, this is an excellent way to work as you can create your template file with all the JavaScript in the head of your document, as added by Dreamweaver, then move the JavaScript to a functions file and just have the link to that file in the head of the template document. When you create new pages from your template they will contain all the necessary JavaScript.

Working with Dynamic Data

In the later part of this book, developing dynamic sites with ASP in Dreamweaver MX will be discussed in detail. Developing with valid XHTML or HTML should make your life easier when incorporating dynamic data into your page. Once data is being pulled from a database, small errors such as unclosed tags and badly nested elements can wreak havoc across your site and become difficult to debug, so starting out with a solid framework as you design your layout should save you time later on in the development process.

A combination of valid (X)HTML and CSS is ideal for a dynamic site, especially those sites that allow users to add information (such as content management systems, or client updateable news pages) as your stylesheets will format the inserted content maintaining the consistency of the look and feel.

What to Watch Out For

There are some caveats when working with dynamic pages:

- When selecting an area to create a Repeat Region, Dreamweaver MX's name for a dynamic, repeating block of code pulled from a database, ensure that you have selected the entire block of code that you want to be repeated, and that the tags are still properly closed and nested when the page is viewed in a web browser with the content.

- When creating areas of your page that will be displayed conditionally, ensure that all tags are closed correctly when the page is loaded under each possible condition.

- If you are creating pages that users of your site will be adding content to, or content authors, via an administration section, then extra care will need to be taken in the design of the application so that the authors do not add anything invalid, or add HTML markup where you are working in XHTML. If you are using ASP, careful use of the `Replace` function can allow you to replace offending items (such as special characters or, if you are allowing people to enter HTML tags, non-valid tags or attributes) with their valid versions.

Validating Dynamic Pages

Dynamic pages should be validated with the online validator at the W3C and, if they include conditional regions, each possible way that the page can be displayed should be validated if at all possible. Your server-side code will not cause you any validation problems at the validator because, by the time it has been parsed by the server, all the validator is seeing is the (X)HTML that is returned to the browser.

If you are maintaining a dynamic site, pages that are frequently modified, either by users or content authors, should be validated occasionally in order to check that your counteracting of invalid items is working effectively.

Working with Third-Party Extensions

The community of extension developers is one of the great strengths of using Dreamweaver. If the product doesn't ship with some functionality that you need, there is often an extension available for download from the Macromedia Exchange that will fill that gap for you, and learning to create your own extensions is something well within the reach of any developer with a good grasp of JavaScript.

> You can learn more about extensions by going to the Macromedia Dreamweaver exchange page at http://dynamic.macromedia.com/bin/MM/exchange/main.jsp?product=dreamweaver – here you can download lots of extensions, and the Extension Manager.

While discussing valid (X)HTML it is worthwhile noting a few points:

- XHTML support is new with this version of Dreamweaver, and not all extensions will have XHTML support so you may need to make some edits in *Code View* in order to ensure your page validates after using the extension.

- Extensions may use browser-specific tags and/or non-valid markup. Validating your page after using the extension will tell you if this is the case and give you some pointers on how to fix the problem in *Code View*.

Summary

With Macromedia Dreamweaver MX, creating valid and accessible web sites with HTML and XHTML is within the realm of every designer and developer's abilities. In this chapter we discussed:

- The differences between HTML and XHTML

- Why HTML 4.01 is the last version of HTML as we know it and that future standards in markup for the web will be XHTML

- How to write valid XHTML and HTML in the Dreamweaver environment.

- The rules that you need to follow in order to migrate from HTML-based sites to XHTML Transitional, and looking towards the future to XHTML Strict

- Why valid, accessible code matters

This chapter provides some essential building blocks for good practices in web development, which will assist you as we move onwards to styling your pages with CSS and to adding dynamic data to your web sites. By following best practice not only will your web sites be more accessible to all web users, but you will also find your working methods and debugging streamlined and simpler.

3

- Why use CSS?

- The basics of CSS

- CSS tools in Dreamweaver MX

Author: Rachel Andrew

CSS in Dreamweaver MX

In *Chapter 2* we looked at how markup is evolving to meet the needs of the Web today. Part of that process is to remove the practice of styling documents using HTML tags within the documents as this leads to messy, inflexible markup that is difficult for some devices to parse. However, this does not mean that we are left with plain, boring documents – far from it!

In this chapter we will build on the skills used in *Chapter 2* and look at Cascading Style Sheets (CSS) and how to implement them on your web site using Dreamweaver MX. We will look at different ways of using CSS and discuss common browser issues, and how to deal with these problems.

What Is CSS?

CSS is a language that defines how HTML documents are presented in a browser. They can be thought of as a template with which you define how you want an element to look across your entire site and, on any page to which you attach that stylesheet, the element will look the same. This helps to create consistency across the pages of your site. As an example, suppose that you wanted all your level one headings, those contained in `<h1>` tags, to be purple in color and use the Verdana font face. Using only HTML you would need to code every single instance of the `<h1>` element like this:

```
<h1><font color="#663366" face="Verdana, Arial, Helvetica, sans-serif">my
heading</font></h1>
```

Using XHTML and CSS you would only need to use:

```
<h1>my heading</h1>
```

in your markup and define the `<h1>` tag once to be colored purple and using Verdana as the main font face in your stylesheet:

```
h1 {
  color: #663366;
  background-color: transparent;
  font family: Verdana, Arial, Helvetica, sans-serif;
}
```

Because we only need to define elements once for all pages that you are linking to, you can trim down file sizes and therefore page load times immensely. However you don't need to have all elements defined in the same way; you can specify 'classes' to apply to elements, which we will be covering later in this chapter.

History

The CSS1 Specification became a W3C Recommendation in December 1996. CSS1 mainly provides methods of styling text – thus replacing the `<font>` tag. CSS2 became a Recommendation in May 1998, and builds on the CSS1 specification adding support for positioning elements, a new selector specification, and support for different 'media descriptors' in order to provide different stylesheets to be used depending on the device that the page will be displayed on.

You can find the CSS recommendations here: http://www.w3.org/TR/REC-CSS1 *and here:* http://www.w3.org/TR/REC-CSS2.

The first browser to support any CSS at all was Microsoft's Internet Explorer 3. Netscape did not add in support until Netscape 4 and used an implementation that relies on JavaScript being enabled in the browser – if JavaScript is turned off in any version of Netscape 4, CSS will not be displayed either!

The majority of current web browsers support CSS1 very well and much of CSS2. We haven't reached that utopian point of being able to design once and it will look good in every current browser, but things are far better than they ever have been. For a listing of browser support for CSS1 and 2 visit *http://www.westciv.com/style_master/academy/browser_support/basic_concepts.html*.

The W3C

The W3C (World Wide Web Consortium) created the CSS recommendations along with recommendations for other web technologies, taking into account the point of view of developers and of companies such as Microsoft, Netscape, Apple, and around 500 other member organizations. If you want to read up more about CSS, HTML, XHTML, or you want to find online validators and see what new recommendations there are, then the W3C web site at *http://www.w3.org* is a good place to visit.

Why Use CSS?

CSS allows the separation of content and the structure of that content from presentation. HTML was not designed as a language to allow the visual formatting of documents further than the creation of an easy-to-read, structured document. Formatting tags, such as `<font>`, were added by the browser companies (notably Netscape) in order to extend the capabilities of HTML, and many of these later became part of the official specifications.

Separating Document Structure from Presentation

You will see this phrase a lot when stylesheets are discussed. In practice, it means that all information that describes how the document is presented to the user is removed from the HTML and put into stylesheet rules, and all information that defines the content and document structure remains in the HTML. Elements such as headings `<h1>` through to `<h6>`, paragraphs `<p>`, tables for tabular data `<table>`, lists `<ul>`, `<ol>`, `<dl>`, and so on, are used to describe the structure and content of the document. Other elements and attributes are typically used for presentational purposes, such as the `color` and `font` attributes for setting text colors and fonts, and `align`, `margin`, `border`, and `padding` attributes for positioning content.

By removing these presentational HTML elements and attributes and replacing them with stylesheets, your pages will become smaller, far easier to read and to debug. Separating content and document structure from presentation is the reason behind many of the plus points listed here.

Accessibility

CSS allows precise control over layout, obviating tag misuse. We discussed this misuse of HTML tags in *Chapter 2* (in the section *Best Practices for Markup*). Screen readers and other technologies interpret the markup by using the HTML tags that are present on the page; if inappropriate markup is used, the experience for a person who is blind is going to be one of confusion because the structure and meaning of your document will be far from clear.

Modern browsers allow users to override your styles with a user stylesheet. You might at first think this is not a good thing – why would you want someone to replace the carefully created work of art that is your stylesheet with theirs? However, users with defective vision, for example, can apply a stylesheet that uses large fonts or high contrast, meaning that they can then easily navigate your site and make a purchase at your online store.

By using CSS you can easily change the font sizing, colors, and even layout of your site – simply by changing the stylesheet. Many sites are now offering different 'themes' including those that provide a high contrast color scheme, or large text in order to assist those who have difficulty reading small, low-contrast text if that is a design choice for your site. In this way designers can begin to overcome problems of making things look great for those using conventional web browsers and yet provide a meaningful experience for those who are using something else entirely, or who need specific devices in order to be able to use your site comfortably. We will return to the issue of displaying different stylesheets later in this chapter.

More Flexibility in Design

By using HTML tags to lay out and style our pages we had limited ways in which to resize and position page elements. Using `<font size="xx">` would allow resizing, but with CSS it is possible to specify the spacing between words, letters, and lines of text, to add or reduce the amount of padding around `<h1>`, or other structural tags. Moving into the realms of CSS2 allows positioning of page elements outside of the 'grid' layout made necessary by using tables as a layout tool.

Smaller File Sizes

As I demonstrated at the beginning of this chapter, moving to CSS allows you to control the visual appearance of all the elements across your entire site with one definition in the stylesheet. More advanced use of CSS can produce effects that previously you would need to use an image for – such as the layering of page elements.

Browser Support

As I have already mentioned when discussing the history of CSS, browser support for CSS1 and much of CSS2 is excellent in current browsers, and even in older browsers there is a good degree of support. It is hard to get accurate statistics for browser use as it varies greatly between sites however, according to Browser News (*http://www.upsdell.com/BrowserNews/stat.htm*), as of May 16, 2002, over 95% of visitors to the three sources (sites that use a hit counter, EWS – Engineering Workstations Server at the University of Illinois, and upsdell.com) studied are using a browser with reasonable CSS support, as shown in the figure below. I have included Netscape 4 in this total, even though it arguably has terrible CSS support, because it does support the text styling properties that we will discuss in the first part of this chapter.

Browser Stats (use with caution)			
	Source 1	Source 2	Source 3
IE6	34%	32%	36%
IE5	55%	58%	41%
IE4	3.3%	2.5%	1.3%
IE3	.05%	.05%	.6%
IE2	.05%	0	.1%
Gecko (NN6, Mozilla, ...)	1.1%	1.1%	7.6%
NN4	4.2%	5.0%	5.2%
NN3	.05%	1.3%	.35%
Opera	.8%	.1%	.6%
(other)	1.4%	.1%	7.3%
'-' indicates no data '0' indicates <<.1%			

CSS is very browser friendly. If a browser or device does not support CSS it will just ignore the stylesheet and render the content with its default settings. Apart from certain bugs in traditional web browsers (which are well-documented and we will discuss ways to cope with these later), the use of CSS will not render your pages inaccessible to someone who is using an older browser or non-CSS supporting device.

Shortening Development Time

Once you have set up a stylesheet for the common elements across your site, adding new pages that are consistent with the rest of the site is simple, as any page that has the stylesheet linked will take the same styles for headings, paragraphs, borders, and other elements. Should you need to change the font face, or the color scheme used throughout the site, only that one stylesheet will need to be altered for the changes to be reflected across the entire site consistently.

The Basics of CSS

Before we dive into working with CSS within Dreamweaver MX, it is worth understanding some of the basic concepts of designing with CSS. If you have used CSS in the past then this section may serve as a refresher to your knowledge.

Ways to Implement CSS

There are three ways in which to implement CSS in your web site or document – inline, embedded, or externally.

Inline

An inline style definition is a one-time style definition placed in your code to style just the element that it is attached to. By using this method you will lose many of the benefits of CSS, because you will need to style each element individually, in the same way that you would use font tags or other presentational HTML. However, it can be useful and necessary for some DHTML effects – such as the timeline code in Dreamweaver MX. An example of inline CSS is:

```
<h1 style=" font-family: Verdana, Arial, Helvetica, sans-serif; color: #663366;">
```

This markup would only affect that particular `<h1>` tag on that page. If there were a second `<h1>` tag on the page it would be displayed in the default style for the user's browser.

Embedded

An embedded stylesheet only controls the elements on that page, and the CSS code is placed in the head of the document. In the code example below, any `<h1>` tags in the document would be colored purple however, this CSS will not be applied to any other pages on the site.

```
<head>
<title>CSS Example</title>
<style type="text/css">
<!--
h1 {
   font-family: Verdana, Arial, Helvetica, sans-serif;
   color: #663366;
}
-->
</style>
</head>
```

If you wanted to use this style on every page of your site and were using the embedded method, you would need to add this code to every page, meaning that changing the `<h1>` from purple to orange would involve changing it on every page of the site.

External Stylesheets

An external stylesheet is the most useful and flexible way to use CSS. By linking to a single external stylesheet from all pages of your web site, each page will use the definitions from that stylesheet. To change our purple `<h1>` tags to orange, site-wide, involves one simple change to the external stylesheet. We will discuss the design and implementation of external CSS later in this chapter. A simple link to an external stylesheet looks like this:

```
<link href="global.css" rel="stylesheet" type="text/css" />
```

We will cover attaching stylesheets to our documents in more detail later in the chapter.

'Cascading' Stylesheets

The cascading in CSS refers to the fact that styles defined closer to the element will overwrite other rules set, therefore if we set:

```
h1 {
    font-family: Verdana, Arial, Helvetica, sans-serif;
    color: #663366;
}
```

in an external stylesheet, but then decide that on one particular page of my site we want all `<h1>` tags to be green, we could add a style rule in an embedded stylesheet in the head of that document. If instead, we simply want a single `<h1>` tag to be green, we could use an inline style on that specific tag and it would take precedence over styles set in embedded or external stylesheets.

Redefining HTML Tags

We have already seen how redefining HTML tags with CSS rules can change the way these structural tags are rendered, while also preserving the structure of your markup. This method provides a simple way of creating and maintaining a consistent look and feel for your site, without bloating the HTML with presentational markup. If you are working with several content authors who add content to the site, then redefining tags will mean that their content will fit in with the rest of the site, using all the formatting defined in your stylesheet.

Creating CSS classes

CSS classes allow you to create rules for a page element that has that class applied to it. For instance, if in the stylesheet I have:

```
.myborder {
    border-width: 1px;
    border-color: #000000;
    border-style: solid;
}
```

any element, such as the `<img>` below, with a class of 'border' applied will get a 1 pixel wide black border around it:

```
<img alt="me" height="80" width="40" src="me.jpg" class="myborder" />
```

Netscape 4 will render this border in a strange way and will cause the image to become non-clickable if it is a link. This is just one of the problems that you may encounter while using CSS with Netscape 4. Later in this chapter we will discuss ways to cope with old browsers.

CSS Tools in Dreamweaver MX

Dreamweaver MX ships with a number of tools that make working with CSS easy and intuitive. There are many new additions over and above the functionality that was available in previous versions of Dreamweaver.

Setting Preferences

The following preferences will enable you to become comfortable working within the Dreamweaver environment with CSS.

CSS Styles

Go to *Edit* > *Preferences* > *CSS Styles*:

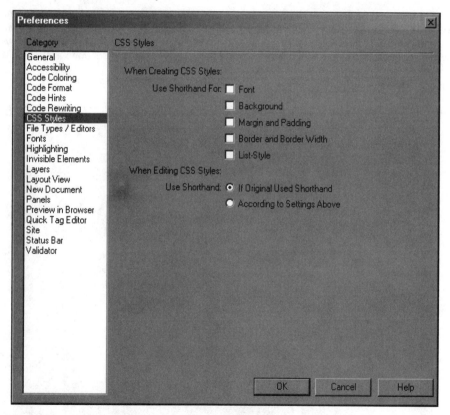

CSS allows shorthand and longhand syntaxes for either brevity or clarity. A snippet of CSS code in longhand syntax looks like this:

```
.longhand {
  font-family: Arial, Helvetica, sans-serif;
  font-size: small;
  color: #660066;
  text-decoration: underline;
}
```

On this dialog box, checking the boxes will force Dreamweaver to use the shorthand syntax:

```
.shorthand {
    font: small Arial, Helvetica, sans-serif;
    color: #660066;
    text-decoration: underline;
}
```

These rules should display in exactly the same way in the browser; which you use is personal preference.

More important are the radio buttons at the bottom. If you are creating a stylesheet in another editor, such as Topstyle, but then make edits in Dreamweaver, you should make sure that any rules Dreamweaver adds are consistent with the style you have used in the rest of your stylesheet. In this situation you should set the 'When editing CSS style: Use Shorthand' property to 'when original is in shorthand'.

You will find that certain rules work when declared in shorthand in certain browsers and not in longhand, particularly in older browsers such as Netscape 4, which accepts some style rules when written in shorthand (for instance `border:` will render, but `border-left:` will not). If you are using the shorthand syntax to cope with these problems then it is important to make sure Dreamweaver is set up to assist you in this.

File Types /Editors

To specify another editor to be your default CSS editor, go to *Preferences > File Types /Editors*:

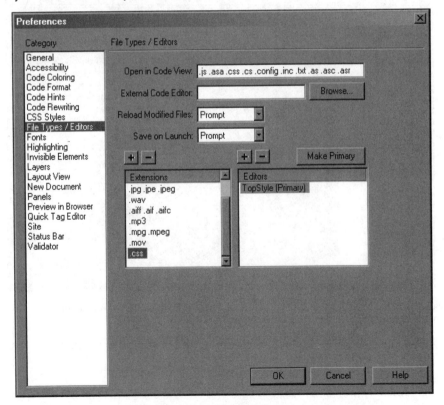

We will discuss integrating an external editor later in this chapter.

The CSS panel

The CSS panel enables you to attach stylesheets to your page, create new styles – either in a new stylesheet, an existing stylesheet, or embedded in your document and to edit styles already created:

Creating a Simple Stylesheet in Dreamweaver MX

To create a new stylesheet click on *New CSS Style* button, which is the second button from the left:

This brings up a New CSS Style dialog box:

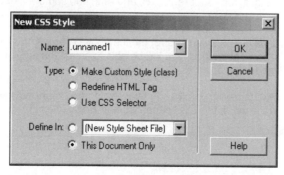

You will need to create a style definition in order to create a new stylesheet, so a good place to start is with the basic font styles for the body text of our page. In the drop-down list select '*body*' and then click the radio button labeled '*Redefine HTML tag*'. Select the radio button to define in '*New stylesheet file*' and click *OK*.

Since this is a new stylesheet, a '*Save As*' box will come up so that you can save your stylesheet. Make sure that you add the `.css` extension on the end of your stylesheet name (in other words, save as `global.css` and not just `global`). Once you have saved it, the following dialog box will appear:

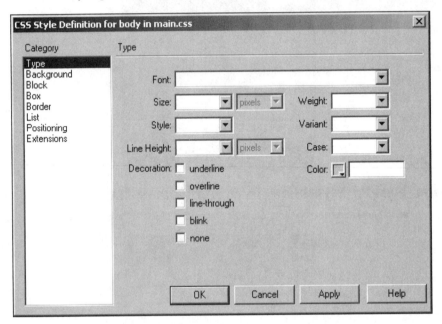

In this CSS Style Definition Dialog, you can set the rules for the tag or class that you are working with. For our body text we will want to select '*Type*' in the left-hand list and then choose a font face, size, and color before clicking *OK*.

If you create a style in a new stylesheet file whilst working in a document, Dreamweaver automatically attaches it to the document, so you should see your changes take effect immediately. We have only specified this style for the body text. Because of differences in the way that browsers (particularly Netscape 4) interpret the inheritance rules, browsers will display this differently and some will apply this rule to all text – including that in tables, paragraphs, and lists, and some will not. To be on the safe side, we need to add this same definition to other page elements where we want to use the same font settings.

Click on the *New CSS Style* button again and repeat the above process for `<p>`, `<td>`, and `<li>`. Now that we already have a stylesheet defined, you will be able to select the name of your newly created stylesheet in the New Style Dialog box.

You can redefine any HTML tags that you wish to by following this methodology. To edit your CSS styles select the radio button, at the top of the CSS panel, labeled *Edit Styles*:

In this tree view of styles in your stylesheet, double-clicking on an item will open up the CSS Style Definition Dialog again with this definition pre-filled so that you may make and save changes. If you would rather make edits in an external editor, and you have specified one in the preferences, then right-click (command-click on a Mac) anywhere on the panel and select *Use External Editor* – if this is checked, double-clicking on a definition will open the stylesheet in your external editor for you to make your changes.

Setting Up Custom Classes

Creating a custom class in Dreamweaver is as simple as redefining an HTML tag. Call up the *New CSS Style* dialog once again, but this time select the *Make Custom Style (class)* radio button and, in the textbox at the top of the dialog, enter a name for your class. This needs to begin with a period.

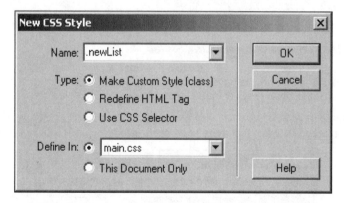

Click *OK* and the familiar dialog will open up allowing you to set the properties for this class. Set some properties and click *OK*. Your new class will appear in the CSS Styles Panel. To apply this class to an element in your document, select the element and then click on the class name in the CSS Styles Panel. The figure overleaf shows a list with my new class applied to one list item <li> tag.

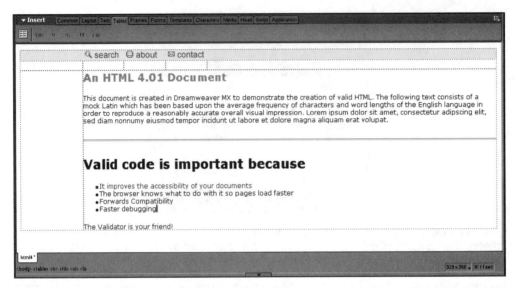

In the HTML below you can see how Dreamweaver has applied `class="newlist"` to the first item. Therefore the other items take our default redefinition of the `<li>` tag, but the one with the class applied takes on the style definition of that class.

```
<ul>
  <li class="newList">It improves the accessibility of your documents</li>
  <li>The browser knows what to do with it so pages load faster</li>
  <li>Forwards Compatibility</li>
  <li>Faster debugging</li>
</ul>
```

Using CSS Selectors To Add Different Link Styles

A common request from new CSS users is how to create nice-looking links with CSS, how to remove the underlines from links and also how to have two or more different styles of links on one page. This can be easily achieved within the Dreamweaver interface and relies on CSS selectors.

Once again, open up the *New CSS Style* dialog, this time select the *Use CSS Selector* radio button. In the first drop-down list you will see that there are 4 items listed:

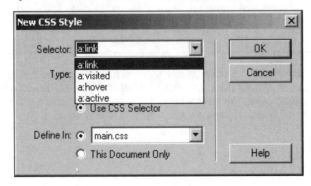

Select *a:link* and click *OK*.

The order in which we will add these definitions is vitally important, compliant browsers will be unable to render your link styles properly if they are not applied in the order of: LINK, VISITED, HOVER, ACTIVE.

You will now be presented with the now familiar dialog and can choose how you would like to style your links. To remove underlines from links, check the *none* checkbox in the *Decoration* section as in this figure:

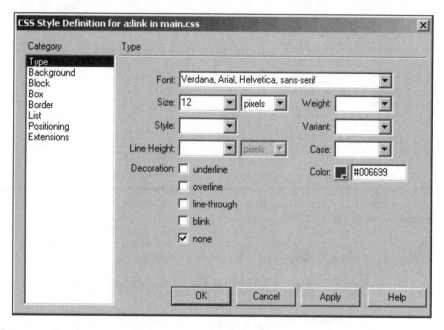

Click *OK* and repeat the process for your other link styles.

If you want to create a hover effect when the user holds their pointer over a link, then you need to use different styles for the a:hover selector. Common ways of styling this hover state are:

- Adding an underline if there is none in the normal state of the link. To do this check *underline* in the *Decoration* section.

- Adding a background color on hover. You can do this in the *Background* pane of the CSS Properties dialog when working on the *a:hover* selector.

After creating styles for all 4 states the markup in your stylesheet should look like this:

```
a:link {
  font-family: Verdana, Arial, Helvetica, sans-serif;
  font-size: 12px;
  color: #006699;
  text-decoration: none;
}
a:visited {
```

```
    font-family: Verdana, Arial, Helvetica, sans-serif;
    font-size: 12px;
    color: #333366;
    text-decoration: none;
}
a:hover {
    font-family: Verdana, Arial, Helvetica, sans-serif;
    font-size: 12px;
    color: #333366;
    text-decoration: underline;
    background-color: #CCCCCC;
}
a:active {
    font-family: Verdana, Arial, Helvetica, sans-serif;
    font-size: 12px;
    color: #333366;
    text-decoration: none;
}
```

This will have the effect of making all links in the documents that have this stylesheet attached look the same way. Which is fine if you only need one set of link styles throughout your site but it is likely that you will want to have different colored links in a navigation bar, or side panel, that is easily achievable with CSS in Dreamweaver by following these steps.

Launch the New CSS Style dialog box and select *Use CSS Selector* once again. Select the first selector `a:link` but this time, before clicking *OK*, edit the selector like so:

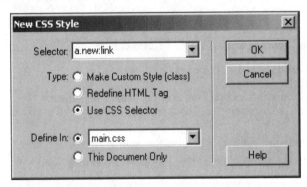

Click *OK* and define some different style rules to those for your first set of links. You need to do this for each selector in turn, remembering to add `.new` after the `a`.

The resulting stylesheet code will look like this:

```
a.new:link {
    font-family: Verdana, Arial, Helvetica, sans-serif;
    font-size: 12px;
    color: #990000;
    text-decoration: none;
```

```
}
a.new:visited {
  font-family: Verdana, Arial, Helvetica, sans-serif;
  font-size: 12px;
  color: #660000;
  text-decoration: none;
}
a.new:hover {
  font-family: Verdana, Arial, Helvetica, sans-serif;
  font-size: 12px;
  color: #660000;
  text-decoration: underline overline;
  background-color: #999999;
}
a.new:active {
  font-family: Verdana, Arial, Helvetica, sans-serif;
  font-size: 12px;
  color: #660000;
  text-decoration: none;
}
```

To apply this styling to an individual link, select the link and use Dreamweaver to apply the class, new, to it:

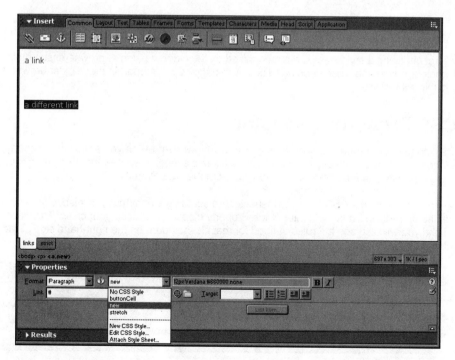

How To Attach a Stylesheet

After you have designed the stylesheet, the next step is to attach it to your documents. To do this, click the *Attach Stylesheet* button on the bottom of the CSS Styles panel.

The dialog that appears allows you to browse for your stylesheet. The two radio buttons underneath allow you to select how you would like to attach the stylesheet; the options are **link** and **import**.

link

Linking to the stylesheet is the usual way of attaching a stylesheet to your page. Selecting this option will attach your stylesheet to your page by way of the following markup:

```
<link href="global.css" rel="stylesheet" type="text/css" />
```

This way of attaching a stylesheet is supported by all CSS-enabled browsers, and is what you should do if you need browsers such as Netscape 4 to be able to apply the styles.

import

If you choose *import,* the stylesheet will be attached with this markup:

```
<style type="text/css">
  <!--
    @import url("global.css");
  -->
</style>
```

This way of attaching a stylesheet is not recognized by the older, version 4, browsers, something that can be used to our advantage when needing to deal with buggy CSS support in these older browsers. We will return to this subject later.

The CSS Property Inspector

The CSS mode of the Property Inspector is new in Dreamweaver MX. If you switch the Property Inspector to CSS mode it will give you easy access to your custom classes, as well as the ability to create new styles and edit styles (in the same way as you can from the CSS Panel).

To apply a class using the CSS Property Inspector, select the element that you wish to apply the class to. Then, in the drop-down list in the center of the Property Inspector, choose your class. The class will be applied and you will also see the rules defined for that class appear on the right-hand side of the Property Inspector, so you can see exactly what is defined for that element.

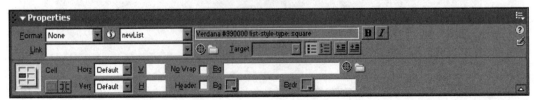

Design Files: Pre-made CSS Stylesheets

Dreamweaver MX ships with a set of ready-made 'Design Files'. These include site designs in both HTML and stylesheets. If CSS is feeling like a rather abstract concept at this point, or you just want a way to quickly get started then these files are really useful.

To use a ready-made stylesheet, select _File > New_ and in the New Document dialog box select _CSS Stylesheets_. A list of pre-made stylesheets will be displayed in the center selector box:

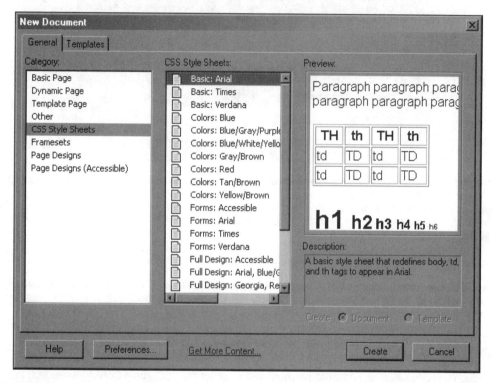

Clicking on any of the stylesheet names will show some of its elements in the right-hand window of that panel, after choosing one that you would like to work with, click _Create_, and the stylesheet will be created as a new document in Dreamweaver. You will need to save this stylesheet within your site.

To get started using your stylesheet you will need to attach it to your page Then any redefined tags will take the rules as set in the stylesheet, and any custom classes defined will be available for your use.

Design Time Stylesheets

Design time stylesheets allow you to apply a stylesheet as you are working in Dreamweaver that will not be visible when the site goes live. They are useful when working on a site that has multiple stylesheets attached, such as sites that use different stylesheets for different browsers, or sites that allow a user to select one of several stylesheets. If you are writing the link to the stylesheet out dynamically with, say, ASP, PHP, or JavaScript, Dreamweaver will not be able to render that stylesheet during the design process, so using a design-time stylesheet allows you to work visually in the Dreamweaver environment.

Working with a Design Time Stylesheet

You can open the design time stylesheets dialog box by either right-clicking (command-click on a Mac) in the CSS Styles panel select *Design Time Style Sheet* in the context menu, or choosing *Text > CSS Styles > Design Time Style Sheets*. The following dialog box will appear:

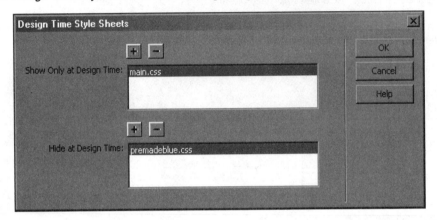

As shown above, you can select stylesheets saved within your site to be shown or hidden at Design Time. To display a CSS stylesheet at design time, click the (+) plus button above *Show Only at Design Time*, then you will be presented with a dialog that will allow you to browse for and select this stylesheet. To hide a CSS stylesheet, click the (+) plus button above *Hide at Design Time*, and once again browse for this stylesheet.

You can remove the stylesheet simply by selecting the stylesheet and clicking the minus (-) button.

The CSS Styles panel updates with the selected stylesheet's name along with an indicator, *hidden* or *design*, to reflect the stylesheet's status. This only affects the view of the document within Dreamweaver, no changes are made to your code.

Integration with Topstyle CSS Editor

Although you can select any editor to be your external editor for CSS within Dreamweaver MX, the product has a close integration with the popular TopStyle CSS editor. A trial version of TopStyle is included on the CD with Dreamweaver MX, or can be downloaded from *http://www.bradsoft.com/*, and it is a very useful application for anyone working extensively with CSS. Unfortunately TopStyle is currently a Windows-only product. There are Mac alternatives including Style Master (*http://www.westciv.com/style_master/index.html*) but they don't offer the tight integration with Dreamweaver MX that TopStyle has at this point in time.

If you are working with TopStyle you will find that changes made to your stylesheet in TopStyle will automatically be updated in Dreamweaver's Design view, and new classes that you add will be available for use immediately.

Replacing Deprecated or Illegal Elements with CSS

In *Chapter 2* we saw that many of the HTML tags commonly used for presentation purposes have been deprecated and are illegal if you wish to validate to a strict DTD. In this section we will look at how to replace those elements with their CSS counterparts.

Our XHTML Strict document shows up many of the problems that appear when all presentational or illegal tags are removed: ugly blue borders around images, our navigation bar falls apart, and text without any styling:

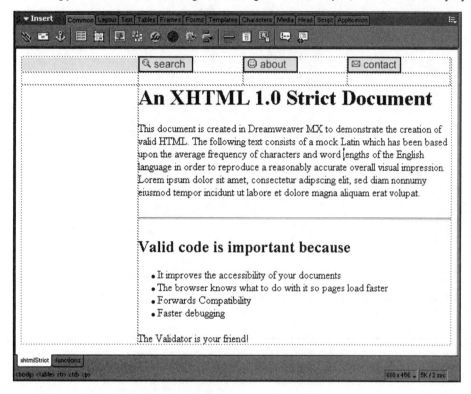

Remove Borders Around Images

In the days of HTML we would use `border="0"` to remove borders on images with links; we can create the same effect with CSS.

Open the *New Style* Dialog box, select *Redefine HTML Tag* and select *img*, as seen here:

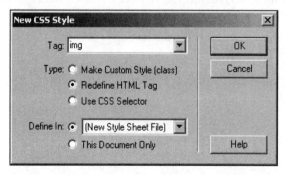

As this is the first style we are adding to this page, create it in a new external stylesheet. After saving your stylesheet, select the *Border* category in the CSS Style Definitions dialog. In the *Style* list select the value *'none'* in the Top dropdown list, and make sure that *Same for All* is checked, as seen here:

79

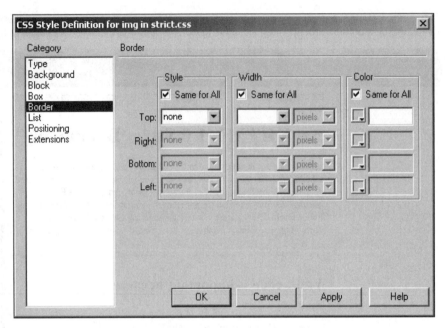

Click *OK* and you will see that your image borders have automatically disappeared within the Dreamweaver Design view.

> Dreamweaver will add a `border="0"` attribute to any image that is a link. If you need to validate to XHTML Strict, or simply do not want this attribute there, you will need to check and remove it when it appears.

Setting Properties of Table Cells

Another issue caused by the removal of presentational tags is that the cells that contain the navigation bar images no longer fit snugly around the images. To change this we will create a custom class to apply to any table cell that is holding a button.

Open the New Style Dialog and select *Make Custom Style (class)* and name this class. You should define it in your new attached stylesheet:

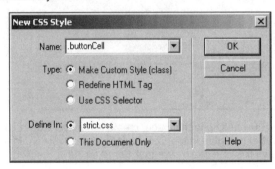

In the CSS Style Definition Dialog, go to *Box* and set the width to the width of your button, the height to the height of your button, and the padding and margin to 0 as seen here:

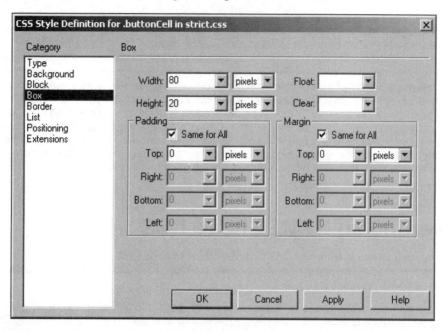

Click *OK* and then, back in your Document window, you need to apply this class to any cell that contains a button:

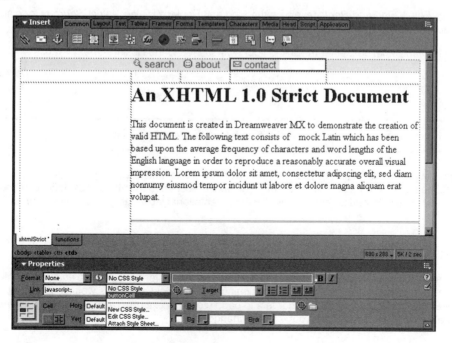

You will also need to create a class that will allow the final cell to stretch to fill the remaining space. Create a class as above and call it .stretch. Set the width of this class to 100%.

When you apply this class to the final table cell, you will notice that Dreamweaver now adds a scrollbar to the bottom of its document window due to not being able to judge the width of the viewport correctly. However, in most modern browsers it should display correctly.

> This might seem like a bit of a 'hack' and it is, but using tables for layout is in itself a hack and you are advised to avoid doing so if at all possible. My purpose here is to show how deprecated elements can be replaced. In practice most people who need to use a table-based layout are likely to stick with an XHTML Transitional DTD for the time being and use a careful combination of CSS and HTML presentational tags in order that they do not lose backwards-compatibility with older browsers. Later on in this chapter, I will explain how to create this kind of layout without using tables for positioning.

Converting an HTML Site to CSS

Once you have started to work with CSS for styling such items as fonts and borders, as opposed to HTML, you will quickly find that your older web sites are much harder to maintain and probably will want to implement CSS across them.

The way that I have achieved this in the past is to create a stylesheet that replaces exactly all your existing defaults for font sizes and face, heading sizes and face, and so on. If you are using Dreamweaver templates then you have a nice easy way to link the stylesheet to all of your pages. If not, and you have a big site, *find and replace* will be your friend!

Choose *Edit > Find and Replace*, and in the Find and Replace Dialog, select *Source Code* and enter *</head>* in the *Search For* box.

In the *Replace With* box, enter the link to your stylesheet and the closing *</head>* tag.

```
<link href="/strict.css" rel="stylesheet" type="text/css" />
</head>
```

> Note: you need to make sure that the path to your stylesheet is correct.

Unless you have redefined tags that have no HTML presentational tags affecting them, you will not see any difference to your page at first – HTML tags take precedence over the styles defined in your stylesheet. You will need to remove any HTML presentational tags that are currently within the document.

CSS for Layout

Hang around any web design-related newsgroup or mailing list for a week or so and you are likely to encounter a heated 'tables versus CSS positioning' debate. Most designers would accept that using CSS to style fonts and to add padding or borders to page elements is a good idea, but to ditch tables? We're good at using HTML tables for layout, so why change?

Why Use CSS for Layout?

Tables are designed to present tabular data, which is the sort of data normally seen in a spreadsheet. The problem occurred because web designers, desperately trying to make the Web look less like so many pages of academic writing, began to use tables in order to create layouts, thus making a tool do a job it really wasn't designed to do. Conventional browsers soon picked up on this and began to render table layouts really well, so we all started to hack tables to create complex layouts and we got good at it. So why should we want to use something different?

Forwards Compatibility

As presentational elements are deprecated and finally removed from the specifications, tables for layout will become harder to use simply because each cell of the table will need to be controlled by way of applying classes to it, as we saw earlier in this chapter. By beginning to use CSS for layout now you will be building web sites in a manner that will enable the greatest forwards compatibility – or future-proofing – for your work.

Accessibility

The W3C, in its document, "*HTML Techniques for Web Content Accessibility Guidelines 1.0*" (*http://www.w3.org/TR/WCAG10-HTML-TECHS/*) recommends that tables should not be used for layout:

5.2 Tables for layout

Checkpoints in this section:

5.3 Do not use tables for layout unless the table makes sense when linearized. Otherwise, if the table does not make sense, provide an alternative equivalent (which may be a linearized version). [Priority 2]

5.4 If a table is used for layout, do not use any structural markup for the purpose of visual formatting. [Priority 2]

Authors should use stylesheets for layout and positioning. However, when it is necessary to use a table for layout, the table must linearize in a readable order. When a table is linearized, the contents of the cells become a series of paragraphs (for instance, down the page) one after another. Cells should make sense when read in row order and should include structural elements (that create paragraphs, headings, lists, etc.) so the page makes sense after linearization.

Also, when using tables to create a layout, do not use structural markup to create visual formatting. For example, the TH (table header) element, is usually displayed visually as centered, and bold. If a cell is not actually a header for a row or column of data, use stylesheets or formatting attributes of the element.

The W3C quite clearly says that tables should not be used for layout. This makes sense if you consider what happens to a table-based layout once it is linearized:

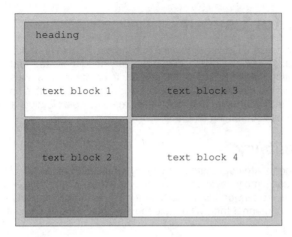

The figure above shows a typical table-based layout, with the data being placed in different cells of the table structure in order to affect the visual display of the page. The layout displayed above would be read by a screen reader as follows:

```
Heading
Text Block 1
Text Block 3
Text Block 2
Text Block 4
```

If the content of blocks 1 and 2 should be following on one from another, this page would become very difficult to understand if text block 3 followed 1!

Platform and Device Independence

As we have already seen, CSS degrades without fault in browsers that do not support CSS at all. In the case of the CSS layout this means that your document will display with the structure that you have given it, ignoring the way that items have been positioned. By carefully structuring your document, and ensuring that the flow of information is meaningful without positioning, you will allow all web users to have access to your content – whether they are on a non-CSS supporting PDA, a text-only browser, or using a screen or Braille reader.

Ease of Redesign

Just as using CSS defined in an external stylesheet will allow you to change the colors or fonts site-wide, using CSS to position page elements will allow you to change the layout of your pages site-wide. If your client decides that the navigation should now be on the right instead of the left – no problem – a few minor edits to one stylesheet and the layout is changed. Compare that to the potentially difficult task of recoding complex nested tables.

Browser Support

Browser support is one of the main issues that divides those who use tables and those who have switched to CSS layouts. There is support for CSS positioning to some extent in all browsers from the version 4 browsers (IE 4/Netscape 44) upwards. As anyone who has attempted to get a CSS layout working with a version 4 browser will know, very few properties are supported, and those properties that are supported may be in a strange or inconsistent way.

CSS Layouts in Dreamweaver MX

In Dreamweaver MX, as in Dreamweaver 3 and 4, you can design your site using 'layers' instead of, or as well as tables. Layers are nothing more than inline CSS positioning and should not be confused with the proprietary `<layer>` tag in Netscape 4, which modern browsers do not support. In order to build a CSS layout in Dreamweaver you can either use 'layers' or build an external stylesheet that contains your positioning and attach that to your page. We will look at the pros and cons of each method here.

Layers

As I have already mentioned 'layers' are simply inline CSS positioning. By using Dreamweaver layers to lay out your page you will not gain many of the advantages of using CSS, as you will still need to edit each document in your site individually to make changes. However, using layers is the easiest way to explore CSS positioning in the Dreamweaver environment, so we'll look at this method initially.

Create a new document. On the *Common tab* of the Insert Toolbar, select *Draw Layer*. To recreate the navigation bar so that it looks similar to the table layout version, draw a wide 'layer' across the top of the document. In the Property Inspector set the size of the layer as 20px in height and 96% wide.

In the Property Inspector you can also set the distance that the 'layer' will be positioned from the top and left of the viewport – see the figure below – I have used 2% for the left position because I want this layer to remain more-or-less central in the browser. Name this layer `nav`:

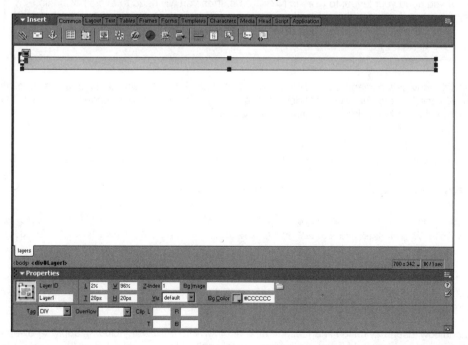

Now we need a new layer, which we will call `content`, to hold the content. Drag it to approximately the correct area on the page. We want this layer to be positioned from the right-hand side of the page, in order to keep our liquid layout. However, Dreamweaver MX doesn't give us the ability to position things from the right-hand side of the page.

To position this layer we'll need to switch into Code view. If you select the layer first, it will be highlighted once you are in Code view and you will be able to find it easily. The `content` layer should look something like this:

```
<div id="content" style="position:absolute; left:180px; top:68px; width:536px;
height:259px; z-index:2"></div>
```

You need to delete the definition for `left` and replace it with one for `right`, like so:

```
<div id="content" style="position:absolute; right: 7%; top:72px; width:70%; z-
index:2;">
```

I have also removed the `height` rule so that the area will resize to the size of the content and set the width of this layer to `70%`.

This will mean that whatever the size of the user's browser window, the content will resize with it. However in the Design view we are now left with a little problem. If you so much as touch that layer, a `left: xxx;` rule will be added to the code which will break the fluidity of the page – it's easy enough to delete it again but a bit of a nuisance.

> If you need your layout to work in Netscape 4, then you will need to avoid positioning elements from the right-hand side of the page, or use an external stylesheet and one of the methods that I will discuss in the '*Browser and Device Issues*' section further on in this chapter.

To add the navigation images, we need to return to our `nav` layer. Select that layer and switch into Code view. We need to add one additional definition to this layer in order for our images to be placed 180 pixels away from the left-hand side of the layer. Edit this line:

```
<div id="nav" style="position:absolute; left:2%; top:20px; width:96%; height:20px;
z-index:1; background-color: #F0F0F0; layer-background-color: #F0F0F0;"></div>
```

and add `padding-left: 180px;` so that you end up with this:

```
<div id="nav" style="position:absolute; left:2%; top:20px; width:96%; height:20px;
z-index:1; background-color: #F0F0F0; layer-background-color: #F0F0F0; padding-
left: 180px;"></div>
```

Switch back into Design view and click inside the layer and you will find that your cursor ends up 180 pixels in from the left. You will see that Dreamweaver has added the rule `layer-background-color: #F0F0F0;`, which is a proprietary Netscape rule and will not validate.

You can now insert navigation images, one after another, into this layer including applying Swap Image behaviors just as you would if you are working in table cells.

Here we can see the end result in Dreamweaver MX:

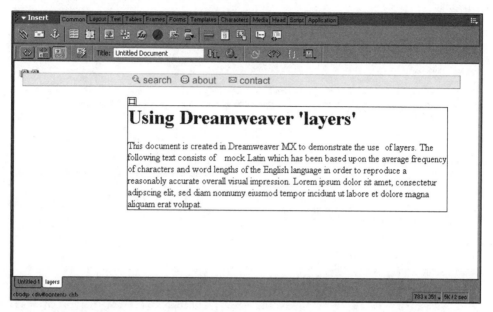

The page looks like this in IE 6:

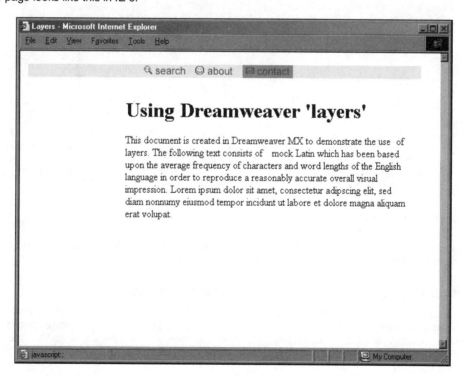

Here is the final code used to create this layout, which is in the code download for this book and saved as `layers.html`:

```
<?xml version="1.0" encoding="iso-8859-1"?>
<!DOCTYPE html PUBLIC "-//W3C//DTD XHTML 1.0 Transitional//EN"
"http://www.w3.org/TR/xhtml1/DTD/xhtml1-transitional.dtd">
<html xmlns="http://www.w3.org/1999/xhtml">
<head>
  <title>Untitled Document</title>
  <meta http-equiv="Content-Type" content="text/html; charset=iso-8859-1" />
  <script type="text/JavaScript" src="functions.js"></script>
  <link href="strict.css" rel="stylesheet" type="text/css" />
</head>

<body
onload="MM_preloadImages('i/button01b.gif','i/button02b.gif','i/button03b.gif')">

  <div id="nav" style="position:absolute; left:2%; top:20px; width:96%;
height:20px; z-index:1; background-color: #F0F0F0; layer-background-color:
#F0F0F0; padding-left: 180px;">

    <a href="javascript:;"
onmouseover="MM_swapImage('img1','','i/button01b.gif',1)"
onmouseout="MM_swapImgRestore()"><img src="i/button01.gif" alt="search this site"
name="img1" width="80" height="20" id="img1" /></a><a href="javascript:;"
onmouseover="MM_swapImage('img2','','i/button02b.gif',1)"
onmouseout="MM_swapImgRestore()"><img src="i/button02.gif" alt="about" name="img2"
width="80" height="20" id="img2" /></a><a href="javascript:;"
onmouseover="MM_swapImage('img3','','i/button03b.gif',1)"
onmouseout="MM_swapImgRestore()"><img src="i/button03.gif" alt="contact me"
name="img3" width="80" height="20" id="img3" /></a>

  </div>

  <div id="content" style="position:absolute; right: 7%; top:72px; width:70%; z-
index:2;">
    <h1>Using Dreamweaver 'layers'</h1>
    <p>This document is created in Dreamweaver MX to demonstrate the use of
layers.
      The following text consists of mock Latin which has been based upon the
      average frequency of characters and word lengths of the English language in
      order to reproduce a reasonably accurate overall visual impression. Lorem
      ipsum dolor sit amet, consectetur adipscing elit, sed diam nonnumy eiusmod
      tempor incidunt ut labore et dolore magna aliquam erat volupat.</p>
  </div>
</body>
</html>
```

Even using inline styles to add positioning to this document, there is significantly less code in comparison with the tables-for-layout version.

CSS Positioning Defined in an External Stylesheet

Using Dreamweaver layers to create a layout, whilst preferable to using tables and presentational HTML, means that each page of the site has to contain the CSS rules markup for positioning the elements. If you remember, defining our CSS styles in an external stylesheet meant that we could change font size or color site-wide by altering one definition. Defining CSS positioning in an external stylesheet is just as powerful.

We can use the page that we created with Dreamweaver's layers in the previous section to get us started.

Switch to Code view and locate the CSS rules for the navigation bar:

```
<div id="nav" style="position:absolute; left:2%; top:20px; width:96%; height:20px;
z-index:1; background-color: #F0F0F0; layer-background-color: #F0F0F0; padding-
left: 180px;">
```

We are going to need to place these rules into an external stylesheet, so if you already have a stylesheet attached to the page, open it either in Dreamweaver or in your external CSS editor. If you have no stylesheet attached, then create one and link it to this page now.

In the stylesheet add the following CSS rules:

```
#nav {
    position:absolute;
    left:2%; top:20px;
    width:96%;
    height:20px;
    z-index:1;
    background-color: #F0F0F0;
    layer-background-color: #F0F0F0;
    padding-left: 180px;
}
```

You will notice that these are exactly the same rules as could be found inline, we have simply moved them into the external stylesheet.

Now, back in our HTML document, delete the style definition so that we are left with:

```
<div id="nav">
```

The same process should be followed in order to place the definition for the content div into the external stylesheet. The page will display in the same way within Dreamweaver and when previewed in the browser as it did when we used inline CSS. The benefits, however, should be obvious at this point – the page will contain less code and will therefore load more quickly, but the main benefit is that every page that links to this stylesheet will display any `<div>` with an id of nav or content in exactly the same way. If you want to put your navigation on the bottom of the page, or change the background color of the content, you need only alter the rules in one place.

Structuring Content Effectively

In using CSS to lay out our pages we are freed from the necessity of structuring the flow of our content in order to create the layout. This leaves us free to consider how we can best structure our document so that people visiting our site with a device that won't use the layout information (for example, screen readers and text-only browsers) are still able to make sense of our content.

In order to structure the content effectively, we need to consider how our information would be presented in a linearized form, devoid of formatting. We should consider how a user would navigate the site should they be having the contents read out to them by way of a screen reader or if they are simply using a text-only browser such as Lynx and needing to tab through each link in order to get to the right one to move onto another document.

It is generally a good idea to place items such as navigation links to get at least back to the homepage or to the main sections of the site near the top of the page in order that a user can quickly go back to the homepage or on to a different section if they realize that this page is not what they wanted. Any content that is not the main focus of the page should go to the end of the document.

Our CSS Layout As Displayed in Lynx

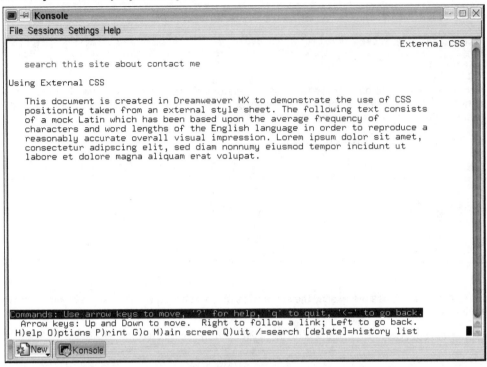

Using the text-only browser Lynx is a good way of testing our document structure. You can see the navigation links at the top of the page; it has taken the text of these from our `alt` text as it does not display images. Then follows our `<h1>` heading and then the content.

.. and On an Ipaq in Pocket Explorer (no CSS Support)

Pocket Explorer does not support CSS, but does display images, so our navigation images appear. However, everything is displayed linearly. It is important when designing with such devices in mind to remember that because the screen is so small, only a small amount of your content will appear when the page loads initially. Hence we need to make sure that there is useful content available quickly to catch the user's attention.

Browser and Device Issues

Browser issues are cited as the main reason that people do not implement CSS on their web sites; this excuse is fast becoming outdated. However, while browsers with no support for CSS should render your content in a readable fashion, there are problems with browsers that have partial or buggy support for CSS and it is these browsers, particularly Netscape 4, that we need to consider.

Versions of Netscape 4 may crash when encountering certain valid CSS declarations, or they may render your page so that it is unusable, or just plain ugly! Thankfully there are ways around this problem.

@import for Netscape 4

Earlier, we looked at two ways of attaching a stylesheet to our page: linking it, or using @import. Netscape 4 does not recognize @import, so we use this fact to our advantage by attaching two stylesheets to the page: one basic, Netscape 4-friendly, stylesheet that we link to our page, and another, more advanced stylesheet, which we attach using @import, and is therefore invisible to Netscape 4.

To attach two stylesheets to your page in this way using Dreamweaver, you need to attach the basic Netscape 4 friendly stylesheet **first**, using the link method:

then attach the second stylesheet, with the declarations for newer browsers using @import:

You have to specify the imported stylesheet *after* the linked stylesheet, so that the basic Netscape 4-friendly CSS is overridden by the second stylesheet.

In Code view the generated code looks like this:

```
<link href="oldbrowsers.css" rel="stylesheet" type="text/css" />
<style type="text/css">
<!--
@import url("newbrowsers.css");
-->
</style>
```

Any CSS that you want to be different for newer browsers must be included in the imported stylesheet. The browser will use the values in the linked stylesheet if no values are found in the imported one for that element.

JavaScript Techniques

It is also possible to use JavaScript to detect what browser is being used, and write out the appropriate stylesheet for that browser. This method relies on the user having JavaScript turned on, but can be very useful if you find that a bug in a particular browser causes a crash or other problem, and you need to isolate that browser by attaching a stylesheet designed to be friendly to it.

We can also use JavaScript to detect whether the user is visiting with a newer, more standards-compliant browser, or a pre-version 5 browser, and display stylesheets accordingly. This method checks to see whether the browser supports the W3C DOM, which newer browsers do, and then writes the appropriate stylesheet into the page.

```
<script language="javascript" type="text/javascript">
if (!document.getElementById) {
document.write('<link rel="stylesheet" href="oldbrowsers.css" type="text/css"
/>');
}
else
{
document.write('<link rel="stylesheet" href="newbrowsers.css" type="text/css"
/>');
}
</script>
```

The first stylesheet in the above code should be the stylesheet for those older browsers that do not support the W3C DOM, the second stylesheet is for all newer browsers.

Media Descriptors

Media descriptors allow us to specify how a document is to be presented on different media: monitor screens, paper, screen readers, Braille readers, or other devices. For example, we can specify that a different stylesheet is used if a page is being printed to that which is used when it's displayed in the browser window. It will allow a stylesheet designed with speech synthesis rules to be served to screen readers, and stylesheets designed with Web TV or PDAs in mind to be served appropriately.

Whether a browser or device will understand the media descriptor varies between devices at present, but there is good support for `print` (and this is the media descriptor you may find most useful currently) and learning to use this method of serving appropriate presentational rules should become more useful in the future as device support grows.

The media descriptors as listed in the CSS2 specification are:

Descriptor	Media
all	All devices
aural	Speech synthesizers (screen readers)
braille	Braille tactile feedback devices
embossed	Paged Braille printers
handheld	Handheld devices (small screen, monochrome, limited bandwidth)
print	Documents to be printed
projection	Projection devices
screen	Color computer screens – standard web browsers
tty	Media using a fixed-pitch character grid or portable devices with limited display capabilities. These are typically older mobile devices, most current devices would fall into handheld
tv	Television

You can use media descriptors in two ways: either by specifying a separate stylesheet for each type that you wish to use, or by using @import.

Specifying a Separate Stylesheet for Each Media Descriptor

If you already have a stylesheet linked to your page for the screen presentation of your document and want to add a stylesheet that will only come into play when the document is printed, you can add a second linked stylesheet for print. You will also need to add the media descriptor screen to your existing stylesheet so that the browser knows that the screen stylesheet is to be used in the browser, but the print stylesheet should be used when the page is printed.

```
<link rel="stylesheet" type="text/css" media="screen" href="screen.css" />
<link rel="stylesheet" type="text/css" media="print" href="print.css" />
```

Using a print stylesheet allows you to, for instance, hide navigation when a document is printed; change the font from a sans-serif typeface (which is more readable on screen) to serif typeface (which is more readable in print); remove a background color or images that would cause the printing to take longer and generally allow you control over the way the page appears when printed.

Using @import With Media Descriptors

The above method means that you need to create a separate stylesheet for each browser; by using @import you can have one stylesheet and specify certain elements for certain types of media. To use the @import method attach your stylesheet to the page like so:

```
<style type="text/css" media="all">@import "all.css";</style>
```

Within the stylesheet all.css you add attributes for each media descriptor, by using @media as in the example overleaf:

```
@media print {
  body { font-size: 10pt; }
}

@media screen {
  body { font-size: 12px; }
}

@media screen, print {
  body { color: #000000; }
}
```

The above declarations will give a font size of 10 points when the page is printed, 12 pixels when the page is viewed in a regular browser and both screen and print will use #000000 (black) as the color of the body text.

Validating Your CSS

Dreamweaver MX has no built-in CSS validator, however you can validate your CSS easily using the CSS Validator on the W3c web site: *http://jigsaw.w3.org/css-validator/*. You can download the validator to use offline, validate your stylesheet by simply pointing the validator to a stylesheet that is uploaded to your web space, upload your stylesheet to the validator, or simply copy and paste the contents of it into a textbox on the site.

As with HTML and XHTML pages, validating your stylesheet will help you to fix issues that could cause problems in some browsers, and is a good thing to do if you are experiencing problems.

Summary

In this chapter I have tried to give a basic grounding in the fundamentals of CSS, both within Dreamweaver and in the raw code in order that you can quickly understand the concepts behind the interface. You should feel confident in understanding:

- What CSS is

- The different ways you can implement CSS on your web site

- The CSS tools within Dreamweaver MX

- CSS for text styling

- CSS for positioning – both using 'Layers' (Inline CSS Positioning) and CSS Positioning in an external stylesheet

- The browser and device issues inherent in using CSS, and some methods to cope with those

There are many resources available that will help you to take your CSS skills to the next level; including the glasshaus book, '*Cascading Style Sheets: Separating Content From Presentation*' (ISBN: 1-904151-04-3), and numerous resources on the Web. Now that Dreamweaver MX brings good CSS support to your development environment, you can be creating sites with CSS in no time at all.

In the next chapter we're going to take a detailed look at constructing accessible web sites with Dreamweaver MX.

4

- Accessibility overview

- Accessibility standards

- Why is accessibility important?

- Accessibility tools in Dreamweaver MX

Author: Bob Regan and Alan Foley

Accessibility and Dreamweaver MX

Creating accessible web pages has never been more important than it is today. With the recent adoption of accessibility standards in the United States, Canada, the European Union, Australia, Japan, and Brazil, designers and developers face mandates to ensure that people with disabilities are able to access the contents of web sites and web applications.

In addition, ensuring that web sites are accessible to people with disabilities is simply the right thing to do. For people with disabilities, the Internet can be a tremendously valuable tool. It can provide access to the world around us, as well as a level of independence not previously possible.

Imagine a task as simple as reading the newspaper. Prior to the Internet, a blind person who wanted to read the paper had two choices. He could get a Braille version of the paper, which was expensive and often hard to find, or he could ask someone to read the paper to him. Today, a blind person is able to use software called a screen reader to read the news to him from a web site each day. Dependence on others is eliminated.

Now, imagine a person with a disability writing a memo to a colleague, or applying for a promotion, or taking a course at a university. For many people with disabilities, accessibility is about much more than convenience. It is about access to employment, education, and the community. It's about being able to lead a normal life.

Dreamweaver MX provides the most complete set of tools available for building, editing, and maintaining accessible web sites and web applications. Dreamweaver MX includes tools that prompt designers to provide important accessibility information when inserting images, forms, media, tables, and frames. Moreover, Dreamweaver MX helps designers understand and comply with accessibility standards, with features that include a reference guide, templates, code snippets, and a built-in accessibility validation tool.

Finally, Dreamweaver MX makes it easier than ever for people with disabilities to create web sites and web applications. With improvements to the authoring environment, Dreamweaver MX now works with assistive technologies such as the Window-Eyes™ screen reader from GW Micro (*http://www.gwmicro.com/*) and the JAWS screen reader from Freedom Scientific (*http://www.freedomscientific.com/*).

This chapter will introduce the topic of accessibility and review the accessibility features of Macromedia Dreamweaver MX. Topics include:

- Accessibility overview
  - Defining disabilities
  - Assistive technologies
  - Accessibility standards
  - Why is accessibility important?
- Accessibility in Dreamweaver MX
  - Accessibility preferences options
  - Adding images
  - Adding media
  - Adding frames
  - Adding forms
  - Adding tables
  - Accessibility validation
  - Accessibility reference
  - Accessible templates
  - Accessible authoring environment

All the code samples seen in the chapter are available in the code download for this book, available from glasshaus.com.

Accessibility Overview

In general terms, accessibility describes how well web sites work for people with disabilities. An accessible site is one in which design elements such as color, font size, or layout do not obscure the site's content. An accessible web site is also compatible with the assistive technologies used by people with disabilities.

More specifically, policies such as **Section 508** of the US Rehabilitation Act (*http://www.section508.gov/*) and guidelines such as the **Web Accessibility Initiative**, or **WAI** (*http://www.w3.org/TR/WCAG10*) specify what constitutes an accessible site with a series of checkpoints. Each checkpoint addresses issues for specific disabilities and technologies.

This section provides a more complete definition of accessibility in terms of the range of disabilities commonly found among web users, the assistive technologies used, and the policies governing web accessibility. Finally, this section reviews a number of reasons for incorporating accessibility into web site design.

Defining Disabilities

A 1997 report by the US Census Bureau (*http://www.census.gov/*) categorizes 19.6 percent of the United States population as having some sort of disability. This percentage is generally considered to be consistent with worldwide statistics. Within the broader category of disability are the following:

- Visual impairments

- Hearing impairments

- Motor impairments

- Cognitive impairments

Each of these categories includes a range of conditions. For example, visual impairments include low vision, color blindness, and blindness. The tools and techniques addressing issues for people who are blind are very different from those that address issues for people who are color-blind. Perhaps the most diverse category is that of cognitive impairments. This group includes people with seizure disorders, as well as people with learning or developmental disabilities. Building sites that are accessible to people with cognitive disabilities can be a complex task as the obstacles to comprehension often lie in the content as well as in the page design.

Disability categories can overlap and might also include temporary disabilities. One group that is often overlooked is the deaf-blind community. For people who are deaf and blind, the Internet can be an immensely important means of communicating with others. In addition, any one of us may find ourselves temporarily disabled – someone with a broken wrist may have difficulty using a mouse but still need access to the Web to meet day-to-day job requirements.

At the same time, it is important to keep in mind that as people get older, most face a disability of some kind. While nearly 20 percent of the total US population has a disability, as the population ages, the proportion of people with disabilities grows higher (see the table below). In fact, almost 75 percent of the population over the age of 80 has a disability. Thus, accessibility is not just about opening doors; it is about keeping them open. Accessibility allows people to maintain a level of independence that age might otherwise make difficult.

Ages	Total Number	With Disability	Percent with Disability
All Ages	267,665,000	52,596,000	19.7%
Under 15 years	59,606,000	4,661,000	7.8%
15 to 24 years	36,897,000	3,961,000	10.7%
25 to 44 years	83,887,000	11,200,000	13.4%

Table continued on following page

Ages	Total Number	With Disability	Percent with Disability
45 to 54 years	33,620,000	7,585,000	22.6%
55 to 64 years	21,591,000	7,708,000	35.7%
65 years and over	32,064,000	17,480,000	54.5%

Source: *http://www.census.gov/hhes/www/disable/sipp/disab97/ds97t1.html*

Assistive Technologies

Users with disabilities frequently rely on hardware and software to access web content. These tools, known as assistive technologies, range from screen readers to touch screens and head pointers.

Blind users of the web frequently use software called a screen reader to read the contents of a web page out loud. Two common screen readers, already mentioned above, are JAWS, from Freedom Scientific, and Window-Eyes, from GW Micro. Screen readers enable users to hear, rather than read, the contents of a web page; however, a screen reader can read only text, not images or animations. It is essential therefore that images and animations be assigned text descriptions that screen readers can read. These text descriptions are called alternative text, or alt text.

Users with impaired mobility may rely on the keyboard instead of the mouse to navigate web pages. For individuals with nerve damage, arthritis, or repetitive motion injuries, use of the mouse may not be comfortable or possible. Using only *Tab* and *Enter* on the keyboard, it is possible for these individuals to negotiate a page with ease. Many users of the Internet have this capability and are simply unaware of it. In Internet Explorer (IE), pressing *Tab* moves the focus of the browser among all available links on a page. The dotted lines around links in IE let the user know where the current focus of the browser is positioned. Pressing *Enter* activates links, giving the same effect as clicking (and releasing) a mouse. In the example below, notice the dotted lines around the link for "*Usable Forms for the Web.*"

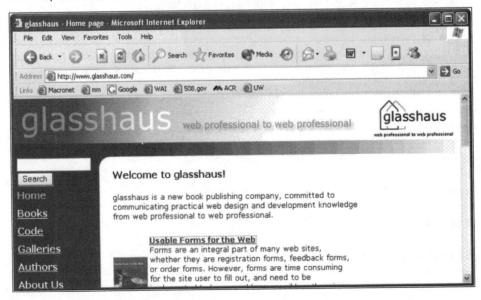

In some cases, users may employ touch screens, head pointers, or other assistive devices. A touch screen allows an individual to navigate the page using her or his hands without the fine-motor control required by the mouse. A head pointer is simply a stick placed in a person's mouth or mounted on a head strap that the person uses to interact with a keyboard or a touch screen.

In these cases, it is very important that essential components of the page work without a mouse. Rollovers, drop-down lists, and interactive simulations are all examples of elements that typically depend on the mouse for user interaction. The designer or developer of these elements must ensure that keyboard-defined events are included along with mouse-defined events. A quick test using the keystrokes available in IE can provide a valuable glimpse of the difficulties a web page may present for users with disabilities. For example, a user can move to any focusable object including links, form controls, and embedded objects by pressing the *tab* key and pressing the *enter* key will activate selected links. Pressing *ctrl + tab* moves between frames.

Accessibility Standards

Accessibility policies vary from country to country, but many countries, including the United States, Australia, Canada, the European Union, and Japan have adopted policies based on standards developed by the **World Wide Web Consortium (W3C)**. In 1994, the W3C began investigating accessibility issues that might be encountered by people with disabilities on the new emerging World Wide Web. This group led to the formation of the Web Accessibility Initiative (WAI). The WAI consists of several efforts to improve the accessibility of the Web. Perhaps the most widely used document is the **Web Content Accessibility Guidelines (WCAG)**.

For each of the fourteen guidelines that constitute the WCAG, there are a series of checkpoints rated as Priority 1, Priority 2, or Priority 3:

- Priority 1 checkpoints are the actions designers *must* take to make a site accessible

- Priority 2 checkpoints are the actions designers *should* take to make a site accessible

- Priority 3 checkpoints are the actions a designer *might* take to improve the accessibility of a site

The Priority 1 checkpoints of the WCAG serve as the basis of accessibility standards in almost every country where a formal policy has been adopted. The exceptions are Canada and the United Kingdom, where web site designers for the national governments are required to follow the Priority 1 and Priority 2 checkpoints of the WCAG.

In the United States, the law governing web accessibility is commonly referred to as Section 508. Section 508 of the US Rehabilitation Act prohibits federal agencies from buying, developing, maintaining, or using electronic and information technologies that are inaccessible to people with disabilities. Originally enacted in 1988, Section 508 made little progress until Congress passed the Workforce Investment Act ten years later. This amendment to Section 508 mandated standards for accessibility and, what is more, gave members of the public and government employees with disabilities the right to sue agencies in federal court and file administrative complaints for non-compliance.

As of 21 June 2002, all federal web sites are expected to comply with the standards mandated under Section 508. These standards are based on the Priority 1 checkpoints of the WCAG, with one Priority 3 checkpoint thrown in for good measure. Section 508 does not make any provision for Priority 2 checkpoints of the WCAG.

The difference between Section 508 and the WCAG is subtle but important. Section 508 was intended to define when a problem was severe enough to serve as the basis of a lawsuit. The WCAG defines a set of goals for accessible design. As a result, the Section 508 standards were designed to be evaluated more easily. This has made the Section 508 standards a popular basis for accessibility policies at the state, local, and institutional level. Designers and developers in these settings are often under no federal mandate to follow the Section 508 standards. Instead, their local accessibility policy may require use of these standards. This distinction can be confusing but important. The consequences for non-compliance may vary significantly from place to place.

The Section 508 standards actually consist of six parts. Each addresses a different type of technology. The full set of standards for each section may be found at the URLs listed below:

- 1194.21 Software applications and operating systems
  http://www.section508.gov/index.cfm?FuseAction=Content&ID=12#Software

- 1194.22 Web-based intranet and Internet information and applications
  http://www.section508.gov/index.cfm?FuseAction=Content&ID=12#Web

- 1194.23 Telecommunications products
  http://www.section508.gov/index.cfm?FuseAction=Content&ID=12#Telecommunications

- 1194.24 Video and multimedia products
  http://www.section508.gov/index.cfm?FuseAction=Content&ID=12#Video

- 1194.25 Self-contained, closed products
  http://www.section508.gov/index.cfm?FuseAction=Content&ID=12#Self

- 1194.26 Desktop and portable computers.
  http://www.section508.gov/index.cfm?FuseAction=Content&ID=12#Desktop

Most relevant to the discussion here are the standards for web content outlined in section 1194.22. These standards are listed below. It is important to note that in cases where plug-ins, such as Macromedia Flash content, are used, the Software and Operating System standards outlined in section 1194.21 apply. To learn more about the Section 508 standards, visit *http://www.section508.gov* or *http://www.macromedia.com/macromedia/accessibility/*.

§ 1194.22

Web-based intranet and Internet information and applications.

- (a) A text equivalent for every non-text element shall be provided (for example, via "alt", "longdesc", or in element content).

- (b) Equivalent alternatives for any multimedia presentation shall be synchronized with the presentation.

- (c) Web pages shall be designed so that all information conveyed with color is also available without color, for example from context or markup.

- (d) Documents shall be organized so they are readable without requiring an associated stylesheet.

- (e) Redundant text links shall be provided for each active region of a server-side image map.

- (f) Client-side image maps shall be provided instead of server-side image maps except where the regions cannot be defined with an available geometric shape.

- (g) Row and column headers shall be identified for data tables.

- (h) Markup shall be used to associate data cells and header cells for data tables that have two or more logical levels of row or column headers.

- (i) Frames shall be titled with text that facilitates frame identification and navigation.

- (j) Pages shall be designed to avoid causing the screen to flicker with a frequency greater than 55 Hz and lower than 2 Hz.

- (k) A text-only page, with equivalent information or functionality, shall be provided to make a web site comply with the provisions of this part, when compliance cannot be accomplished in any other way. The content of the text-only page shall be updated whenever the primary page changes.

- (l) When pages utilize scripting languages to display content, or to create interface elements, the information provided by the script shall be identified with functional text that can be read by assistive technology.

- (m) When a web page requires that an applet, plug-in or other application be present on the client system to interpret page content, the page must provide a link to a plug-in or applet that complies with §1194.21(a) through (l).

- (n) When electronic forms are designed to be completed online, the form shall allow people using assistive technology to access the information, field elements, and functionality required for completion and submission of the form, including all directions and cues.

- (o) A method shall be provided that permits users to skip repetitive navigation links.

- (p) When a timed response is required, the user shall be alerted and given sufficient time to indicate more time is required.

Why Is Accessibility Important?

For most people, the reasons for creating an accessible web site are simple: it is the right thing to do and it is the law. It is often helpful, however, to point out the additional benefits of creating an accessible web site. The following is a list of reasons many find compelling:

- Accessibility is the right thing to do

- Accessibility is the law for many institutions

- Accessibility offers benefits for **all** users, not just those with disabilities

- Accessibility uses innovative technology

- Accessibility creates market opportunity

Accessibility Is the Right Thing To Do

Accessibility represents an important step toward independence for individuals with disabilities. Accessible web pages provide access to fundamental government services and information such as tax forms, social programs, and legislative representatives. Accessible web pages also make possible a broader range of employment and educational opportunities by providing added means of communication. In addition, accessibility allows users with disabilities to participate in day-to-day activities many of us take for granted, such as reading a newspaper or buying a gift for a loved one.

Accessibility Is the Law for Many Institutions

With new national requirements in the United States, Canada, and the European Union, and more to come in the near future, there are numerous legal mandates for accessibility. These policies will likely expand in scope. In the US, for instance, Section 508 sets standards for web pages designed or maintained by federal agencies. State and local governments as well as educational and nonprofit institutions around the US are considering their own accessibility policies. For example, earlier this year the University of Wisconsin at Madison adopted an Accessibility Policy requiring all pages published or hosted by the university to conform to all WCAG Priority 1 and 2 checkpoints.

Accessibility Offers Benefits for All Users

As with many improvements intended for individuals with disabilities, the enhancements of accessible design offer benefits for all users of the Web. Anyone who has pushed a shopping cart out of a grocery store can attest to the value of automatic doors and ramps cut into curbs. Similarly, accessible web pages are often easier to read, easier to navigate, and faster to download, as they are optimized for ease of use, and don't tend to contain so many page elements that are often the culprits behind making sites large in size and slow loading, such as Flash movies, and large images.

Accessibility Uses Innovative Technology

Accessible design is based on the premise that web pages must work with a range of browsers that includes more than just Netscape and Internet Explorer. A page must be accessible whether using a screen reader, a refreshable Braille display, or a head pointer. Making pages work with non-standard browsers often makes them available to other consumer Internet devices, such as WAP-enabled phones or handheld Personal Digital Assistants (PDAs).

The techniques of accessibility are based on recent technologies and design strategies. Older, static HTML designs often intermix content with formatting on web pages. Accessibility guidelines encourage the separation of formatting from content through the use of Cascading Style Sheets (CSS) to allow more flexible use of content and easier implementation of more powerful dynamic models. For more on the use of CSS for accessibility, refer back to *Chapter 3* of this book.

Accessibility Creates Market Opportunity

Accessibility offers potential for organizations and businesses to reach new customers and new markets. As additional policies are adopted, the need among government and educational institutions for goods and services that support an accessibility policy is growing. In the US, businesses providing goods and services to the government via the Web or other information technology should understand Section 508. Businesses that understand accessibility issues and comply with Section 508 have a strong market advantage. This advantage is multiplied as local governments implement new policies.

Accessibility in Dreamweaver MX

For designers and developers trying to build accessible content, Dreamweaver MX is an ideal tool. Dreamweaver MX automates many elements of creating accessible sites and prompts designers to provide information when necessary. Dreamweaver MX also includes powerful validation and reference tools to help designers ensure that their sites are designed properly. Another advantage of Dreamweaver MX is that it has been modified to provide better keyboard access and to work with screen readers. Dreamweaver is the first professional design tool to be accessible to individuals with disabilities.

This section outlines the accessibility features implemented in Dreamweaver MX. Each of the features will be explained and described in terms of the benefits for people with disabilities and for the designers themselves.

Accessibility Preferences Options

Creating accessible web pages requires designers and developers to mark up elements of the page with information to be used by assistive technologies such as screen readers. For example, each image on a page should be given a text equivalent, called 'alternative text' or 'alt text,' which a screen reader conveys to its user in place of the image.

Accessibility features such as alt text are often overlooked when creating web sites. Dreamweaver MX allows designers and developers to set preferences that remind them to provide accessibility information as they are building the page. By activating the first five *Accessibility* options in the *Preferences* dialog box that you can get to via the *Edit* menu (see below), designers and developers will be prompted to provide accessibility-related information for form objects, frames, media, images, and tables as they insert each of these elements – see below for more on these prompts.

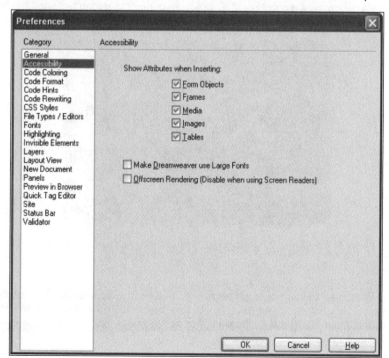

Adding images

With the *Images* option selected, users are asked to provide a text equivalent and a description for each image as it is inserted. When a user inserts an image, the following panel appears:

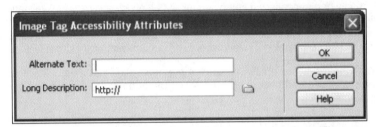

A screen reader reads the alt text in place of the image. In general, it is desirable to describe the image in terms of its function rather than its appearance. This helps the content flow better as it is read to the user. It also spares the user from long descriptions that are not relevant to the content.

In general, alt text (which is contained in the `alt` attribute of an element) should be limited to about 50 characters. If further details are required to convey the content of the image adequately, the designer should consider using a long description. The `longdesc` attribute is a link to a longer description stored on a separate page. Although the long description is not visible to sighted users, screen reader users are notified of the existence of the link.

In the example that follows, the sourcecode listed shows that the image has both an `alt` attribute and a `longdesc` attribute associated with it. The image shows a diver near a coral reef with alt text that reads, "Safe diving near a coral reef." There is also a link to a long description file, `scuba.html`, which might include a more detailed discussion of the techniques demonstrated in the photo.

```
<img src="/images/scuba.gif alt="Safe diving near a coral reef"
     longdesc="scuba.html">
```

For images that convey no content, such as spacer images, the appropriate `alt` attribute is `alt=""`. To set an empty `alt` attribute, Dreamweaver MX has a new pull-down menu on the *Property inspector*. From this pull-down menu, the designer or developer may select `<empty>` as the value for the `alt` attribute.

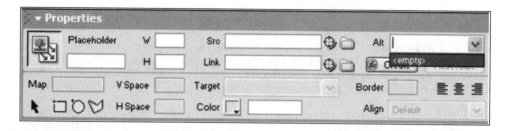

Adding Media

Inserting a media object on a page raises a number of significant issues.

First, it is important to make sure that the object itself is accessible. Under Section 508 standards, any content that is delivered using a plug-in is considered a piece of software. Therefore, media elements such as pieces of Flash or Shockwave must be evaluated using the software standards. For more information on the software standards, visit *http://www.section508.gov*.

Second, designers might want to provide more information about the media element using Dreamweaver MX. As with images, when a media element is inserted, a dialog box appears to collect accessibility-related information.

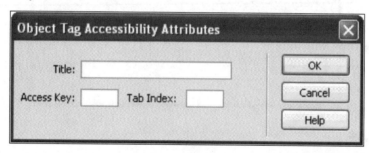

The `title` attribute (see *Title* above) is intended to function in a similar fashion to the `alt` attribute for images; however, support for this attribute in browsers and screen readers is fairly weak (it is supported in Netscape 6+ and IE 4+). It is up to the individual designer to decide if it is worth using.

Access Key (the `accesskey` attribute) provides keyboard users with a quick means of moving directly to the element on the page. For example, if the access key for a Flash movie is set to *'P'*, a user who relies on the keyboard rather than the mouse could press *Alt* and *P* to go directly to the Flash movie. It is necessary, however, for the designer or developer to notify the user of the existence of the access key. In a form, underlining a letter in the label generally identifies the access key; however, media elements do not usually have labels associated with them. Consequently, the designer will have to provide this information on the page itself or on a separate page that provides directions for users with disabilities.

`tabindex` (see *Tab Index* above) is a very helpful attribute, particularly when working with Flash content. The tab index allows the designer to specify the order in which a user encounters the contents of a page when using *tab* to navigate. With Flash content, a problem may arise if the ActiveX architecture traps the cursor inside the Flash movie. If a user enters a Flash navigation bar at the top of the page using *tab*, it is likely that the user will then be unable to access the links on the page below. A common way around this problem is to set the Flash element to appear at the end of the tab order. It is important to remember, however, that a tab order be set for all links, input elements and objects in this instance.

Adding Frames

At one time, frames posed a serious challenge to screen readers; however, most screen readers today can handle frames perfectly well. Most of the challenges that people with disabilities encounter with frames are the same as those for people without disabilities. It is difficult to link to individual pages, and the use of the *Back* button may be problematic.

Ironically, frames can provide a real benefit for accessibility. Most designers and developers use them to segment the page by content. Often the banner appears in one frame, navigation in another, and the content in a third. A screen reader user can easily move from one frame to another, skipping over titles and links to get to the information the user really wants to hear.

Frames are only helpful if titled properly, however. In Dreamweaver MX, as a designer inserts a frameset, he or she is prompted to provide a title for each frame (see below). The pull-down menu at the top of the dialog box contains a list of all of the frames in the frameset. For each of these frames, the designer will need to specify a different name. The names do not have to be long or detailed, but they should be meaningful. Even names as simple as *'banner,'* *'nav,'* and *'content'* will suffice.

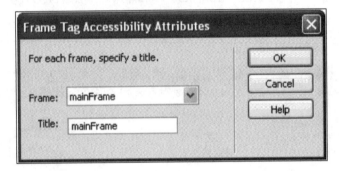

Adding Forms

Creating accessible forms is easy with Dreamweaver MX. With the *Forms* option selected in the *Preferences* dialog box, designers and developers are prompted to provide a label for each form element along with an access key and the position in the tab order.

Traditionally, labels for form elements are simply placed to the left of the element itself. If the layout is more complex, with labels placed apart from the corresponding elements, screen reader users can have a very difficult time determining the purpose of each element. When the designer adds the label for the element using the dialog box seen below, Dreamweaver MX also adds HTML markup that formally associates the text label with the element.

There are two styles available for this label-element association. The first option, *Wrap with Label Tag*, is used when the text label is immediately next to the form object. The second, *Attach Label Tag Using 'for' Attribute*, is used when the layout is more complex.

Input Tag Accessibility Attributes

Label: [   ]

Style: ⦿ Wrap with Label Tag
        ◯ Attach Label Tag Using 'for' Attribute
        ◯ No Label Tag

Position: ⦿ Before Form Item
           ◯ After Form Item

Access Key: [   ]   Tab Index: [   ]

OK   Cancel   Help

Let's take a simple example. We'll create a form with a single form field for an e-mail address and a submit button. In the first example, the text label is immediately to the left of the form field. In this case, the designer would use the first option, *Wrap with Label Tag*, to create the form.

The code to generate this form is shown below. Notice that the `<label>` element contains both the text label *'Email'* and the `<input>` element itself. Also, notice that the *Submit* button has no label. This is because screen readers will read the contents of the `name` attribute as the label for the *Submit* button.

```
<form name="form1" method="post" action="">
  <p>
    <label>Email
      <input type="text" name="textfield">
    </label>
  </p>
  <p>
    <input type="submit" name="Submit" value="Submit">
  </p>
</form>
```

Notice that, in the next example the layout is slightly more complex. The text label is placed above the form element using a table. In this case, the method described above will not work. Instead, the designer should use the `for` and `id` attributes to associate the text label with the form field. This is most easily accomplished by choosing the second option, *Attach Label Tag Using 'for' Attribute*, in the *Input Tag Accessibility Attributes* dialog.

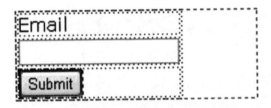

The code used to generate this example is shown below. Notice that the `<label>` element contains only the text label, "*Email*". The `for` attribute within the `<label>` element has the same value as the `id` attribute in the `<input>` element – "*textfield*". This is how the screen readers will know which label will go with which form field in more complex layouts such as this one.

```
<form name="form1" method="post" action="">
  <table width="10" border="0">
    <tr>
      <td><label for="textfield">Email</label></td>
    </tr>
    <tr>
      <td> <input type="text" name="textfield" id="textfield"></td>
    </tr>
    <tr>
      <td><input type="submit" name="Submit" value="Submit"></td>
    </tr>
  </table>
</form>
```

Adding Tables

Creating accessible tables for presenting data is perhaps the most complex issue for designers and developers. Dreamweaver MX has greatly simplified this process, adding all the necessary markup for simple tables with one or two sets of headers.

When inserting a data table within Dreamweaver MX, designers are immediately asked to provide a caption, summary information, and the position of headers in the table. A table caption is used to provide a title for the table. These captions are visible and placed at the top of the table. Summaries should be used to provide a general description of the data in the table. This information is not visible but is easily accessible to screen reader users.

Identifying headers make it significantly easier for screen readers to navigate tables. This step is tremendously important but often overlooked by designers. When the designer specifies a header using the *Tables* dialog box, Dreamweaver MX identifies the row or column of headers and adds the `scope` attribute for that header. The `scope` attribute associates data in the data cells with the corresponding headers so that a screen reader will read the headers along with the data.

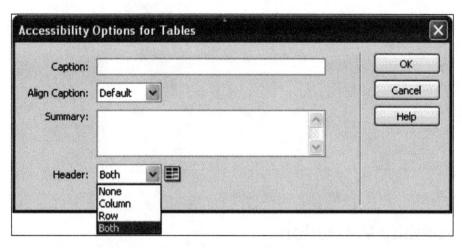

In the example below, we have a relatively simple table with a single row of headers along the top, "*Last Name*", "*City*" and "*State*". Under these headers, we have a brief list of individuals.

Participants 2003		
Last Name	**City**	**State**
Flynn	Raleigh	NC
Marsh	Madison	WI
Gandin	Madison	WI
Rick	Columbus	OH

In the code used to generate this table, notice that in the first row all of the cells use the `<th>` element. This lets the screen reader know that these cells are headers for the information displayed below. In addition, each of these `<th>` elements contains the `scope` attribute with the value set to "*col*". This lets the screen reader know that the header organizes a column of information, as opposed to a row, and that all of the cells below use this header.

```
<table width="150" border="1" summary="This table shows three columns of data
displaying last name, city and state.">
  <caption>Participants 2003</caption>
  <tr>
    <th scope="col">Last Name</th>
    <th scope="col">City</th>
    <th scope="col">State</th>
  </tr>
  <tr>
    <td>Flynn</td>
    <td>Raleigh</td>
    <td>NC</td>
  </tr>
  <tr>
    <td>Marsh</td>
```

```
      <td>Madison</td>
      <td>WI</td>
   </tr>
   <tr>
      <td>Gandin</td>
      <td>Madison</td>
      <td>WI</td>
   </tr>
   <tr>
      <td>Rick</td>
      <td>Columbus</td>
      <td>OH</td>
   </tr>
</table>
```

Accessibility Validation

Built-in to Dreamweaver MX is a comprehensive set of tools for validating the accessibility of a single page, a group of pages, or even an entire site. The new Accessibility Reports tool (seen below) validates web pages for compliance with Section 508 standards and the WCAG Priority 1 checkpoints.

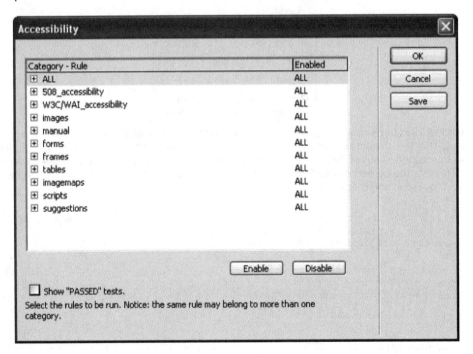

The accessibility report identifies all areas with obvious errors, such as missing alt text, as well as areas that require a manual evaluation, such as for color combinations. In addition, when a designer or developer selects an individual item from the report, the corresponding part of the page is highlighted to point the designer directly to the area in need of attention:

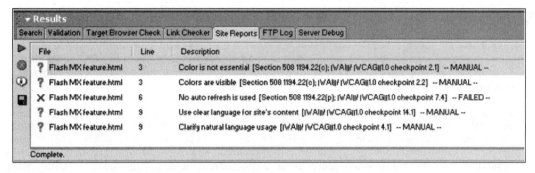

Beyond the validation tools built directly into Dreamweaver MX, there are a variety of third party products available that perform more sophisticated types of validation functions and also help to automate the repair of sites. One such product is LIFT for Dreamweaver from UsableNet. LIFT allows designers to validate a page as it is being constructed, pointing out problems as they appear on the page. LIFT also helps designers automate the repair of some of the most complex accessibility issues. For example, LIFT offers designers the ability to quickly repair complex tables using the headers and ID attributes quickly, with a graphical interface. For designers who regularly work with these types of complex problems, LIFT can be a very valuable tool.

Accessibility Reference

Dreamweaver MX includes a built-in accessibility reference, as seen below. This reference explains each of the rules used to check pages for accessibility and includes links to more detailed information about each issue. This reference tool makes it easier for designers and developers to master the specific accessibility issues relevant to their sites. The reference tool can be used together with the accessibility report, so that the designer or developer may request more information about a rule listed in the report, and the response will appear in the accessibility reference panel.

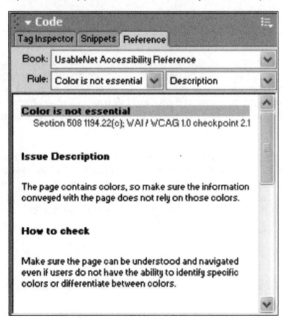

Accessible Authoring Environment

A significant improvement to Dreamweaver MX over its predecessors is its cooperation with assistive technologies. With improved labeling and sequencing of buttons, Dreamweaver MX is now the most powerful web development environment for users of assistive technologies such as the Window-Eyes and JAWS screen readers.

Several features have been added to Dreamweaver MX to facilitate web page creation by users with disabilities. Among these features are two new shortcut keys that allow users to access Dreamweaver MX panels using the keyboard. The first of these shortcuts, *Control+Alt+Tab*, allows the user to access the panel groups in Dreamweaver MX. For example, pressing *Control+Alt+Tab* once takes the user to the Design panel group. From there, pressing *Tab* moves the user among the buttons of the open panel. Pressing *Control+Tab* will move the user among the different panels in the group.

The second shortcut allows the user to return to the page window by pressing *Control+Alt+Home*. Users will need this keystroke after moving among individual panels and panel groups.

Two other useful new features of Dreamweaver MX specifically support users with impaired vision, and screen reader users. Both of these options are available in *Edit > Preferences* under the accessibility category. The first, *Make Dreamweaver Use Large Fonts*, increases the default font size within the Dreamweaver application. The menu options and panels are then easier to read for those with low vision.

The second, *Offscreen rendering (Disable when using Screen Readers)*, offers improved performance for screen reader users in Dreamweaver MX. To prevent flickering, Dreamweaver uses double buffering, which draws the screen in memory before displaying it to the user. Screen readers work best with this option disabled since they will only read the foreground screen, not the screen generated in the background.

Summary

This chapter has outlined the accessibility features in Dreamweaver MX. Dreamweaver MX is a powerful tool both for people with disabilities who are creating web sites and for the development of accessible web sites and web applications. Dreamweaver MX automates many elements of creating accessible sites and prompts designers to provide information when necessary. Dreamweaver MX also includes powerful validation and reference tools to help designers ensure that their sites are designed properly.

The development of accessible web sites will ensure that site content is not obscured by design elements; furthermore, an accessible web site is compatible with the assistive technologies used by people with disabilities such as screen readers, touch screens, or head pointers. Dreamweaver MX has been developed to provide better keyboard access and to work with screen readers and is the first professional design tool to be accessible to individuals with disabilities.

5

- Introduction to dynamic web pages:

  - variables

  - operators

  - dynamic forms

  - cookies

  - sessions

Author: Omar Elbaga

Server-Side Overview

In this chapter you will be given a swift introduction to the basics of coding dynamic web applications (using ASP/VBScript as our language of choice). This is essential to your Dreamweaver MX learning experience – before using the pre-built Dreamweaver MX server behaviors, it is important to have a firm understanding of how dynamic web pages work. This will enable you to use Dreamweaver MX to its fullest capacity and will also save you time!

In this chapter we will look at:

- Static versus Dynamic web pages

- Variables

- Commenting Code

- String, Integer, and Boolean Data types

- Built-in Functions & Typecasting

- Operators

- Conditional Logic

- Looping Logic

- HTML Forms

- URL Parameters

- Cookies

- Sessions

- Environment Variables

No More Static

At this point in the book, we are now ready to shed our old ways for the new. Have you ever wondered how to implement all those cool dynamic features you see on so many web sites these days, such as logins, registrations, personal folders, greeting cards, e-mail, and so on?

Some of us have sat and thought hard about how to imitate these features in some extraneous way utilizing your knowledge of plain old HTML, but it isn't easy. There have been sites where the user is prompted to *Click here to sign my guestbook!*, and on doing so, be presented with a note saying *E-mail me and I will post it as soon as possible*. The site moderator would then have to post the message manually! The next step would be to prompt the user's e-mail client. When we got tired of that we discovered the next best thing, free CGI programs.

This story may sound familiar to some of us but not others, but whatever situation you are in, there is no need to fret any longer about dynamic web content. By the end if this chapter you will have working knowledge as to how many of these cool features you always drooled at are done.

What's Wrong with HTML?

Nothing. HTML is awesome! HTML is and will probably always be the main language of the Web. The question is not "what's wrong with HTML" but simply "what can't HTML do?" And the answer to that is "a lot" if you expect to be offering user-interactive applications and/or data that will be constantly changing. How can we expect HTML to send an automatic e-mail to you when a user clicks the feedback button? Remember that HTML is not a programming language – it is actually a simple markup language – its main job is to format text.

The only way we can expect something to automatically happen based on user interaction, is by a program or "web application" that is built specifically for the task at hand. These web applications are built using one of the many web-scripting languages available. Dreamweaver MX supports five of the most popular of them – **ASP**, **ASP.NET**, **JSP**, **Cold Fusion**, and **PHP**.

> *"Does this mean I don't need HTML anymore?"*
>
> *No. HTML is necessary and as you will see, these scripting languages work hand in hand with HTML. As a matter of fact, they cannot do much online without HTML!*

Static Versus Dynamic

In simple terms **static** means "fixed" or "stationary" while **dynamic** means "changing." Anything that only executes on the client browser is considered static, for example, the text contained in HTML cannot be manipulated unless the site's author goes into the sourcecode and manually changes it. That's pretty darn "stationary." Although client-side JavaScript is much more sophisticated than HTML (it is an actual scripting language), it is also "stationary" because it only executes on the client browser. Even JavaScript programs are considered client-side unless they are used with Microsoft's **Active Server Pages** (**ASP**), which we will discuss later in this chapter (ASP is executed server-side). Client-side JavaScript programs actually execute wholly within the browser and can be viewed in the sourcecode. This is why web developers usually refer to web development that only utilizes these types of technologies as "client-side development".

On the other hand, "server-side" refers to web development that utilizes technologies that do not execute within a client browser but on an actual live server. Server-side technology is considered **dynamic** because its execution can change depending on what it receives from the client. One of the most important aspects of server-side technology is that it allows you to connect to databases and view and update the data, all from the client browser.

The web scripting language is embedded within the sourcecode along with the HTML. It executes on the server once the page is accessed by a browser (some languages such as VBScript, Javascript, PHP, and Coldfusion execute line by line, whereas JSP and ASP.NET pages are compiled to native code on the server). The dynamic output and the generic HTML is then sent back to the clients. Here is an example in PHP:

```
<!-- sayHello.php -->
<html>
  <body>
    <?php
      $sayHello = "Hello friends!";
      echo $sayHello;
    ?>
  </body>
</html>
```

We could have simply written "Hello friends!" in the body, but instead, we stuffed the text into a PHP variable and then printed that variable. When a client accesses the page, the PHP engine reads the following PHP code:

```
<?php
  $sayHello = "Hello friends!";
  echo $sayHello
?>
```

It then sends the text to the client browser as HTML. If you create this page and then execute it on a live server, you will not see any PHP in the sourcecode; rather you will only see the following HTML:

```
<html>
  <body>
    Hello friends!
  </body>
</html>
```

This why they are called server-side languages: the server parses the embedded server-side script and sends the result as HTML to the client browser.

Now let's explore the workings of dynamic web pages in much more detail, looking at ASP in particular.

Exit Free CGI Hunting, Enter ASP

We will not be learning all of the five web scripting languages Dreamweaver MX supports. Instead, we will illustrate the construction of dynamic pages in Dreamweaver MX throughout this chapter (and the rest of the book) using **ASP**.

As we learned above, ASP is one of Microsoft's own server-side technologies. ASP files end with an `.asp` extension and are effectively HTML pages, but have script contained within them, inside special delimiters (see later for more on these). ASP pages can be coded with any scripting language that has support for the ActiveX Scripting Engine – VBScript, JavaScript, JScript (Microsoft's version of JavaScript), Perl, Rexx, and Python. The two predominant choices are VBScript and JavaScript – both have native support for ASP.

VBScript seems to be the preferred one, and the one we will use throughout this book – it has gotten to the point where nearly all ASP resources use VBScript, so using VBScript makes it easier to find help when it's needed, especially for beginners. It is the default language for ASP.

It's important to note that Dreamweaver MX actually generates ASP code for you, so you may wonder why you need to know anything about ASP. This is the mistake many Dreamweaver users make. They use it to build dynamic pages without knowing a thing about web programming and find themselves in all kinds of jams.

Think about it. Wouldn't it be hard to use Dreamweaver's objects to build HTML pages if you didn't know what a table or form was? You must have some basic understanding of code and design before using something that generates code and design for you. Dreamweaver MX speeds up your application building time if you know when and how to use it. If we don't know what a recordset is, then how can we know when and how to use the Dreamweaver MX Recordset Server Behavior? (I will explain this server behavior in *Chapter 7*.) This is why I am taking the time out to introduce you to web programming with ASP so that you can fly through your web applications when using Dreamweaver MX. Don't worry – you will soon get how to tell it to do all the "dummy" work for you.

ASP/VBScript Basics

Now let's go straight on to our look at dynamic web programming with ASP/VBScript, Dreamweaver MX style.

What I Need To Get Started

To begin coding in VBScript all you need is any text editor (even Notepad will do). In order to execute ASP what do we need? As you may recall, we mentioned earlier that web-scripting languages execute on a live server, therefore we will most certainly need a **web server**:

- If you use **Windows 95/98** there is a mini-server Microsoft makes available for free called **Personal Web Server** (PWS). You can download it here: *http://www.microsoft.com/msdownload/ntoptionpack/askwiz.asp*. You can choose the Windows 95 option for both 95 and 98.

- Microsoft does not distribute Personal Web Server (PWS) with, or support its use with **Windows ME**. Please see this tech note: *http://support.microsoft.com/support/kb/articles/Q266/4/56.asp*. While Microsoft does not recommend installing PWS on a Windows Me system, there are third-party tutorials on how to do so. Please use these tutorials at your own risk. You can find one at *http://billsway.com/notes_public/PWS_WinMe.txt*.

- If you use **Windows 2000** you are in luck. While PWS will work fine for Windows 95/98 users, Windows 2000 comes with a full-blown web server called **Internet Information**

Services (IIS). IIS is not installed by default on Windows 2000, but you can install it by going through the following steps:

1. Start
2. Control Panel
3. Add/Remove Programs
4. Add/Remove Windows Components
5. Check off the Internet Information Services option
6. Click Next.

- If you are using **Windows XP Professional**, you can install IIS also by inserting the Windows XP Professional CD-Rom into your CD-Rom Drive and following the same steps as for Windows 2000 above.

*Please note that you cannot run ASP on **Windows XP Home Edition**.*

Unix does not support ASP out of the box, but there is software available that will enable the deployment of Active Server Pages on a Unix server. If you have to use a Unix server for ASP you may find **ChiliASP** useful. See *http://www.chiliasp.com* for more details.

Once you have completed your installations, make sure the server works by simply pointing your preferred web browser to *http://localhost* – if successful we will see the default web server page.

Now let's try running an ASP through our web server – try it now! Create the following file and save it as `Myasppage.asp`.

```
<html>
  <head>
    <title>My ASP Page</title>
  </head>
  <body>
    Can you see me? I'm the first ASP page to be executed on this server!
  </body>
</html>
```

Now place this file into the home directory of your web server. This is usually *C:\inetpub\wwwroot* – the folder `wwwroot` is the root of your virtual web site. Whenever your domain is accessed online, the server begins serving pages here. By default, the server will execute pages with the names `default` or `index`.

Point your browser to `http://localhost/Myasppage.asp`, and you should be presented with this:

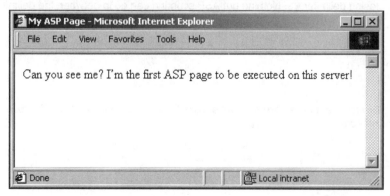

As long as the page loads and you see the text within the body you're OK. If you do not, please double check that you installed the web server properly. Make sure your web server is running by going to *Control Panel > Administrative Tools > Internet Services Manager* (or *Personal Web Manager*). You can start or shut down the web server by finding the *Default Web Site* in the tree, and using the "Start" and "*Stop*" buttons in the display.

You should also make sure that the home directory has read access and can execute scripts. Right-click your *Default Web Site*, select the *Properties* option, and click the *Home Directory* tab. Make sure the *Read* option is checked, and also make sure that *Scripts only* is selected from the Execute Permissions menu under *Application Settings* (*Scripts and Executables* will also work, but allowing execution of programs on your web server by others can be a major security risk – this is good practice).

Specifying Your Scripting Language

Because ASP web pages can be scripted using various languages, it is necessary to inform each page which language will be used. Since VBScript is the default language for ASP, it is not obligatory to specify that you will be using VBScript, but it is good practice to specify it anyway – the server will assume that you are using VBScript if the language is not specified. You specify use of a language besides VBScript by adding in a line of code at the top of your page with the following syntax: `<% @ Language = "language_name" %>`. For example, if you use JavaScript you would type:

```
<% @ Language = "JavaScript" %>
```

Keep in mind that this line must be the first line in your sourcecode. If you do not specify your language at the top of each page, your page will throw an error when executed if it is coded in a language other than VBScript. Of course, it will also throw an error if you code with a language other than that which is specified in this page directive.

Dreamweaver MX will automatically insert this line for you every time you create a new dynamic ASP web page using either VBScript or JavaScript.

The <% %> Delimeters

All ASP script code must go in between delimiters – the server then executes all code within the delimiters. Once it sees the first opening delimeter `<%`, the ASP script engine begins its work until reaching the closing delimiter `%>`. Nothing but ASP scripting can go in between the delimiters. Here is an example:

```
<%
   Dim MyVariable
%>
```

We use the `Dim` statement to declare a variable. `Dim MyVariable` is one line. The following is equivalent to the above:

```
<% Dim MyVariable %>
```

We can also break up multiple lines with their own delimiter blocks.

```
<% Dim MyVariable %>
<% MyVariable = "Hello" %>
```

This is equivalent to:

```
<%
  Dim MyVariable
  MyVariable = "Hello"
%>
```

I think you get the idea. It's up to you how you want to format your code – just remember to be consistent throughout your application, and format your code in a manner that makes it easy for you and others to read your code. Keeping as much ASP code as possible in one block is what you should always aim for, rather than opening a new block for no apparent reason, although sometimes when embedding ASP code within HTML, multiple blocks are necessary.

> Keep in mind that one ASP line cannot be broken up into separate delimiter blocks.
> `<% Dim %> <% MyVariable %>` will throw an error, because a variable must come after the `Dim` statement.

Variables

Variables are one of the most important concepts in any language. A variable is like a placeholder or an allocation set in memory for a value – it can hold a value of your choice. It is not an exaggeration to say that variables are the essence of what dynamic information is all about. This is because a variable is likely to change or vary – we expect the values of variables to change, which is why we refer to the values of variables by variables in our web applications and not their literal values. Have I confused you yet?

Picture this: I have a **car**. You might ask "Erm, OK…what *kind* of car?" Well, it can be a Porsche, BMW, Acura, Audi, etc. In a real-life situation I would probably mention the *kind* of car I have. However, in the vast world of the WWW it's better to just say that I have *a car*.

Why? Because when I am writing a dynamic web application that deals with cars (for example, a database application that collects and stores details of people's cars), I probably won't be just talking about *my car*, but the cars of the thousands of visitors to my site who wish to use my application. I don't know what kind of car will be introduced by the client/user so I would rather have a placeholder that can contain any value that I can refer to or edit at anytime.

Declaring Variables

Let's declare our first variable in VBScript. Create a new dynamic page in Dreamweaver MX, selecting ASP/VBScript. From *File* select *New*, and choose the options seen overleaf:

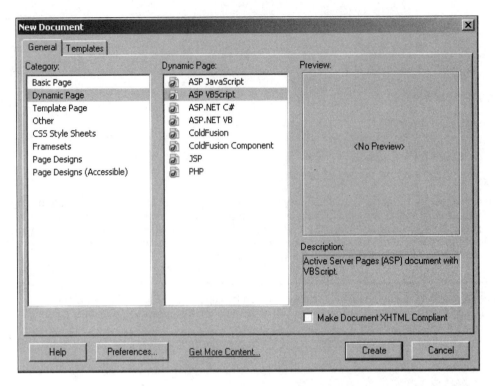

Keep the code and design panes in view. We will code our VBScript directly into the code pane.

> ASP code can go anywhere on your page, but for the examples in this chapter, all ASP code should be typed within the `<body>` tags of the document.

In VBScript we declare a variable using the `Dim` statement as you saw in the example above. Create a new ASP/VBScript page and save it as `my_variable.asp`. Type the following within the `<body></body>` tags.

```
<%
   Dim MyVariable
   MyVariable = "I am the value of an ASP variable"
%>
```

View the page live on your server. You may hit *F12* as a shortcut in Dreamweaver MX to load the page in a browser window.

What did you see? If you said nothing...great! You shouldn't have seen anything but a blank screen, because all we did is declare a variable called `MyVariable`, with a value of "I am the value of an ASP variable".

What we have not done yet is print out the value of the variable – let's do that now. Modify your code like this:

```
<%
   Dim MyVariable
   MyVariable = "I am the value of an ASP variable"
   Response.Write MyVariable
%>
```

The `Response.Write` statement simply says "write out the content of `MyVariable` on the page". View your page now – you should see the following displayed in your browser:

I am the value of an ASP variable

You can also include HTML within the value of a variable like so:

```
<%
   Dim MyVariable
   MyVariable = "I am the value of an <strong>ASP</strong> variable"
   Response.Write MyVariable
%>
```

Variables can be assigned values without having been previously declared in a `Dim` statement, however, best practice suggests that by routinely "Dimming" variables explicitly, it becomes easier to debug a page long after it has been written and published, as the code is more readable and better organized.

The following example will work fine.

```
<%
   MyVariable = "I am the value of an ASP variable"
   Response.Write MyVariable
%>
```

Unfortunately, Dreamweaver MX does not stick to this convention. It often generates ASP code without declaring its variables.

Syntax Rules for Variables

There are some rules regarding the syntax of variables:

- Do not use spaces, periods, or dashes anywhere in the variable. `My variable` is unacceptable

- Variables must begin with a letter. `2myvariable` is unacceptable

- Reserved words cannot be used as variable names. `Dim` is unacceptable because it is reserved in VBScript. For a list of VBScript reserved words, see the following link: *http://support.microsoft.com/default.aspx?scid=kb;EN-US;q216528*

125

Variable Naming Conventions

There are some conventions that have become popular for naming variables. Naming variables according to their data types is often done. We will learn more about data types later in this chapter.

For example, if the variable is a string then adding `str` to the beginning of the variable name is not uncommon – for example `strMyVariable` or `str_my_variable`. The same would go for an integer variable – `intMyVariable` or `int_myvariable`.

In addition, some variables are named after the author. My initials are **OE** so I might name my variable as such: `OE_MyVariable` or `oe_my_variable`.

Macromedia adds its initials to most of its variables. Macromedia uses **MM** so you will often find variables such as `MM_RedirectPage`, `MM_ConnectionString`, etc.

You will get used to seeing this when sifting through the sourcecode. Do not become confused by this; it is simply a naming convention. It doesn't really matter how you name your variable. The best advice when naming your variables is to keep it **simple, appropriate, and obvious** – whether or not you decide to add prefix letters to your variables is up to you. You can see an interesting article about naming conventions at *http://msdn.microsoft.com/library/default.asp?url=/library/en-us/script56/html/vbscodingconventions.asp*.

> Avoid naming your variables by sole initials such as `RP`, `ag1`, `str_cdp`, etc.
>
> Make sure that what the variable represents is obvious, just from glancing at it, such as `RedirectPage`, `ArabicGreeting`, etc.
>
> Then you may feel free to add your own prefixes, however you want, for example `str_RedirectPage`, `OE_ArabicGreeting`, etc.

VBScript is Case-Insensitive

Unlike JScript, VBScript is **case-insensitive**. This means that it doesn't matter whether you use lowercase or uppercase characters in VBScript code. `Dim Myvariable` is the same as `DIM mYvariaBle`. Certainly, this makes things easier for the web developer, especially because it gives you one less thing to worry about when it comes to debugging time!

However, even though VBScript is case-insensitive you should maintain some sort of unity within your code. Code becomes confusing to the eye when you have a variable written `myvariable` in one place and then the same variable written `MYVariable` in another. Choose one style and stick with it.

The <%= Shortcut

You can use `<%=` in place of `Response.Write` as long as this is the only action you wish to perform inside a new block of code. For example, to print the date and time using the `Now()` VBScript function, both of these are equivalent:

```
<% Response.Write Now() %>
```

and

```
<%= Now() %>
```

We can also rewrite our variable declaration example above to the following, utilizing the shortcut to output the variable:

```
<%
   MyVariable = "I am the value of an ASP variable"
%>
```

```
<%= MyVariable %>
```

This shortcut often comes in handy, as we shall see throughout the course of this chapter.

Commenting Code

Commenting code is a manner of displaying textual information in relation to your code without it being parsed. Every programming/markup language offers the ability to comment code, even HTML. The following is an HTML comment:

```
<!-- This table is to hold the main navigation of the page -->
<table><tr><td> home / about / contact </td></tr></table>
```

Everything within the `<!-- -->` delimiters will not be parsed as HTML code. Of course, these HTML comments are viewable in the sourcecode – as you can see, comments are for informing anyone viewing the code of the purpose of the different code sections.

ASP/VBScript comments are done by putting a single quote in front of a line. This causes the entire line to be completely ignored by the web server. For example, let's add a comment to our `my_variable.asp` page, and comment out our `Response.Write` line:

```
<%
   MyVariable = "I am the value of an ASP variable"

   'Response.Write MyVariable
   ' Here is a comment
%>
```

Dreamweaver MX should turn commented lines gray in Code View.

When you view this page in the browser now, the variable will not be outputted – only the first line will execute. Note that ASP comments are **not** viewable in the client browser at all, as the server has already parsed the code.

Commenting code is very important, especially when it comes to debugging. It allows you to block out code quickly in case you want to test isolated code sections for whatever reason. It also gives you the opportunity to document your code. This is helpful when the time comes for you (or someone else) to look back through the code and update it.

Dreamweaver MX often comments code generated by its server behaviors.

Concatenation Using the Ampersand (&)

You can also concatenate variables – all concatenation means is putting things together. As a note, it is **not** adding things mathematically. It is simply putting them together, side by side.

For example, let's try concatenating two strings into one variable. Create the following file and save it as `my_greeting.asp`:

```
<%
   Dim Mygreeting
   Mygreeting = "Hello" & " World"
   ' We need to leave a space before the W in World.

   Response.Write Mygreeting
%>
```

View the page in your browser and you should see the following display:

Hello World

We have concatenated two values to become one value for our `Mygreeting` variable. We can also concatenate two variables to become the value of a third variable. Create the following file and save it as `my_second_greeting.asp`:

```
<%
   Dim MyHello, MyWorld, Mygreeting
   MyHello = "Hello"
   MyWorld = "World"
   Mygreeting = MyHello & " " & MyWorld

   Response.Write Mygreeting
%>
```

View the page in your browser and you should again see:

Hello World

You can also concatenate variables with values during output. For example:

```
<%
   Dim MyHello
   MyHello = "Hello"

   Response.Write MyHello & " World"
%>
```

Every single part in concatenation must be separated by an ampersand (&) symbol.

The following is **incorrect** and will throw an error:

```
<%
   Dim MyHello, MyWorld, Mygreeting
   MyHello = "Hello"
   MyWorld = "World"
   Mygreeting = MyHello & " " MyWorld
   ' there is a missing ampersand between the quotes and the MyWorld variable

   Response.Write Mygreeting
%>
```

Note that it is allowable to concatenate strings using the plus sign (+), but not preferred over the ampersand (&). Because the plus sign is also used to mathematically add integers, using the (+) plus sign to concatenate integers can cause erroneous results.

Data Types: String, Integer and Boolean

Every variable has a data type. It is important that you know the difference between **strings**, **integers**, and **booleans**. There certainly are more data types than these three but these are the ones you will usually be working with. Some other data types (that we will not be dealing with here) are: Currency, Date, Object, Decimal, Byte, Array, Empty, Null, Long, Single, and Double.

Data type is also referred to as variable type. Variables will act according to their types – there are things you may try to do with a string that will not give you the results you intended due to the data type.

A string contains alphanumeric characters or numbers (strings **must** be surrounded by quotes), integers contain whole numbers (integers are **not** surrounded by quotes), and booleans hold values that are either True or False. Let's look at an example of each. Create the following page and save it as asp_datatypes.asp:

```
<%
   MyString = "Hi my name is Omar!"
   MyInteger = 34
   MyBoolean = False
   ' notice how only strings are surrounded by quotes.

   Response.Write MyString & " I am not " & MyInteger & " That is " & MyBoolean
%>
```

You should see the following on your screen:

Hi my name is Omar! I am not 34 That is False

Please be aware that although strings can contain numbers, you can't perform any direct mathematical computations on them. Numbers with a string data type are not treated as integers; rather, they take on alphanumeric values. Let's take a look at an example – create the following file and save it as string_numbers.asp:

```
<%
   MyString1 = "20"
   MyString2 = "20"
   Response.Write MyString1 + MyString2
%>
```

You will see the following:

2020

The plus sign (+) will simply force a concatenation of the two strings. We didn't want 2020 – we wanted 40! You can only receive this kind of response by giving the 20's **integer** data types. For example:

```
<%
  MyNumber1 = 20
  MyNumber2 = 20
  ' we must not add double quotes

  Response.Write MyNumber1 + MyNumber2
%>
```

This page should give you the following in your browser:

40

You might be asking yourself, "What if I wanted to add a quote within the value of a string?" Of course you can do so, but you must **escape** it because once the ASP script engine hits the second double quote it will think it is the end of the value and cause undesirable results. You can escape quotes within string values by adding an additional double quote in front of it. For example:

```
<%
  MyString1 = "Jennifer said, ""ASP is cool!"""
  ' double quotes have additional double quotes in front of them

  Response.Write MyString1
%>
```

VBScript's House of Built-In Functions

VBScript has a number of built-in functions that you can use at your disposal. They simplify things for you tremendously and give you the ability to manipulate your variables as required. There are different types of built-in functions: Date/Time functions, Conversion functions, Format functions, Math functions, Array functions, and String functions. For a list of the many built-in functions VBScript has to offer, go to *http://msdn.microsoft.com/library/default.asp?url=/library/en-us/dnexpvb/html/usingvbscriptfunctions.asp*.

You don't need to remember all these functions, since even retired ASP developers will use a reference! Let's go ahead and look at some examples.

Conversion Functions

This type of function converts one data type to another. For example, let's say we wanted to convert a number that was a string to an integer, then we can use the `CInt()` function. Create the following file and save it as `convert_to_int.asp`:

```
<%
  MyString = "23"
  MyNewInt = CInt(MyString)
  'convert to integer data type, declare new variable

  Response.Write MyNewInt
%>
```

You should see the following in your browser:

23

The variable `MyNewInt` is not a string any longer, but an integer. We took the number that had a string data type, converted it to an integer data type and created a new variable out of it. This might be hard to believe unless you see it with your own eyes, so let's use another function to display the data type of the variable – `TypeName()`.

Let's print out the data type of our variables before and after the conversion – add the following code to the above example:

```
<%
   MyString = "23"
   Response.Write TypeName(MyString)
   'print out variable data type

   MyNewInt = CInt(MyString)
   'convert to integer data type, declare new variable

   Response.Write MyNewInt
   Response.Write TypeName(MyNewInt)
   'print out variable and its data type
%>
```

You should see the following in your browser:

String23Integer

String Functions

These functions allow us to do some cool things with strings. Let's take a quick look at the following string functions: `Len()`, `Trim()`, and `Left()`.

The `Len()` function returns the number of characters of a string. Create the following file and save it as `len.asp`:

```
<%
   MyString = "I am cool"

   Response.Write MyString
   Response.Write "<br>There are <strong>" & Len(MyString) & "</strong> characters
in the above statement."
%>
```

You should see the following results:

I am cool
*There are **9** characters in the above statement.*

Keep in mind that even empty spaces count as characters. The `Trim()` function removes spaces that may appear on both the left and the right side of a string. Create the following file and save it as `trim.asp`:

```
<%
   MyString = "  I am cool  "

   Response.Write "." & MyString & "."
   Response.Write "<br>." & Trim(MyString) & "."
%>
```

You should see the following results:

. I am cool .
.I am cool.

While printing the variables out, I added a period before and after the string value so the empty spaces are more obvious. As you can see the first print-out still contains the empty spaces to the right and left, while the second print-out does not because of the `Trim()` function. On this note, there are also `RTrim()` and `LTrim()` functions that can trim a specific side only.

The `Left()` function allows you to return a specified amount of characters from the left. It accepts the number as an attribute after the string, For example, `Left(string, 5)`. Create the following file and save it as `left.asp`:

```
<%
   MyString = "I am cool. Didn't you know that I was valedictorian of my High
   School class. Not only that but I also have a bachelor's degree in Creative
   Writing."

   Response.Write Left(MyString, 10)
%>
```

You should only see the following results when printing the variable:

I am cool.

We cut the rest of our friend's soliloquy. This comes in handy when you want to display only a certain amount of text, especially when text comes from a database field. (You will learn more about how to connect your pages to a database in *Chapter 6*). Feel free to explore the many VBScript functions. They have a lot to offer.

Operators

Operators allow you to manipulate data within your code. Operators have three main classes: Logical, Comparison, and Mathematical. Here is a list of the often-used operators. If you need to view the results of the examples live, type the code and save it in an ASP file.

Assignment

There is only one assignment operator and that is the equal sign (=). It simply stores whatever is to the right of the operator inside the variable to the left. You have been doing this throughout the examples in this chapter, so you will be used to it by now. For example:

```
<%
  Dim myGreeting
  myGreeting = "Hello"
%>
```

The assignment operator above simply stores the string `Hello` inside the variable called `myGreeting`. Here is another example:

```
<%
  Dim myNumber
  myNumber = 23
%>
```

The assignment operator above simply stores the number `23` inside the variable called `myNumber`. The equal sign can also be a mathematical operator in which it stands for equality. (See *the mathematical operators* section later.)

Logical

And, Not, Or – let's have a look at these in order.

AND

For example (`AND.asp`):

```
<%
  number1 = 4-1
  number2 = 6-2
  If number1 AND number2 = 3 Then
    Response.Write "correct"
  Else
    Response.Write "false"
  End If
%>
```

Logical operators simply join what is on the left to what is on the right. The example above checks to see whether both the variables `number1` *and* `number2` equal 3. Since they don't both equal 3, *false* is returned.

OR

We can change the above example using OR (`OR.asp`):

```
<%
  number1 = 4-1
  number2 = 6-2
  If number1 OR number2 = 3 Then
    Response.Write "correct"
  Else
    Response.Write "false"
  End If
%>
```

The above code checks to see whether either 4-1 or 6-2 equals 3. Since at least one of them does, it prints out *correct*.

NOT

The NOT operator simply says the opposite of the statement to the right of it. For example, in the following code (`NOT_1.asp`):

```
<%
  number1 = 4-1
  If number1 = 3 Then
    Response.Write "correct"
  Else
    Response.Write "false"
  End If
%>
```

Certainly, 4-1 equals 3 so *correct* will print out. Now let's add NOT to the code:

```
<%
number1 = 4-1
If NOT(number1 = 3) Then
Response.Write "correct"
Else
Response.Write "false"
End If
%>
```

Now *false* is returned – `number1` still equals 3, but the NOT operator causes the code to return the opposite of what would otherwise be expected.

You will learn more about `If...Then` statements later in this chapter.

Comparison

Operator	Meaning
=	Equal to
<	Less than
>	Greater than
<=	Less than or equal to
>=	Greater than or equal to
<>	Not equal to

For example:

```
<%
X = 1
Y = 3
If x < y Then
    [' Execute this code ]
End If
%>
```

Comparison operators compare 2 arguments, and see if a specified condition is met.

Mathematical

Operator	Meaning
^	Exponentiate
*	Multiply
/	Divide
\	Integer Divide
MOD	Modulus
+	Plus
–	Minus
&	Concatenate

For example:

```
x = 54
y = 67
z = x + y
Response.Write z
```

Mathematical operators perform a mathematical operation between what is on the left and right side such as the plus sign (+) in the above example.

While Divide (/) divides one number by another and returns the result, Integer Divide (\) returns only the quotient and Modulus (MOD) returns only the remainder.

For example, 5 divided by 3 is 1 with a remainder of 2. Integer Divide will return 1, while Modulus will return 2.

Let's use the following code to see this for ourselves (`divide.asp`):

```
<%
  number1 = 5/3 ' Divide
  number2 = 5\3 ' Integer Divide
  number3 = 5 MOD 3 ' Modulus

  Response.Write number1 & "<br>" & number2 & "<br>" & number3
%>
```

This gives us the following readout:

1.66666666666667
1
2

For further reading on VBScript operators, go to:

http://msdn.microsoft.com/library/default.asp?url=/library/en-us/script56/html/vbsoperators.asp.

135

Operator Precedence

As you know, ASP code executes from left to right, line by line, although operators execute according to their own order. This order is called operator precedence. While Comparison operators all have equal precedence (they will execute in the left-to-right order), Mathematical and Logical operators execute in order of precedence, regardless of a left-to-right order, as seen here:

Precedence Order	Operation
Mathematical	
1	Exponentiation (^)
2	Multiplication (*), Division (/), Integer Divide (\)
3	Modulus (Mod)
4	Addition (+), Subtraction (-)
Logical	
1	Not
2	And
3	Or

For example (`operator_precedence1.asp`):

```
<%
   intOrderTest = 3 + 2 * 4
   Response.Write intOrderTest
%>
```

In a left-to-right order the answer should be 20, but since multiplication has a higher precedence than addition, the answer will be 11. Using parentheses to group expressions will allow you to force operators to execute before others that may be higher in precedence – for example, to force addition before multiplication, we could change our example to this (`operator_precedence2.asp`):

```
<%
   intOrderTest = (3 + 2) * 4
   Response.Write intOrderTest
%>
```

Expressions in parentheses are always evaluated before expressions that are not in parentheses. It is important to note that operator precedence is still maintained between multiple expressions that are all in parentheses. You should always group expressions with parentheses instead of relying on the natural precedence to make your code more readable.

Note: Multiplication, division, and integer divide will execute in a left-to-right order when they occur together in the same expression.

Conditional Logic

Like variables, this section is also one of the most important aspects to your language. Conditional logic gives the coder the ability to control the flow of his or her program depending on certain criteria or conditions. You can only imagine how pertinent this is when we are talking about dynamic web sites where you have no idea how your users will interact with your web applications. You will need to make decisions based on the input your web application receives. Let's take a look how we can control our output.

If...Then Statement

This is the mother of all control! It says "**If** this is true **then** do this". Create the following file and save it as `if_then.asp`:

```
<%
   MyExpectedOutput = "This web site is cool"
   If MyExpectedOutput = "This web site is cool" Then
      Response.Write "Thanks for your kind words."
   End If
%>
```

You should see the following result:

Thanks for your kind words.

The `If` statement checks to see whether the `MyExpectedOutput` variable equals our desired value. If so, we thank the user. Keep in mind that when you compare between two strings, every character is taken into account, even spaces. You can also set the conditions around embedded HTML using multiple blocks instead. We can arrange the example above to look like this:

```
<%
   MyExpectedOutput = "This website is cool"
      If MyExpectedOutput = "This website is cool" Then
%>

Thanks for your kind words.

<%
   End If
%>
```

You should see the same results as for the example above.

We can add the `Else` keyword to the statement to introduce another output if the expression does not meet our criteria. Create the following file and save it as `if_then_else.asp`:

```
<%
   MyExpectedOutput = "This website sucks."
      If MyExpectedOutput = "This website is cool" Then
         Response.Write "Thanks for your kind words."
      Else
         Response.Write "Hey, don't be so mean."
      End If
%>
```

137

You should see the following results:

Hey, don't be so mean.

The `If` statement checks to see whether the `MyExpectedOutput` variable equals our desired value – if not, we add a comment. Again, you can set the conditions around embedded HTML using multiple blocks like we did in the previous example, for example:

```
<%
   MyExpectedOutput = "This website sucks"
      If MyExpectedOutput = "This website is cool" Then
%>

Thanks for your kind words.

<% Else %>

Hey, don't be so mean.

<%
   End If
%>
```

You should see the following result:

Hey, don't be so mean.

If...Then...ElseIf Statement

The `If...Then...Else` statement will give you the ability to provide two possible code continuations. If you need more than two you have two choices. You could add another `If...Then...Else` statement, but the code would be in danger of becoming inefficient and sloppy. A better method is to use the **ElseIf** statement. It allows you to combine multiple `If...Then...Else` statements in one. Create the following file and save it as `if_then_elseif.asp`:

```
<%
   UserRating = 9
     If UserRating = 4 Then
        Response.Write "Why have you rated my website so low."

     ElseIf UserRating = 6 Then
        Response.Write "Cmon. You can do better than that."

     ElseIf UserRating = 9 Then
        Response.Write "Close, but I deserve better."

     ElseIf UserRating = 10 Then
        Response.Write "There you go!"

     End If
%>
```

You should see the following results:

Close, but I deserve better.

You can use an `Else` keyword for your last check in an `ElseIf` statement. It would act as the default program flow if none of the other conditions match. Be aware that, if you use it, it must be the last statement, and can never come before an `ElseIf`. The following example is ok:

```
<%
  UserRating = 9
    If UserRating = 4 Then
      Response.Write "Why have you rated my website so low."
    ElseIf UserRating = 6 Then
      Response.Write "Cmon. You can do better than that."

    ElseIf UserRating = 10 Then
      Response.Write "There you go!"

    Else
      Response.Write "I'm looking for a ten rating."

End If
%>
```

Looping Logic

This type of logic has the ability to loop blocks of code and have it execute multiple times while certain conditions are `true` or until they are met. For example, you may need to loop through records in a database to display them, or you may need to loop through variables until the last record is reached. There are several loop statements in VBScript that basically accomplish the same task – we will go through a couple of the most commonly used ones – the **Do While ... Loop**.

Do While ... Statement

This loop allows you to create a loop while a condition you specify is `True`. The `Do While` loop takes the following form:

```
Do While your condition
  Code to be executed
Loop
```

Let's take a look at an example. Create the following file and save it as `do_loop.asp`:

```
<%
Dim intCount
intCount = 1

Do While intCount <= 15
  Response.Write intCount
  intCount = intCount + 1
Loop
%>
```

You should see the following results:

123456789101112131415

In the above example we looped the number 1 based on the condition that it is less than or equal to 15. In between the loop we printed the variable out and incremented it by 1. The code continues to execute over and over, (printing out the variable and then incrementing by 1) until the condition becomes `False`.

While ... Wend

Dreamweaver MX uses this loop in the Repeat Region server behavior for looping through database records. This loop works exactly like the `Do ... While` loop. You can simply replace the `Do While` with `While` and the `Loop` with `Wend` in the above example:

```
<%
Dim intCount
intCount = 1

While intCount <= 15
   Response.Write intCount
   intCount = intCount + 1
Wend
%>
```

See Chapter 7 for more on Repeat Region.

Response.End & Response.Redirect

These are two cool features in ASP that also allow you to control the flow of your programs. **Response.End** ends a web application immediately. Once the script engine hits it, no code after that line is executed. You can see why we would want to do this – for example, if you have a web application that streams a download to a user after payment, the application may check the database for the user's payment. If it is not found, you can automatically end the program so the rest of the script is not executed.

Response.Redirect works in the same manner except that instead of simply ending the program, it allows you to immediately redirect the browser to a specified URL. It's similar to `Response.End` in that no code is executed on the current page after it is processed.

Response.End

Let's try a few examples. Create the following file and save it as `check_password.asp`:

```
<%
  Password = "45gh4"
  UserInput = "45gh4"

    If UserInput <> Password Then
      Response.End
    Else
%>

Here is the very secret code only for users who knew the password: <br><strong>The
bird flew west when seeing the tarantula.</strong>

<%
  End If
%>
```

You should see the following results when viewing the page:

Here is the very secret code only for users who knew the password:
The bird flew west when seeing the tarantula.

What we did was set a password, then check it against the "user input". We then said that if the two variables are not equal end the code, or else continue and display the secret code.

> *At this point you might be wondering how the user submitted that value of the `UserInput` variable anyhow – you will learn about adding this kind of interactivity in the next section.*

Now change the `UserInput` password to make it deliberately incorrect and see what happens:

```
<%
  Password = "45gh4"
  UserInput = "12345"

    If UserInput <> Password Then
      Response.End
    Else
%>

Here is the very secret code only for users who knew the password:<br /><b>The
bird flew west when seeing the tarantula.</b>

<%
    End If
%>
```

When you view the page you should see nothing, because the web application was shut down due to the password being incorrect – isn't that cool!

Response.Redirect

Now how does `Response.Redirect` work? As we said before, it's done the same way, but simply redirects to another URL, after stopping code execution on the original page. Create the following file and save it as `redirect_wrong_user.asp`:

```
<%
  Password = "45gh4"
  UserInput = "12345"

    If UserInput <> Password Then
      Response.Redirect "http://www.google.com"
    Else
%>

Here is the very secret code only for users who knew the password:<br><b>The bird
flew west when seeing the tarantula.</b>

<%
    End If
%>
```

141

When you view the page, you should see that good ol' Google logo (as long as you are online, of course!). You can also redirect to another page within your own web site of course, such as an error page or the index page. This is done by simply changing the URL specified in the `Response.Redirect` line.

You can use these features however you like. For example, you might simply want a redirect to occur after executing some code as standard, rather than waiting for a condition to be met – it's all up to you how you want to use `Response.End` and `Response.Redirect`.

Whatever you do, make sure that you test your code for the appropriate results as sometimes due to simple mistakes a web application may do the complete opposite of what you intended – like streaming a download to non paid-up users, and disallowing access to paid-up users.

Applying Our ASP Knowledge

Thus far our web applications have been very limited. We were using small examples to demonstrate ASP and VBScript features, but now we will move onto a more fun (dynamic) section where you will finally see some practical ASP examples, to allow users to actually interact and submit data to your web applications!

Cool Web Forms

As we all know, **forms** provide users with the opportunity to submit information to a web site, but during our "static" days we really had no idea how to make real use of them, or we tried to look for some CGI script to do our work for us. Forms are pretty much the only way you can receive information from your users on your server. They are also the basis of how users do things such as registering with, logging in to, and sending feedback to your web site.

The good news is that with our newfound knowledge of ASP and VBScript, these forms suddenly become way more useful.

Your first question should be **"How do we display information submitted by forms?"** This is the key. If we know how to display it, we know how to retrieve it and if we know how to retrieve it we can do many things with it, as you will see in the later chapters.

get Versus post

The method of a form can be set to `get` or `post`. By default, a form's method is set to `get`, which appends the form fields to the URL as URL parameters (see the *URL Parameters* and *Request.QueryString* sections for a much more in-depth explanation).

Using the `get` method makes things simpler because the values are easily seen in the address bar, which also makes it easy to troubleshoot. However, be mindful that the client can also see these values, and the URLs are also cached by the browser (this means that you should not use this method when submitting sensitive information – see the *Cookies* section for more on this).

The size of the values passed is restricted to the maximum length of characters allowed in the address bar.

Using the `post` method submits the form field values in the HTTP header. This is the preferred method because the data submitted is not directly visible to the client. Another advantage is that you can send much larger bits of information using `post` than you could using `get`.

Request.Form

`Request.Form` retrieves any form element submitted with a `post` method. Whenever you create a form element you give it a name. For example, `<input type="text" name="username">` will create a textfield named **username**. In order to display the value that was inputted in this textfield and submitted to the ASP, you need to use `Request.Form("username")`. That username is contingent upon the name of the textfield – if you change the name of that textfield then you must change the name in the ASP code. They must match each other.

> Always make sure that the name of the form element and the value of the intended `Request.Form` match.

Dummy Login Form

Now let's look at some code in action – we will create a dummy login form and display the username on the next page. Create the following files:

```
<!-- login_user.asp -->

<form name="form1" method="post" action="welcome_user.asp">

    username: <input type="text" name="username" /><br />
    password: <input type="text" name="password" /><br />
    <input type="submit" name="submit" value="submit" />

</form>
```

```
<!-- welcome_user.asp -->

Welcome <strong><%=Request.Form("username")%></strong>!<br />
I know your password too but I won't display it ;)
```

If you access `login_user.asp` through your web server and enter your username as *Omar*, you would see the following result on the `welcome_user.asp` page after pressing *Submit*:

*Welcome **Omar**!*
I know your password too but I won't display it ;)

The `<%=Request.Form("username")%>` code in `welcome_user.asp` retrieves the value of the `<input type="text" name="username">` form element in the `login_user.asp` page. Certainly you can retrieve the other form elements on this page ("password" and "submit") using `Request.Form("password")` and `Request.Form("submit")`.

> `Request.Form` will only retrieve values of form elements that were directly submitted to it. In other words, you cannot display the form element values on a third page using `Request.Form` unless you passed the values from the second to the third page with another form that had its default values the same as the first form.

Listbox Selection Form

We can also retrieve the values of other types of form elements such as checkboxes, listboxes, and other types. We will display the value selected from a **listbox**. Create the following files:

```
<!-- sex_selection.asp -->

<form name="form1" method="post" action="display_sex.asp">

  <select name="sex">
    <option>male</option>
    <option>female</option>
  </select>
  <input type="submit" name="submit" value="submit" />

</form>
```

```
<!-- display_sex.asp -->

You are <strong><%=Request.Form("sex")%></strong>
```

`sex_selection.asp` allows you to select your sex from a drop-down listbox, and `display_sex.asp` displays the result.

Listbox Selection Form with Conditional Logic

We can also do some tricks depending on what the user selects utilizing our knowledge of conditional logic. We can change the code for the `display_sex.asp` to redirect to different pages depending on the user's sex. Let's change that page.

```
<!-- display_sex2.asp -->

<%
If Request.Form("sex") = "male" Then
    Response.Redirect "http://www.menshealth.com"
  ElseIf Request.Form("sex") = "female" Then
    Response.Redirect "http://www.ivillage.com"
  End If
%>
```

The code above redirects the user to *http://www.menshealth.com* if the sex selection was male and *http://www.ivillage.com* if the sex selection was female. Since there are only two options you could also use the following code:

```
<%
If Request.Form("sex") = "male" Then
    Response.Redirect "http://www.menshealth.com"
  Else
    Response.Redirect "http://www.ivillage.com"
  End If
%>
```

Instead of checking for both we only check for the first. Since there are only two options, we know that if it doesn't equal "male" it must equal the second option. You will find other uses for these tactics in your own web development.

Checkbox Selection Form

Checkboxes are also very useful – each checkbox that is in a checked state when the *Submit* button is pressed submits a value. This can come in handy when we want a user to make a simple selection. Create the following files:

```
<!-- send_note.asp -->

Send us a note!

<form name="form1" method="post" action="thank_you.asp">

    name: <input type="text" name="name" /><br />
    email: <input type="text" name="email" /><br />
    message: <br /><textarea name="message" rows=2 cols=20 wrap=hard></textarea><br />
    register for newsletter: <input type="checkbox" name="newsletter" value="1" />
    <br />
    <input type="submit" name="submit" value="submit" />

</form>
```

```
<!-- thank_you.asp -->

Thank you <strong><%=Request.Form("name")%></strong>.<br />
You submitted the following message:
<strong><%=Request.Form("message")%></strong><p>

<% If Request.Form("newsletter") = 1 Then %>

You also signed up for our newsletter.

<% End If %>
```

When `send_note.asp` is submitted, `thank_you.asp` displays our name and message. In addition, if the user does tick the checkbox the value `1` will be submitted associated with its name `newsletter` and the `thank_you.asp` page will display the following:

You also signed up for our newsletter.

In this section, you learned how to retrieve form elements submitted in a form via the `post` method with an ASP – the possibilities are endless. In the next three sections, we will learn how to submit form elements using the `get` method, and retrieve them from a URL parameter. We will do the latter first, to keep it simple to start with.

URL Parameters

Another way we can receive data from users (as we have seen before) is via the `get` method, using **URL parameters**. This can be (and very often is) used to pass data between pages. We can allow users to pass data or we can embed our own data to be passed in the sourcecode via an `href` attribute. Before we talk about anything you may want to know what a URL parameter is. A URL parameter or **QueryString** is any attribute and value passed after a question mark (**?**) attached to the end of a URL. Here's an example:

```
http://www.website.com/webpage.asp?name=omar
```

The URL parameter in the above URL is `name=omar`.

Every URL parameter is made up of a name and a value just like any variable. The **name** of the URL parameter above is `name` and the **value** of the URL parameter called name is `omar`. Hence, we can also refer to this as a **name/value pair**.

Multiple name/value pairs can be passed by adding an ampersand (**&**) between parameters. Here's an example:

```
http://www.website.com/webpage.asp?name=omar&id=23
```

Request.QueryString

This is all well and good, but what we want to know is how to retrieve these URL parameters. It's simple and exactly like `Request.Form`, but we use **Request.QueryString** instead. So for example, if the following URL parameters were passed: `http://www.website.com/webpage.asp?id=23` we can display it using `Request.QueryString("id")`.

Create the following pages:

```
<!-- display_users.asp -->

<a href="get_id.asp?id=12">omar</a><br />
<a href="get_id.asp?id=15">rahim</a><br />
<a href="get_id.asp?id=145">michael</a><br />
<a href="get_id.asp?id=148">terry</a><br />
```

```
<!-- get_id.asp -->

Look at the URL Parameter in the address bar<br />
The ID you selected equals <strong><%=Request.QueryString("id")%></strong>.
```

Now when you click on one of the links in `display_users.asp`, the ID value contained in the corresponding URL is retrieved and displayed by `get_id.asp`.

Submitting a Form Using get

When the `get` method is used in submitting a form, and the form fields are appended to the action page's URL as name/value pairs, the name sent will be the name of the form field and its value will be the value entered or set for that particular form field. For example, let's look at a form with a textfield named `name`, whose value has been set to "omar", and a *Submit* button named `submit` that has a value set to "send". If we go and submit this form to a page called `thanks.asp`, the URL will look like this after submission: *thanks.asp?name=omar&submit=send.*

These values cannot be retrieved with `Request.Form`, rather they are retrieved like normal URL parameters are with `Request.QueryString`. For example, add the following to two new ASP files:

```
<!-- send_note2.asp -->

Send us a note!

<form name="form1" method="get" action="thank_you2.asp">
```

```
id: <input type="text" name="id" /><br />
name: <input type="text" name="name" /><br />
<br />
<input type="submit" name="submit" value="submit" />

</form>
```

```
<!-- thank_you2.asp -->

Thank you <strong><%=Request.QueryString("name")%></strong>.<br />
Your ID is: <strong><%=Request.QueryString("id")%></strong>
```

When the page is submitted, the form fields will be appended to the QueryString of the action page as URL parameters.

It's as simple as that. You change the value associated with your `Request.QueryString` depending on the URL parameter you want to display. If the URL parameter has an attribute called **name** then you can display its value with `Request.QueryString("name")`. URL parameters will be extremely important when you begin to display database records on your pages. You will usually need to pass that data to other pages.

Cookies (not made out of dough)

Whether you are an experienced web developer or simply an Internet enthusiast, you have no doubt heard about cookies. Cookies are not our favorite snack food in this context; rather they are simply a term used to describe another great feature, which is not only native to ASP, but usable with almost any web scripting language (Netscape created the original cookie).

Cookies are simple text files that you can create and store on the client machine. They allow you to store simple data such as usernames, dates, etc. Values of cookies can be created by the web application or accept parameters submitted by the user. However, they must be used with care.

How do we actually make use of them? Cookies are comparable to the forms and URL parameters we discussed earlier – they allow you to maintain data across pages. When cookies are created they are automatically stored in a specific folder in the user's hard drive, which cannot be changed – on Windows 2000 you can find this folder by going to `C:/Documents and Settings/Administrator/Cookies`. You will probably find dozens already there. Each cookie contains specific data stored by various web applications while you were using the Internet.

Response.Cookies and Request.Cookies

Response.Cookies is all you need to create a cookie. You just need to name the cookie and give it a value, for example `Response.Cookies("MyCookie") = "Hello World"` would create a cookie called `MyCookie` with a value of `Hello World`. This example creates a specific value, but certainly you can store information entered by a user as the value if desired.

For example, if a user submits a form with a textfield called *username*, you can store the value of that textfield as the value of a cookie like so: `Response.Cookies("MyCookie") = Request.Form("username")`. This way you will have that data stored on the user's computer and you can retrieve it any time so long as it is not deleted.

At this point, you are probably asking, "Now that I know how to create a cookie, how do I retrieve it?" **Request.Cookies** will retrieve any cookie you created, identifying it by name. For example, if we wanted to retrieve the cookie named `MyCookie` that we created earlier we can do so like this: `Request.Cookies("MyCookie")`. How easy is that? If we want to output it on screen we simply use `Response.Write Request.Cookies("MyCookie")`.

Let's have a look at an example to put this theory into practice – create the following file:

```
<!-- my_first_cookie.asp -->

<%
Response.Cookies("username") = "omar"
%>

<%=Request.Cookies("username") %>
```

You should see the following results:

omar

We created a cookie named `username` and gave it a value of `omar` – then we displayed the cookie. Now let's create some cookies based on what a user might submit in a form. We will use another dummy login form:

```
<!-- cookie_login.asp -->

<form name="form1" method="post" action="login_create_cookies.asp">

username: <input type="text" name="username" /><br />
password: <input type="text" name="password" /><br />
<input type="submit" name="submit" value="submit" />

</form>
```

```
<!-- login_create_cookies.asp -->

<%
Response.Cookies("userid") = Request.Form("username")
Response.Cookies("pwd") = Request.Form("password")
%>
userid cookie: <strong><%=Request.Cookies("userid") %></strong><br />
pwd cookie: <strong><%=Request.Cookies("pwd") %></strong>
```

After submitting the data, when you view the `login_create_cookies.asp` you should see the values you entered. We have seen something similar before, but this time we didn't display them simply using `Request.Form`, rather, we stuffed the values into 2 cookies, then retrieved the values from there.

Note that now these cookies have been created, we can retrieve the data from any page without having to prompt the user again (until the cookies are deleted). This may come in handy if we wanted to, say, display the `username` across several pages.

> Many web developers use `ck` to prefix cookies when naming them. For example: `ckUserID`, `ckPassword`, etc.

Cookie Expiration

Cookies will delete themselves once the user shuts down his or her browser if you do not specify an expiration date. This is fine if you only want the information for a single session, but you may want the information to be maintained for days, weeks (or even years). For example, you can specify a cookie named `userid` to expire after 7 days like so: `Response.Cookies("userid").Expires = Date + 7`.

We can add expiration dates to our first cookie example in the `my_first_cookie.asp` page like so:

```
<%
  Response.Cookies("username") = "omar"
  Response.Cookies("username").Expires = Date + 7
%>

<%=Request.Cookies("username") %>
```

You can increase the amount of days as you require, from 7-365 or more. Still, be aware that a user may still delete cookies from his or her computer every so often.

Updating Cookies

You cannot create 2 cookies on the same computer with the same name, but you can update cookies by simply rewriting their values. See the following example:

```
<!-- rewrite_cookie.asp -->

<%
  Response.Cookies("ckRememberMe") = True
  Response.Cookies("ckRememberMe") = False
%>

<%=Request.Cookies("ckRememberMe") %>
```

If you view the page, you should see the following results:

False

We created a cookie called `ckRememberMe` and gave it a value of `True` and then rewrote the value to `False`.

Deleting Cookies

We can delete cookies by simply giving them an empty string value. See the following example:

```
<!-- delete_cookie.asp -->

<%
  Response.Cookies("ckRememberMe") = True
  Response.Cookies("ckRememberMe") = ""
%>

<%=Request.Cookies("ckRememberMe") %>
```

Nothing should display on the screen, since the cookie does not exist. ASP doesn't throw an error when trying to retrieve a cookie that does not exist.

Cookies are useful and fun. They have many uses and can help web developers in many different situations – don't be afraid to use cookies if you see a good use for them in your web application.

A Word of Warning About the Use of Cookies

However, when using cookies you should be careful not to use them to store any sensitive information, such as usernames and passwords, or heaven forbid, credit card details! They are not dangerous *per se*, but it is the potential of *how* they can be used that makes them a potential security risk. Since they are only unencrypted text stored in a file on a user's computer, it is a possibility that some unscrupulous web users (as long as they have the cookie's name) could access them at anytime. Hence companies can share with other companies whatever is stored in your cookies.

Despite this, as long as you are wise in your use of cookies and heed these warnings, you should be fine – besides, cookies are beneficial to any web developer. They are quite handy for persisting data, and what's more, they do not take up server space like sessions (see later) that are stored on the server. For more specific information you may visit Netscape's legal notice on cookies at *http://www.netscape.com/legal_notices/cookies.html*.

Session Variables

Session variables provide another way to maintain state across several pages within your web application. Once a user accesses a page on your site, memory is allocated on the web server for this user inside what is called a **Session Object**. Any variable stored in this session object is called a session variable. Session variables can be used to maintain state for the duration of a user's visit to the web site. You can store values into session variables that will be **unique** to each user (in the same way cookies are). Every user gets his or her own session when they access your web site.

Unlike cookies, sessions live on the server, not on the client's computer. They die if there is no request from the user to the server within a session timeout interval set either in IIS or an ASP page. In IIS, 20 minutes is the default timeout for sessions. This value can be increased or decreased by the web developer.

You can change the default timeout from inside your web server program. For example, in Internet Services Manager:

- Right-click *Default Web Site*

- Choose *Properties* from the shortcut menu

- Select the *Home Directory* tab

- Click the *Configuration* button

- Select the *App Options* tab

- Make sure the *Enable session state* option is checked

- Set the *Session timeout* in minutes

- Click on *OK* to exit the *Application Configuration* dialog and *OK* again to exit the properties dialog

You can also programmatically set the session timeout from within an ASP page by adding the following code at the top of your ASP page:

```
<% Session.Timeout = 10 %>
```

Creating and Retrieving Session Variables

Session variables are created just as easily as the other variables. You can write a value into a session variable with the following code: `Session("session_name") = "my value"`.

Retrieving session variables is very easy. You simply need to print out the session – for example `Response.Write Session("session_name")`.

Let's create an example similar to our cookie login, but instead of storing the values in cookies, we will store them in session variables.

```
<!-- session_login.asp -->

<form name="form1" method="post" action="login_create_sessions.asp">

username: <input type="text" name="username" /><br />
password: <input type="text" name="password" /><br />
<input type="submit" name="submit" value="submit" />

</form>
```

```
<!-- login_create_sessions.asp -->

<%
  Session("userid") = Request.Form("username")
  Session("pwd") = Request.Form("password")
%>
userid session: <strong><%=Session("userid") %></strong><br />
pwd session: <strong><%=Session("pwd") %></strong>
```

Access `session_login.asp`, enter some values and submit the form. After submitting the data, when you view the `login_create_sessions.asp` you should see the values you entered.

Updating Session Variables

Session variables can be updated by simply rewriting the value, just like with cookies. See the following example:

```
<!-- rewrite_session.asp -->

<%
  Session("svRememberMe") = True
  Session("svRememberMe") = False
%>

<%=Session("svRememberMe") %>
```

When viewing the page you should see *False*.

Deleting Session Variables

You can destroy a particular session variable with **Session.Contents.Remove.** For example, the following code would destroy a session named `MM_Username`:

```
<% Session.Contents.Remove("MM_Username") %>
```

151

You can also destroy all values stored in the session object, which will destroy all sessions on the server that were set for the user, by using **Session.Abandon**. Use this with caution because it will delete *all* session variables associated with the user:

```
<% Session.Abandon %>
```

If you send the user to a page that contains this code, the user's sessions will be destroyed and memory will be freed. For example, if you create a page named `delete_sessions.asp` with the above code, access it and then go back to your `rewrite_session.asp` page you will find the sessions empty.

You can also destroy the entire session object with the following code:

```
<% Session.Contents.RemoveAll %>
```

Note On Sessions

Be mindful when using sessions. Because sessions can take up a lot of server memory, you should use them sparingly, especially if you are expecting a lot of users at your site. The problem can sometimes arise in not knowing how long to set the timeout interval for. If you keep the time too short while the session holds login information for example, the user will find themselves having to log in again if he or she leaves the system idle for any length of time. On the other hand, setting the timeout interval too long will eat up server resources even if the user is no longer at your site.

Sessions will last according to their timeout scope. This means that if a user logs onto your site, therefore creating a session, but then leaves your site after 1 minute, that session will still last for 19 more minutes regardless, eating up your server memory (provided the time is set to its default value, or course!). For this reason the length of session timeouts should be kept short – anything over 25 minutes is way too much under normal circumstances. The key is using a balanced timeout interval and destroying the session in your ASP once you no longer need it. Don't let this scare you too much – as you become more experienced you will know when and how to use them more efficiently.

Environment Variables

Environment variables are pieces of information that the web server makes available to any program that requests them. These variables can offer very useful information such as the name of the web server, or the user's IP address. You can then access these variables within your ASP script. What follows is some of the more commonly used environment variables:

Environment Variable	Description
HTTP_REFERER	The URL of the page that sent the user to the current one.
QUERY_STRING	The URL parameters following the (?) in the URL.
REMOTE_HOST	The client's IP Address.
SCRIPT_NAME	The URL of the current page.
SERVER_NAME	The server hostname.
URL	The URL of the ASP page (excluding the querystring.)

For a list of the many more environment variables see the list at
http://www.aspfree.com/asp/servervariables.asp.

You can retrieve a specific environment variable using the following syntax:

```
Request.ServerVariables("VariableName")
```

Create the following files to utilize some of the environment variables:

```
<!-- link_page.htm -->

<a href="http://localhost/env_variables.asp">link to env_variables.asp</a>
```

```
<!-- env_variables.asp -->

The URL of this page is: <strong><%=Request.ServerVariables("URL") %></strong>
<br />
Your IP address is: <strong><%=Request.ServerVariables("REMOTE_HOST") %>
</strong>
<br />
Go back to the page you came from:
<strong>
  <a href="<%=Request.ServerVariables("HTTP_REFERER") %>">
  <%=Request.ServerVariables("HTTP_REFERER") %></a>
</strong>
```

Environment variables are really beneficial in that they can give you pertinent information. For example, you could put the user's IP address as the value of a hidden field in a feedback form so that you have the IP address of the submitter. This is helpful in identifying a particular user – if a particular user is, say, posting abusive/offensive messages on your site, you can use it to ban them from accessing the site anymore, by excluding their IP address.

Here is an example:

```
<!-- send_note3.asp -->

Send us a note!

<form name="form1" method="post" action="thank_you.asp">

  name: <input type="text" name="name" /><br />
  email: <input type="text" name="email" /><br />
  message: <br><textarea name="message" rows=2 cols=20 wrap=hard></textarea><br />
  register for newsletter: <input type="checkbox" name="newsletter" value="1">
  <br />
  <input type="submit" name="submit" value="submit" />

  <input type="hidden" name="ipaddress"
value="<%=Request.ServerVariables("REMOTE_HOST") %>" />
</form>
```

When you run this page, view the HTML sourcecode to see the form's hidden element value so you can see that your IP address is in fact being stored in the form ready to be submitted with the other fields.

Feel free to make use of these variables!

Summary

You did it! We learned a lot in this chapter. You were introduced to the differences between static and dynamic web sites, and the most important aspects of creating ASP files with VBScript, such as:

- Declaring variables
- Commenting code
- Conditional logic
- Built-in VBScript functions
- Web forms
- URL parameters
- Creating, Updating, and Deleting Cookies
- Creating, Updating, and Deleting Sessions
- Utilizing Environment Variables

The understanding of basic ASP principles you gained from this chapter will make things much easier for you when you begin to use Dreamweaver MX to generate ASP code for you. In *Chapter 7*, we will take a lengthy stroll on how to automate ASP code, using most of Dreamweaver MX's built-in Application behaviors. Before we do that however, you will learn the basics of connecting dynamic pages to databases.

Resources

The following list of links is here to give you places to go if you want to read further on the subjects we have glossed over in this chapter. You don't need to know much about how the actual code works to build great dynamic web sites in Dreamweaver MX, as you will see in later chapters. However, it is highly recommended that you look into the "code beneath the hood" in more depth, as it will help no end in increasing your understanding of what's actually going on, giving you more control over your sites, and giving you greater flexibility.

ASP Resources

- *http://www.w3schools.com/asp/*
- *http://www.aspin.com*
- *http://www.4guysfromrolla.com*
- *http://www.devguru.com/Technologies/asp/quickref/asp_intro.html*
- *http://msdn.microsoft.com/library/default.asp?url=/library/en-us/iisref/html/psdk/asp/aspguide.asp*
- *http://www.asptoday.com*

VBScript Resources

- *http://www.w3schools.com/vbscript/*

- *http://www.devguru.com/Technologies/vbscript/quickref/vbscript_intro.html*

- *http://msdn.microsoft.com/library/default.asp?url=/library/en-us/script56/html/vtoriVBScript.asp*

6

- Database design

- Creating databases

- SQL queries

- Connecting web pages to a database

- Accessing databases in Dreamweaver MX

Author: Rob Turnbull

Databases Overview

People generally think that a database is something that is created in a special piece of software such as **Microsoft Access**. However, a database could be defined as any store of data that is organized in such a way as to make easy entry and retrieval possible. This means that files created in **Notepad** or **Excel**, could be used as databases – although when used as such, we tend to refer to them as "datastores" to make it clear that they simply **store** data, leaving it up to us to organize how we go about updating or retrieving it.

Using a database application has the added advantage of providing a surrounding network of code for accessing the data – something a flat text file, for instance, does not. If you need ease of use from your database application (and let's face it, who doesn't?) then you should be looking to take advantage of a database application, such as the two we are going to look at in this chapter (and throughout this book). They are **Microsoft Access 2000** and **Microsoft SQL Server 2000**.

How Do I Create a Database?

First, we need to establish a difference between creating a database and creating the database content. When you create your database, you are creating the container in which your data can reside, and no data will be created at this point. Only after you have created the container can you proceed to creating the content.

In Microsoft Access

Microsoft Access 2000 offers up a myriad of wizards and templates for you to choose from to get your job done. Creating your database is as simple as clicking the mouse a few times (and pressing a couple of keys too, unless you want to create a database called `db1.mdb`, which is Access 2000's default name for the first database it is asked to create).

When you open Access 2000 you will see the dialog shown below:

This dialog offers you a few options to choose from. You can open any existing databases you may have on your system by selecting the *Open an existing file* option and then either choosing *More Files...* in the list to search your system for other databases, or selecting one you have previously worked on that is displayed in the list.

You can also create a database for your project using the *Access database wizards, pages, and projects* option. This presents you with a choice of example databases to choose from, which might suit your particular needs (see below):

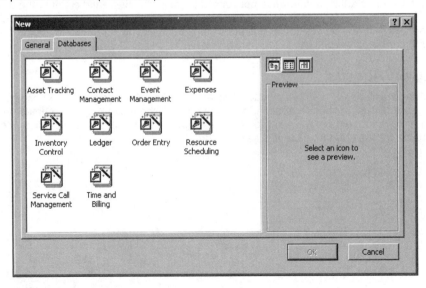

For the purposes of this book, however, we are going to create our own database from scratch so (assuming you've opened the Wizard up) press *Cancel* on the dialog shown above, and instead select the *Blank Access Database* option and click *OK*.

You are then asked to give your database file a name and select the location to store it. I'm going to call mine `webprodmx.mdb` (not to be confused with our `webprodmx_data` database we use in the next chapter!) and store it in my databases folder in `C:\databases\`.

That done, you're ready to begin creating your database structure (tables etc.) and content. We'll get to that in a minute – first, let's just cover the creation process in SQL Server.

In Microsoft SQL Server

We will use **Enterprise Manager** to create our databases in SQL Server. This is one of SQL Server's main interfaces, but you could, if you so desired, use the **Query Analyzer** to create your databases instead (using the SQL command `CREATE DATABASE`, for instance). In fact, SQL queries could be written into the Query Analyzer to perform everything else you could possibly think of to do with your database. However, although it is an extremely powerful tool, We're not going to use the Query Analyzer here because the benefits it offers really lie beyond our needs at this stage.

Launch Enterprise Manager.

> *If you need to log on to your SQL Server, please ensure that you are logged in as Administrator, since this affects all the objects that you are going to create. By logging in as Administrator any object that you create will be prefixed with* dbo.*, meaning that* dbo *– the Database Owner – is recorded as the owner of that object.*

When the console has opened (Enterprise Manager runs under **Microsoft Management Console** (**MMC**)) you will see two panes. The left pane is a tree view as shown here and the right pane shows the contents of the left pane's selected element.

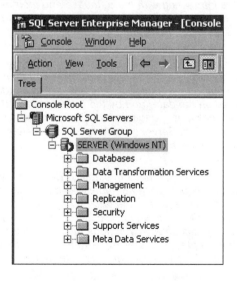

Once you have expanded your tree view to look something like the one above (your server name will no doubt be different to mine), right-click on the *Databases* node and select *New Database...* from the context menu.

At a very basic level, all you need to do to create your SQL Server database is enter a name in the *Name* box on the *General* tab and click *OK*, which in many cases may well be perfectly acceptable.

Where it may not be acceptable is when your network administrator specifies the places that you must create all your files. In such a case, leaving the default locations of the *Data* files and the *Transaction log* files is not an option. To change the location of these files, you need to click onto each tab in turn and use the ellipses button (...) in the *Location* column to select the new storage location. You can also specify alternative names for the files here, instead of the default database name, which will have been pre-entered for you if you have already entered the database name on the first tab.

This shouldn't be an issue for us, so – unless you have this worry – simply enter `webprodmx` as the name for our new database, leaving all the defaults in place, and click *OK*.

A little explanation of what SQL Server is going to do with your data is in order at this point – stay with me.

*One of the main differences between Access and SQL Server is the way data is managed. Access uses a single file (the `.mdb` file) to store everything – the limitations of which will become apparent shortly – whereas SQL Server uses several files: at least two. It has a **data** file and it has a **transaction log** file.*

Without getting way too deep into the workings of SQL Server (which isn't within the remit of this book), what basically happens is, User1 logs into SQL Server and performs some actions on the data in one of its databases. Those actions are written to a transaction log and applied to the data at a subsequent point. If anything should go wrong while User1 is interacting with the database and their modifications cannot be completed successfully, the transaction will not be applied and so the data will remain unaffected (this is called "transactional roll back").

*SQL Server locks its data at the row level so that many users can use the same database – and even the same data – simultaneously. It can then schedule multiple user access requests to that data. It does this by order of merit (depending on what action is to be performed on the data) and by the order in which those requests were originally made. This is known as "concurrency". (You can read more about this subject in **Books Online** – SQL Server's impressive help system, which can be found under the Microsoft SQL Server menu.)*

*Access, on the other hand, does not have this ability. Because it was designed for desktop use, Access locks its data at the database level, so that only one user can use the database and make modifications to the data at any one time. This may seem restricting (and it can be), but if your web traffic is low, this **One-user-at-a-time** principle still shouldn't be noticeable. A web page uses a single database connection – regardless of how many people are interacting with the site – so as far as the database is concerned, it's the same user making data requests each time.*

This is one of the reasons why Access is widely used as a database manager for small web sites – despite its limitations it holds up remarkably well under small loads. If you're just learning, or you expect very low web traffic on your web site (for example, if it's a personal web site), you might consider using it. That said, for anything resembling mainstream work where the need for good performance and reliability is paramount, you would be well advised to use a tool like SQL Server, which was designed for such work.

Expanding the *Database* node in the left pane of the SQL Server console will show you your newly created database and its internal structure.

Preparing a SQL Server Database for Internet Use

A new SQL Server database is created containing eleven objects, two of which are pre-populated with data. If you click on the *webprodmx* database name under *Databases* in the left pane, you'll see the items associated with each database listed on the right – this is how it'll probably look (you can change this view by right-clicking in the pane and selecting *View*):

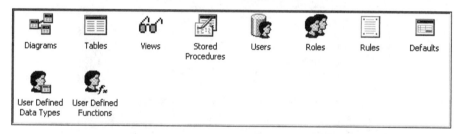

The **Users** object contains an item called *dbo* (Data Base Owner). This object stores the database owner's account, and is created so that this user can administer the new database. For security reasons, other user accounts should be added to your database, which are each given just enough access for them to get their required job done. This prevents the risk of accidental damage being done by someone with too many permissions. You can assign permissions on a new account manually, on an object-by-object basis, but it is often easier to simply assign a new account one of the predefined **Roles** that SQL Server makes available. A role is an array of permissions that are pre-set for each of the database objects, and represents one of a number of common database-related job roles. Roles become very useful if you are creating many user accounts.

To reduce clutter in the left pane, you may want to exclude from view all the system databases and objects. To do this, right-click the SQL Server name and select the Edit SQL Server Registration properties... option. On the resulting dialog, there are three checkboxes at the bottom. You need to deselect the middle one marked Show system databases and system objects. Now you will only see items that you create yourself.

We need to set up a special account in SQL Server in order for our web application to be able to talk to our database. This is the *IUSR\MachineName* account – the **Internet User** account. This account acts as an alias for all the traffic brought to the database from your web application.

Creating the IUSER Account in SQL Server

1. In the left pane of the SQL Server console, click *Security*, then the *Logins* node.

2. In the right pane, which now shows the current users of this database, right-click and select *New Login...* and the following dialog will open:

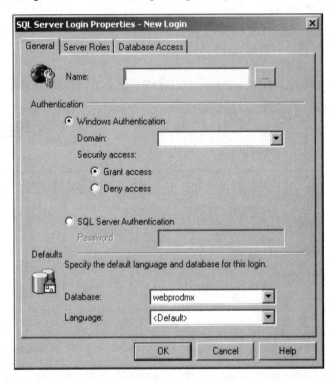

3. Click the ellipses button (...) next to the *Name* box. This will open a window entitled *SQL Server Login Properties – New Login*. If it is not selected already, select your machine name from the drop-down list entitled: *List Names From*. In the *Names* list, scroll down the list of logins until you find the *IUSR_MACHINENAME* login (with the name of your computer in place of *MACHINENAME*). Select it and click *Add*.

4. Click *OK* and the dialog will be filled out for you, showing the login details for *IUSR*. The name will be displayed as *DOMAINNAME\IUSR_MACHINENAME* (where the domain that this computer is a member of appears instead of *DOMAINNAME* and the name of the machine replaces *MACHINENAME*). We don't want this login to be domain-specific, however – we want people on the Internet to be able to use it and they won't be logged in to our domain.

5. To change this, select the radio button called *SQL Server Authentication* to make this login an SQL Server authenticated login.

6. Enter a password.

7. Select *webprodmx* in the Database drop-down list.

8. Click the *Database Access* tab. Scroll down the list until you can see *webprodmx*. Tick the checkbox next to it and your new login details will be added to that database:

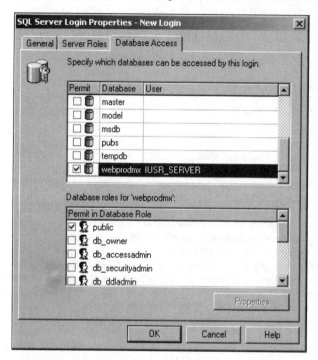

9. With that done, click *OK* and your new Internet User login is created.

You can now set up a web site that has the ability to connect to this database. We will be doing exactly that, later in this chapter, in the section entitled **Making The Connection**.

Database Design

There is far more to good database design than just following a good naming convention. If you were to spend some time asking people their thoughts on the dos and don'ts, you would end up being able to fill an entire book. Lo and behold, someone beat you to it: perhaps one of the best books you could buy on the subject is *Database Design For Mere Mortals* by Michael J. Hernandez (Addison-Wesley Publishing Co; ISBN: 0201694719).

We won't go into great depth here, but we'll see a couple of things that you should consider when designing your database – if only to save you headaches later on!

Object Naming Conventions

SQL has a number of reserved keywords that must be avoided at all costs when creating names for your database objects and their properties. For a complete list, launch **Books Online**, go to the *Index* tab and enter '*keywords, reserved for SQL Server*' and click *Display*.

Using a good naming convention can help you to understand what is going on when you come to use your database later on, or when you return to a project you wrote months ago.

For example, if you have a few database tables named as follows:

```
tbl_Customers

tbl_Customer_Orders

tbl_Customer_Order_Details

tbl_Products
```

it wouldn't take a genius to figure out that `tbl_Customer_Orders` would be a good place to look if you wanted to view some customer orders. Naming things logically makes it easy to quickly assess what an object contains and what it should be used for. This is especially useful when accessing these objects from external programs such as Dreamweaver MX.

In the above example, We have prefixed each table name with `tbl_`, which is short for 'Table'. We do this so that we know it's a table and not a **View**, **Stored Procedure,** or any other database object. For views, I use a prefix of `view_`, for stored procedures, I use a prefix of `sp`. Note that I do not use an underscore after the `sp` prefix, the reason being that SQL Server uses that prefix for its own internal system stored procedures. If you were to adopt the `sp_` convention yourself, there's the danger that you give one of your own stored procedures the same name as a system stored procedure. In such a circumstance SQL Server will run the system stored procedure in preference to your own – possibly causing untold damage to your database.

Table column names are another area that can cause serious problems later on if you are not careful. For example, say we have a table that contains customer orders and we want to include a column to store the date that an order was placed. We can't simply use `Date` as our column name, since Date is a reserved word in SQL Server. We get around this by using `CO_Date` instead (`CO_` signifying that it belongs to the `Customer_Orders` table): this avoids any naming conflicts and the column name still makes sense. (We would also be able to distinguish between the date of a customer order and any other dates we might want to store in our database, of course.)

Avoid the use of spaces in object and property names. The examples shown here use the underscore character in place of spaces. You could use the capitalization method instead, which, for our `tbl_Customer_Orders` object, would look like this: `tblCustomerOrders`. The start of each new word is capitalized instead of being separated with underscores.

Creating Tables

A table structure defines the order and sequence in which data is stored and retrieved from your database. Each entry consists of a record, which you can think of as a horizontal row in your table containing data in a series of columns, known as "fields". Each field stores equivalent items of data for each record. It is common practice (and one that we will adopt from here on) to make the first field a unique identifier for the record it belongs to: known as a **Primary Key**. This field will be useful to use later on when we begin to build relationships between the tables we have created.

We summarize all this below, with two imaginary records – the first one highlighted.

Primary Key	Field 1	Field 2	Field 3	Field 4
1	Value for field one	Value for field two	Value for field three	Value for field four
2	Value for field one	Value for field two	Value for field three	Value for field three

Of course, we could store all the data for a given record in exactly the same form, and if we were dealing with a comma-delimited text file, that would be exactly what we would do. However, the values in each field of a record are almost always different in nature, depending on what each field is supposed to store, so the use of **data types** (such as `integer` or `date`) can greatly improve the efficiency of our database and help prevent inappropriate data types being entered in a given field (we will be looking at data types shortly).

Let's say we want to create a table for an e-commerce site called `tbl_customers`, which stores all our customer details. In it, we will have the following fields:

- A primary key, which we will call `CustomerID`

- The name of the customer, be it an individual or business – we'll call this field `CustomerName`

- The customer's address, in a field called `PostalAddress`

- Their postal code, which we store separately in a field called `PostalPostcode`, since it can be used to quickly group customers by geographical region

- Their nationality, `PostalCountry` – again, so that customers from a given country may be more easily grouped together

As we'll see, Access doesn't give us as much scope about what data types we can use as SQL Server does, but setting the correct data types for each of these fields and determining how much space each one can take up will help us maintain the integrity of the data, save on storage space, and could even speed up data access.

Data types are set at table level, so let's now take a look at the process of creating a table and the different data types that can be stored in the fields within it. We'll look at Access first.

Creating Tables Using Access

With your empty database open select *Tables* in the left column of the database window, click *New*, and select *Design View* from the pop-up dialog (you could also have double-clicked the *Create Table in Design View* icon in the *Tables* window).

You will be presented with the Table Design View.

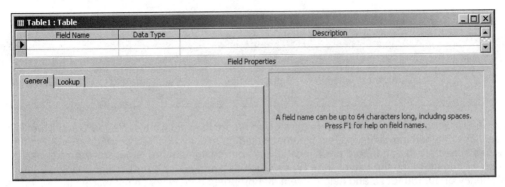

I've said that we can think of a record as rows of fields, running horizontally. You'll note, however, that we're stacking the field definitions vertically as we create them, which may seem a little counter intuitive at first. There are three values that you can assign to each field:

- The *Name*, which Access uses to identify a given field within a table and retrieve its data

- The data type – a very general class of data into which the data falls, such as `Number` or `Currency`

- A *Description* – some text that you can use to remind yourself of what a given field was intended to hold. What you enter here has no wider use within the database itself, and is entirely optional

Click inside the *Data Type* box for the topmost field and click the down arrow – you'll see a list of the general data types that Access recognizes. If you select a general data type and then move down to the *Field Properties* dialog and select *Format* (for most of the general types) or *Field Size* (in the case of *Number* data types), you'll see another down arrow appear. Click on this and you'll see all of the subtypes you can assign to your data. For instance, the subtypes of a *Number* data type are:

- Byte

- Integer

- Long Integer

- Single

- Double

- Replication ID

- Decimal

If you've done any programming before, you may well be familiar with the concept of using different data types to optimize how your data is stored and handled within your code. If not, don't worry, you can play around with the different data types and field lengths at your leisure – most of them are fairly easy to grasp – and you won't need a thorough grounding in this for the simple table we're about to create.

Let's now take a look at creating that `tbl_customers` table in Access.

To create the primary key, in the first *Field Name* box in Design View, type *CustomerID*. Give it a *Data Type* of *Autonumber*. Access will now ensure that the value created here for each record will be unique. The field size will be set as *Long Integer* by default, so leave it like that. Now click on the gray square to the left of your *Field Name* to highlight the entire row. Right-click, and you'll see that the first entry in the pop-up menu that appears is *Primary Key*. Select this, and you'll see that a small key icon appears in the gray square to the right of your field name. This signifies that Access will now treat this field as the primary key for this table. To maintain integrity, Access only allows you to assign this property to one field in a table at any one time.

Move down to the next field and name it *CustomerName*. Give it a *Data Type* of *Text* and you may wish to increase the *Field Size* (the number of individual characters) to *100* or so, from the default value of *50*. Always aim to make a field no bigger than the maximum size of value you expect it to ever have to hold.

Name the next field *PostalAddress* and give it a *Field Type* of *Text* and a size of *250*. Be aware that textfields can only hold a maximum of 255 characters anyway, so if you feel this field should be able to hold more characters than this, you would need to use a *Memo* data type. For this example however, use a *Text* type to keep things simple.

Name the next field `PostalPostcode`. Give it a *Field Type* of *Text*. A *Field Size* of *20* should be sufficient.

Name the next field, called `PostalCountry`, and give it a *Field Type* of *Text* and a *Field Size* of *50*.

You save your newly created table by selecting the *File* option from the menu, choosing *Save As...* and entering *Tbl_Customers* as your new table's name. You can now view your table in *Datasheet View* by selecting *View | Datasheet View*. If you had simply tried viewing your table in *Datasheet View*, straight away, Access would have prompted you to save you table first. Either way, you have now created your new `tbl_Customers` table.

Creating a Table in SQL Server

Select the empty database *webprodmx* we created earlier, under *Databases*, in the left pane. In the right-hand pane right-click on the *Tables* icon and select *New Table*. The *New Table* dialog will open.

This is hopefully fairly clear: you enter the field name in the *Field Name* column and when you then move into the *Data Type* column and select the down arrow that will appear, you will see a list of all the types of data types that SQL Server supports. Unlike Access, SQL Server does not have general data types, which then break down into more specific subtypes. It also has a great many more actual types. This reflects the fact that SQL Server is optimized for fast data retrieval and efficiency of storage.

If you refer back to our example table, `customers`, you'll recall that it has a primary key field named `CustomerID`. This screenshot shows how our *New Table* dialog box looks just after we've created this field:

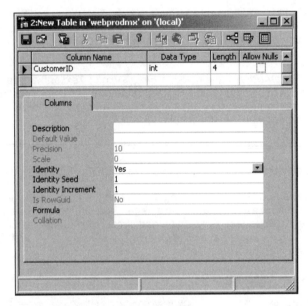

As shown, give this field a data type of *int*, then go down to the *Identity* box in the *Columns* tab and set this to *Yes*. Identity is the name for SQL Server's built-in primary key data type. This defaults to an Identity Seed (the number from which the identity field will begin counting when the first record is created) and Identity Increment (the rate at which the value is increased with each new record), of *1*, in each case. This means that the first record will be given a primary key of 1 and each successive record will have a primary key one bigger. This is fine, but SQL Server still provides the ability to customize things to a very low level.

We selected an *int* data type because this occupies 4 bytes by default. You'll find that you can't change the value in the *Length* column, for this reason. If this were a textfield, such as a *char* type (character), we could set how many characters it occupies and, thus, what kind of load on the total storage space this field will exert for each record. As you saw when carrying out this process in Access, the decision about how big a field should be must be taken with care. An *int* can store up to around 2 billion values, which may seem like overkill (even if this were Amazon.com that we were designing for!), but remember that any value stored here can never be used again, and customers will come and go. In the lifetime of your database, the use of an *int* for a field of this kind is appropriate – especially since the next smallest size available is *tinyint*, anyway, which can only store up to 256 different values.

Now let's create the other fields: `CustomerName`, `PostalAddress`, `PostalPostcode` and `PostalCountry`. For normal fields like this, you can permit the value to be a *Null*. Null is literally an unknown value. It is not an empty string (that is, a character string with no content, "") then it contains nothing. The use of a `null` explicitly stores the fact that no value was entered here. You can also specify a *Default Value* in the *Columns* tab, which is a value that will always be entered in this field, should no other value be provided in its place.

Create `CustomerName` as a *char* data type of length 100. You may think this is too much, but it depends whether you would expect to be receiving commercial customers or not. A *char* data type is of fixed length, which is to say that this field will always hold 100 characters, even if the customer name was simply *John Smith*: the rest of the field would be filled up with spaces. This may sound very inefficient, and we could have made this field a *varchar* data type instead, meaning that each field for a given record would occupy only as many characters as are needed to store its value. However, the use of fixed length fields allows SQL Server to search for and retrieve values much faster, since it does not have to check for the end of each field all the time. Make sure you uncheck the *Allow Nulls* column and don't bother entering any default values, since neither of these options are appropriate for this field.

Now create `PostalAddress` as a field of type *char* and give it a length of 250 characters. `PostalPostcode` and `PostalCountry` can also be fields of type char with lengths of 20 and 50 characters respectively. If this were a real example, you might wish to assign `PostalCountry` with a *Default Value* – if you expected the majority of your customers all to come from your home country, for instance.

Your finished *New Table* dialog should look like this.

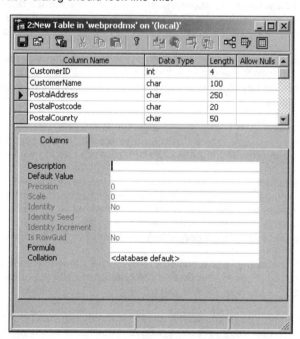

Save this table by clicking the *Save* icon in the top left of this dialog; name it `tbl_Customers`. Close the dialog and now click on the *Tables* icon in the right-hand pane. Your new `tbl_Customers` table will be listed in the resulting display.

Relational Databases and Referential Integrity

Relational databases allow you to store lots of information in a structured and organized way, removing the need to store multiple copies of the same data. The use of primary keys is crucial to how we achieve this.

For example, say in our e-commerce site, a customer places an order for five items. You would want to store the customer's delivery details, an overview of their order, and the details of their order (the individual items they bought).

You could store all this information in one table and have the customer's name and address entered with each record of the order, but that's a lot of repetition. Fortunately, thanks to relational databases, you can split the information over several tables:

* The `tbl_Customers` table we've just created would have just one record per customer and would store their contact and delivery details

* The `tbl_Customer_Orders` table would have one record per order and might detail the order total, the date and time the order was placed, and whether the order has been fulfilled or not

* The details of the order, a record of each individual item ordered, would be kept in the `tbl_Customer_Order_Details` table

In this case, you would set up two relationships to show how the entries relate to each other: one would be between `tbl_Customers` and `tbl_Customer_Orders` and the other would be between `tbl_Customer_Orders` and `tbl_Customer_Order_Details`. We do this using the value of `CustomerID`, the primary key from the `tbl_Customers` table. The `tbl_Customer_Orders` and `tbl_Customer_Order_Details` tables will each contain a field that stores the `CustomerID` values of the customers who placed these orders – the same `CustomerID`s we stored in `tbl_Customers`. This is known as a **foreign key**. A foreign key is simply a primary key from one table as recorded as a field within another table.

Like a lead connects a dog to its owner, the foreign key in the `tbl_Customer_Orders` and `tbl_Customer_Order_Details` tables ties the order records to the customers to whom they belong – from this we can retrieve the details of each customer, along with their orders.

So you would have columns in `tbl_Customer_Orders` and `tbl_Customer_Order_Details` called `CustomerID`, which would hold foreign keys: the value of `CustomerID` for the relevant record in `tbl_Customers`. These foreign key columns are not *Identity* or *Autonumber* columns (unique values only) because we might have to store several records with the same `CustomerID` in these tables (if the customer were to place more than one order).

So, let's recap. Using the example of a customer buying five items from our store, there would be one record created in `tbl_Customers`, one record created in `tbl_Customer_Orders` and five records created in `tbl_Customer_Order_Details`.

Let's see how this is done. You might want to create some dummy tables called `tbl_Customer_Orders` and `tbl_Customer_Order_Details`, so that you can try this next example out for yourself. You can give each one dummy fields, to reflect how you think they would be structured, if you like, but all they really need is primary keys of their own (`OrderID` and `OrderDetailsID`) and a field called `CustomerID`, for the foreign key, in each case.

Creating a Relationship in Access

To create a relationship in Access, click the relationships button on the toolbar:

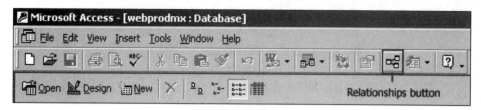

You will now be looking at a large blank gray canvas onto which you need to add the tables you want to relate to each other.

We will follow on from the examples seen before and relate the `customers` table to a `customer orders` table, which would be the first of two relationships we would set up if we were to follow the examples through to their conclusion.

Right-click and select *Show Table* from the context menu. From the dialog, select `tbl_Customers` and click *Add*. You should also add `tbl_Customer_Orders`.

In the list of columns in the `tbl_Customers` object, left-click and drag from the `CustomerID` field to the `CustomerID` field in the `tbl_Customer_Orders` object and then let go. As you start to drag between the objects the cursor changes to a small horizontal bar. When you have finished dragging and have dropped (released the click you started on `tbl_Customers`), the *Edit Relationships* dialog opens up for you to specify the details of this relationship in:

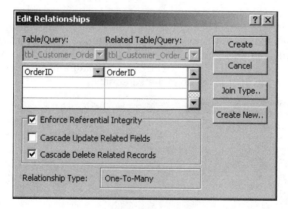

We want to set up a **One-To-Many** relationship between `tbl_Customers` and `tbl_Customer_Orders` and the columns that have the related data in them are both called `CustomerID` in this case. They don't have to be the same, they just have to contain the same data and be stored using the same data type.

As seen above, you also want to specify *Cascade Delete Related Records* in the referential integrity area so that if a record is deleted from my `tbl_Customers` table, all the related records from my `tbl_Customer_Orders` table will be deleted as well.

Click *Create* to create the relationship and you will see a black line drawn between the two tables to signify the relationship. Notice that above the end of the line that ends at `tbl_Customers` is a *1* and above the other end is an infinity symbol (which looks like a sideways 8). These visually signify the one-to-many relationship you have created between these two tables:

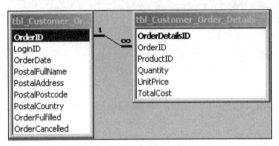

Creating a Relationship in SQL Server

As ever with SQL Server, there is more than one way to achieve your objective. To visually design your relationships, you can, from the *Table Design* view, click *Manage Relationships...* on the toolbar and use the resulting dialog to create them, or you can go though the process of creating a *Database Diagram*, as we are about to.

In Enterprise Manager, in the left pane, expand the `webprodmx` database then click on the *Diagrams* object.

Right-click in the right pane and select *New Database Diagram* from the context menu to launch the *Create Database Diagram Wizard*. Click *Next*.

Now you can select the tables to add to your diagram by clicking on them and clicking the *Add* button in between the left and right lists. If you check the *Add Related Tables Automatically* option, it will automatically add any tables to the diagram that are related to a table you wish to add. You can also specify how many levels of related tables it should add automatically. The default is *1*. We want to add `tbl_Customers` and `tbl_Customer_Orders` to our diagram, so select them and click *Add* to put them into the list on the right, as seen in the screenshot.

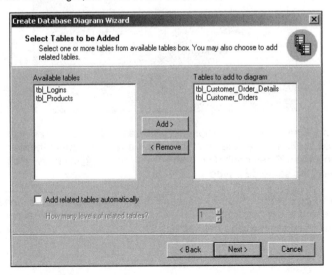

Click *Next* to check the details then click *Finish* if everything looks OK (if you made a mistake, click *Back* to go back and correct it). SQL Server will now generate a basic diagram for you.

This now works in pretty much the same way as you saw in Access. Once again, from the list of fields in the `tbl_Customers` object, left-click and drag from the `CustomerID` field to the `CustomerID` field in the `tbl_Customer_Orders` object and let go. A dotted line is drawn between the objects you are connecting as you do so. When you drop the drag, the *Edit Relationships* dialog opens up for you to specify the details of this relationship in:

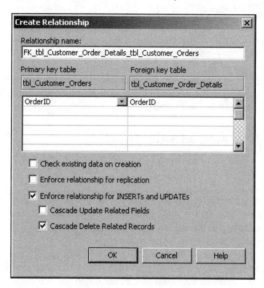

One of the very useful options here is the first checkbox, *Check existing data on creation*. This allows you to ensure that any data already in these tables conforms to this relationship. If you know it doesn't, make sure this checkbox is left unchecked. When creating relationships on empty tables it does not matter if you left it checked of course.

If you plan to use this database in a replication environment (a replication environment being a collection of databases that synchronize their content at predefined intervals), you can specify that this relationship should be enforced by checking the second checkbox. We are not going to be getting involved with replication in this book, so I have unchecked that box also.

Finally, we have the *Cascade Update* and *Cascade Delete* options. I have de-selected the *Update* option as it won't affect this relationship in this instance. We cannot change the `CustomerID` value for a record in our `tbl_Customers` table because it is the `Identity` value, which is a read-only value. Therefore, *Cascade Update* for this relationship isn't possibile.

Click *OK* to create the relationship.

The diagram now shows a line with a gold key at one end and an infinity symbol at the other to visually signify the one-to-many relationship you have created between these two tables:

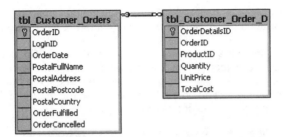

You then need to save the diagram: you can use the default name of *Diagram* 1 if you want to, although a descriptive name may help you in future if you create many diagrams in your database.

When you save your diagram, some behind-the-scenes modifications need to be applied to the tables involved in it to ensure that the relationships you just specified will be adhered to. You need to click *Yes* to allow these changes to be saved.

SQL Server Views and Access Queries

Views or **Queries** are the ideal way to bring together the data you need to retrieve from the tables in your database.

Using Views or Queries in your database allows us to store some of the SQL work within our database rather than having that entire statement passed to the database from your web page. This means that to change the data displayed on a page, you might only need to modify the code in your database, rather than editing the SQL in your web page.

The need to build very complex SQL queries can rear its head quite quickly in large projects, which is why I almost always use Views or Queries to gather together the data I want and then use a simple select statement to grab all of those records in my web page. I may even pass a filtering parameter into the View to narrow down my recordset even further. The beauty of doing it this way, is that the complex SQL statement stays in the database and the run-time performance of the queries can be increased (your web pages will load faster).

Say, we want to view my sales by seeing who has bought products from my online web store along with how much they spent in total. We don't need to know what they bought or where they live at this point in time, we only want to see the crucial data: their name and their total purchase cost.

To generate the recordset for a web page to show me this data in Dreamweaver MX, we could open the **Recordset Builder** and switch to *Advanced View* and go about building up the following statement:

```
SELECT dbo.tbl_Customer_Orders.OrderID, dbo.tbl_Customer_Orders.PostalFullName,
       SUM(dbo.tbl_Customer_Order_Details.TotalCost)
AS TotalPurchaseCost
FROM dbo.tbl_Customer_Orders INNER JOIN dbo.tbl_Customer_Order_Details
ON dbo.tbl_Customer_Orders.OrderID = dbo.tbl_Customer_Order_Details.OrderID

GROUP BY dbo.tbl_Customer_Orders.OrderID, dbo.tbl_Customer_Orders.PostalFullName
```

The Recordset Builder is great in that it will get us a long way towards creating this SQL statement, but it won't be able to do it all, so we would have to add in some of this code by hand. As we've said before, it's often easier to get visual tools to do the job for us. We will be looking at how to use the **Simple Recordset Builder** and the **Advanced Recordset Builder** later in this chapter.

A simpler way to do this would be to create a View called view_Purchase_Totals in SQL Server or a Query in Access to house the SQL code above and then to use the Dreamweaver MX Recordset Builder to build a recordset with the following code:

```
SELECT * FROM view_Purchase_Totals
```

I know which I'd prefer!

Views and Queries become more and more useful when you need to gather data from more and more tables. Using a View or Query to select records from a single table may offer only slight benefits, and only if the table is large, with many columns, and you are selecting most of them: if it's a small table, then the benefits are often much fewer. I'm sure you get the idea.

Simple SQL

Later in this chapter you will see just how easy Dreamweaver MX makes building SQL statements to create recordsets for your web pages. To give you a fuller understanding of this creation process and the final SQL code that it produces, I think a quick primer in some simple SQL is in order.

All the SQL statements you will see here can be used in the **Advanced Recordset Builder** of Dreamweaver MX. Some of them can be created in the **Simple Recordset Builder**, too – the difference being that when you need to specify more than one criterion in your statement, you'll need to be using the advanced *Recordset Builder*.

SQL Server uses a strict naming convention for its objects if you have programmed a language that uses dot notation before, then you will recognize this and understand it easily. If not, it really is quite logical.

To reference an object in SQL Server you use the following standard:

```
databaseowner.objectname
```

For example:

```
dbo.tbl_Customer_Orders
```

> *Access doesn't need this extra information, nor would it understand it if you used it. The reason is that Access doesn't use the Ownership metaphor or permissions principles that SQL Server does: it's intended as a single-user database manager. SQL Server ensures that only the people with the relevant permissions can perform actions on the database objects, but in Access, it's a free-for-all!*

The following examples assume that the owner of the database objects in SQL Server is *dbo*. Also, we will be addressing the same table object, tbl_Logins, in each case.

Selecting All Records from a Table

Probably the simplest SQL Statement there is.

Access:

```
SELECT * FROM tbl_Logins
```

SQL Server:

```
SELECT * FROM dbo.tbl_Logins
```

This statement says "Select all the records contained in `tbl_Logins`". Here, * means all columns. This is not to be confused with the mathematical * which looks the same but performs a very different role (that is, multiplication).

Selecting All Records That Meet 1 Criterion

This is almost as easy as the first example, but there are a couple of crucial rules to bear in mind. We are going to use a similar statement to the one above, but we only want to return those records that contain a specific value in the specified column. You use the keyword `WHERE` to specify this.

Access:

```
SELECT * FROM tbl_Logins WHERE LoginUsername = 'value'
```

SQL Server:

```
SELECT * FROM dbo.tbl_Logins WHERE LoginUsername = 'value'
```

Strikingly similar aren't they?

This statement says "Select all the records contained in `tbl_Logins` where the value contained in the `LoginUsername` column matches the value specified (in place of `value`)".

What you may need to watch out for in SQL statements is the data type of the column that stores the value you need to match. In the example opposite, the column `LoginUsername` has a text-based data type, which means that the value I'm going to compare with the value in that column needs to be enclosed in single quotes. If it had been a numeric column, I would not have used the single quotes.

To illustrate this point, the following SQL code will show you the correct way to use a numeric value in the value area of this statement.

Access:

```
SELECT * FROM tbl_Logins WHERE LoginID = value
```

SQL Server:

```
SELECT * FROM dbo.tbl_Logins WHERE LoginID = value
```

This statement says "Select all the records contained in `tbl_Logins` where the value contained in the `LoginID` column matches the value specified (in place of `value`)".

The `LoginID` in our database is a numeric value, therefore the comparison value needs to be numeric too. By removing the single quotes from around the value, the SQL Statement becomes valid. If you left the single quotes around the value and tried to execute the statement, you would get a data type mismatch error because the SQL will see that you are trying to use a non-numeric value in a comparison statement with the value contained in a numeric column.

Bearing these facts in mind, let's quickly step through a couple of increasingly complex, yet still very straightforward, examples.

Selecting All Records That Meet Several Criteria (Using AND)

The `AND` keyword allows you to create SQL statements that specify that more than one criteria must be met in order to return any results.

Access:

```
SELECT * FROM tbl_Logins WHERE LoginUsername = 'value' AND LoginPassword =
'anothervalue'
```

SQL Server:

```
SELECT * FROM dbo.tbl_Logins WHERE LoginUsername = 'value' AND LoginPassword =
'anothervalue'
```

This statement says "Select all the records contained in `tbl_Logins` where the value contained in the `LoginUsername` column matches the first value specified (in place of `value`) `AND` the value contained in the `LoginPassword` column matches the second value specified (in place of `anothervalue`)".

Selecting Records That Meet One or More of Several Criteria (Using OR)

The `OR` keyword allows you to create SQL statements that specify that one or more criteria of **either** of the specified criteria must be met in order to return any results.

Access:

```
SELECT * FROM tbl_Logins WHERE LoginUsername = 'value' OR LoginPassword =
'anothervalue'
```

SQL Server:

```
SELECT * FROM dbo.tbl_Logins WHERE LoginUsername = 'value' OR LoginPassword =
'anothervalue'
```

This statement says "Select all columns for all the records contained in `tbl_Logins` where the value contained in the `LoginUsername` column matches the value specified (in place of `value`) OR the value contained in the LoginPassword column matches the value specified (in place of `anothervalue`)".

If you were to build a slightly more complex SQL statement that utilized the OR keyword **and** the AND keyword, you would be well advised to use parenthesis to encapsulate the OR criteria. If you don't do this, you may get erroneous results. The following Access-based examples will explain this. To use this example in SQL Server, just add `dbo.` in front of the table name.

```
SELECT * FROM tbl_Logins WHERE (LoginUsername = 'value' OR LoginPassword =
'anothervalue') AND LoginAccessLevel = 'yetanothervalue'
```

This would correctly return all columns for all records from the `tbl_Logins` table that meet the criteria of having a matching `LoginUsername` value OR a matching `LoginPassword` value AND also having a matching `LoginAccessLevel` value. Compare it with this, which could return incorrect results:

```
SELECT * FROM tbl_Logins WHERE LoginUsername = 'value' OR LoginPassword =
'anothervalue' AND LoginAccessLevel = 'yetanothervalue'
```

Here, the SQL might be saying what the first example said, or it might be interpreted as saying "Return all records from the `tbl_Logins` table that meet the criteria of having a matching `LoginUsername` value AND also having a matching `LoginAccessLevel` value OR a matching `LoginPassword` value". If you say the whole statement out loud with a big emphasis on the OR keyword, you'll understand the point I'm making here.

Basically, the more complex your SQL statements become, the more careful you will have to be in creating them.

Useful SQL Keywords

There are far too many SQL keywords in total for me to cover in this section of the book. However, a quick glance at some of the more commonly used ones, that you will no doubt come across time and again, might help you to understand how to achieve the results you are after. To see all the SQL keywords, check out Books Online.

COUNT

If you want to count how many login records you have stored in your `tbl_Logins` table, for example, you could use the COUNT keyword in the following way:

Access:

```
SELECT COUNT(LoginIncluded) AS TotalLogins FROM tbl_Logins
```

SQL Server:

```
SELECT COUNT(LoginIncluded) AS TotalLogins FROM dbo.tbl_Logins
```

This actually illustrates two very useful SQL keywords in one go, COUNT and AS.

The COUNT(LoginIncluded) section will count how many rows there are in the table tbl_Logins, while the AS TotalLogins section will return the COUNT value to an alias column called TotalLogins. TotalLogins doesn't exist as a column in our database but we are declaring it as an alias by using the AS keyword.

The above SQL statement might be more useful to us if we used a selection criteria to count how many rows there are in our tbl_Logins table that are 'Included' – this would be signified by a True value in the LoginIncluded column as follows:

Access:

```
SELECT COUNT(LoginIncluded) AS TotalLogins FROM tbl_Logins WHERE LoginIncluded = 1
```

SQL Server:

```
SELECT COUNT(LoginIncluded) AS TotalLogins FROM dbo.tbl_Logins WHERE LoginIncluded
= 1
```

SUM

If you want to add up the values of several rows (such as a total value of a customer's orders) to create a grand total, you could use the SUM keyword in your SQL statement as in the following example:

Access:

```
SELECT SUM(TotalCost) AS GrandTotal FROM tbl_Customer_Order_Details WHERE OrderID
= 2
```

SQL Server:

```
SELECT SUM(TotalCost) AS GrandTotal FROM dbo.tbl_Customer_Order_Details WHERE
OrderID = 2
```

The SUM(TotalCost) section will add together all the rows contained in the table tbl_Logins that match the WHERE criteria and return a single row contained in a column we called GrandTotal using the alias keyword AS. In this example, the rows that match must have an OrderID of 2.

TOP

The TOP keyword is very useful if you want to specify that only a certain number of rows should be returned to your recordset. Obtaining exactly the right amount of data you require and nothing more is good for performance reasons.

For example, if we had a table that contained hundreds of thousands of rows of data and we know that over ten thousand of those rows will match my specific WHERE criteria but we only want to view a sample of those records rather than view all of them, then the TOP keyword can arrange that for us.

All you need to decide is how many records you want to retrieve. Let's say that we want 100. Here's what we'd do:

Access:

```
SELECT TOP 100 * FROM tbl_Products WHERE ProductCategory = 'DVD'
```

SQL Server:

```
SELECT TOP 100 * FROM dbo.tbl_Products WHERE ProductCategory = 'DVD'
```

The process this statement goes through is fairly straightforward. It filters the table `tbl_Products` with the criteria we specified (`ProductCategory` must equal `DVD`) and then, from that resultset it selects the first (`TOP`) 100 records.

You'll notice the `*` immediately after the `100` figure in the statement. This signifies which columns of the table we want returned. We could have specified 1 or more column names here to narrow down even further the data that is returned, but we wanted all of the columns, so used `*`.

That's all well and good but what if you didn't want the top 100 records? Say you wanted to view the last 100 **DVDs** added into your products database between two dates. To do that, you could either specify the dates in your SQL statement using the `BETWEEN` keyword, or you could use the `ORDER BY` keyword. We will look at both of these in turn.

BETWEEN

The `BETWEEN` statement has a lot of uses and just a couple of simple stipulations in how it is used. Let's look at an example of `BETWEEN` in use and then break it down to see what's going on.

Access:

```
SELECT TOP 100 * FROM tbl_Products WHERE ProductCategory = 'DVD' AND
ProductDateAdded BETWEEN #01 MAY 2002# AND #31 MAY 2002#
```

SQL Server:

```
SELECT TOP 100 * FROM dbo.tbl_Products WHERE ProductCategory = 'DVD' AND
ProductDateAdded BETWEEN '01 MAY 2002' AND '31 MAY 2002'
```

We want to `SELECT` all columns of data for the `TOP 100` records that are returned that match the criteria specified – in this case, specifying that `ProductCategory` is `DVD` and the `ProductDateAdded` column must contain a date that is `BETWEEN` the dates of the 1st and the 31st of May 2002, inclusive.

There are a couple of things that you need to keep an eye out for when using `BETWEEN`:

- It must specify inclusive values
- It must be compared to the same data type

180

In the example above the `ProductDateAdded` has a `Date` data type so the first and second values must be date values also.

For a slightly more in-depth look at dates and how they are used in SQL, see the *Going on a DATE* section later in this chapter.

ORDER BY

`ORDER BY` is a powerful keyword that you can use to order the way your records are returned to you. You might want to order them in the order in which they were entered into the database, using the primary key value, which is usually a sequential number for each row. You might want to specify multiple columns by which to order your data. The way in which that data would be returned to you is dependent on the order in which you specify the columns in the `ORDER BY` statement.

A couple of examples will help to illustrate this powerful keyword.

Access:

```
SELECT TOP 100 * FROM tbl_Products WHERE ProductCategory = 'DVD' AND
ProductDateAdded BETWEEN #01 MAY 2002# AND #31 MAY 2002#

ORDER BY ProductCategory, ProductPrice
```

SQL Server:

```
SELECT TOP 100 * FROM dbo.tbl_Products WHERE ProductCategory = 'DVD' AND
ProductDateAdded BETWEEN '01 MAY 2002' AND '31 MAY 2002'

ORDER BY ProductCategory, ProductPrice
```

Using the same example as the `BETWEEN` example, we have added the `ORDER BY` keyword in there so that all the results returned meeting the criteria specified will be ordered by their `ProductCategory` and within that, ordered by their `ProductPrice`.

This means that the DVDs that match the overall statements criteria will be returned ordered with the cheapest DVD in the first category listed first, up to the most expensive DVD in the first category, then the cheapest DVD from the second category up to the most expensive DVD from the second category, and so on until all the matching records have been sorted into order. Then the `TOP 100` DVDs **from that set** will be retrieved.

You can also specify the direction in which a sort order is used, either from the smallest value to the largest value, or from the largest value to the smallest value.

This is achieved by using the `ASC` or `DESC` keywords (short for ASCending and DESCending).

The default sort order is ascending, you can use it in your SQL statements but it is not necessary unless you are specifying more than one sort order.

To sort the previous example so that the most expensive DVDs are listed first and the cheapest are listed last within each category, and still having the categories in ascending order, you can add the `ASC` and `DESC` keywords to the statement, as in the following example:

Access:

```
SELECT TOP 100 * FROM tbl_Products WHERE ProductCategory = 'DVD' AND
ProductDateAdded BETWEEN #01 MAY 2002# AND #31 MAY 2002#

ORDER BY ProductCategory ASC, ProductPrice DESC
```

SQL Server:

```
SELECT TOP 100 * FROM dbo.tbl_Products WHERE ProductCategory = 'DVD' AND
ProductDateAdded BETWEEN '01 MAY 2002' AND '31 MAY 2002'

ORDER BY ProductCategory ASC, ProductPrice DESC
```

IN

The IN keyword is useful for those times when you might have several criteria that you want to use as a filter on your data.

You could write a long WHERE clause that uses many OR statements, or you could write a much shorter WHERE clause that uses the IN statement. The following examples illustrate this point.

First we'll look at solving this problem by using the OR keyword:

Access:

```
SELECT ProductName, ProductCategory, ProductDescription, ProductPrice FROM
tbl_Products WHERE ProductCategory = 'Cat 1' OR ProductCategory = 'Cat 2' OR
ProductCategory = 'Cat 3' OR ProductCategory = 'Cat 4' OR ProductCategory = 'Cat
5'
```

SQL Server:

```
SELECT ProductName, ProductCategory, ProductDescription, ProductPrice FROM
dbo.tbl_Products WHERE ProductCategory = 'Cat 1' OR ProductCategory = 'Cat 2' OR
ProductCategory = 'Cat 3' OR ProductCategory = 'Cat 4' OR ProductCategory = 'Cat
5'
```

Now we'll solve this problem using the IN keyword. You specify the values to compare against the column within parenthesis.

Access:

```
SELECT ProductName, ProductCategory, ProductDescription, ProductPrice FROM
tbl_Products WHERE ProductCategory IN ('Cat 1','Cat 2','Cat 3','Cat 4','Cat 5')
```

SQL Server:

```
SELECT ProductName, ProductCategory, ProductDescription, ProductPrice FROM
dbo.tbl_Products WHERE ProductCategory IN ('Cat 1','Cat 2','Cat 3','Cat 4','Cat
5')
```

If the data type that you are comparing a value against is numeric, it doesn't require single quotes around it. The above example uses them because the `ProductCategory` column is a text-based column.

GROUP BY

The GROUP BY keyword will group together identical values in a column in your resultset. In this regard, it is quite similar to the ORDER BY keyword. Where it differs, is in the data that is not allowed to be specified in the overall SQL statement. For example, in Access you cannot include a Memo field in a Group By clause. In SQL Server, the equivalent would be a Text field.

The data will be sorted first in the order of the columns specified in the GROUP BY statement, then in an ascending order, row by row, unless you also specify an ORDER BY as well.

For example, in the `tbl_Products` table you might have many products that share the same category and you might want to return a resultset that groups together the results by category and then by price, as in the ORDER BY example previously. The difference between the two is in the data that can be returned to your resultset. ORDER BY will allow you to return any and all columns of data if you so wish. GROUP BY will need to look at the data first to see if a grouping is allowed on the data required and, unfortunately, not all data types can be grouped. For example, a memo field in Access or a textfield in SQL Server cannot be returned in a GROUP BY statement unless they are being used as an expression of criteria to be met (that is, I want all the records where the description column is not empty).

A valid GROUP BY statement might be created as follows.

Access:

```
SELECT TOP 100 ProductName, ProductCategory, ProductPrice FROM tbl_Products GROUP
BY ProductName, ProductCategory, ProductPrice
```

SQL Server:

```
SELECT TOP 100 ProductName, ProductCategory, ProductPrice FROM dbo.tbl_Products
GROUP BY ProductName, ProductCategory, ProductPrice
```

You can see that we have had to specify the columns that we want to be returned by this statement. We cannot use the * wildcard to return all columns because we cannot include all the columns of this table in a GROUP BY clause.

The following example shows the use of the GROUP BY statement in conjunction with the use of a column that contains data that cannot be returned to the resultset but that can be used to filter that resultset.

Access:

```
SELECT TOP 100 ProductName, ProductCategory, ProductPrice FROM tbl_Products WHERE
(ProductDescription IS NOT NULL) GROUP BY ProductName, ProductCategory,
ProductPrice
```

SQL Server:

```
SELECT TOP 100 ProductName, ProductCategory, ProductPrice FROM dbo.tbl_Products
WHERE (ProductDescription IS NOT NULL) GROUP BY ProductName, ProductCategory,
ProductPrice
```

We still select the same columns as before but the results will be filtered to only show records that have a value that is NOT NULL, in the ProductDescription column.

The use of the NOT keyword comes into play here. It is used to reverse the logic of the statement it is contained within. In this case we reversed the normal IS NULL statement by specifying IS NOT NULL so that all records that have a ProductDescription will be returned.

DISTINCT

DISTINCT is used to prevent duplicate rows being returned to the resultset.

If you absolutely must have a resultset that contains at least one unique value on every row then DISTINCT can be the answer. However, it isn't always necessary to use DISTINCT because, generally, you will return the primary key value of each record in your query. If the need arises for a resultset that doesn't include the primary key value, then DISTINCT will ensure that no duplicate records are returned.

The following is an example of using the DISTINCT keyword.

Access:

```
SELECT DISTINCT ProductCategory FROM tbl_Products
```

SQL Server:

```
SELECT DISTINCT ProductCategory FROM dbo.tbl_Products
```

This will select all the individual categories from the ProductCategory column in the tbl_Products table. You may have thousands of rows of products in that table; each of them stored in, let's say, 20 categories. This example will return those 20 distinct rows to your resultset.

Going On a DATE

Dates are notoriously awkward – this, of course, refers to a date as a type of data, and not that person you've been having occasional late night drinks with! If you live anywhere outside of the countries that follow the US date format, you can find yourself in all sorts of trouble when storing dates in your database.

In the examples shown for the keyword BETWEEN earlier in this chapter, we have specified the date in a manner that leaves no ambiguity over how the date should be read. However, 01/05/2002 could mean the first of May or the fifth of January, depending on where you are in the world.

Access and SQL Server always try to store the date in the US format, Month, Date, and Year. If they come across a date that cannot be stored this way, such as 17/05/2002, then it is converted into the Month, Date, and Year format, whilst keeping the date accurate. To save yourself a lot of trouble, just use non-ambiguous dates like 01 May 2002.

When using dates in your SQL statements, such as performing a search for matching items that have a date that falls between two dates that you specify, you will need to remember the following strict rules about how each database application needs dates to be presented to it:

- Access needs the date value to be wrapped in hash symbols, that is `#01 May 2002#`

- SQL Server needs the date value to be wrapped in single quotes, that is `'01 May 2002'`

Making the Connection

To be able to use data on your web pages you need to tell your web application where to look for that data (note that *Chapter 7* includes a recap on using these connection types in the context of a real web application).

There are two ways of doing this. You can either tell Dreamweaver MX that a System DSN (Data Source Name) has been set up on your computer and you wish to use that, or you can define a custom connection string that encapsulates all the information required to connect to the data source, including where the database is and security information needed to access the data. We will concentrate on using a System DSN.

There are no real advantages to be had in using one method over the other. It might simply come down to your hosts not allowing you to create a system DSN on their servers. If this were the case you would then need to use a custom connection string, known as a DSNLess connection.

This can all be done from Dreamweaver MX but it's just as easy to go out to your operating system and set it up from there – the dialogs that are used are exactly the same but getting to them requires less clicks on your part, and far less explanation on mine.

Setting Up a DSN To an Access database

- Open the *Data Sources (ODBC)* administrator on your computer

- Click the *System DSN* tab then click *Add*

- Select Microsoft Access Driver (*.mdb) from the list and click Finish

- Now you get to enter the name of this DSN. I'm going to call mine *DSNwebprodmxAccess*

- Leave the description field empty unless you really want to enter something in there. It's not necessary for this to work

- Next, click *Select* to select the location of your database. Use the dialog to find the database and select it. Click *OK* and the full path to your database is now shown above the *Select* button. Mine is `C:\databases\webprodmx\webprodmx.mdb`

- Click *OK* to close that dialog and the click *OK* to close the main dialog

Your DSN is set up and ready to use.

Setting Up a DSN to a SQL Server database

- Open the *Data Sources (ODBC)* administrator on your computer

- Click the *System DSN* tab then click *Add*

- Scroll the list to the bottom, select *SQL Server* and click *Finish*

- For the name, I'm going to call mine *DSNwebprodmxSQL*

- Either type the name of your SQL Server into the *Server* drop-down list or click it to select your server, then click *Next*

- If you've followed this chapter from the start then the next few screens are all filled in for you. The database is already set to *webprodmx* because that is what we set it to when we created our login in SQL Server. The other settings you can leave in place. Click *Next*, then click *Finish*

- You now have the chance to test these settings to make sure no errors have crept in. Click *Test Data Source…* and, all being well, you should see a screen that contains the words *Tests Completed Successfully*

- Click *OK* then *OK* again, to get back to the original DSN screen, where you will see your newly created DSN in the list

- Click *OK* to close this screen

Connecting To Dreamweaver MX

The final stage for connecting your web site to the database is to define a connection in Dreamweaver MX that will use the DSN on your computer that you just set up. This connection will be stored in a **Connections** folder in your site definition and will be referenced on every page that you create that needs to talk to the database. The beauty of doing it this way is that if your connection details change for some reason, you will only need to change one connection file to bring your entire site up to date, rather than modifying every single page by hand.

To define your connection, open the *Databases* panel in the *Application* panel group. Click the plus (+) button and select *Data Source Name (DSN)* from the pop-up menu.

In the dialog that pops up you are going to name this connection and select which DSN on your computer that it should use. You will also need to provide the **Username** and **Password** that the DSN needs to authenticate itself with in the database, if required. In my Access examples, I didn't set a username or a password so these can be left blank. In my SQL Server example, I had to specify the username but I left the password blank.

For Access databases, fill out the dialog as shown opposite, and click *OK*.

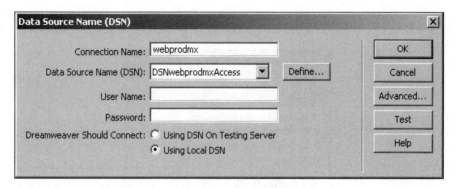

For SQL Server databases, fill out the dialog as shown here:

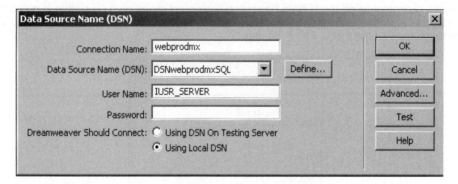

Now click *OK*. Once your connection file has been created within your site, you can start to build recordsets.

> *Note: If you start to build a recordset before a connection file has been created for your site, then the connections drop-down list in the recordset dialog will be empty but you can create the connection by clicking the Define... button next to the connections drop-down list and then following the steps outlined above.*

The Simple Recordset Builder

The Simple Recordset Builder allows you to build an SQL statement to request data from your database. You won't always need to specify a WHERE clause in your SQL statement but if you do need to then the Simple Recordset Builder allows you to specify a single WHERE clause. If that is not enough for your purposes then you will need to use the **Advanced Recordset Builder**. We'll get to the Advanced Recordset Builder in the next section.

There are only a few preparatory steps you need to follow to be able to use dynamic data on a web page. The first thing to do in Dreamweaver MX is to set up a site definition in which you are going to build your web application. After you have created your site definition, you will create a new page. You will specify that this page is a dynamic page and also, which server-side scripting language you are going to use. See *Chapter 8: Creating a Basic Dynamic Web Site* for further information on all of the steps briefly mentioned here.

Once you have created a page that you can add data to, you then need to create a recordset. Rather usefully, the *Bindings* panel found in the *Application* panel group tells you this, as seen here:

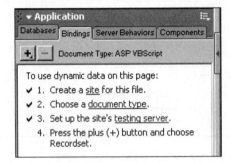

To build a recordset using the Simple Recordset Builder, click the plus (+) button in either the *Bindings* panel or the *Server Behaviors* panel and select *Recordset (Query)* from the pop-up menu. It is the first option on the menu, as seen below:

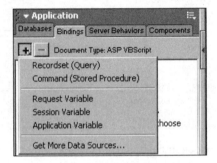

This will present you with the Simple Recordset Builder interface where you can set about defining what data you want to retrieve from the database. To retrieve the whole of the tbl_Products table you would complete the dialog in the same way as shown here:

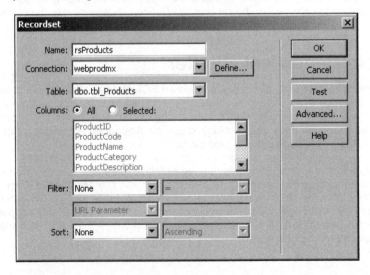

The Simple Recordset Builder also allows you to specify a single WHERE clause and a single ORDER BY clause.

To illustrate just how easy this is, let's specify that we want to apply a filter to the ProductCategory column and specify that the category must equal DVD. We'll also set an ORDER BY clause to sort these records by their price starting with the cheapest.

To do this, select ProductCategory from the *Filter* drop-down list and select the equality operator (=) from the drop-down list to the right of it. Then select *Entered Value* from the list below the *Filter* drop-down list and in the textbox to the right of that, type *DVD*. In the bottom left drop down list labeled *Sort*, select *ProductPrice* and in the bottom right drop-down list, select *Ascending*. You should now have something that looks like this:

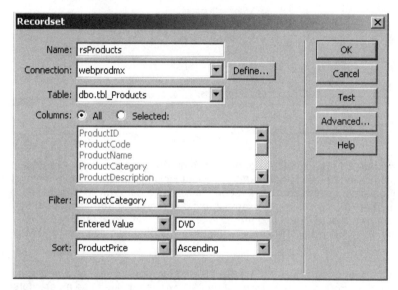

When you click *OK*, having selected all the relevant settings, the recordset is created for you and is added to the *Bindings* panel. If you then click the plus icon next to the recordset name, you can see all the columns of the tbl_Products table and, if we so desired, we could start adding these pieces of data to our web page, as seen overleaf:

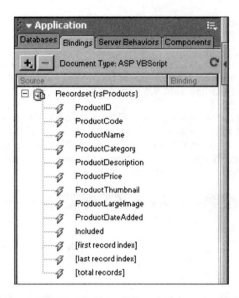

Not only did this retrieve all of the columns from the `tbl_Products` table, it also added three extra items. They are *[first record index]*, *[last record index]*, and *[total records]*.

These three elements are useful for signposting data. For example, if you create a search results page that will display 10 results per page, you could include these three elements on the page somewhere to indicate which section of records the user is currently looking at which is *Currently viewing 1 to 10 of 73 records*. In this example, the *1* is produced from [first record index], the *10* is produced from [last record index] and the *73* is produced from [total records]. If you used a link to get the next page of records *(next 10)*, then the first two signposts would change. that is, *Currently viewing 11 to 20 of 73 records*.

To make this simple recordset a lot more flexible and far more useful for a web page, instead of specifying that the `ProductCategory` must be DVD, we can make it use a parameter that our web page must pass to this recordset to use as the filter.

Open up the *Recordset* dialog for this recordset again by double-clicking the recordset name in the *Bindings* panel. Where we previously selected *Entered Value* from the drop-down list, this time, select *URL Parameter*. Where we previously entered DVD in the textbox to the right of that drop-down list, we are now going to type *cat*. This will be the name of the URL parameter that this recordset will use to filter database with:

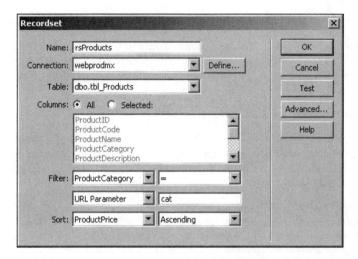

If this recordset were on an actual web page that displayed data and you browsed to that page specifying a URL parameter of *cat=DVD*, the recordset would be filtered to show only products in the DVD category. If the URL parameter were *cat=CD* then only products from the CD category would be shown.

Easy, flexible, and powerful – what more could you want?

The Advanced Recordset Builder

The Advanced Recordset Builder is the place to build those recordsets that require more detail than can be offered by the Simple Recordset Builder, in terms of their SQL statement. The Simple Recordset Builder is only capable of creating recordsets that use either none or one criterion.

Once you know how to work it, creating simple or advanced recordsets in this dialog is only limited by your knowledge of SQL. The basic layout of the SQL statement is put into place as you click through the building process. After that you will need to dive into the code and enter the final details. Don't worry; it's easier than it might sound.

We'll build the same recordset as we did with the Simple Recordset Builder but this time we'll add an extra parameter into the mix to illustrate the power that the Advanced Recordset Builder affords you.

We start the same way as before, click the plus (+) button in either the *Bindings* panel or the *Server Behaviors* panel and select *Recordset (Query)* from the pop-up menu. On the right-hand side of the Simple Recordset Builder dialog there are five buttons – press the *Advanced...* button to switch to the Advanced Recordset Builder.

> Note: When you build a recordset and click OK, the dialog you used to build that recordset is the one you'll see the next time you go to build a recordset.

Now you will see the empty Advanced Recordset Builder in which you are going to build your SQL statement.

The first thing we need to do is name the recordset. I'm going to call mine *rsProducts* again.

Now we need to select the database connection so that we can view the database objects in the *Database Items* window at the bottom of this dialog. If you were to click the plus (+) icons next to the three items in there, *Tables*, *Views,* and *Stored Procedures* before you have selected your connection, they will contain nothing. Once you have selected your connection, they will be populated with your database objects and you can then go ahead and build your SQL statement.

Select your connection from the *Connections* drop-down list.

In the *Database Items* window of this dialog, click the plus (+) icon next to *Tables* and a listing of all the tables in your database will be displayed (maybe after a short delay as the connection is made to the database). Click the plus (+) icon next to *tbl_Products* and the list will be updated to show all the columns of the `tbl_Products` table.

Ordinarily, you would click on the table name to highlight it and then click the *SELECT* button to the right of the *Database Items* window to start creating your SQL Statement. However, we have a little shortcut here: we want to select all the columns for all the records in this table that have a value in the *ProductCategory* column that matches our criteria, so the quick way to generate the SQL statement for this is to click the *ProductCategory* column and click the *WHERE* button to the right of the *Database Items* window.

The *SQL* window will now show the beginnings of your SQL statement, as seen here:

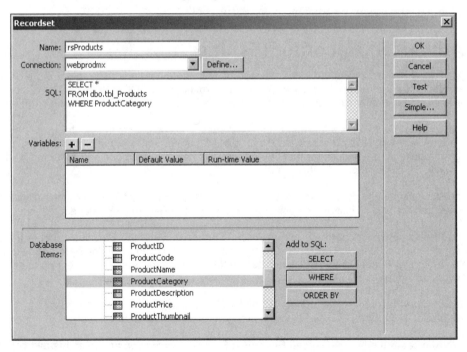

We now have an incomplete `WHERE` statement that if left as it stands would make this recordset fail. We need to define what that `ProductCategory` should equal.

Click to place the cursor after *ProductCategory* in the *SQL* window and type:

> = 'varCategory'

You have total control over the naming of your variables I chose to give mine meaningful names and to prefix them with var so as to let me know that it is a variable and to give me a good idea about what the contents of that variable is just by looking at the name.

We know this variable is going to contain a text-based value so it must be wrapped in single quotes to identify it as such.

Now we need to define what value varCategory should pass to this SQL statement. We do this using the Variables window below the *SQL* window. Click the plus (+) icon above the *Variables* window. A new variable line is added to the *Variables* window that we are going to fill in with the following details:

> Click in the *Name* column of this new variable line and type: *varCategory*
>
> Click in the *Default Value* column (or press *Tab*) and type: *xyz*
>
> Click in the *Run-Time Value* column (or press *Tab* again) and type: *Request("cat")*

Now to explain what is going on here...

In our SQL Statement in the *SQL* window, we have said that the column ProductCategory should equal the value contained in the variable called varCategory.

The *Default Value* we supplied serves two purposes. First, it allows us to test our completed SQL statement to make sure that we are getting the results that we expect back, and second, when the page is used in a live environment, it acts as the actual variable value if the *URL* parameter called *cat* doesn't exist.

The *Run-Time Value* column is where we specify what should be used as the actual value to filter this recordset. As previously mentioned, if this parameter doesn't exist then the default value will be used to filter the recordset. I use a default value of *xyz* to ensure that the recordset will be empty if the *cat* parameter does not exist. You may want to use a default value of an existing ProductCategory to ensure that this recordset always contains data.

In the Simple Recordset example, we added a sort order to our records that would return the cheapest first. To accomplish this, select *ProductPrice* in the *Database Items* window and click the *ORDER BY* button to the right. As previously discussed, *ORDER BY* defaults to *ASCENDING* so we don't need to add that unless we are adding more than one *ORDER BY* clause.

Our finished Advanced Recordset Dialog should look like this:

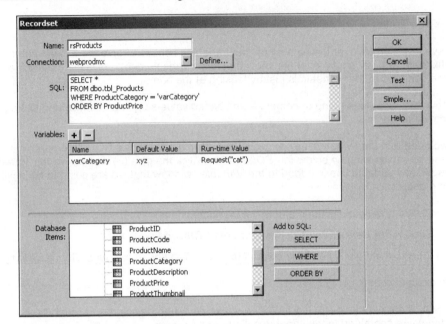

Click *OK* to close the dialog and create the recordset.

Hopefully you can see what the advantages are of using the Advanced Recordset Builder over using the Simple Recordset Builder. You can use multiple parameters in your statements. You can also just write your SQL statement directly in the *SQL* window by hand if you so desire.

Using Commands

At some point in your web site development you will no doubt want to add, edit, or delete data from your database. In Dreamweaver MX there are two ways you can do any of these actions. The first, and perhaps most common way would be to use the standard *Insert, Update,* and *Delete* Server Behaviors.

The other way would be to use a **command**.

Commands can be created to perform all of the same database operations as their Server Behavior counterparts with the addition of being able to utilize **Stored Procedures** (more on those in the next section of this chapter).

So, why might you choose to use commands over server behaviors?

If you are comfortable writing syntactically correct SQL statements by hand or even if you just have an understanding of the correct formation of SQL, then you will find the Command interface a breeze. It is very much like the Recordset Builder interface.

If you need to have more than one of the same database interactions on the same page, then you will need to use one command per database interaction. For instance, you might want to INSERT a new record into your database that needs to be split over two tables: you could set up two commands on a page to do this for you. The server behavior versions of these database interactions can only be included on your web page once.

Perhaps the major benefit of commands over server behaviors is the amount of code produced. Server behaviors tend to produce bulky code because they need to cater for a lot of different scenarios, whereas their command counterparts produce a very small amount of code whilst maintaining adaptability.

The following examples will introduce you to the usage of each of the commands available to you with the exception of the Stored Procedure Command, which is covered later.

The creation process of each of these commands begins in exactly the same way.

> *Your command will only be listed in, and therefore editable from, the Server Behaviors panel after creation, no matter which panel you choose to start the creation process with.*

Click the plus (+) button in either the *Bindings* panel or the *Server Behaviors* panel and select *Command* from the pop-up menu. You will see the *Command* dialog, which looks like this:

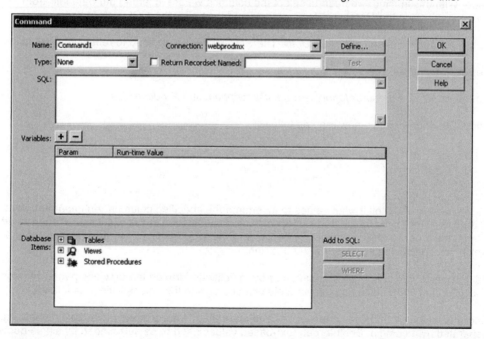

The first thing to do in creating any command is to name it, which you can do in the top-left box of the dialog. All commands are given a default name but it's not too descriptive so we'll be changing that to something that makes more sense to me.

Inserting a Record

This Insert command will add a new product record to my database so I'm going to call it *cmdInsertProduct*.

My connection is already selected for me because I have already set up a connection for this site. If yours is not, then you will need to set up a connection before continuing, which you can do by clicking the *Define...* button in this dialog or you can follow the steps outlined earlier in this chapter in the section headed *Making the Connection*.

From the *Type* drop-down list we want to select *Insert* because this is an INSERT command (easy, isn't it?). Immediately after you select *Insert* from the list, the basic INSERT statement is added to the *SQL* window. All we are going to do is populate this statement with the relevant information. We can ignore the checkbox next to *Return Recordset Named* as this is only used for Stored Procedures.

The buttons in the lower-right of the dialog, under the heading of *Add to SQL:*, change to reflect the type of statement we are building. For the INSERT statement only one of the two buttons is active and it is called *COLUMN*.

In this case, we want to insert only certain pieces of information into my tbl_Products table and in all likelihood, those pieces of information would have been submitted from a form on the previous page. With this in mind, we need to select the columns we are inserting our data into from tbl_Products in the *Database Items* window and then click the *COLUMN* button.

Select *ProductCode* and click *COLUMN*. The *SQL* window is updated to reflect your selection.

Select *ProductName* and click *COLUMN*.

Do the same for *ProductCategory*, *ProductDescription,* and *ProductPrice*.

The *SQL* window should now read as follows:

```
INSERT INTO dbo.tbl_Products (ProductCode, ProductName, ProductCategory,
ProductDescription, ProductPrice)
VALUES ( )
```

All we need to do is tell it what values to insert into the specified columns. An important point to note is that you cannot mix up the items between lists; they must be in the exact same order. In other words, the order in which you specify the items in the INSERT INTO line must be the same order in which you specify the items in the VALUES line.

To get values into this INSERT command from a fictitious form on the previous page, we need to Request that information and use variable placeholders in the values listing, as follows.

Click inside the parentheses after *Values* and enter the following string of variable names, each separated by a comma. Don't forget, text-based values need to be surrounded by single quotes.

'varProductCode','varProductName','varProductCategory','varProductDescription',varProductPrice

Now we need to define where these variables are going to get their information. This example still assumes that we are getting our information from a form on the previous page and that the form elements were named as shown in the *Request* parts of the following details.

- Click the plus (+) button above the *Variables* window, then click in the *Name* column and type *varProductCode*. Tab to the *Run-Time Value* column and type *Request("ProductCode")*.

- Add another variable line for `varProductName` with the *Run-Time Value* of *Request("ProductName")*.

- Do the same for `varProductCategory` with a *Run-Time Value* of *Request("ProductCategory")*.

- Once again for `varProductDescription` with a *Run-Time Value* of *Request("ProductDescription")*.

- Finally, once more for `varProductPrice` with a *Run-Time Value* of *Request("ProductPrice")*.

- Your *Command* dialog should now look like this:

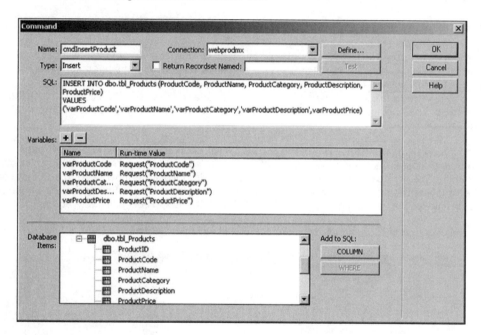

With all that done, click *OK* and your command is applied to the page.

Now, when the form on the previous page submits its information to this page, it will be inserted into the database.

Updating a Record

This UPDATE command will allow us to add a filename to the `ProductThumbnail` column of a record (for instance, the one we just inserted with the INSERT command that didn't include one).

With the *Command* dialog open, name this command `cmdUpdateProduct` and select *Update* from the *Type* drop-down list. Your connection should already be selected in the *Connection* drop-down list. The two buttons in the *Add to SQL* area have got the labels *SET* and *WHERE* because that's the syntax of the *UPDATE* statement, as you'll see in a minute.

In the *Database Items* window, expand the *Tables* listing and then expand the `tbl_Products` table. Click to highlight the *ProductThumbnail* column and click *SET*. Your *SQL* window is updated to show the following SQL code. (This example is using SQL Server, the Access version of this would be the same but without the `dbo.` prefix on the table name.)

```
UPDATE dbo.tbl_Products
SET ProductThumbnail
WHERE
```

Now we need to tell it what value `ProductThumbnail` should be set to and we need to identify which record this statement should be applied to. We do this by typing *= 'varProductThumbnail'* after *ProductThumbnail*. The *SET* line of the *SQL* window will now read as follows:

```
SET ProductThumbnail  = 'varProductThumbnail'
```

`varProductThumbnail`, as you've probably guessed by now is a variable that will get its *Run-Time Value* from a field called `ProductThumbnail`, which we will assume has been submitted from the previous page. Click the plus (+) button above the *Variables* window and add `varProductThumbnail` as the variable name and `Request("ProductThumbnail")` as the *Run-Time Value*. The only thing left to do is to make sure that we are going to update the right record in our database.

We do this by using the ID number of the record, which will also have been passed through to this page from the previous page. Click *ProductID* in the *Database Items* window and then click *WHERE*. Click in the *SQL* window after *ProductID* and add *= varProductID*. We now need to add that variable to the variables list, so click the plus (+) button above the *Variables* window again and on the new variable line set the variable name to *varProductID* and the *Run-Time Value* to *Request("ID")*.

Your finished update *Command* dialog should look like this:

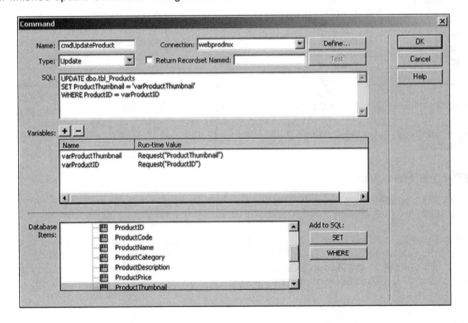

Updating Multiple Records (Simple Example)

Let's say we have a page that displays all of our web site users and against each one is a checkbox. What we might want to be able to do is to deactivate several accounts and it makes a lot of sense to be able to update more than one user at a time. For details of how to set up this page, please refer to the *Administration Options* section in *Chapter 8*. This example explains how to do this.

With the *Command* dialog open, name this command `cmdUpdateMultiUsers` and select *Update* from the *Type* drop-down list (your connection should already be selected in the *Connection* drop-down list). Expand the *Tables* listing in the *Database Items* window, highlight *LoginIncluded* and click *SET*.

Your *SQL* window should now look like this:

```
UPDATE dbo.tbl_Logins
SET LoginIncluded
WHERE
```

Now type *= 0* after *LoginIncluded*. This column of the database is a binary column so a *1* (SQL Server) or *–1* (Access) in this column would mean that the record is included – a zero means it is excluded.

Now we need to specify which records to update. We will be using the `IN` keyword in this case which was covered in detail earlier in this chapter (see *Useful SQL Keywords* for further information). In the *Database Items* window, click *LoginID* and then click *WHERE*. *LoginID* is added to the *SQL* window. Click in the *SQL* window to place the cursor after *LoginID* and type the following:

```
IN (varLoginID)
```

Your SQL should now look like this:

```
UPDATE dbo.tbl_Logins
SET LoginIncluded = 0
WHERE LoginID IN (varLoginID)
```

All you need to do now is add the *varLoginID* to the variables window.

Click the plus (+) button above the *Variables* window and enter the variable name in the *Name* column – *varLoginID*. In the *Run-Time Value* column, type *Request("LoginID")*.

199

Your finished multiple update *Command* dialog should look like this:

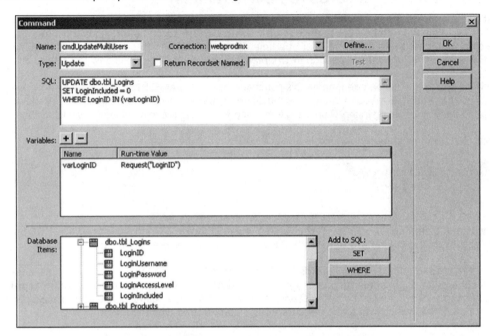

Now, when multiple checkboxes are ticked on the page that submits to this page, a list of *LoginIDs* will be delivered in a comma-delimited string and all the records that match one of those *LoginIDs* will have their *LoginIncluded* column updated to contain a *0*. These people can no longer login – as long as the correct logic is in place to assure that the *LoginIncluded* column is used, of course! We will deal with how to do this in **Chapter 8** in the **Administration** section.

Deleting a Record

Deleting records is sometimes a necessary step for keeping your database up to date. The following example shows you how passing the ID number of a product record to a DELETE command will delete that product.

With the *Command* dialog open, give the command a name of *cmdDeleteRecord* and select *Delete* from the *Type* drop down list. Your connection should already be selected in the *Connection* drop down list. The shortcut detailed in other commands doesn't work for the DELETE command, we have to specifically click the table name in the *Database Objects* window and click the *DELETE* button to add the table name to the SQL.

Then, expand the *tbl_Products* table in the *Database Objects* window and click the *ProductID* column. Click *WHERE* to add this column to the *SQL* window.

Your *SQL* window should look like this:

```
DELETE FROM dbo.tbl_Products
WHERE ProductID
```

You now need to place the cursor after *ProductID* and type *= varProductID*.

Add the variable to the *Variables* window by clicking the plus (+) button above it. In the *Name* column, type *varProductID* and set the *Run-Time Value* to *Request("ProductID")*.

Your final *Command* dialog should look like what we see here:

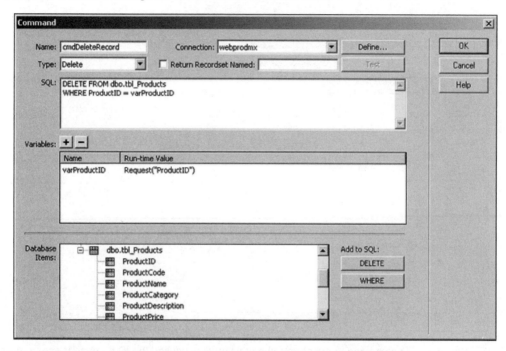

Click *OK* to apply this command to the page. When this page is passed the ID number of a record in the *ProductID* parameter, that record will be deleted.

Deleting Multiple Records (Simple Example)

Following on from the previous example, a common scenario would be the need to delete multiple products from your database. You could do them one at a time if you want, but if you need to delete lots of products then I wouldn't recommend it. What I would recommend, however, is using a command to delete multiple products, as shown in the following example.

With the *Command* dialog open, give the command a name of *cmdDeleteMultiProducts* and select *Delete* from the *Type* drop-down list. Your connection should already be selected in the *Connection* drop-down list. In the *Database Items* window, select the table that you are deleting the products from, in this case it is *tbl_Products*, and click the *DELETE* button. Then click the *ProductID* column and click the *WHERE* button.

Your SQL window should now look like this:

```
DELETE FROM dbo.tbl_Products
WHERE ProductID
```

Now place the cursor after *ProductID* and type: *IN (varProductID).*

Click the plus (+) button above the *Variables* window to add a new variable line. Click in the *Name* column and type *varProductID*. Tab to the *Run-Time Value* column and type *Request("ProductID").*

Your final *Command* dialog should look like this:

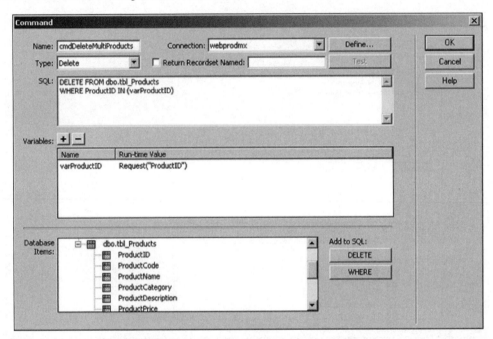

Click *OK* to apply this command to the page. When this page is passed the ID number of one or more records in the *ProductID* parameter, those records will be deleted. You can pass a comma-delimited string of numbers into this command and it will delete each record whose ID is contained in that string.

Stored Procedures

Stored procedures are pre-compiled SQL statements that are stored in the database – Access doesn't support them, SQL Server does. They have the benefit of being much faster to execute than a standard piece of SQL code because they are compiled the first time they are executed, and because they are modular in design they can be reused from various web pages without you needing to recreate the SQL statements contained within the stored procedure each time.

Where they show their real power is in their ability to utilize parameters. You can define parameters within your SQL statement and then pass values into the stored procedure for use in the SQL statement.

An example of putting a stored procedure to good use would be if you needed to perform a repetitive task over and over again, such as inserting multiple rows of data into a database table. Ordinarily, you might create a web page to manually feed each record into the database one at a time. With a stored procedure and the right piece of coding, you could pass a file of data to a web page, have that page loop through each line of the file and pass each line in turn to the stored procedure through the use of parameters, which would insert each row of data into your database tables according to your SQL statements.

To take that example a stage further, let's suppose we have two related tables in our database, the first called `tblUsers` and the second called `tblUserDetails`. Now, supposing that all the code on our web page was in place to take the contents of a text file and pass those contents, line by line, to a command that had been programmed to pass a single line of information to a stored procedure in my database. That command would have been set up to use a variable for each piece of information on that line.

We would then need to have a stored procedure in our database that could accept the data being passed in the variables from this command and insert it into our two tables.

On top of all that, because the two tables are related, we need to grab the primary key value after a new record has been inserted into `tblUsers` to use in `tblUserDetails` as that record's foreign key.

A stored procedure to do exactly that could be coded like this:

```
CREATE PROCEDURE dbo.spAddUser(
@UName nvarchar(100),
@UEmail nvarchar(250),
@UUsername nvarchar(100) = NULL,
@UPassword nvarchar(100) = NULL,
@DAddress1 nvarchar(100) = NULL,
@DAddress2 nvarchar(100) = NULL,
@DAddress3 nvarchar(100) = NULL,
@DTown nvarchar(100) = NULL,
@DCounty nvarchar(50) = NULL,
@DCountry nvarchar(50) = NULL,
@DPostcode nvarchar(20) = NULL,
@DPhone nvarchar(20) = NULL,
@DFax nvarchar(20) = NULL,
@DWebAddress nvarchar(250) = NULL,
@DDescription nvarchar(1000) = NULL)
AS
Declare @NewID Int
INSERT INTO dbo.tblUsers(UName, UEmail, UUsername, UPassword) VALUES(@UName,
@UEmail, @UUsername, @UPassword)
SELECT @NewID = @@IDENTITY
INSERT INTO dbo.tblUserDetails(UserID, Address1, Address2, Address3, Town, County,
Country, Postcode, Phone, Fax, WebAddress, DDescription) VALUES(@NewID,
@DAddress1, @DAddress2, @DAddress3, @DTown, @DCounty, @DCountry, @DPostcode,
@DPhone, @DFax, @DWebAddress, @DDescription)
GO
```

Starting from the top, we tell SQL Server that we want to create a stored procedure called `spAddUser`. We then set about defining all of the parameters that we are going to use in this stored procedure, assigning them the correct data type for the data that they are going to hold and specifying `NULL` against those values that are allowed to store `null` values. These parameters will get their values passed to them from the command that is calling this stored procedure. We then say what we would like to create this stored procedure `AS`, which is where the SQL statements come into play. We declare a local variable called `NewID`, which is going to store the primary key value from the first table. That value is an integer and so the variable is declared as an integer.

The next line takes the first four values passed to the stored procedure and inserts them into the `tblUsers` table. Then the local variable called `NewID` is assigned the value of the last created identity value (`@@IDENTITY` is an internal SQL Server variable that stores the last identity value created), which is the primary key value from the first table. The rest of the details passed from the command to this stored procedure are then inserted, along with the `NewID` value, into the second, related table.

The final statement `GO` tells SQL Server to execute this batch of SQL statements.

In order for your web application to be able to use this stored procedure, you're going to have to grant the `Exec` permission to your IUSR account, which you can do from the *Stored Procedure Properties* window. You can either right-click the *Stored Procedure Name* then select *Properties* from the context menu, or you can simply double-click the *Stored Procedure* name. Then you click the *Permissions* button in the top-right corner of the *Properties* dialog and click to place a tick in the *Exec* column for the *IUSR* user. Click *OK* to get out of the dialogs.

The Stored Procedure Command

This brings us neatly to the command that we haven't yet covered – the Stored Procedure Command. It is a little different to the other commands but it's still fairly easy to understand.

Open a *Command* dialog by selecting *Command* from the *Bindings* or the *Server Behaviors* panel. In the *Name* box, type *cmdSPInsert* and select *Stored Procedure* from the *Type* drop-down list.

In the *Database Items* window, expand the *Stored Procedures* node to view all stored procedures in your database that you have permission to use. If your list is empty, you will need to close the *Command* dialog, assign the *Exec* permission to your stored procedure and then start creating your command again.

Click to select the stored procedure called *dbo.spAddUser* then click the *PROCEDURE* button to the right. All sorts of things happen now. Your stored procedure is added to the *SQL* window and all of its parameters are added to the *Variables* window, which has suddenly grown a few extra columns. Most of the details are filled in for you with 'best guess' items but you should feel free to change anything that you need to. In our case, we do not want to return any values so all these variables should have their *Direction* column value set to *IN* because they are to be fed *IN* to the stored procedure.

You need to specify the length of each item in the *Length* column. These should be the same as the lengths declared in your stored procedure after the data type declaration of each parameter.

The need to specify a default value depends entirely upon your web application – if you are positive that all values that need to be passed to the stored procedure will actually be passed then you can leave the *Default Value* column blank. If not, then a value in this column might be a good idea. If, as in our example, your Stored procedure can accept `NULL` values in some of its columns, then default values will not be necessary for those columns. In our example, only the name and the e-mail address are definitely required by our stored procedure and a default value for those would probably be a bad idea. So to get around that you would make sure that they contained a value by using form validation on the page that submits the data.

The final column to fix is the *Run-Time Value* column. This is the important one and works in exactly the same way as the *Run-Time Value* columns for all the previous examples of command usage – you set each parameter's run-time value to the place it should look for its data. As previously mentioned, this column has already been filled with best guess data, but in all likelihood it will be wrong because it uses the parameter names you have used as its guess, for the form element names that you will probably need to use in this column. You should check them all carefully before continuing.

With all that completed, your *Command* window should look like the following:

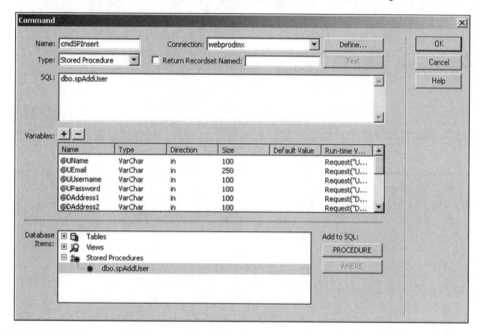

Click *OK* in the *Command* dialog to apply it to your page.

One final thing worth a mention is in regard to the following line that is part of the code automatically generated for you by commands.

```
cmdSPInsert.Prepared = true
```

The `Prepared` property of a command, when set to `true`, means that it will be compiled when first run. This is of benefit to you in terms of the speed at which your application will perform if you plan to use the same command object several times – If you plan to use it only once, it may slow your application slightly because of the delay caused by compilation.

Most databases support prepared commands but if yours does not, it may return an error if you try to send a prepared command to it. SQL Server does support them so you won't encounter this problem using this database.

Summary

This chapter has given you an insight into the basics of the SQL language and has shown you a few pointers on the database design pitfalls to avoid.

Hopefully I may have prompted a few ideas of the possibilities available to you when working with commands and stored procedures by detailing some simple examples and explaining their usage.

When it comes to using the power afforded us by SQL, we have only really touched the surface here and I heartily recommend that you seek out a good book solely dedicated to the subject of SQL to take your knowledge on to the next level.

With careful planning and good database design, the knowledge you have gained from this chapter can take you a long way in your web application development projects.

7

- Defining a web site
- Server behaviors
- Application objects

Author: Omar Elbaga

The Application Panel

Now that you are familiar with ASP / VBScript coding and database structures, you can delve into the fabulous server behavior features Dreamweaver MX has to offer. We will be taking a stroll through the *Application* panel, whilst giving you a good understanding as to what each behavior has the capability of doing.

It is wrong to think that each server behavior does only one single thing. On the contrary, other than a few specific server behaviors (such as *Log In User*), each server behavior can have multiple uses for many different kinds of web applications. The behaviors are generic blocks of code that can be called upon for use in various aspects of your web applications.

It is important to know when and how to use the Application panel. We will look at full-blown applications in later chapters, but here we will concentrate on these areas:

- Databases / Connections – how Dreamweaver deals with connecting to databases, via Data Source Names or Custom Connection Strings

- Bindings – Dreamweaver makes binding data to pages via recordsets, and Application, Request, and Session variables very easy – learn how in this section

- Server Behaviors – these are pre-written pieces of server-side code that you can add straight to your applications, speeding up web site development no end

Before Moving On – Creating a Virtual Directory

Please create a physical directory named `webprodmx_files` on your PC where you will save all the file examples for this chapter. To test examples locally we should create a virtual directory called `webprodmx` pointing to the physical directory you just created. For example, in PWS:

- Go to *Start* > *Settings* > *Control Panel* > *Administrative Tools* > *Personal Web Manager*

- Go to *Advanced* > *Add*, and you should see the following dialog box:

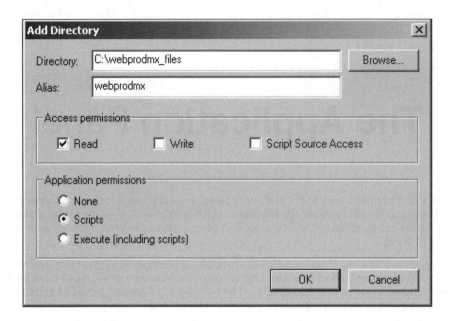

- Click *Browse...* and select the physical directory named `webprodmx_files` that you created above

- Type `webprodmx` for the *Alias*

- Check *Read* under *Access Permissions* and *Scripts* under *Application Permissions*, and click *OK*

- Close the Personal Web Manager

You should now be able to access the physical directory by pointing your web browser to *http://localhost/webprodmx*. Make sure your server is running. When this virtual directory is accessed through the browser it will point to the root physical folder `webprodmx_files` that you created on your PC (for more on setting up web servers, see *Chapter 5*).

Defining Your Site

While your server is running, open Dreamweaver MX. If you have not created a site, your *Application* Panel should display numbered bullets listing the process to set up a site. The first one says, "*Create a site for this file.*" Click the hyperlink named *site*. If Dreamweaver MX loads a different site that you have already created, go to *Site > New Site*. You should be presented with a *Site Definition* dialog box. This dialog box has seven screens, but we will only be covering the first three here – this will be sufficient for setting up a basic site – we will now go through each of these in turn:

Local Info

The Local info screen looks like this:

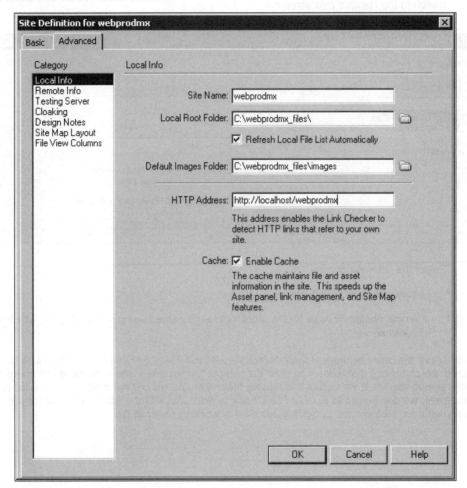

Fill it in as follows:

- *Site Name*: Name your site `webprodmx`.

- *Local Root Folder*: Browse for the local root folder named `webprodmx_files`, which you created above.

- *Default Images Folder*: Browse for the folder that will hold your images – it is best to call it images, and put it inside the root of your web site, `webprodmx_files` – this is good practice for effective site layout – we will know where all our images are.

- *HTTP Address*: Type *http://localhost/webprodmx*.

Also, make sure the site cache is enabled (that is, the checkbox is checked)

Remote Info

- Switch to the *Remote Info* screen:

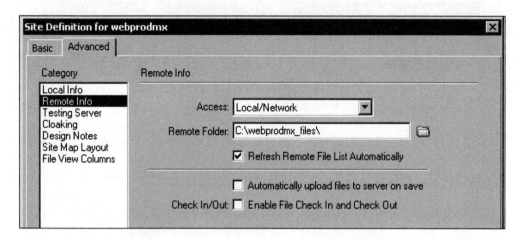

- Select the following options:

  - *Access*: Select Local/Network.

  - *Remote Folder*. Browse for the local root folder named `webprodmx_files`, which you created above.

We can leave the other settings at their defaults – *Refresh Remote File List Automatically* is selected, which means that when you view the remote file list in the site window, it will make sure you are seeing the latest version of the remote files. Also, as we are not working in a collaborative environment, we don't need to *Enable File Check In And Check Out* – which is useful for just such environments as it allows you to quickly see who is working on what file.

Testing Server

Switch to *Testing Server*:

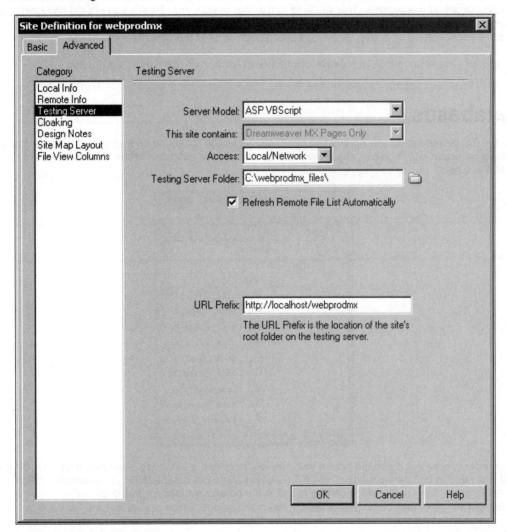

Select the following options:

- *Server Model*: Select ASP VBScript

- *Access*: Select Local/Network

- *Testing Server* Folder: Browse for the local root folder named `webprodmx_files` that you created

- *URL Prefix*: Type *http://localhost/webprodmx*, and click *OK*

Let's recap briefly what you should have done so far. You should have created a physical directory on your PC where you will save all the file examples named `webprodmx_files`. You should also have created a virtual directory named `webprodmx` that will be accessed from the browser from *http://localhost/webprodmx*. This will lead to the root of your site. Finally you should have defined a site in Dreamweaver MX named `webprodmx` that will be tested on your local server. *Chapter 8* has more about setting up a site, including a discussion of what the other four panels do.

Now let's move on to look at how we connect our site to, and use it with, a database.

Databases

The *Databases* tab on the *Application* panel shows all the database connections you have created for a particular site. You can easily view the names of your database tables and columns too, as we can see here:

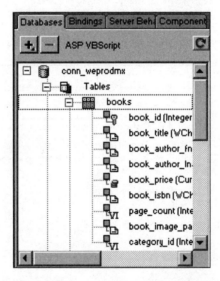

In order to create a database-driven web site we first need a database. Feel free to review *Chapter 6* if you need to before proceeding. We will be using a sample database for our examples called `webprodmx_data.mdb`, which can be found in the code download for this book on *http://www.glasshaus.com*. This database has three tables, which are as follows:

Table 1: categories

category_id	Autonumber (primary key)
category	Text

Table 2: books

book_id	Autonumber (primary key)
book_title	Text
book_author_fname	Text
book_author_lname	Text
book_price	Currency
book_isbn	Text
page_count	Number
book_image_path	Text
category_id	Number (foreign key)

The book_image_path column will contain the path to the book image. To save time for the moment, we will use a default image for each record. Let's put this image in the directory images/book_images/book_image.gif – create this path in the root of your site now.

You may create your own image, save it as book_image.gif *and put it in the* book_images *folder, or download the book image provided in the code download for this book, on glasshaus.com.*

Table 3: users

user_id	Autonumber (primary key)
username	Text
user_pwd	Text
first_name	Text
last_name	Text
email	Text
access_group	Text
dtstamp	Date/Time

Connections

Before you can utilize your database within your ASP web applications, you need to create a connection from the ASP page to your database. Fortunately Dreamweaver MX makes it simple for you. There are two ways you can create a connection to your database: **Data Source Name (DSN)** or **Custom Connection String** (often referred to as a "DSN-less connection").

Before you can create connections you must make sure the PC that hosts the database and serves the connection has the appropriate data access drivers (**Microsoft Data Access Components –** **MDAC**) installed – look for driver details in the following places:

- Windows 95, 98, or NT – go to *Start* > *Settings* > *Control Panel* > *ODBC Data Sources (32-bit)*

- Windows 2000 – go to *Start* > *Settings* > *Control Panel* > *Administrative Tools* > *Data Sources (ODBC)*, then click the *Drivers* tab

- Windows XP – go to *Start* > *Control Panel* > *Performance and Maintenance* > *Administrative Tools* > *Data Sources (ODBC)*, then click the *Drivers* tab

If you see the ODBC icons then the appropriate drivers should already be installed. These drivers are usually installed as standard, but if you find yourself without the right drivers you can download the latest ones from *http://www.microsoft.com/data/download.htm*.

Custom Connection String

The connection string is simply a string containing variables that contain information to connect to the database such as the provider type, physical location of the database on the server, and username and passwords if any. You will choose between two provider types, an **ODBC** (**Open Database Connectivity**) or an **OLE DB** provider. OLE DB is simply built on the success of ODBC by providing access to more kinds of data. The providers allow you to make a connection between your application and your database by specifying the database driver and database location. The string must then be embedded in every page that will retrieve database records. When you give Dreamweaver MX the string you want to use, it creates a separate folder called *Connections* with a file named after your connection. Whenever you create a recordset, Dreamweaver MX by default includes the string at the top of your page. (You will learn about *Recordsets* in the next section.) Hence you will not have to worry about it adding the connection string to each page.

The connection string syntax will vary depending on the provider and database you use. Since Access and SQL Server are the two database types most often used with ASP, we will show the syntax for both of them for both the ODBC and OLE DB providers:

ODBC

Microsoft Access

```
Driver={Microsoft Access Driver
(*.mdb)};Dbq=C:\folder_name\dbname.mdb;Uid=username;Pwd=passcode;
```

SQL Server

```
Driver={SQL Server};Server=server_name;Database=dbname;Uid=username;Pwd=passcode;
```

OLE DB

Microsoft Access

```
Provider=Microsoft.Jet.OLEDB.4.0;Data Source=c:\folder_name\dbname.mdb;User
Id=username;Password=passcode;
```

SQL Server

```
Provider=SQLOLEDB;Data Source=machine_name;Initial Catalog=dbname;User
ID=username;Password=passcode;
```

The strings should be written in one line. If you are not protecting your database with a username and password you can leave that part out of the ODBC string: `Uid=username;Pwd=passcode;` or the following out of the OLE DB string: `User ID=username;Password=passcode;`.

Password-Protected Access Database

As you may know you can set a password for an Access database through Access tools. For **ODBC** connection strings, if you set a password on an Access database you can leave this part out of the string: `Uid=username;` and simply fill in the password. Here is an example:

```
Driver={Microsoft Access Driver (*.mdb)};Dbq=C:\folder_name\dbname.mdb;Pwd=123456;
```

For **OLE DB** connection strings, if you set a password on an Access database you need to manipulate the string a bit. You should replace the following part: `User ID=username;Password=passcode;` with: `Jet OLEDB:Database Password=12345`. Here is an example:

```
Provider=Microsoft.Jet.OLEDB.4.0;Data Source=c:\folder_name\dbname.mdb;Jet
OLEDB:Database Password=123456;
```

> Many web developers have performed tests to compare between the providers and it turns out that the OLE DB provider is recommended as being a faster connection than ODBC.

For more connection strings, go to *http://www.basic-ultradev.com/articles/ADOConnections*.

Your database should be located above the `wwwroot`, because if it resides underneath the `wwwroot` folder, it will be available to viewers of your web site. Anyone who knows the name of the database can attempt to download it! If it resides above the `wwwroot` directory, you can retrieve the physical path to the database by using the code `Server.MapPath`. You should know the name of your database and the folder it resides in. You can create a file containing a line of ASP similar to the one below within the `wwwroot` of your site to display the physical path to the database:

```
<!-- display_dbpath.asp -->

<%=Server.Mappath("folder_with_database\webprodmx_data.mdb") %>
```

So How do we Actually Connect to a Database?

Before we add a connection we must open a page. Create a new dynamic ASP web page and save it as `categories.asp` in your `webprodmx_files` directory. The file will now be associated with your `webprodmx` site (save all future files under this directory and site). You can create a connection to a database using a custom connection string by writing the appropriate string in the field of the custom connection string dialog box – click the plus sign (**+**) under the *Databases* tab from the *Application* Panel. Click the *Custom Connection String* option, as seen overleaf:

You should then see the following dialog box:

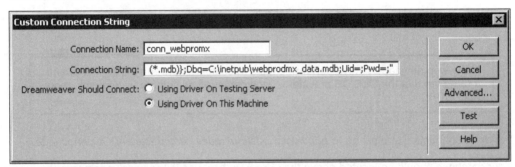

Here you must enter a name for your connection and the custom connection string in the appropriate fields. Name your connection `conn_webprodmx`, and enter the appropriate string (see above), making sure that you adjust the database location and ID and password as needed.

> As a convention, the prefix `Conn` is often attached to the beginning of the connection name such as: `conn_webprodmx`, `ConnWebProDmx`, etc.

At this point you should test your connection, by hitting the *Test* button. If it is successful you will see the following alert box:

Now hit *OK*, and *OK* the *Custom Connection String* box. If everything was successful you should see your connection added in the panel space under the *Databases* tab.

Data Source Name (DSN)

While a custom connection string is a faster connection, it requires us to know some detailed information about the database we are connecting to such as the physical path of the database on the server – this is not always readily available. The next best thing would be to simply create a DSN, which is basically a pointer to a System Data Source you set up in the ODBC manager on the server. Once you set one up on the server, you only need to know the DSN name and the username/password (if any) in order to create the connection. The connection string simply becomes `DSN=dsn_name`. Dreamweaver MX will generate this string for you as it does custom connection strings.

As you will see, the DSN must be created on the server that actually holds the database. You can create one on your own machine if you are hosting your own site and have access to the Data Sources administration. But if your site is being hosted remotely by a hosting company with which you don't have access to administration you can tell your web host to create the DSN(s) for you if it comes with your web hosting package. However some hosting companies give their users the ability to create their own DSNs through some sort of virtual control panel.

In any case, following these instructions creates a DSN:

- Open your *Data Sources (ODBC)* administrator from your *Control Panel* (see earlier in the chapter for a description of exactly where this is)

- Click the *System DSN* tab

- Click the *Add...* tab to add a new DSN

- The *Create New Data Source* dialog box will now appear, listing all the drivers currently loaded on the system. Select the driver appropriate to your database, for example *Microsoft Access Database (*.mdb)* for Access, and then click *Finish*

- In the final dialog box that now appears, first enter a *Data Source Name* and *Description* for the DSN (I chose *Webprodmx* for my DSN name). Second, click the *Select...* button and navigate to your chosen database. Click *OK*, and the new DSN should be added to your *System DSN* list; it should now be available for use in Dreamweaver MX

Now let's go back into Dreamweaver MX and create a connection using our DSN. Select the *Databases* tab and click the plus sign (+). Select the *Data Source Name (DSN)* option and the following dialog box will pop up.

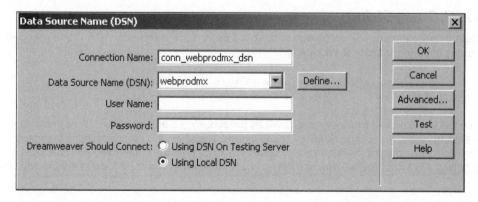

Fill in a name for your connection and select your DSN from the list. If your database is protected with a username and password enter them in the fields; if not, leave them empty (we didn't have to do this when we were using a custom connection string because this information is already provided by the string). Again, it is advised that you test the connection – if it is successful hit *OK*, and *OK* out of the *Data Source Name (DSN)* pop-up.

The connection will then be added to the connections list underneath the *Databases* tab. You can create connections to different databases for the same site, but one usually suffices since all your data will most likely be stored in one database. Creating a connection to your database is the **first** thing you need to do when preparing a database-driven web application – until then, none of the other ASP application behaviors will be made available.

Bindings

The *Bindings* tab of the *Applications* panel holds dynamic content in a safe place for you to easily access and bind as you build your documents. For example, when you create a recordset, it will be listed under the *Server Behaviors* tab, and accessible under the *Bindings* tab. You will be able to bind recordset columns into your document (see the *Server Behaviors* section of this chapter for more on recordsets).

Recordsets are not the only dynamic content you can store in the Bindings area; you can also store other dynamic text such as Request Variables, Session Variables, and Application Variables. Request Variables include cookies, querystrings, form variables, and environment variables. (If you need a refresher on Request and Session Variables, see *Chapter 5*.)

Bear in mind that the Bindings area does **not** create the variables for you. It simply allows you to store dynamic variables you have already created throughout your applications so that you can access them easily as you build documents. For example, the *Log In* Server Behavior creates a session variable named `MM_Username` that holds the username of a successful login. You can then add `MM_Username` to the bindings area so you can use it with ease on any documents you create.

Request Variables

Now let's test some dynamic variables and store them in the *Bindings* tab, so we can get a feel of how this all works. To start off with, we will look at Request variables.

Request.QueryString

Create a new dynamic ASP web page and save it as `create_request_variables.asp`. Add the following code to the body of your page:

```
<a href="create_request_variables.asp?my_id=23&my_name=omar">create
query_strings</a>
```

When this link is clicked two query strings will be passed: `my_id` and `my_name`. Store these variables in the Bindings area by selecting *Bindings*, then *Request Variables* (this can be found in the menu underneath the + button). Select `Request.QueryString` from the *Type* menu and type `my_id` in the *Name* field. Click *OK*. You will now see the `my_id` variable listed under *Request* in the *Bindings* window.

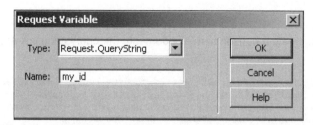

Follow the same steps to also add the `my_name` querystring and it will be added to the *Request* list.

Now we can start using and reusing our dynamic variables wherever we want – drag and drop them from the *Bindings* window anywhere you like in your document, and Dreamweaver MX will generate the ASP code to display the variables. For example, if we drag one instance of each variable we created above into `create_request_variables.asp`, our code will now look like this:

```
<a href="create_request_variables.asp?my_id=23&my_name=omar">create
query_strings</a>
<%= Request.QueryString("my_name") %>
<%= Request.QueryString("my_id") %>
```

Now if we load our page up in a browser and click the hyperlink, the values of the parameters should appear wherever you placed them on your page:

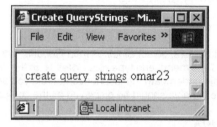

Go back to the code. Create a form and place one textfield and a hidden field inside the form. In Design View, select the textfield and then from Bindings select the `my_name` querystring variable. Finally click the *Insert* button at the bottom of the *Bindings* window – this will bind the `my_name` querystring variable as the value of the `<textfield>` element. Do the same to bind the `my_id` querystring variable to the hidden field. When this page is viewed live and the querystrings are passed, the textfield and hidden form elements will be populated with the querystring variables.

This tactic may be used to maintain state between pages by passing data held as querystring variables inside a form. Of course, instead of the form, you could create another hyperlink and simply pass the current querystrings to a second page. These methods are often used to pass data from page to page, because remember that, unlike sessions and cookies, querystrings and form elements cannot be retrieved on a page unless they are manually passed from a prior page. As a note, they can be passed from the same page too.

Dreamweaver MX makes it easy to reuse the dynamic querystring variables on pages throughout our site. After adding them to Bindings, we can simply drag and drop them from the Bindings window. Henceforth instead of typing out `<%=Request.QueryString("querystring_name") %>` when you click the *Request Variable* option from *Bindings,* you see that there are other request variable types besides querystrings. We can store those request variables in the Bindings window just as we have with querystrings.

Request.Form

On the same page, create a horizontal rule underneath the querystring link and form, and then insert the following code:

```
<form name="form1" method="post" action="create_request_variables.asp">
  username: <input name="username" type="text" id="username" /><br />
  password: <input name="user_pwd" type="password" id="user_pwd" /> <br />
  <input type="submit" name="Submit" value="Submit" />
</form>
```

Now select *Bindings*, then *Request Variables*. In the pop-up box that appears, select `Request.Form` from the *Type* menu and type *username* in the *Name* field. Click OK. You will then see the `username` variable listed under *Request* in the *Bindings* window. Follow the same steps to also add the `user_pwd` form field and it will be added to the *Request* list.

As with the other variables, you can now call these variables to anywhere you want in your page by dragging and dropping them from the *Bindings* window into your code. When you enter values into your form and *Submit* it, the values will appear wherever you placed the variables.

Request.Cookie

On the same page, insert a horizontal rule below the form you just created. In Code View add the following code above the opening `<html>` tag:

```
<% Response.Cookies("ckSayHello") = "Hello" %>
```

In the same manner as we did before, select *Bindings* then *Request Variables*, choose `Request.Cookie` from the *Type* menu, and type `ckSayHello` in the *Name* field. If you now drag and drop the `ckSayHello` variable underneath the last horizontal rule you added, and view your page through a browser, the cookie variable should be displayed as the cookie is created once the page loads.

Request.ServerVariable

On the same page, insert a horizontal rule below the dynamic cookie variable you just created. In the same manner as before, bring up the *Request Variables* pop-up box. Select *Request.ServerVariable* from the *Type* menu and type `remote_host` in the *Name* field. *OK* this, then we should be able to drag and drop the `remote_host` variable from the *Bindings* window onto your page. View the page in a browser, and the `ServerVariable` should be displayed once the page loads.

Session Variables

You can also store session variables in the Bindings window. Of course we have to create one first. Create a new dynamic ASP web page and save it as `create_session.asp`. In Code View add the following code above the opening `<html>` tag:

```
<% Session("svSayGoodbye") = "Goodbye" %>
```

Select *Bindings*, then *Session Variables*. Type `svSayGoodbye` in the *Name* field and click OK. The variable should be listed under a "*Session*" heading in the *Bindings* window. Now we can drag and drop the `svSayGoodbye` variable onto our page, just like we did before with our Request Variables – now view the page in a browser, and the Session Variable should be displayed as the session is created once the page loads.

The Bindings area is another useful timesaving feature of Dreamweaver MX – use it as much as you can. It organizes your dynamic variables and keeps them accessible as you build documents. Another good reason to use it is that you won't have to remember the names of the dynamic variables after you have created them! Once you create a dynamic variable, always add it to the *Bindings* window for easy access to its value.

Server Behaviors

The *Server Behaviors* tab contains all the pre-built ASP code blocks that help us build our web applications except a few others that reside under *Application Objects*. The first and foremost server behavior we need to learn about is the **Recordset** behavior.

Recordset (Query)

The *Recordset* behavior creates a recordset, which is a subset of database records. It is the object that sends an SQL query to a database, which then returns the data requested. The recordset is a part of the ADO (ActiveX Data Objects) set of objects that Microsoft created to provide ease of access to data stored in a wide variety of database sources. This object is called from our ASP page. Fortunately we do not need to know the ASP syntax to create a recordset object. In fact, you do not even have to know the SQL, but thanks to *Chapter 6* you should be familiar with it.

Dreamweaver MX gives us two ways to create a recordset: **Simple** and **Advanced** modes. In simple mode you do not need to manually add the SQL. You will be able to manually write your SQL in advanced mode. It is up to you which mode you use, but if you know SQL then it is suggested that you use advanced mode. Simple mode only allows simple queries to be constructed. We will now create a sample recordset from the database. Once we create our recordset we will be able to drag and drop the records onto our page.

Let's retrieve the list of categories stored in the table named `categories`. Create a new Dynamic ASP, and call it `categories.asp`. Now, from the *Bindings* or *Server Behaviors* tab click the plus sign (+) and select *Recordset (Query)*, and you should be presented with a pop-up box like this:

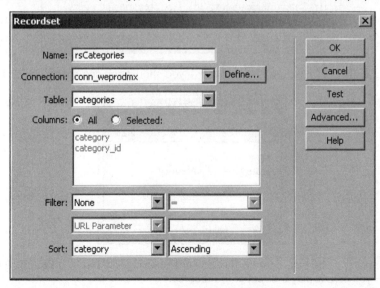

- Name your recordset `rsCategories` (it is a convention to prefix recordset names with "rs")

- Select the *Connection* you will be using (let's use the one we created earlier)

- Select the `categories` table, and select both fields

- We will not be filtering for any records as we just want to retrieve all the records, but it would be nice to sort the records in alphabetical order. From the first *Sort* drop-down menu select the *category* column; from the second one, select *Ascending*

> For future reference, only select the columns that you need. Retrieving columns that will not be used only slows down the execution time.

Hit the *Test* button, and Dreamweaver MX will sent the query to the database to test it – if successful, a box should pop up showing you all the records retrieved for that recordset.

Now *OK* the test box and click the *Advanced* button to take a look at the SQL Dreamweaver MX generated. We could have typed this in ourselves, but it has been done for us, saving us time. Switch back to *Simple* mode and click *OK*.

Click the *Bindings* tab from the *Application* Panel and you will see that the records are now available for our page, displayed in expandable tree form. Now, on our ASP, create an HTML table with 2 rows and 2 columns with 50% width, similar to what you see below. Drag and drop the appropriate fields from *Bindings* into each table column respectively; it should look something like this in Design View:

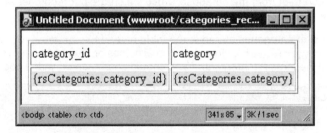

Now view `categories.asp` through a browser – you should see something similar to this:

You may wonder why the first record is the only one showing – in the next section we will find out why and how you can display the rest of the records.

Repeat Region

Although our recordset does in fact retrieve all the records from our categories table, it will not automatically display all the records. When you try to display the database columns, ASP will display the first record retrieved. In order to display all records in the table we must loop through the records (recall "*Looping Logic*" from *Chapter 5*). Fortunately, there is a server behavior that does this for us, called **Repeat Region**. This server behavior will generate the ASP code necessary to loop through our records. Now that we have dragged the variables onto our page, we must add a repeat region behavior to the dynamic texts.

We should first select the area that we want repeated. Select the dynamic text in the left column, hold shift and select the dynamic text on the right. This will highlight the second row of the table, which is what we want to repeat. If this does not work for you, place your cursor in the second row and select the <tr> tag from the status bar towards the bottom of the document. Click the plus sign (+) from the *Server Behaviors* tab and select *Repeat Region – OK* the *Repeat Region* dialog box that pops up, as it is fine for what we want here. View the page in your browser, and it should look something like this:

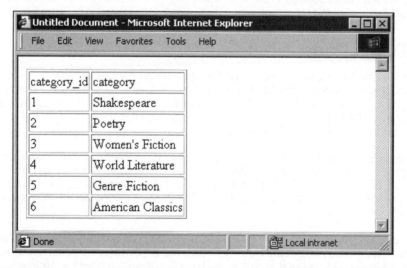

We have displayed our categories dynamically from our database. We created a recordset to retrieve the records, and then we created an HTML table and placed the dynamic text into the table columns, adding a repeat region behavior to display all the records.

It didn't take too long to do this, but Dreamweaver MX has another feature that can save us even more time! It is called the **Dynamic Table Object**. You can find it by going to *Insert > Application Objects*, and its icon can be found under the *Application* tab in the *Insert* toolbar at the top of the display. Using it, you can recreate the page we just created but with only 2 steps. Let's do that now.

Create a new dynamic ASP web page and save it as `dynamic_table.asp`. We must create the same recordset we created in the first example. Name the recordset `rsCategories`. After creating the recordset, place your cursor in the document where you want to place your dynamic table and select *Insert > Application Objects > Dynamic Table*. You will be presented with this pop-up box:

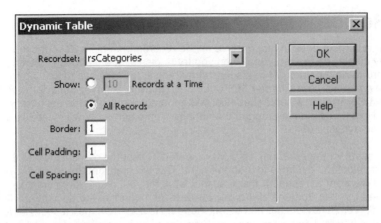

Select the recordset you created, select the *All Records* radio button and click *OK*. What do you see? The same table we created in the first example. Dreamweaver MX generates the table, adds the dynamic fields from the recordset, and finally adds a repeat region all in 1 step!

Go To Detail Page

This behavior usually consists of two pages: the **Master** and the **Detail** page. This concept is based on the one-to-many table relationship, that is, two tables where the primary key of a record is stored as a foreign key in a second table that contains additional information associated with that record – we can retrieve information from both tables as long as we have the key present (if you need a refresher on this, please review *Chapter 6*).

You can also use this server behavior to retrieve different numbers columns from the same table on different pages. For example, you may like to display minimal information about records on your master page, but have more info present when you drill down on detail pages – you pass the primary key onto a detail page, open the same recordset, but retrieve more columns than those retrieved on the master page.

In our `webprodmx_data` database, the `categories` and `books` tables have a one-to-many relationship – the primary key of the `categories` table is stored as a foreign key in the `books` table. The schema is set up like this so that each book is associated with a particular category. In a real-world web application we would display the categories on a master page and pass the primary key ID of a selected record to a detail page that displays the books associated with that ID.

Master Page

We already have a working master page that displays the categories from our database named `categories.asp`. We need to adjust it so that we make each category link to a detail page passing the Unique ID of the record (which will be the primary key: `category_id`) as a **URL parameter**. (If you need a refresher on URL Parameters, please review *Chapter 5*.)

Let's take a new copy of `categories.asp` and call it `categories2.asp`. Now, highlight the `category` dynamic text within the HTML table and select *Server Behaviors*, then *+*, then *Go To Detail Page*, as seen here:

The *Go To Detail Page* dialog box looks like this:

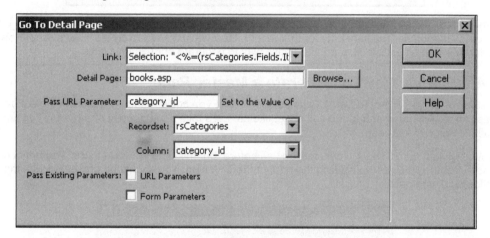

Fill in the fields as shown. We have not created the *Detail page* yet, but write books.asp in that field (we will create this page next). By default, the URL parameters passed (*Pass URL Parameter*) should be the category_id. You can change the name of the URL Parameter, but it's easier for us if we name the URL Parameter after the database column name. You could also manually change the value of the *Pass URL Parameter* field and the *Column* selector to pass a different column as the URL Parameter, but you will usually pass the primary key of the table since this is the unique key. Passing other columns is usually done in addition to passing the unique column. Make sure *Recordset* and *Column* are set to rsCategories and category_id respectively.

Leave the checkboxes besides *Pass Existing Parameters* unchecked, since we have no existing URL parameters already appended to the URL of this page or form parameters that we want to pass to the books.asp; we have no existing URL or form parameters. If there were we could choose to pass them along with the category_id URL parameter we are passing here. Hit *OK* and the category dynamic text will turn into a hyperlink.

Before we create the detail page (books.asp) let's have a look at categories2.asp in a browser so we can see what has happened. If you hover your mouse over the category hyperlinks, you will see that each one has its own URL – see the status bar at the bottom of the browser window overleaf:

227

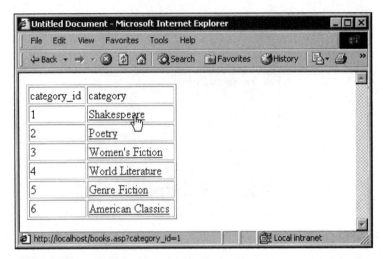

The number passed as the `category_id` value will be relative to the category, and is in fact the Access autonumber (primary key) for that record. Now we just need to create `books.asp`! However, before we do that, let's look at an alternative way to generate our dynamic links.

An Alternative Way To Generate a Master Page

Instead of using the *Go To Detail Page* behavior here, you could manually generate the action of passing a URL Parameter to a detail page, like so. Let's take another copy of `categories.asp` and call it `categories3.asp`.

Now, highlight the `category` dynamic text as before, but this time go down to the *Properties* window and select the little yellow folder to the right of the *Link* field. You should be presented with the following dialog box:

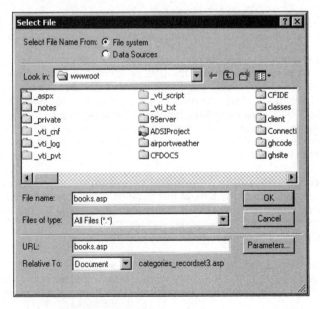

Type in `books.asp` for the filename and click the *Parameters* button to the bottom right – you should now see something like the following:

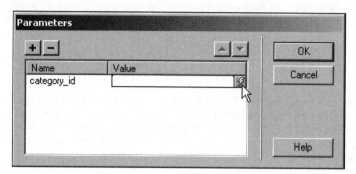

Under Name, fill in the name of our URL Parameter, `category_id`; for the `value` field, we want to pull the appropriate values out of our database – click the lightning bolt icon to the right of the field, to bring up the following:

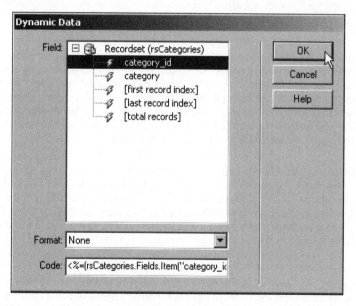

From here, expand the `rsCategories` recordset, select the `category_id` column and hit *OK*. Hit *OK* again to close the *Parameters* dialog box, now that we have filled in our *Value* column, and hit *OK* a third time to close our *File Select* dialog box.

Now if you look at the *Link* field in the *Properties* window, you should see that it has been filled in (with something like `books.asp?category_id=<%=(rsCategories.Fields.Item ("category_id").Value)%>`). You should also notice that our hyperlinks have been created in our page, the same as when we used the *Go To Detail Page*.

You can pass URL Parameters with either method. The *Go To Detail Page* behavior is nice because it saves time but it has a shortcoming – you cannot pass more than one URL Parameter when using the behavior – for example, we might want to pass the `category` name as a URL Parameter along with the `category_id`. When you do it manually you have the option of adding multiple Parameters.

Now let's create our `books.asp` detail page!

Detail Page

Create a new dynamic ASP page and save it as `books.asp`. We must now create a recordset that opens the `books` table and filters for the category ID passed as a URL parameter. Select *Server Behaviors > + > Recordset*, and switch to *Advanced* mode when the dialog box pops up. Name your recordset *rsBooks* and select the `conn_webprodmx` connection from the menu. Enter the following **SQL** in the space provided:

```
SELECT book_image_path, book_title, book_author_fname, book_author_lname,
book_price
FROM books
WHERE category_id = MMColParam
ORDER BY book_title ASC
```

While creating SQL queries you may utilize the `SELECT`, `WHERE`, *and* `ORDER BY` *shortcuts from the bottom half of the dialog box under Database Items by selecting the database table or column and clicking the desired button. For example, if you want to build a* `SELECT` *statement to select some fields from the* `books` *table, simply expand the database tree until you can see all the fields in the* `books` *table, then in turn, click on each one you want to* `SELECT`, *and press the SELECT button. The fields will be added to the* `SELECT` *statement in the SQL query above.*

Next, add the following variable directly into the Variables area – you need to click the + button to add a variable. Now enter the *Name* as `MMColParam`, the *Default Value* as 0, and the *Run-time Value* as `Request.QueryString("category_id")`. The variables area gives you the ability to list the names and values to represent dynamic variables you may use in your SQL. Dreamweaver MX will then simply use a variable named `MMColParam` in the SQL to represent the dynamic URL parameter variable `Request.QueryString("category_id")`.

When you add your own variable in the list make sure it matches the variable in the SQL exactly, otherwise the code will throw an error when executed live. For example, `MMColParam` in the SQL must match `MMColParam` in the variable list. `MMColParam` is not equal to `mmColparam`. This goes for any variable you may add in the SQL.

The dialog box should now look like this:

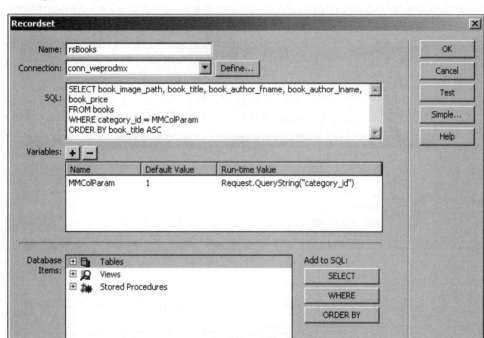

So, we are retrieving five columns from our `books` table – `book_image_path`, `book_title`, `book_author_fname`, `book_author_lname`, and `book_price`. We will list the books in alphabetical order by title. We have filtered our recordset to pull only the records whose `category_id` is equal to the `category_id` URL parameter passed from the previous page.

`MMColParam` is just a variable that will contain the value of the URL Parameter. You can name this variable whatever you like. (See *Chapter 5* for a refresher on variables and URL Parameters.)

Switch to Simple mode and click *Test* – you should see this screen as follows:

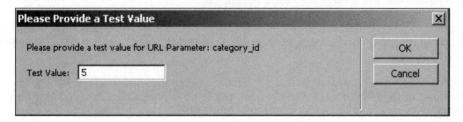

Enter the number 5, click *OK*, and you should see the records associated with the category whose `category_id` is 5. This test simulates a passed URL Parameter – in the real-world application, the ID will be passed in the querystring from a hyperlink. Hit *OK* to leave the test box, and *OK* again to submit your recordset.

Now, in your document create a table with two rows and two columns. Place your cursor in the second row of the left column, and choose *Image* from the *Insert* menu – the following dialog box shall appear:

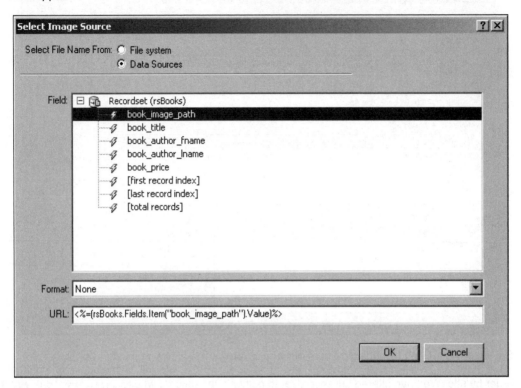

As seen above, click the *Data Sources* radio button from the top. You will see all the recordsets you created for this particular page – there should only be one currently – rsBooks. Expand the tree for this recordset, and select the database column that holds the URL path to the image – book_image_path. Hit *OK*.

Dreamweaver MX will place an image placeholder for the dynamic image on your page. When the page is viewed live, the appropriate image will appear.

Next, place your cursor in the second row of the right-hand column. From *Bindings*, drag and drop book_title, book_author_fname, book_author_lname, and book_price into the column, format the text as you like.

Highlight book_price on your page, then in *Bindings* you should see this field highlighted. Click the upside-down arrow to the right of it and you will see some formatting options (you may have to scroll the *Application* panel to the far right to see it) like so:

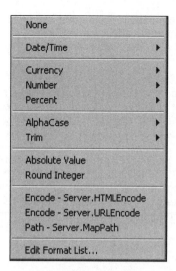

Select *Currency > Default*. This will format the text to display as currency, using a VBScript built-in function. (See *Chapter 5* for a refresher on VBScript built-in functions.)

Lastly we need to add a repeat region so that all the records will display. Repeat the second row of your table by selecting the entire second row of the table, selecting `<tr>` from the status bar of the Dreamweaver MX document, and selecting *Server Behaviors > Repeat Region*. Choose the `rsBooks` recordset from the recordset menu and display all the records. Hit *OK*. You might also want to add a link back to the master page somewhere on your detail page.

Load the `categories3.asp` page in your browser and click the *Genre Fiction* link – you should be taken to the detail page (`books.asp`) and it should display a list of the books associated with that category (ours looks like this):

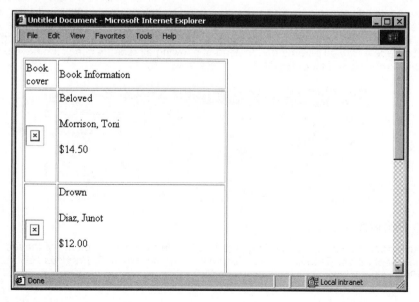

Isn't that cool? You didn't have to manually create that long list of books with static HTML and update it manually – ASP generates the HTML for you, and Dreamweaver MX generates the ASP for you! All you have to do now to display new information through your web application is to add new records to your books table.

You can manually add a record to the database in Access, or you could create an online content management system for yourself to make it easier to update your records at any time. You will learn more about this kind of extension in the sections on the Insert, Update, and Delete behaviors later in this chapter.

Some of our categories have no books under them at the moment, for example the World Literature category, so when you click on it, the books.asp page will be empty. We are be able to make this page more user-friendly for recordsets that come up empty by utilizing the *Show If Recordset Is Empty* server behavior. We will deal with this server behavior in the Show Region section, but before we get to this let's play with this page even more using some other cool server behaviors!

Recordset Paging

So far we have displayed our categories dynamically. When a category is clicked the user is taken to a complete list of all books associated with the respective category. Thus far we only have 20 different records to display in total – this is easy to deal with, but what about in future, when we want to display lots more? Also bear in mind that when we add the thumbnail images, they will increase the page loading time even further, so it will eventually become unmanageable to display all the records for each category every time.

So what if we wanted to remedy this by say, displaying 4 records at a time? This is all no problem at all – that's what the **Recordset Paging** set of behaviors is for.

Displaying a Few Records At a Time

Let's make some adjustments to our books.asp page by having only 4 records display at a time. Before we go any further we have to edit our repeat region. Double-click the *Repeat Region* behavior listed in the *Server Behaviors* list from the *Application* Panel. This will re-open the dialog box that selects our *Repeat Region* parameters. Instead of showing all records check the radio button above it and show **4** records at a time. Hit *OK*.

Move To Previous Record

Place your cursor in a suitable place (we chose a place in the second column of the first row of your table) and select *Server Behaviors > + > Recordset Paging > Move To Previous Record*, which should bring up the following dialog box:

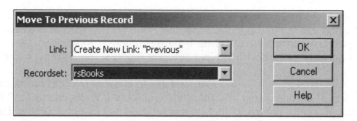

Leave the value for the *Link* field the way it is; it will create the text for us. Make sure the `rsBooks` recordset is selected in the *Recordset* field and hit *OK*. The *Previous hyperlink* will be added to your page where you put your cursor.

Move To Next Record

Choose another suitable space (we chose a space just to the right of the *Previous* hyperlink) and select *Server Behaviors > + > Recordset Paging > Move To Next Record*, and click *OK*. A *Next* hyperlink will be added to the right of our *Previous* hyperlink.

Before we view the page in our browser, let's use an *Application Object* called the **Recordset Navigation Status**. This object creates a display of how many records exist and how many are being displayed currently. It shows the user where he or she is in the context of all the records collectively. Before we add it, let's make some room for it by adding a third row above the row that contains the *Previous* and *Next* links. Do this by placing your cursor in the first row, right-clicking, and selecting *Table > Insert Row* – an empty row should be created above the other two.

Now that we have created the empty row place your cursor in the second column of the first row. Select *Insert > Application Objects > Recordset Navigation Status*, and *OK* the dialog box that appears, to add the object to our page. Now when we view the `books.asp` page in a browser we should see something like this:

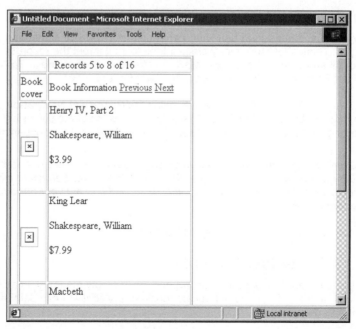

Although the page looks great, there is one slight problem that needs fixing – did you notice it? The problem is that when you get to the detail page, the *Previous* hyperlink is displayed even though there are no previous records (when records 1-4 are displayed). In addition, when you scroll through the records and get to records 12-16, the last group of records, the *Next* hyperlink is still displayed.

What we really want to happen is for the *Previous* link to show only if you are **not** at the first record, and the *Next* link to show only if you are **not** at the last record. Well guess what? Dreamweaver MX has another group of server behaviors that do this for us! They can be found under *Server Behaviors > + > Show Region*.

Show Region

Show Region contains a set of server behaviors that allow you to show regions of your document based on a few conditions. In our application, we'll utilize two, to sort out the problems discussed above:

Show Region If Not First Record

Highlight the *Previous* hyperlink that was generated by the *Move to Previous Record* behavior. Select *Server Behaviors > + > Show Region > Show Region If Not First Record*, and *OK* the box that appears.

Show Region If Not Last Record

Highlight the *Next* hyperlink that was generated by the *Move to Next Record* behavior. Select *Server Behaviors > + > Show Region > Show Region If Not First Record*, and *OK* the box that appears.

Now view the `books.asp` page in a browser, and you should see that the *Previous* hyperlink does not appear until you get to the second group of records. Similarly the *Next* hyperlink does not appear when you get to the last group of records.

Recordset Navigation Bar

Before we move onto another server behavior, I am going to show you something else Dreamweaver MX can do for you. Think about how many steps it took to implement the recordset Paging – we had to work with four different server behaviors: *Move To Previous Record*, *Move To Next Record*, *Show Region If Not First Record*, and *Show Region If Not Last Record*.

Brace yourself...we could've done this in one step using the **Recordset Navigation Bar** object! It can be found under *Insert > Application Objects*. This object utilizes the same server behaviors we used before, but selecting it inserts fully functional *First*, *Previous*, *Next*, and *Last* hyperlinks – instantly.

> *Dreamweaver MX has some other Application Objects that save us extra steps, as we shall see later. However, I want you to be able to use the server behaviors individually before using the additional timesaving Application Objects, to aid your understanding – I hope you forgive me!*

Now let's continue our look at the *Show Region* behaviors.

Show Region If Recordset Is Empty

There may be some instances where a recordset comes up empty meaning it has retrieved no records based on the query. I left one of the categories empty so that I can demonstrate this server behavior for you.

If you click on the *World Literature* category on your master page you will see that the detail page is empty because there are no books associated with this category. If this were a real-world application, you would most likely want to display a message when a query comes up empty. For example, you might display, "Sorry, no records found. Please go back and select another category." Without further ado, let's do that now.

Before we add the server behavior let's add the text, "Sorry, no records found. Please go back and select another category." Add another row above the other rows in your table. You should now have an empty first row. Place your cursor in the second column of this row and type your message there. Highlight the row by selecting the `<tr>` tag from the page status bar while your cursor is in the row. Select *Server Behaviors > + > Show Region > Show Region If Recordset Is Empty*.

View your page live now by loading the `categories3.asp` page. Select the *World Literature* category. You should see your message displayed because the recordset will be empty.

There is another issue on the page that calls for the use of another server behavior. I don't know about you but I think it looks a bit messy having the rest of the table showing but empty when the records come up empty. If you don't mind you can leave it, but we can easily hide it when the recordset is empty like so:

Show Region If Recordset Is Not Empty

Return to your document in Dreamweaver MX and highlight the second row of the table. Select *Server Behaviors > + > Show Region > Show Region If Recordset Is Not Empty*. Repeat this process for the third row of the table. Now if you view the page in a browser, the rest of the table should not display when the recordset on the detail page is empty.

So far we have learned how to:

- Create recordsets to retrieve database records

- Display database records dynamically on our web pages

- Filter recordsets by parameters passed and show and hide regions based on conditions

It would be great if we could now add a system to allow us to update our data without having to manually go into our database to do so – create a web application with Dreamweaver MX that will allow us to insert, update, and delete database records.

Insert Record

The *Insert Record* behavior can be found under *Server Behaviors*. It does exactly what its title suggests. With this behavior you do not have to open a recordset – it creates all the code necessary to insert a record into your database. The only thing you need to do is create an HTML form. Each column will be paralleled with a form field except the autonumber column, which is automatically generated by the database. Any other column that will be automatically generated should be left alone. For example, some database tables have a column that holds the date and time the record is added, generated automatically by Access.

As we mentioned above, the form should parallel the database table you will be inserting data into. Each column will receive its value from the form field; therefore you have to take into account the database column's data type.

We will attempt to insert a new category into our `categories` table – let's take a look at our `categories` table again:

category_id	Autonumber (primary key)
category	Text

There are only two columns. One of the two is an autonumber so we will only need to insert into one column using one form field. A single textfield will therefore serve this purpose just fine.

For sake of time, we will add the insert record form on this page. In a real-world application you may decide to add the insert record form on a separate page. There is no major difference. The only difference is that depending on the type of web application you will most likely only want certain people inserting records into your database. Nevertheless this has nothing to do with where we put our insert record form. You will have to hide or disallow access to administrative features through user logins. You will then be able to allow or disallow users to certain areas based on some database column. You will learn this concept later in this chapter. In the meantime, we just want to learn how to simply allow a user to insert records into your database online.

Add a Horizontal Rule at the bottom of your `categories3.asp` page. Insert a table with one column, 2 rows, and 50% width underneath the horizontal rule. In the first row type the text, "*Add Category*". Insert an empty form in the second row. Insert a new table with 2 rows and columns with 100% width inside the form. (Make sure you insert the table inside the form.)

Type the text "*category:*" in the left column of the first row. Insert a textfield in the right column of the first row by placing your cursor there and selecting *Insert > Form Objects > Text Field*. Name the textfield "*category*". Insert a button in the right column of the second row, and change the label of the button to "*Insert Category*". The form should now look something like this:

Add Category	
category:	[ ]
	[Insert Category]

> Giving form fields that insert data into database columns the exact same name as the database columns themselves can make things easier on yourself, because it makes it easier to recognize which form field send data to which database columns. It also allows the Dreamweaver MX *Insert Record* behavior to automatically associate the form fields with their respective database columns without having to do so manually. Still, it is important to note that this does carry with it the associated problem of revealing the name of your database columns to anonymous users through the HTML sourcecode. Revealing anything about the structure of your database can be sensitive information. If this does not sit well with you then avoid this tactic. You may use names that help you recognize what the form field is for without using the exact name of the database column.

Now that we have created our form we can add the *Insert Record* Behavior. Select *Server Behaviors > + > Insert Record*, and you will be presented with the *Insert Record* dialog box:

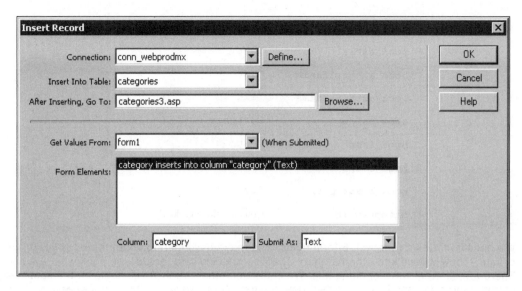

As seen above:

- Select the `conn_webprodmx` connection from the *Connection* menu

- Select the `categories` table to insert the form values into. Put `categories3.asp` (to redirect to after insertion) in the *After Inserting, Go To* field, by browsing or typing (you could redirect to any page you like. For example you might decide to redirect to a page that thanks the user for the insertion before showing the results)

- Select the correct form in your document that holds the insert record form. By default it will be named `Form1` unless you changed the name yourself. Since we named our form field the same as our database field, Dreamweaver MX should automatically choose the textfield named *category* to be the source of data to be inserted into the `category` database table (in situations where they are not called the same thing, you can make the association manually here, by changing the text in the *Form Elements* field)

- The category should be submitted as *Text* (see the *Submit As* field)

Hit *OK*. View your `categories3.asp` page in a browser and try to insert a new category – the new category should automatically appear in the categories list. Not only this, but it will automatically be placed in the list alphabetically. Hover your mouse over the new category and look at the stats bar; you will see its new ID number that was generated by the database. Click the new category to go to the `books.asp` page; you should receive the message, "*Sorry, no records found. Please go back and select another category*" because we have not added any books under this category yet.

You now know how to insert records into your database online. Before we move onto the *Update Record* behavior, let's try to insert records into the `books` table for our new category. Of course, before we add the necessary *Insert Record* behavior we need to create an HTML form that reflects the database table – let's take another look at the columns for the `books` table:

`book_id`	Autonumber (primary key)
`book_title`	Text
`book_author_fname`	Text
`book_author_lname`	Text
`book_price`	Currency
`book_isbn`	Text
`page_count`	Number
`book_image_path`	Text
`category_id`	Number (foreign key)

We need to create a form with 8 form fields. You may be wondering about the `category_id` column – how will we know the category ID of the specific category for the book we are adding? There are different ways of doing this. We could open the `categories` table on the same page of this insert page and bind the categories to a list menu. We would bind the `category_id` as the value of each `<option>` tag, and have this list menu insert into the `category_id` of our books table.

However, one of the things to aim for when building web applications is code reuse. We should always try to build code that will be reusable for other options. In this case, we already opened the `categories` table on `categories3.asp` so why do it again? Once we select a category on this page, the `category_id` is automatically passed to the `books.asp` page as a URL parameter.

Therefore, it makes sense to have the facility for inserting new books on the `books.asp` page, because here we have already chosen the `category_id` we are dealing with, so we don't need to worry about it again. We can bind the `category_id` URL Parameter to a form textfield or hidden field. It is very important that the category id is inserted properly because it is how books are associated with their respective categories.

So, let's create our facility for inserting new books into the database! Insert a horizontal rule at the bottom of your `books.asp` page. Insert a table with 2 rows, 1 column and 50% width underneath the horizontal rule. Type the text "*Add Book*" in the first row of this table. Insert an empty form in the second row, and insert a new table inside this form, with 8 rows, 2 columns, and 100% width.

In the left-hand column of this table, type out the following in each respective row: `book_title`, `book_author_fname`, `book_author_lname`, `book_price`, `book_isbn`, and `page_count`. Leave the last two left-hand rows empty. Insert a textfield into each right-hand row that has text entered into the left-hand row (the first six). Insert a hidden field in the seventh right-hand row (for the `category_id` – see below) and a button in the eighth right hand row. Our form should now look like this:

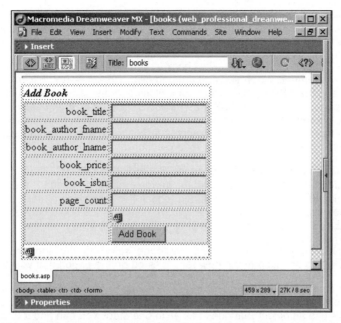

Now rename each textfield and the hidden field with the names of their respective database columns. Change the label of the *Submit* button to "*Add Book*". Lastly, we need to make sure the value of the hidden field is the category ID that will be coming from the URL Parameter named category_id, passed from the categories3.asp page. Highlight the hidden field for the category_id and change its value to the following:

```
<%= Request.QueryString("category_id") %>
```

Now we need to add the *Insert Record* Behavior. *Select Server Behaviors > + > Insert Record*. Choose the conn_webprodmx connection, insert into the books table, and redirect to the books.asp page. Make sure the form fields are sending their data to the relevant database columns by checking through the statements in the *Form Elements* box. Your *Insert Record* dialog box should now look like this:

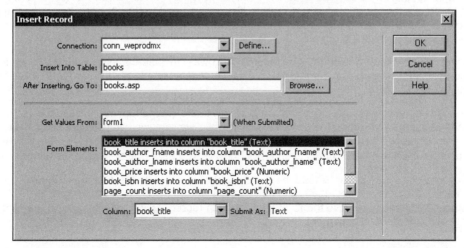

The Server Behavior will add another hidden field into the form – do not delete this field. Dreamweaver MX uses this method for the *Insert Record*, *Update Record,* and *Delete Record* server behaviors. You can simply ignore the hidden field added by Dreamweaver MX for these three server behaviors.

If you recall from *Chapter 5*, you can easily check to see if a form has been submitted to the page using a condition statement. When you add the behavior, Dreamweaver MX uses the name of the form as a variable in the ASP *Insert Record* code block and also adds it as a hidden field in the form itself. When the page is loaded, the ASP *Insert Record* code block then checks through a conditional statement to see whether this field has been submitted, which essentially means that the *Insert Record* form has been submitted. If so it executes the entire insert code block, otherwise it loads the page normally without executing the insert record action.

We can now add books for a particular category. Regarding the `book_image_path` column, as you know, we have created a static path to a default image that will be used for each book. This path will be the default value for each new record added (check this by looking at the `books` table in Access). Hence, we will not insert a `book_image_path` from the form. You could change this of course, to either change the path manually, or upload an image from this form.

Test this now by loading your `categories3.asp` page, selecting any category you like, and trying to insert a new book. You should see the new record listed on the page once you submit the form.

It took a while to create the insert form for the `books.asp` page. We had to format it, add and rename all the fields, and finally add the *Insert Record* Behavior. Well, as luck would have it, Dreamweaver MX has an object that does this all in one step! You can find it under *Insert > Application Objects > Record Insertion Form*. You will not have to manually create the form to reflect the database table. The object will create the form and add the *Insert Record Server* behavior for you. When you get a chance, go ahead and try it.

Now that we know how to insert records let's update them!

Update Record

Updating records is different from inserting records in that when we insert we don't need to retrieve records, we just need to insert a completely new record into a specific table. Since the *Insert Record* does this it basically does everything we need. Due to this people assume the *Update Record* must also do everything on its own, but it doesn't. Unlike inserting records, when we update a record we need to retrieve the record we want to update, that is, we need to **find** it, **open** it and then **update** the record. The *Update Record* behavior will do the third part, but it will not automatically find and open the record you want to update.

However, we now know how to retrieve records don't we – this means that we always need to create a recordset before we use the *Update Record* behavior. We have to tell the *Update Record* behavior which record to update.

So how did we retrieve the book records associated with the categories? We passed the `category_id` to the `books` page and filtered the `book` table by this ID. Similarly we can pass the `book_id` to a new page that will reopen the `books` table and filter for the specific `book_id` we passed. We will then bind the values of the database columns to an HTML form and add the *Update Record* behavior.

Open your `books.asp` page. Reload the `rsBooks` recordset (go to the *Bindings* window, and double-click the *rsbooks* recordset), and make sure you add the `book_id` column to the SQL SELECT statement. We need to retrieve the ID number of each record, as we will pass this to the next page. OK out of the *Recordset* dialog box.

Now go back to your page, and add the text "*edit*" within the repeat region besides the other dynamic text. It will be repeated besides each record when the page is viewed live. Turn the "*edit*" text into a hyperlink that points to a page called edit_book.asp, which we will create in a second.

We want to pass the book_id as a URL Parameter. You already know how to do this. You could use the *Go To Detail* Page behavior or manually add it from the *Link* dialog box. Let's do it manually:

- Highlight the edit link and click the yellow folder besides the *Link* field from the *Properties* window – this should bring up the *Select File* dialog box

- Make sure edit_book.asp is entered for the *File Name*

- Click the *Parameters* button besides the URL field towards the bottom to bring up the *Parameters* dialog box

- Add a new URL parameter by clicking the + button and name it book_id

- Click on the *Value* field, then click the lightning bolt to the right of it; in the *Dynamic Data* dialog box that appears, select the book_id column from your rsBooks recordset. (If you don't see it, it means that you haven't added it to the recordset.)

OK all the dialog boxes to close them. Now view the updated categories3.asp page in a browser, and click through to a books.asp page. Hover your mouse over each of the *edit* hyperlinks that appear, and you'll notice that the appropriate book_id is attached to the end of each URL.

Now let's create our edit_book.asp page.

Go back to Dreamweaver MX and create a new dynamic ASP web page – save it as edit_book.asp. Create a new recordset called rsUpdateBook, making sure the conn_webprodmx connection is chosen. Enter the following SQL in the *SQL* box:

```
SELECT book_id, book_author_fname, book_author_lname, book_isbn, book_price,
book_title, page_count
FROM books
WHERE book_id = MMColParam
```

Now add a new variable, with the following values – MMColParam for *Name*, 0 for *Default Value*, and Request.QueryString("book_id") for *Run-time Value*.

Hit *OK*. This query will retrieve the information for the book whose ID is equal to that passed in the URL Parameter.

Just as for the *Insert Record* behavior, we have to create a form that reflects the database columns and table we want to update. But I've been having you do things the long way. Now that you know how to use the individual server behaviors, instead of creating the form we will use one of Dreamweaver MX's timesaving Objects – the *Record Update Form*.

Select *Insert > Application Objects > Record Update Form*, and you will be presented with the following dialog box:

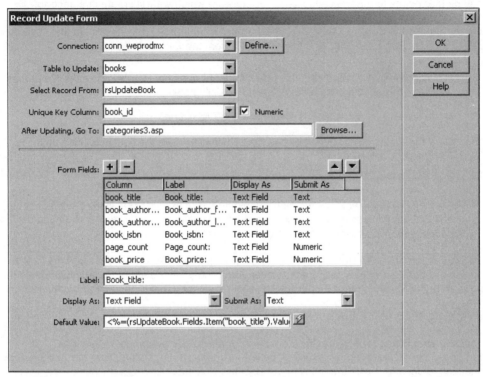

As seen above, select the `conn_webprodmx` connection, `books` table to update, `rsUpdateBook` recordset, `book_id` as the unique key column and redirect to `categories3.asp` after updating.

Remove the following form fields from the list: `book_image_path`, `category_id`, and `book_id` (you should always remove unique IDs from the *Update Record* behavior because no one should ever be allowed to edit these values in normal circumstances. Also, we don't need to edit the image path through this form). Hit *OK* and the *Update Record* form should be created for you in your document.

Test your page in a browser, and try editing some of your book records.

We left the `category_id` out of the update to start off with, as explained above, but we might want to update this – that is, we might want to place a book into a different category. Let's do that now. We need to do three things: add the `category_id` column to the `rsUpdateBook` recordset, create a new recordset to retrieve the categories, add a field for the category ID in our update form, and add the `category_id` column to the *Update Record* behavior.

On the `edit_book.asp` page, get up the details for the `rsUpdateBook` recordset again, and add the `category_id` column to the `SELECT` SQL statement. Your SQL should now look like this:

```
SELECT book_id, book_author_fname, book_author_lname, book_isbn, book_price,
book_title, page_count, category_id
FROM books
WHERE book_id = MMColParam
```

We also need to add a form field to the update form. Before we do that we should think about how we want to display the categories for display. The only thing stored in the book record that associates the book record with a particular category is the `category_id`. Most likely we will not have memorized the ID numbers of our categories – it would be more practical to retrieve the categories and select which category we want to place the book in from a listbox field. Thus we need to create a new recordset and retrieve the categories.

Create a new recordset called **rsGetCategories**. Make sure the `conn_webprodmx` connection is selected, and type the following SQL into the appropriate field:

```
SELECT category, category_id
FROM categories
ORDER BY category ASC
```

Hit *OK*. In your form, add a row above the seventh row that contains the *Submit* button (there should now be eight rows in all), and type the text "*category*" in the left column of this row. Now add a listbox field to the update form in the right column of this row (use *Insert > Form Objects > List/Menu*).

We want to populate the labels and values of the listbox from the `rsGetCategories` recordset – rename the listbox field "*category_id*". Select the listbox field and click the button labeled *Dynamic* from *Properties* to open the *Dynamic List/Menu* Server Behavior. (You could also get this Server Behavior by going to *Server Behaviors > + > Dynamic Form Elements > Dynamic List/Menu*.) You should see the following:

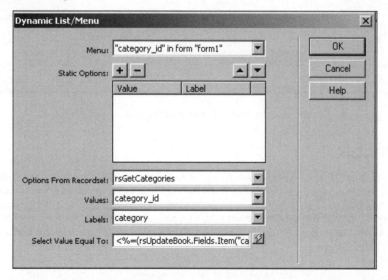

Select the right listbox field is selected from the menu labeled *Menu*, as seen above. Leave the *Static Options* empty. In the next field, select `rsGetCategories`. Populate *Values* with the `category_id` column and *Labels* with the `category` column (we would rather see the category name in the listbox).

The next option, *Select Value Equal To* is very important. We want to make sure that when we load the page, the listbox selects the category that it is currently in by default, otherwise we could change the category by accident when we submit the form. Select the lightning bolt to the right of the field to bring up the recordsets that have been created for this page. Select the `category_id` column from the `rsUpdateBook` recordset, rather than from the `rsGetCategories` recordset.

Finally, we need to reload the *Update Record* behavior to make sure it is included in the update. Double-click *Update Record* from the *Server Behavior* list in the *Application* Panel. When the dialog box opens, make sure that the field labeled *category_id* (which is the listbox field) submits to the `category_id` column numerically in the *Form Elements* option list (see it highlighted below). If you don't do this, the category_id may be ignored by default. The *Update Record* dialog box should now look like this:

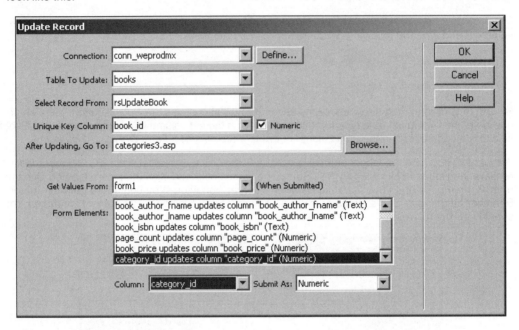

Test your pages in a browser, and try moving some books into new categories.

Delete Record

The *Delete Record* Behavior works very similar to the *Update Record* except that it deletes the record from the database. Just like the *Update Record*, you have to retrieve the record you want to delete and then add the server behavior. Open your `books.asp` page, and right next the "*edit*" hyperlink, add a "*delete*" hyperlink that links to a page called `delete_book.asp` (which we will create in a minute) and pass the `book_id` as a URL Parameter, as we've done before. Name the URL Parameter `book_id`.

Create a new dynamic ASP web page and save it as `delete_book.asp`. Create a new recordset and name it *rsGetBookForDelete*. Make sure the `conn_webprodmx` connection is selected, and add the following SQL:

```
SELECT book_id, book_title, book_author_fname, book_author_lname
FROM books
WHERE book_id = MMColParam
```

Add a variable directly below named `MMColParam`, with a *Default Value* of `0`, and a *Run-time Value* of `Request.QueryString("book_id")`. Hit *OK*.

Drag and drop the `book_id`, `book_title`, `book_author_fname`, and `book_author_lname` onto your document as you wish. You might also want to add a message like, "*Are you sure you want to delete this book?*" for example. Below this text, insert an empty form and insert a button inside the form. Change the button's label to "*Delete Book*". Name the form "*frm_delete_book*". Add the *Delete Record* behavior by selecting *Server Behaviors > + > Delete Record*. Make sure the `conn_webprodmx` connection is selected, set *Delete From Table* as books, and *Select Record From* the *rsGetBookForDelete* recordset. Select the **book_id** as the *Unique Key Column*, *Delete By Submitting* the *frm_delete_book* form, and redirect to `categories3.asp` after deleting. Your *Delete Record* dialog box should now look like this:

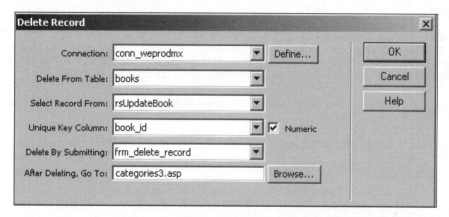

Hit *OK* – we are now finished! Test your delete function live – it should look something like this:

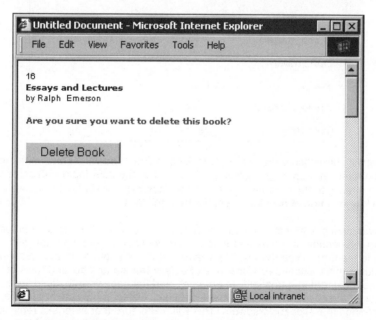

We now have completed a pretty thorough web application that allows us to view and update a book database via the Web. We have the ability to insert categories or books, and update and delete books. We can even move books into different categories.

One way to extend our application would be to add a facility for user logins – this leads us to the next group of server behaviors.

User Authentication

The User Authentication group of server behaviors contains four server behaviors that make creating a login extremely easy. Once we have a login set up, we will be able to restrict access to pages or even parts of pages. Let's create a login and play with these behaviors.

Log In User

This server behavior generates the entire code that will open a table, verify a user, and redirect him or her to a desired page. All we have to do is create the login form. The *Log In User* behavior also does something else – it creates one session by default and another optionally. The session created by default holds the username of the person logging in – it is called `MM_Username`.

You can also optionally make Dreamweaver MX set a session for the column that holds access levels. The session will be called `MM_UserAuthorization`.

Both of these sessions can be accessed later on with this code: `Session("MM_Username")` and `Session("MM_UserAuthorization")`. Before we begin, let's take a look at the database table that will store the users:

user_id	Autonumber (primary key)
username	Text
user_pwd	Text
first_name	Text
last_name	Text
email	Text
access_group	Text
dtstamp	Date/Time

Login In User will authenticate the user by checking to see if the values submitted in the login form match the username and `user_pwd` columns. I have filled the user table with some values. You can add your own directly to the database, or create an *Insert Record* behavior (as we saw earlier in the chapter) to allow insertion of new login records from the Web.

Create a new dynamic ASP web page and save it as `login.asp`. Create a login form by inserting an empty form in the document – rename the form "*frm_login*", and insert a table with 3 rows and 2 columns inside the form. Type the text "*username:*" in the left column of the first row and "*password:*" in the left column of the second row. Insert textfields in the top and second rows of the right hand column. Name the username textfield "*username*", and the password textfield "*user_pwd*", as these are the names of the corresponding database columns. Select the password textfield and, from *Properties*, change the *Type* to *Password*. This will make sure that asterisks replace characters typed when the page is accessed live. This is important so that the password is always hidden even while logging in. Insert a button in the bottom row of the right-hand column – change the label of the button to "*Login*". The form should now look like this:

Add the *Log In User* behavior by selecting *Server Behaviors > + > User Authentication > Log In User*. Fill in the resulting dialog box so it looks exactly as shown here:

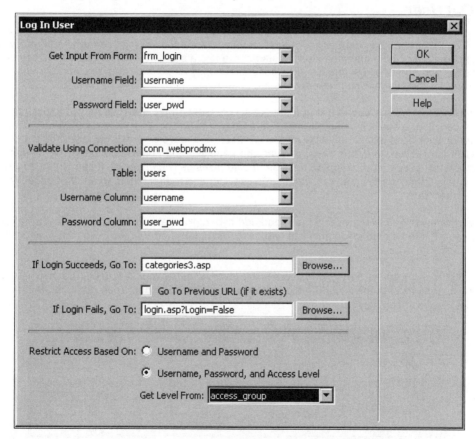

As you can see, we have selected access_group as the column to *Get Level From* – this will make the behavior create the optional session we talked about earlier, MM_UserAuthorization. It will hold the value of the access_group column for the successful user into a session (you can simply restrict access based solely on username and password, but for this example we will restrict based on Access Levels too). Hit *OK*.

Our Login application is complete, but before we test it in a browser, open the `categories3.asp` page. Select *Bindings* > *Session Variable* and type in `MM_Username` and click *OK*. You will now see the Session available under Bindings. This does nothing but make it easier for us to add the code `Session("MM_Username")` to our pages, to identify the user currently in session.

Somewhere at the top of this page type the text, "*Welcome username!*" Highlight the username text and select the `MM_Username` session from *Bindings* and click *Insert* (at the bottom of the *Application* Panel).

The username text should be replaced with the code `<%=Session("MM_Username")%>`. You can now test your login in a browser – load the `login.asp` page, type in "*omar*" for the username and "*123456*" as the password. You should be taken to the `categories3.asp` page.

Log Out User

Of course, we need to give our users the option to logout. However, forget the server behaviors for a second –What does *Log In User* do? It does nothing but authenticate a username and password against the *users* table and then stuff the username into a session. This session is the key, as it gives the opportunity to personalize the user's experience as long as we have stored a unique identifier for the user, which in our case is the username.

On this note, logging a user out is nothing but simply clearing the session. As you know from *chapter 5* you can clear a session using `Session.Abandon` or `Session.Contents.Remove()`. The *Log Out User* behavior does this for us. It clears the `MM_Username` session and if we restricted access based on Username, Password, and Access Level when applying the *Log In User* behavior, it adds code to clear the `MM_UserAuthorization` session. It also gives us two options – it can log a user out but keep them on the same page, or it can sign a user out and redirect them to another page. We will do it the latter way.

Create a new page called `logout.asp`, and add hyperlinks that point to `logout.asp` on all pages that you want to be able to log out from (we have just put one on `categories3.asp`, and labeled it "*Log Out*".)

On `logout.asp`, select *Server Behaviors* > + > *User Authentication* > *Log Out User*. When the dialog box opens click the second radio button labeled **Page Loads**. When done, redirect to `login.asp`, as seen here:

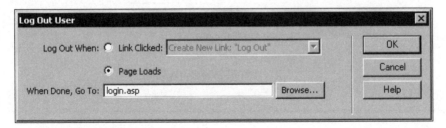

Test your pages in a browser – log in and surf your web pages; sign out when you are ready. You will be redirected back to `login.asp`.

Restrict Access To Page

Now that we have the login application working, we can restrict access to pages based on user logins. For example, we can disallow access to certain pages. You will recall that we restricted access based on Username, Password, and Access Level (the Access Level parallels the `access_group` column stored in the database).

If you look at the *users* table you will see that users have different values for the `access_group` column. Only "*omar*" has the value "*admin*", while others have the value "*member*". This is how the author chose to identify access levels – you could add more access levels and use different values; you could even use numbers if you wanted.

Some sites don't require access levels as there may be no need for them – for example, if all users will have access to the same information, there is no point.

However, it is good to learn this concept because it is often needed. We use the `access_group` column to simply give each a user a level of power. "*admin*" means the user is an administrator, and should have full site access, while a mere "*member*" should not have access to certain site functions, such as inserting, updating, and deleting categories or books. Let's test this out now – we will modify our site so that only "*admin*" users will have access to the update and delete pages.

> *Before we begin using this server behavior make sure you are logged out (login sessions are cleared).*

Open the `edit_book.asp` page and select *Server Behaviors > + > User Authentication > Restrict Access To Page* to bring up the following dialog box:

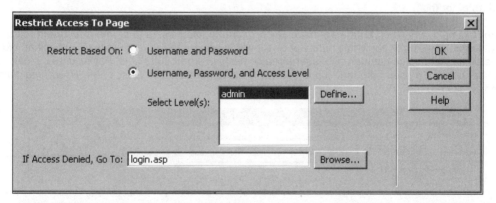

Select the second radio button labeled "*Username, Password, and Access Level*". Define and then highlight the access group values you want to have access. Hit the *Define* button, when the *Define Access Levels* dialog box opens, click the plus sign (+) to add your access group values. It will only allow access to those who have the text "*admin*" in the `access_group` column. If a user gets denied redirect him or her to the `login.asp` page. Hit *OK*.

Close this document and open the `delete_book.asp` page. Now go through the same steps as above to give this page the same access restrictions as `edit_book.asp`.

Now that we have restricted access to our pages let's test it out – load your `categories3.asp` page and try to edit or delete a book – you should be redirected to the `login.asp` page. Also, try logging in as a user who is not an administrator (for example, username "*superman*", password "*sup432*" and try to edit or delete a book – again, you should be redirected to the `login.asp` page.

You may also be wondering how to make it so that mere "members" can't even see the functionality that they won't be allowed to use, such as the "*edit*" and "*delete*" links, and the form for inserting new books. You would rather only show them to administrators, right?

You can use your knowledge of VBScript conditional logic to show the links only to users whose `MM_UserAuthorization` session equals "*admin*". You can surround the functionality that you want to hide from "*members*" with the following code:

```
<% If Session("MM_UserAuthorization") = "admin" Then %>
HTML to be shown to administrators only would go here.
<% End If %>
```

(For a refresher on VBScript Conditional Statements see *Chapter 5*.) Next time around you may decide to put the insert record form on a separate page to the existing records, and simply restrict access to them. You have now safeguarded the administrative options of your site by giving access to them to administrators only, all with a few server behaviors.

Check New Username

I will not be demonstrating use of the *Check New Username* server behavior because it works with a user registration form, the likes of which we have not yet created (you will have to wait till the next chapter for this).

For example, when you create an *Insert Record* form to allow users to create a record in the *users* table you can simply apply this behavior and it will allow you to redirect users to a specified page if a particular field value inputted by a user already exists in a particular field. For example, it can stop a user choosing a username that someone else is using already. The *Check New Username* dialog box looks like this:

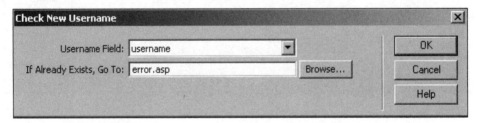

Summary

In this chapter, we have learned:

- How to use the *Application* Panel efficiently while building dynamic content

- How to create a connection to a database

- How to use the *Bindings* window to store and display the dynamic variables you may create throughout your site

- How to use Server Behaviors and Application Objects to generate large blocks of ASP code

We used a wide variety of the server behaviors available in Dreamweaver MX to create a simple but effective online content management system. This chapter has demonstrated some of Dreamweaver MX's more powerful features – we hope you are now fully equipped to start creating your own database applications.

However, it's not over yet. In the next few chapters we will show you how to use Dreamweaver MX to build some more complex complete web applications.

8

- Setting up a working sample web site:

  - Home page, including log out functionality

  - User registration page

  - User log in page

  - User account edit page

  - Administration page (only accessible by Administrators), including deleting users

Author: Rob Turnbull

Basic Dynamic Web Site

This chapter takes the knowledge we learned in the previous chapters a step further, by showing how to create a fully operational dynamic web site – the site we are going to create can act as a skeleton site that we can add content to later. It features many functions that are commonly desired for dynamic sites, to save you time in future work. The pages are as follows:

- **Home page** – this page will contain links to all the other pages bringing them all neatly together. It will contain some code to show or hide certain parts of the page dependant upon the user being logged in and their access level

- **User registration page** – allows new users to enter their registration details to create a login account to access our web site

- **User login page** – checks the details submitted by a user against those stored in the database and contains the necessary logic to only allow successful login attempts to continue

- **Edit my account page** – gives registered users the opportunity to change their registration details

- **Administration page** – a page accessible only by site administrators, which gives them the power to remove any registered user login accounts

These pages will, of course, need a database to talk to in order for them to work – our database will, for the purposes of this chapter, contain just one table, to store all of the details that the users have to enter in the registration process.

> Note that you will already have seen usage of a number of the server behaviors featured in this chapter in *Chapter 7* – however, we thought a recap would be useful to you, plus we are now showing you their use in the context of a complete web site.

Creating the Database

First we need to create a blank database in our chosen database package (we are covering MS Access and SQL Server). If you are unsure how to do this, follow the instructions outlined in *Chapter 6* (under the heading *How do I create a database?*). Now we need to populate the database. Let's go through doing this in Access and SQL Server.

Using Access

With your empty database open (we have called ours `ProdmxCh8`), select *Tables* in the left column of the database window, click *New*, and select *Design View* from the pop-up dialog (you could also have double-clicked on *Create Table in Design View* in the *Tables* window).

Add the following fields to the database:

Field Name	Data Type	Field Size	Allow Zero Length	Default Value
UID	Autonumber	Long Integer	Automatically No – there is no option	
UName	Text	50	No	
UEmail	Text	255	No	
UUsername	Text	50	No	
UPassword	Text	50	No	
UAccessLevel	Text	50	No	SiteUser
UAddress1	Text	100	Yes	
UAddress2	Text	100	Yes	
UAddress3	Text	100	Yes	
UTown	Text	50	Yes	
UCounty	Text	50	Yes	
UCountry	Text	100	Yes	
UPostcode	Text	20	Yes	
UPhone	Text	20	Yes	
UFax	Text	20	Yes	
UWebAddress	Text	255	Yes	

The field size, default value; and allow zero length properties are set on the *General* tab at the bottom of the design window. You need to specify the primary key field in this table, which you do by clicking in the UID row of the Design View and then clicking the gold key button on the tool bar, or by right-clicking the column and selecting *Primary Key*.

When we insert records into this table dynamically from our web site, we will insert into all columns, except UID and UAccessLevel – this is because UID is our unique record identifier and cannot be inserted into, and UAccessLevel specifies the users access level and is used to restrict access as required – we won't be giving user's the option to choose their access level!

Save this table with a name of tblUsers and close the Design View – now we are ready to create the web pages that will use this database table.

If you are going to use this Access database for the basic site, you can skip the next section (which takes you through setting up the same database table in SQL Server), and move straight on to the section headed *Setting up the Site*.

Using SQL Server

Launch *Enterprise Manager* and expand the tree view in the left pane until you can see the *Databases* node.

We are going to add the table into a blank database (we've called ours ProdmxCh8.) With the *Tables* node of the database selected in the left pane, right-click in the right pane and select *New Table* (or select it in the *Action* menu). This opens up the table Design View for you to create the table in.

Add the following fields to the database:

Field Name	Data Type	Length	Allow Nulls	Default Value
UID	Int	4	No	
UName	varchar	50	No	
UEmail	varchar	255	No	
UUsername	varchar	50	No	
UPassword	varchar	50	No	
UAccessLevel	varchar	50	No	SiteUser
UAddress1	varchar	100	Yes	
UAddress2	varchar	100	Yes	
UAddress3	varchar	100	Yes	
UTown	varchar	50	Yes	
UCounty	varchar	50	Yes	
UCountry	varchar	100	Yes	
UPostcode	varchar	20	Yes	
UPhone	varchar	20	Yes	
UFax	varchar	20	Yes	
UWebAddress	varchar	255	Yes	

You need to specify the primary key field in this table, which can be done by clicking in the `UID` row of the table Design View and then clicking the gold key on the tool bar (or by right-clicking and selecting *Set Primary Key*).

You also need to make the *UID* column an Identity column, which performs the same function as an Autonumber column in Access. To do this, make sure the `UID` row is selected by clicking in it, then select *Yes* in the *Identity* drop-down list (in the *Columns* panel at the bottom of the design window). The *Seed* and *Increment* will both be set to 1, which is fine. This means that the first record should start at number 1 (*Seed*) and every new record added to the table should have this value incremented by 1 (*Increment*).

Save this table with a name of `tblUsers` and close the Design View.

Finally, we need to assign the relevant permissions for the *IUSR* user on this table. If we do not, the actions we want to perform from the web pages, such as Insert and Update, will fail because we do not have permission to make these changes to this database object.

With *Tables* selected in the left pane, double-click `tblUsers` and then click the *Permissions* button. Put a tick in all four columns (*Select*, *Insert*, *Update,* and *Delete*) for the *IUSR* user, click *OK* and *OK* again.

Now we are ready to create the web pages that will use this database table.

Setting Up the Site

Dreamweaver MX makes web site creation and management a breeze thanks to its ease of use and intuitive site management tools. Once you have created a site, Dreamweaver MX keeps track of everything within it for you. If you move a file from one place to another, any links to the file can be automatically updated, should you wish – a very useful feature, I'm sure you'll agree.

We need to create a site to house our web pages. To do this, we will use the site definition wizard, which has two views, *Basic* and *Advanced* – we'll use the Advanced view here. You can access the Site Definition wizard in one of two ways, either by using the menu option: *Site > New Site*, or by following these steps:

- In the *Files* panel group, click the *Site* panel to bring it to the front if it is not already.

- In the *Sites* drop-down list, select the bottom option – *Edit sites...*

- In the pop-up dialog, click the top right button, *New...* (this step will be skipped if this is the first site you have created on a fresh Dreamweaver MX installation)

- If the *Advanced* tab is not already selected, click it to bring the *Advanced* panel to the front

There are seven screens or windows to go through in this site definition process and they are listed in the categories window on the left of the define sites dialog. In the previous chapter, we looked at only the first three, which are the bare minimum you need to set up a fully functioning Dreamweaver MX web site – here we will go over all seven windows, to show you what their purpose is.

Local Info

The *Local Info* window looks like this:

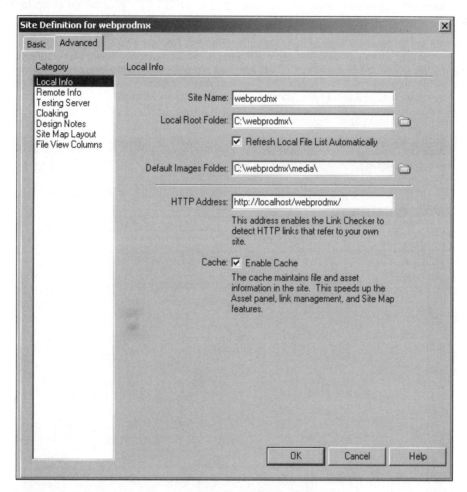

Enter your chosen *Site Name* – we're going to call ours `ProdmxCh8`. Now enter a *Local Root Folder* to store your web content in (we are choosing `C:\inetpub\wwwroot\ProdmxCh8\` – if you haven't created the folder yourself, Dreamweaver MX will create it for you).

Next, choose a location for all your images to be stored in – like the local root folder, either create the folder yourself then use the folder icon to navigate to it, or type in the path you want it to be at, and let Dreamweaver MX create it for you. The images folder is created for ease of site management, plus it should be inside the local root folder, otherwise Dreamweaver MX will give you a warning when you click *OK* or move to another category of the dialog.

Set the HTTP address to *http://localhost/webprodmx/* and make sure the site cache is enabled (that is, the checkbox is checked).

Remote Info

In the *Access* drop-down list, select *Local/Network*. Now click the folder icon next to *Remote Folder* and browse to `C:\Inetpub\wwwroot\ProdmxCh8\`, which is where your server setup for this site will look for the files to serve (for more on setting up web servers, see *Chapter 5*.)

We can leave the other settings at their defaults – *Refresh Remote File List Automatically* is selected, which means that when you view the remote file list in the site window, it will make sure you are seeing the latest version of the remote files. Also, as we are not working in a collaborative environment, we don't need to *Enable File Check In And Check Out* – which is useful for just such environments as it allows you to quickly see who is working on what file.

Your final *Remote Info* panel should look like the following:

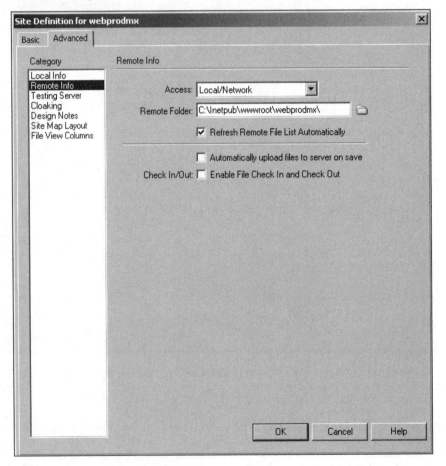

Testing Server

In the *Server Model* drop-down list, select *ASP VBScript*, and in the *Access* drop-down list, select *Local/Network*. Your testing server folder should be set to *C:\Inetpub\wwwroot\ProdmxCh8*, which is where your web server will look for the files to serve for this site. Your URL prefix should be set to *http://localhost/webprodmx/*.

Your final Testing Server panel should look like this:

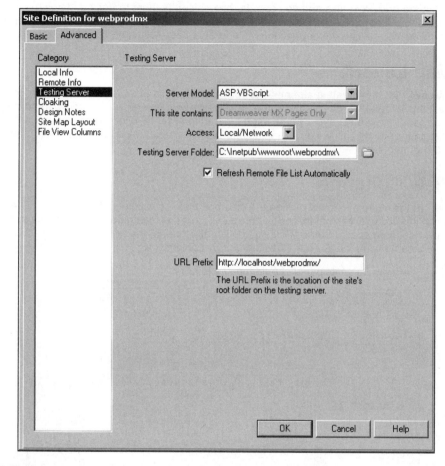

Cloaking

We can leave this at its default setting – *Cloaking* is enabled by default. Cloaking is a means of hiding files and folders within your site from operations such as GET, PUT, Check In, and Check Out. Cloaked files will also be excluded from operations such as report generation. The only way to override cloaking on cloaked files and folders, besides turning off cloaking, is to specifically select cloaked files or folders and perform the intended operation. We don't really need to have cloaking enabled on this basic site, but we can leave it enabled anyway because it doesn't do us any harm.

Design Notes

I personally don't use design notes but Dreamweaver MX does, so we will leave this option selected.

Whether you use them or not, they will be created and used by the application in certain circumstances – some third-party extensions require that design notes are turned on in order for them to function correctly. In instances such as these, the design notes will store information that a particular extension requires, such as variable values or interface settings. They are very small files and will not get in the way of anything so just leave them alone.

They are stored in a folder called `_notes` and are there for you to use in almost any way you see fit. Notes files are basic text files and you can, for example, use them to track updates of pages, or leave reminders for future reference about particular parts of a page. As a naming example, if your page is called `index.asp` the design notes file for that page would be called `index.asp.mno`.

Site Map Layout

Dreamweaver MX can create a site map for you and to do this, it needs to know where to start. You provide it this information by specifying the home page of your web site. If you want to create a site map, you need to already have a home page created in order to select it – as we are yet to create a page, we cannot do this. However, we will come back to this after we have built all our pages, and define a site map then.

File View Columns

Here we get the chance to show or hide the columns that are visible in the site window. As we will not be making use of notes or file `Check In` / `Check Out`, we can hide these columns to give the other columns more space. Select *Notes* in the list of columns, then deselect the checkbox below. Now do the same thing, but for the *Checked Out By* column.

Your final *File View Columns* panel should look as follows:

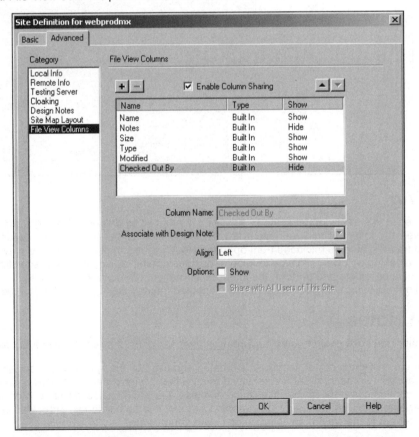

Click *OK* at the bottom of the *Site Definition* dialog to save the definition. Now click *Done* in the *Edit Sites* dialog, and our site is complete and ready to use!

All we have to do now before we can start building up our web pages is connect to our database – this has been covered in detail in *Chapter 6* (in the section headed *Making the Connection*), so please refer there for full details if you are unsure how to complete this step.

Now we've got our database connection sorted out, it's time to build some web pages for our site!

Home Page

This will be the page that holds it all together for us, providing navigation links to all the other pages in our basic web site. Obviously, because we have yet to build the other pages, most of the links won't currently work, but we'll build the overall page now, then complete each of the other pages in turn.

The page content will consist of a simple table with text in the cells – we will be making the text into links as we progress through the chapter. We will also create a simple stylesheet that can be used on all the pages we create. Let's do this first.

Styling Pages with a Cascading Style Sheet

Click *CSS Styles* and then click the *New CSS Style* button. (CSS has been covered in great detail in *Chapter 3*. If you are not familiar with the CSS palette and its options, please refer back to there.)

Let's define the first style of our new stylesheet now – click the *New CSS Style* button, call it `.maintext`, and define it in an external stylesheet called `ProdmxCh8.css`. Save this file in an appropriate place, such as in a `CSS` folder in the root of your site's root folder. Now finish defining the style – in the *CSS Style Definition* dialog box, set the font to *Verdana*, the size to *10px*, and the color to black. Click *OK*, and you will see that `maintext` is listed in the CSS palette.

While we are at it, we will create two more styles to make use of in our pages:

- First, define an `H1` style – set the font to *Verdana*, the size to *14px*, and the color to Black. Give it a weight of *Bold* from the *Weight* drop-down list

- Also, define a style called `.redtext` – set the font to *Verdana*, the size to *10px*, and the color to red

Make sure that all pages we create in our chapter from now on are linked to the `ProdmxCh8.css` stylesheet in this way.

Along with links to the other pages in the site, we'll be adding some other visual elements – for example, after we have created the login page, which will enable us to actually log in to the site, we will display a headline on this home page telling us that we are logged in. You get the idea, I'm sure.

Creating Our Home Page

To start, create a new ASP / VBScript dynamic web page, and make it XHTML-compliant (check the *Make Document XHTML Compliant* checkbox before you click *Create*). Save this file inside the root folder of your site as `index.asp`.

Add a table with six rows, two columns, and a width of 450 pixels. Center the table by setting *Align* to *Center* in the *Property Inspector* window for the table. Select the entire table and click *maintext* in the CSS panel to apply that style to the table.

The following screenshot shows the text to add to this table layout:

Home page	You are currently logged in as:
	Your access level is:
Register	
Login	Logout
Edit account	
Remove users	

The Home page text has had the *h1* style applied to it to clearly define it as a heading.

Let's deal with the simple links first:

- *Register* needs to be turned into a link that points to `UserReg.asp`

- *Login* needs to be turned into a link that points to `Login.asp`

- *Edit* account needs to be turned into a link that points to `EditAccount.asp`

- *Remove Users* needs to be turned into a link and pointed at `RemoveUsers.asp`

We now need to add some data bindings to this page to enable us to display what the user is currently logged in as and what their access level is. These will be taken from session variables that get created once the user has logged in. You will learn more about these session variables later in this chapter when you tackle the user login page.

We need to add two session variables to the page (we can only add one at a time). To add one, select *Bindings > + > Session Variable*, then we type `MM_Username` in the *Name* field and *OK* out of the dialog – it should have appeared in the *Bindings* panel. Repeat the process to bind a session variable called `MM_UserAuthorization` to the page.

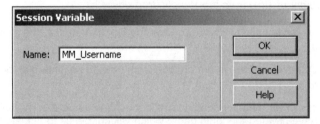

Now we can insert these session variables onto our page at the relevant points. Put the cursor at the end of the line with the text "*You are currently logged in as:*", add a space, and then drag and drop `MM_Username` onto the end of the line. Repeat these steps to add `MM_UserAuthorization` to the end of the text "*Your access level is:*".

To make the word *Logout* actually log the user out, select it, then select *Server Behaviors > + > User Authentication > Log Out User*. All you need to do is tell it which page to go to when the user logs out. For our example we are simply going to direct the browser to the same page, so type `index.asp` in there, or browse to this file using the browse button, then *OK* out of the dialog.

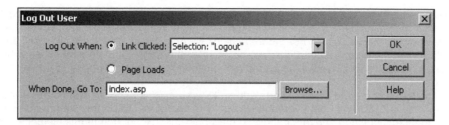

You could select any page to go to after the user logs out, but in our case it makes sense to stay on this page – where else could we go? You could also make this behavior run immediately when the page loads by selecting the other radio button seen above in the dialog. You might want to do this in circumstances where, say, you want to ensure that the last user is logged out (that is, the session is cleared) before a new user uses the page, and has access to that other user's details.

On this page we have a *Login* link, and a *Logout* link. It would be a nice touch to only show the *Login* link when the user is not logged in and only show the *Logout* link when they are. To do this we need to add some simple code around each link to check the contents of the `MM_Username` session variable. The code is only slightly different in each case but make sure you get it the right way around or it won't work!

Select split view and, in the design part of the view, select the *Login* link text. Immediately before the now highlighted *Login* text, type the following code:

```
<% IF Session("MM_Username") = "" THEN %>
```

Immediately after the *Login* link, type the following code:

```
<% ELSE %> <% END IF %>
```

The final code will look like this:

```
<td><% IF Session("MM_Username") = "" THEN %><a href="Login.asp">Log in</a><% ELSE
%> <% END IF %></td>
```

Follow the same steps for the *Logout* link – add the following code before it:

```
<% IF Session("MM_Username") <> "" THEN %>
```

Add the following code after it:

```
<% ELSE %> <% END IF %>
```

The final code will look like this:

```
<td><% IF Session("MM_Username") <> "" THEN %><a href="<%= MM_Logout
%>">Logout</a><% ELSE %> <% END IF %></td>
```

What we've done here is test the value of the session variable MM_Username. For the *Login* link, we test to see if the value of MM_Username is equal to nothing. If it is, we know the user isn't logged in so we can display the *Login* link. For the *Logout* link we just test MM_Username to see if contains a value. If is does, the user is logged in so we can display the *Logout* link. In both cases, where the test fails a non-breaking space will be added to the cell to make sure the table cell doesn't collapse!

Now we just need one more piece of code adding to wrap up this page for the moment. We need to hide the *Remove users* link from everyone except Administrators. To do this we are going to replicate the steps outlined above for showing the *Login* link, except that in this instance, the first line is changed to use the MM_UserAuthorization session variable – it needs to test for an exact value, "Administrator". Add the following code before the *Remove users* link text:

```
<% IF Session("MM_UserAuthorization") = "Administrator" THEN %>
```

We only want administrators to see this link and this code will make sure that happens. Now add the following code after the *Remove users* text to finish.

```
<% ELSE %> <% END IF %>
```

That's it. If the value of the MM_UserAuthorization session variable is *Administrator*, this link will be visible on the page; otherwise, a non-breaking space is added to the table.

Once you have completed the other pages in this chapter and made all the links on this page work, which we will return to after building each of the other pages, this finished page will look like this when you first browse it:

After you have registered and logged in (which you will be able to after you have completed the sections that follow), providing that you give yourself an access level of *Administrator* (try it – go into the database and change your details manually) you will see this page a little differently, as shown in the next screenshot.

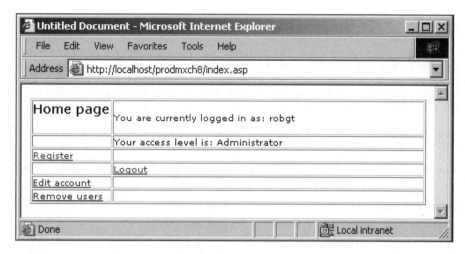

If you leave the Access Level at the default of `SiteUser` then log in, your page will reflect this, and the *Remove Users* link would not be visible.

We have quickly created a simple home page that can link all of our other pages together and make it feel more like a small web site. In displaying the session variables on the page we have covered the creation of data bindings other than those that talk to the database, and we have also covered the *Log Out User* server behavior.

Now we'll move on to building the other pages in our basic dynamic web site, starting with the user registration page, in which we'll experience usage of the *Log In User* server behavior.

User Registration Page

These days, user registration pages are very common on the Internet – many sites require you to register with them so that you can gain access to members-only content, and they can send you updates, and offers, etc.

Our user registration page is going to require users to fill in the bare minimum of information to set up the user account (it's a usability nightmare to require users to fill out pages and pages of forms, and will often lead to them going somewhere else to get what they want). It will offer the user the option of entering further details about themselves, but these details will be optional. These optional details can have their uses – for example, if we were building an online store, we might require our users to register with the site in order to use it. If the user then makes a purchase, we are going to need their full details so that we can fulfill their order. If they supply these details at registration time, they won't have to be bothered with supplying them later, making for a smoother shopping experience.

Let's get started – create a new ASP / VBScript dynamic web page, and make it XHTML-compliant. Save this file inside the root folder of your site, as `UserReg.asp`.

Adding User Registration Functionality

On our `UserReg.asp` page, first add a blank form – don't worry about the attribute values yet, when we have finished with this page they will have been filled in for us by Dreamweaver MX. Now add a table to the document inside the form, with 20 rows, 2 columns, and a width of 300px. Center the table by setting *Align* to *Center* in the *Property Inspector* window for the table. Select the entire table and click *maintext* in the CSS panel to apply that style to the table.

Now drag the cursor over the two top cells of the table to highlight just those two cells – press the *M* key to merge them together. Do the same to the cells of row five as well.

Type a heading of *User registration* into the top row of the table, and apply the *h1* style to it. Leave the next row empty – we'll just use it for spacing out our form.

The following screenshot shows how you need to fill the table in:

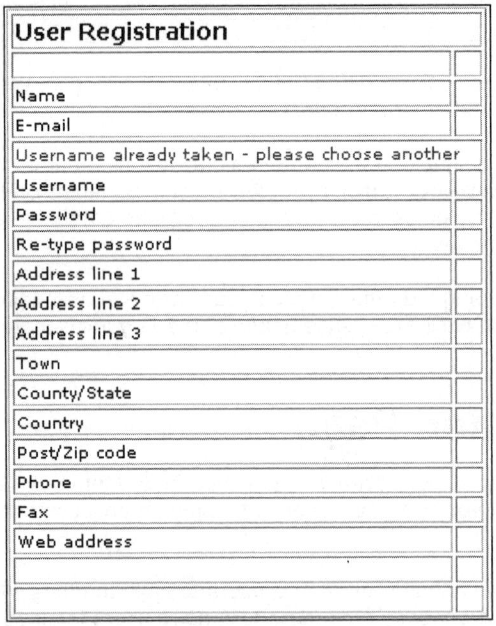

Assign the `.redtext` CSS style to the "*Username already taken, please choose another*" text.

Next, you need to insert textfields in the cells of the right-hand column, and give them *Name* and *Max Char* values as follows:

Row	Textfield name	Max chars value
3	UName	50
4	UEmail	255
6	UUsername	50
7	UPassword	50

Row	Textfield name	Max chars value
8	UPassword2	50
9	UAddress1	100
10	UAddress2	100
11	UAddress3	100
12	UTown	50
13	UCounty	50
14	UCountry	100
15	UPostcode	20
16	UPhone	20
17	UFax	20
18	UWebAddress	255

The `UPassword` and `UPassword2` textfields should be `Password` type textfields. This will replace anything the user types with asterisks and is the primary reason for having a second password box – to make sure they typed what they thought they were typing without any errors. You make a textfield a `Password` type by selecting the *Password* radio button in the property inspector for the textfield.

We will leave the 19th row empty for spacing purposes. In column 2 of the 20th row, insert a *Submit* button.

Sending Registration Details to the Database

For our user registration page to be of any use, it needs to insert the details that are entered into the database. We will use the *Insert Record* server behavior to do this, the usage of which has been seen already in *Chapter 7*.

Go to *Application > Server Behaviors > + > Insert Record*. In the dialog box that appears, select your connection (*ProdmxCh8*) in the *Connection* drop-down list, and make sure `tblUsers` is selected in the *Insert Into Table* drop-down list. In the *After Inserting, Go To* field type `login.asp` – we will be creating this page next. Next, check that your form is already selected in the *Get Values From* list.

Now you need to bind the form elements to the relevant database columns so the right content is entered into the right column. If you have followed the naming convention that has been used in this chapter, these bindings will already have been made for you. If not, use the following table as a guide. To manually bind a database column to a form element, select the form element you want to bind to, then select the database column from the *Bindings* window that corresponds to it and click the *Bind* button at the bottom of the *Bindings* window.

Form Element	Database Column	Submit As
Uname	UName	Text
Uemail	UEmail	Text
Uusername	UUsername	Text
Upassword	UPassword	Text
UPassword2	<ignore>	
UAddress1	UAddress1	Text
UAddress2	UAddress2	Text
UAddress3	UAddress3	Text
Utown	UTown	Text
Ucounty	UCounty	Text
Ucountry	UCountry	Text
Upostcode	UPostcode	Text
Uphone	UPhone	Text
Ufax	UFax	Text
UwebAddress	UWebAddress	Text

UPassword2 is ignored because we are only using this to ensure that the user typed their password correctly. We will use a validation technique to make sure that these two password fields match each other, before allowing the *Insert* to take place. We will do this as follows:

Validating the User Password

Jaro von Flocken (a fairly well renowned extension developer) has created what is regarded as the best form validation extension available for Dreamweaver MX – **Check Form**. It is a highly functional behavior that allows you to validate the data entered in your forms, be that a number within a range, an e-mail address, a specifically formatted date or time, etc. It goes way beyond the capabilities of the standard form validation, which is why I recommend you use it. It is available for download at *http://www.macromedia.com/software/dreamweaver/special/extensions*, or on Jaro's own web site at *http://www.yaromat.com*. You need to install this extension to add the validation to your page.

Installing the Extension

Installing extensions is really straightforward thanks to the Extension Manager application that looks after this side of things for all your installed Macromedia applications, such as Dreamweaver MX, Flash MX, and Fireworks MX.

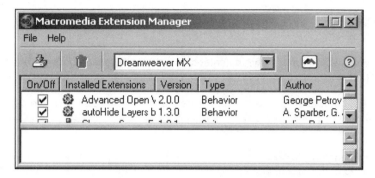

This great little tool, which installs by default when you install Dreamweaver, enables you to quickly install or uninstall extensions in any of the Macromedia applications on your computer that support the .mxp (Macromedia eXtension Package) type of extension. The drop-down list in the middle lists those that it can find and changing this selection will change the panels beneath it to reflect the extensions that you have installed into the other applications. The extension manager itself can be downloaded at *http://www.macromedia.com/exchange/*.

After you have downloaded the extension you can install it in one of two ways – either locate the file on your computer and double-click it to launch the Extension Manager and begin the installation process, or launch the Extension manager application first then click the *Install New Extension* button at the top left of the application, then locate the extension to begin the installation process.

The top panel shows all the extensions installed for the selected application and the bottom panel can display information about the extension selecting in the top panel, if any information exists – usually it does and might be a short introduction to the extension such as what it does, how to use it, and where to locate it in the application interface.

You can remove extensions from Dreamweaver MX without uninstalling them if you need to. This is achieved by un-ticking the tick box in the On/Off column. You might want to do this if you install a lot of extensions and things start to slow down for you. This action simply tells Dreamweaver MX not to load the extension when it starts up. To re-enable disabled extensions, just tick the box again.

On With the Show

With the *Check Form* extension installed, place your cursor anywhere inside your form. Now, in the tag selector, click on the <form#form1> element, which will highlight everything contained within your form on the page.

Go to the *Design* panel and select *Behaviors > + > Yaromat > Check Form*. Now we need to set this form validation behavior to check our form and specify what the acceptable values are. Firstly, when we created our database table that this form inserts into, we specified that Name, Email, Username, and Password were all required fields – therefore, you need to select these fields in turn from the listbox at the top, and check the *Required (empty values not allowed)* checkbox. In addition:

- For *UName*, leave the radio button on *Anything*. You can leave the error message a user will see at the default if you want but you can also type your own – we chose "*Please enter your name*"

- For *UEmail*, select the *E-mail Adress* (sic) radio button, and type "*Please enter your e-mail address*" as the error message

- For *UUsername*, leave *Anything* selected and type "*Please choose a username*" as the error message

- For *UPassword*, leave *Anything* selected and type "*Please choose a password*" as the error message

- For *UPassword2*, select *Text must be the same* and choose *UPassword* from the corresponding fields list. Type "*The password fields do not match - enter them again*" as the error message

That's it! Now, when you click *OK* the behavior is applied to your page and listed in the *Behaviors* panel. It is applied to the `onSubmit` event, which is fine because we want to check that the contents of this form are valid when it is submitted.

Avoiding Duplicate Usernames

We can't allow more than one user to have the same username so we need to check that the username they have chosen is unique before we go ahead and allow the record to be inserted. Luckily for us, Dreamweaver MX includes a server behavior to check this for us. To apply this Server Behavior to our page, select it from *Server Behaviors > + > User Authentication > Check New Username*. The resulting dialog box looks like this:

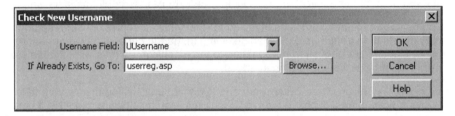

It's a very simple dialog to complete, as seen above – select the form element that contains the possible duplicate username (in our case it's `UUsername`) and then choose the redirect page to go to if it is a duplicate and the user has to try again. Set the *If Already Exists, Go To* field to `UserReg.asp`.

What we're going to do is grab the parameter that is passed to the redirect page through the querystring and display some text on the page to indicate to our user that their username selection was already taken. This parameter is called `requsername` and is created for us by Dreamweaver MX when we use this server behavior. The text to display has already been added to the page on row five of the table. We will have to do some hand-coding at this point, but don't panic! It's quite easy to do.

First, switch to split view so you can see the page in design mode and also the code. Now highlight the row that contains the red text "*Username already taken, please choose another.*" In the tag selector at the bottom of the page, you should be able to click the `<tr>` tag to the left of the highlighted `<td.redtext>` tag to select all the code of the table row. (Unfortunately this doesn't always happen and you may need to click in the Code View on this highlighted line of code and then click the `<tr>` tag to get the desired result. If this fails, you can manually highlight the code using the cursor in the Code View.) This highlighting is for illustrative purposes only in this instance just to show you which section of code you will be working with.

The result is the following lines of code being highlighted in the Code View part of the split view:

```
<tr>
  <td colspan="2" class="redtext">
    Username already taken, please choose another.
  </td>
</tr>
```

We are going to surround this section with some server-side code. This server-side code will determine whether or not to show this entire table row based on the content of the requsername parameter. Now we need to insert:

```
<% IF Request ("requsername") <> "" THEN %>
```

before the code we just highlighted, and:

```
<% END IF %>
```

after the code we just highlighted. What this is doing is checking the parameter called requsername to see if it contains a value. If it does, this table row will be displayed; if it doesn't, it will not be displayed. It will only contain a value if the user has entered a username that already exists in the database.

Your final code segment should look like this:

```
<% IF Request ("requsername") <> "" THEN %>
<tr>
  <td colspan="2" class="redtext">
    Username already taken, please choose another.
  </td>
</tr>
<% END IF %>
```

Persisting Already Entered Data in the Form

One further thing we should do is to think about the usability of this form. If the user enters a username that is already taken, we only really want them to have to re-enter a new username to try and complete the registration process and not all of the other information as well. Wouldn't you get a bit annoyed if each time you tried to register on a web site it asked you to re-enter ALL the information again rather than just entering a new username to try? I would!

Getting around this involves a little bit more coding but again, it is quite simple. You just need to be very careful of the syntax. Let's do it now.

Double-click our *Check New Username* server behavior to open up the dialog box. In the *If Already Exists, Go To* field, you should currently have UserReg.asp entered – we're going to append a rather complex querystring to the end of this, to persist the already entered data in the form when the user has to enter another username.

Replace `UserReg.asp` with the following string:

```
userreg.asp?UName=" & Request("UName") & "&UEmail=" & Request("UEmail") &
"&UPassword=" & Request("UPassword") & "&UPassword2=" & Request("UPassword2") &
"&UAddress1=" & Request("UAddress1") & "&UAddress2=" & Request("UAddress2") &
"&UAddress3=" & Request("UAddress3") & "&UTown=" & Request("UTown") & "&UCounty="
& Request("UCounty") & "&UCountry=" & Request("UCountry") & "&UPostcode=" &
Request("UPostcode") & "&UPhone=" & Request("UPhone") & "&UFax=" & Request("UFax")
& "&UWebAddress=" & Request("UWebAddress") & "
```

This code will add whatever the user enters into our form, excluding the username, on to the end of the querystring as URL parameters – we can then automatically fill the form with these values to save the user typing them in again.

To automatically fill the form with these values, we need to add some more server-side code to our page – the *Value* properties of the form elements need to be filled in as follows:

Textfield	Value
UName	<%=Request("UName")%>
UEmail	<%=Request("UEmail")%>
UPassword	<%=Request("UPassword")%>
UPassword2	<%=Request("UPassword2")%>
UAddress1	<%=Request("UAddress1")%>
UAddress2	<%=Request("UAddress2")%>
UAddress3	<%=Request("UAddress3")%>
UTown	<%=Request("UTown")%>
UCounty	<%=Request("UCounty")%>
UCountry	<%=Request("UCountry")%>
UPostcode	<%=Request("UPostcode")%>
UPhone	<%=Request("UPhone")%>
UFax	<%=Request("UFax")%>
UWebAddress	<%=Request("UWebAddress")%>

Make sure you leave the `UUsername` property inspector value blank; this is the field the user will need to fill in again because their first choice was taken, which is why they are seeing the red text.

Your users will thank you for this extra forethought; believe me!

That's it for `UserReg.asp` – now if you look at it in a browser, you should see the following:

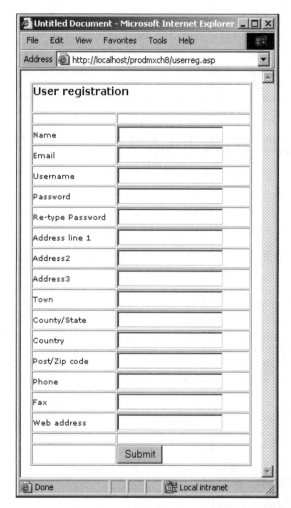

We have made the page only require a bare minimum of information, while at the same time offering the user the opportunity of supplying us with more information. We have also made the page user-friendly by making sure that they only have to enter their information once if they end up having to choose another username.

Now that we've got their details stored in our database, your users are going to need a page that they can use to log in with so that they can see all your wonderful content, which is exactly where we are headed right now!

User Login Page

The login page is quite an easy page to create, as you will soon see. Create a new dynamic ASP VBScript page, make it XHTML-compliant, and save it as Login.asp, in the root of your site. In the CSS panel, click *Attach Style Sheet*, and choose the stylesheet we created earlier to link to Login.asp – your CSS styles should now be listed in the CSS panel.

Now add a form to the page, and add a table inside the form with 8 rows, 2 columns, and a width of `300px`. Center the table by selecting *Align: Center* in the property inspector for the table. Select the entire table and click *maintext* in the CSS panel to apply that style to the table.

Next, highlight the top two cells of the table, and press *M* to merge them together – do the same for the cells of row three. In the top row, which now spans both columns of the rest of the table, type a heading of *User login*, and apply our *h1* style to it. Leave the next row empty; we'll just use it for spacing out our form.

In the single cell on the third row, type "*Login failed, please retry*", and assign the *redtext* style to it. Now insert the following headings into rows 4,5, and 6:

Row	Column	Heading
4	1	Username
5	1	Password
6	1	Remember me

Next, add the form elements next to the corresponding headings and set the names of each in the property inspector, as shown in the following table.

Row	Column	Type	Name	Value
4	2	Text field	Username	
5	2	Text field	Password	
6	2	Checkbox	RememberMe	remember
8	1	Hidden Field	Login	`true`
8	2	Button		

Set the checkbox *Initial State* to *Checked*, and leave the seventh row empty for spacing purposes. Now we need to apply the *Log In User* server behavior to this form, which is located in *Server Behaviors > + > User Authentication > Log In User*.

In the *Log In User* dialog box that appears, set all the elements as follows:

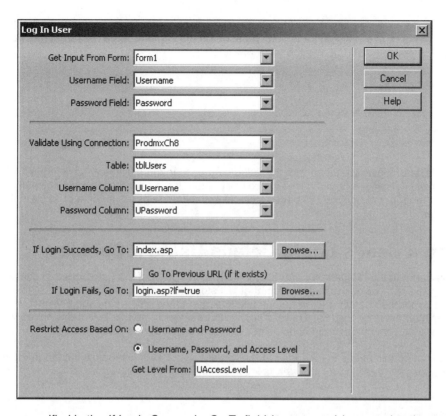

The page specified in the *If Login Succeeds, Go To* field (`index.asp`) is created at the start of this chapter. This should be your site's home page.

One thing that is out of the ordinary here is the *If Login Fails, Go To* value. We have set this to `login.asp?lf=true`, which will come back to this page and pass a parameter called `lf` with a value of `true` – the purpose of this will come clear below.

We are now going to check for the value of `lf` on our login page – if it is `true`, we will display the table row that contains the *login failed* text. Switch to split view so you can see the page in design mode and also the code.

Now select the row that contains the red text *Login failed, please retry*. In the tag selector, at the bottom of the page, you should be able click the `<tr>` tag to the left of the highlighted `<td.redtext>` tag to select the following code:

```
<tr>
  <td colspan="2" class="redtext"> Login failed, please retry.</td>
</tr>
```

Again, you may need to manually select the code from the Code View again to get the `<tr></tr>` tags highlighted as well – at least you can use the Design View to easily find the code we are interested in.

As before, we are going to surround this table row with some server-side code, which will determine whether or not to show this entire table row based on the content of the `lf` parameter we passed earlier. The code to insert before the table row is:

```
<% IF Request("lf") = "true" THEN %>
```

and the code to insert after the table row is:

```
<% END IF %>
```

This code determines whether or not the value contained in the parameter `lf` is equal to `"true"` – if it is the row is displayed, and if it isn't the row is hidden. If the user fails to login correctly for whatever reason, the `Login.asp` page redirects to itself and passes a value of `true` in the `lf` parameter.

Storing a User's Login Details Using a Cookie

Now we can add the "*Remember Me*" functionality to the page. If the user ticks this checkbox we need to write two cookies to their system that will store their login details so that the next time they visit this page, their details can be automatically added to the *Username* and *Password* fields to save them typing them in every time. There is no server behavior to do this in Dreamweaver MX as yet, so we need to do some more hand coding I'm afraid. Let's look at how to do this now.

The code to do this needs to be added at the top of `Login.asp`, just below the language declaration (`<%@LANGUAGE="VBSCRIPT" CODEPAGE="1252"%>`), and is as follows:

```
<%
IF Request("Login") <> "" THEN
  IF Request.Form("RememberMe") = "remember" THEN
    Response.Cookies("ckUsername") = Request.Form("Username")
    Response.Cookies("ckUsername").Expires = Date + 30
    Response.Cookies("ckPassword") = Request.Form("Password")
    Response.Cookies("ckPassword").Expires = Date + 30
  ELSE
    Response.Cookies("ckUsername") = ""
    Response.Cookies("ckUsername").Expires = Date - 1
    Response.Cookies("ckPassword") = ""
    Response.Cookies("ckPassword").Expires = Date - 1
  END IF
END IF
%>
```

This code says "if the value of `Login` exists then check the value of the `RememberMe` form element. If it equals `remember`, write two cookies that contain the `Username` and `Password` respectively, and set each of these cookies to expire 30 days from now. If it doesn't equal `remember`, then remove the cookies so the user will not be remembered any more. If the value of `Login` does not exist then skip all of this and move on." The value of `Login` can only exist after the form has been submitted. For more details on cookies, see *Chapter 5*.

Every time a user logs in, the cookies on their machine will be overwritten with up-to-date information so the user will always be remembered providing they have logged in inside the last 30 days.

To finish the *Remember Me* functionality we need to retrieve the information stored in the cookies and populate the form elements with it, if it exists:

- Select the *Username* textfield and in the *Init Val* field in the Property Inspector type:
  `<%=Request.Cookies("ckUsername")%>`

- Select the *Password* textfield and in the *Init Val* field in the Property Inspector, type:
  `<%=Request.Cookies("ckPassword")%>`

The `Request` items are actually data bindings and therefore you can set them up in your data bindings palette and then use the point-and-click features of Dreamweaver MX to bind these to the textfields on the page.

To do it this way, click *Bindings > + > Request Variable*. Select *Request.Cookie* from the dialog drop-down list, type the name of the cookie in the *Name* box, and *OK* out of the dialog.

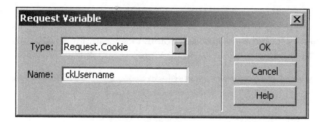

This will add a *Request* node to your bindings palette under which should be listed the *Cookies.ckUsername* cookie. You can obviously add as many items as you need ready for use on your web page – in this case, another one for the `Password` cookie might be useful.

To bind a cookie to a form element, select the element you are interested in, *Username*, then select *Cookies.ckUsername* in the bindings palette and click the *Bind* button at the foot of the bindings palette.

That's it! Your login page is now complete. If you view `Login.asp` in a browser, it should look like this:

Feel free to test it – if you log in with the *Remember Me* checkbox ticked, the next time you go to log in, your details will already be shown in the form. If you deselect the checkbox, you will have to re-enter them.

Here we have taken a basic login page and added a couple of extra frills on top to make it more user-friendly. The page is set up to check the specified database table columns for the correct login information and if a match is found, the user is granted access to the web site and is redirected to the first page you want them to view after login. Their access level is stored in a session variable called MM_UserAuthorization, which we will be using later on, in the Administration page.

A useful extra benefit that comes with using the *Log In User* server behavior is the creation of a session variable called MM_Username that holds the username of the logged-in user. We will see just why this is so useful to us in the next section.

A Note on Session Variables

If you want to create your own session variables based on data stored in the user's record in the database, you can add them into the *Log In User* code yourself. There are two things you would need to add – the first is to add the database column name into the SQL that the behavior selects, and the second is the line to create the session variable and assign it a value.

For example, to create an extra session variable to store the UserID, you would need to locate the following line of code in the *Log In User* Server Behavior:

```
MM_rsUser.Source = "SELECT UUsername, UPassword"
```

Then you can add your column name on to the end of this line:

```
MM_rsUser.Source = "SELECT UUsername, UPassword, UID"
```

Now, to create the session variable you need to find:

```
Session("MM_Username") = MM_valUsername
```

and insert the following new line directly below this to create your session variable:

```
Session("svUserID") = MM_rsUser.Fields.Item("UID").Value
```

That's all there is to it. From now on, if you need to use the UserID for anything on your site, you can refer to the session variable (I called it svUserID).

Open up the home page again; add a link to this page from the Login text and save the page again.

Now we shall move on again, and create a page to allow users to edit their account information!

Edit My Account Page

Now we are going to create a page that allows our users to change all of their registration details, with one exception. They will not be able to change their username, as that needs to be unique in the database and would make this page very complex if it were to be included.

Create a new XHTML-compliant dynamic ASP VBScript page, and save it as `Editaccount.asp` in our site's root folder. Link our cascading style sheet to this page, as we did with previous pages.

Now, add a form to the page, and insert a table inside the form, with 17 rows, 2 columns, and a width of 300px. As with the previous pages, center the table in the page, and apply the *maintext* style to the table.

Next, merge the top two cells of the table together – enter a heading of *Edit account* into this merged cell, and apply our *h1* style to it. To save time, the following screenshot shows what else should be added to the table:

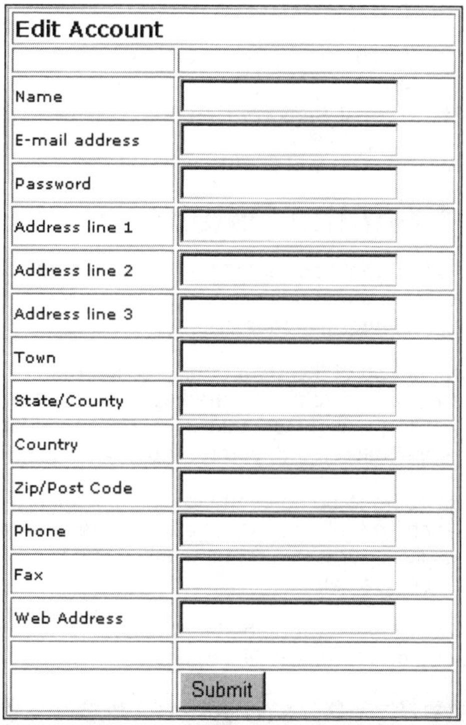

Edit Account	
Name	
E-mail address	
Password	
Address line 1	
Address line 2	
Address line 3	
Town	
State/County	
Country	
Zip/Post Code	
Phone	
Fax	
Web Address	
	Submit

The textfields seen above need to be named as follows, so they will display the right details for editing:

Row	Textfield name
3	UName
4	UEmail
5	UPassword
6	UAddress1
7	UAddress2
8	UAddress3
9	UTown

Table continued on following page

281

Row	Textfield name
10	UCounty
11	UCountry
12	UPostcode
13	UPhone
14	UFax
15	UWebAddress

Give the `Password` textfield a *Type* of *Password*, so that it will be hidden from prying eyes while the user is changing it.

Getting the Data from the Database

To make this page display the correct user data for our users to edit, we need to create a recordset that grabs the data from the database and filters it to a single record. This page might cause us all kinds of problems if the incorrect information is displayed.

As was briefly mentioned at the end of the *User Login* section of this chapter, when you use the *Log In User* server behavior a session variable is created upon successful login. This session variable is called `MM_Username` and, not surprisingly, contains the user's username. To be perfectly sure that your recordset only contains a single record, you must apply a filter to it that uses a unique value.

The reason `MM_Username` is going to be so useful to us is because we have set up our user registration page to check each and every username to ensure there are no two the same in the database – when a user logs in to our web site, their username is stored in the `MM_Username` session variable, giving us a unique value!

Let's get to it – launch the *Recordset (Query)* builder (as seen in *Chapter 7*) and we can begin building our recordset. Fill out the *Recordset* dialog box as follows:

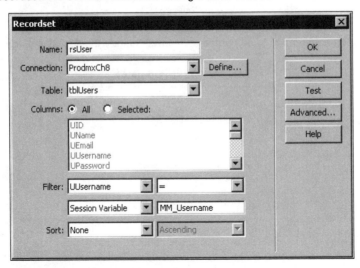

It is quite easy to follow what is happening here. We are creating a recordset called `rsUser`, which uses the `ProdmxCh8` connection to the database. We want to retrieve the values from all the fields of the `tblUsers` table to enable us to bind them to their corresponding form elements on our page. We are specifying a filter that says the value in the `UUsername` column of the database must match the value held in the `MM_Username` session variable. We do not require a sort order, as there should only be a single record that matches the criteria. *OK* out of the *Recordset* dialog.

Writing Our Data To the Form

Now we have built our recordset, we need to bind the data held in it to the form elements on our page, so the user can view their current details. Click the *Bindings* tab in the *Application* panel and expand your recordset so all the columns become visible.

Let's do this the easy way – to bind our recordset to our form, drag and drop each column in the recordset onto its relevant form element – the following table shows which recordset column needs to be bound to each form textfield (the values in the right-hand column are the headings associated with each textfield):

Recordset column	Form field to bind it to
UName	Name
UEmail	E-mail address
UPassword	Password
UAddress1	Address line 1
UAddress2	Address line 2
UAddress3	Address line 3
UTown	Town
UCounty	State/County
UCountry	Country
UPostcode	Zip/Post code
UPhone	Phone
UFax	Fax
UWebAddress	Web Address

The form fields turn blue as they are bound to the recordset columns and they display a dynamic data placeholder within them.

The placeholder displayed depends on the preference that you set. By default you will see {}, but you can change this to show the name of the recordset field inside the curly braces if you prefer. You change this by going to Edit > Preferences > Invisible Elements, *then changing the value selected in the drop-down list next to the "Show Dynamic Text As" heading.*

The final binding we need add to this page is the username – we will bind that directly to the page so it is not going to be editable by the user, but they can easily see that it is their record they are editing.

Click the `UUsername` recordset column and drag it onto the page to the right of the *Edit account* heading. Next, we need to add an *Update Record* server behavior so that any changes the user makes are recorded in the database – select *Server Behaviors > + > Update Record*. You should then fill out the dialog box that appears as follows:

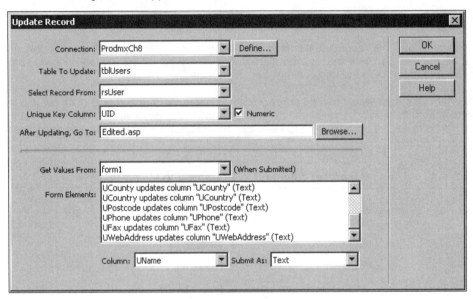

Make sure that the bindings in the *Form Elements* point to the right columns (the form element and column values should be the same in each case, and should be submitted as text). Click *OK* to close the *Update Record* dialog box, and apply the behavior.

Adding Validation To the Edit Page

All that remains to add to this page is the *Check Form* validation, just like we did for the registration page.

We need to do this to ensure that our users cannot remove any data that is required by our database – their name, username, password, and e-mail address. Using this form, they have the ability to change their name, password, and e-mail address and we need to ensure that any changes they make to these three elements are valid.

Select the entire form by clicking on the page somewhere, then clicking the `<form#form1>` tag in the tag selector. Now select *Design > Behaviors > + Yaromat > Check Form*. Set the following in this dialog box:

- With `UName` selected, tick the *Required* checkbox, leave the *Anything* radio button selected, and type "*Please enter your username*" as the error message

- With `UEmail` selected, tick the *Required* checkbox, select the *E-mail Address* radio button, and type "*Please enter your e-mail address*" as the error message

- With `UPassword` selected, tick the *Required* checkbox, leave the *Anything* radio button selected, and type "*Please enter your password*" as the error message

That's us finished – click *OK* to apply the form validation behavior and close the dialog. That completes the creation of the edit account page. To test this page in a browser you will need to log in first, which you can do from the index page of this site. Once you have logged in, the index page displays a link to the *Edit account* page, which should look like this:

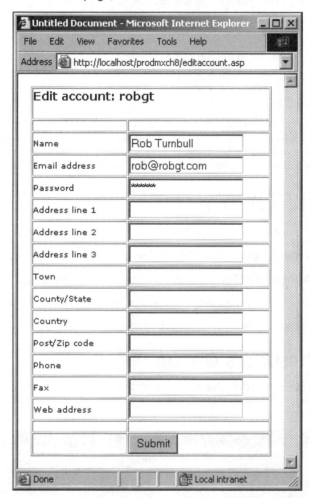

This page performs some complex actions but was created quickly and easily because of the flexibility afforded to us by Dreamweaver MX. We have allowed the user access to their account information so that they may change anything that is incorrect in their record. In doing so, however, we removed the ability for the user to change their username simply because we need to ensure that each user's username is unique in our database.

Another of Dreamweaver MX's built-in objects that we could have used to give us a head start in building this page is the *Record Update Form* Application Object. Please refer to *Chapter 7* for details of how to use this object.

Open up the home page again; add a link to this page from the *Edit account* text and save the page again.

The final part of this chapter follows: a site administration page!

Administration Page

To round off this chapter, we are going to create a page that gives a site administrator the power to remove any or all of his users – this page will require the following items:

- A list of all our users

- A way of selecting one or more users to delete

- A button to delete the selected users

- A message to display to those people who stumble across this page accidentally

Let's get to it – create a new XHTML-compliant dynamic ASP VBScript page, and save it in your site's root folder as RemoveUsers.asp. Link our cascading style sheet to the page as before. Add a blank form to the page, and add a table into it, with 5 rows, 3 columns, and width 500px. Center the table as before, and apply the *maintext* style to it. The table needs to be filled in as follows:

- Merge the top three cells of the table, and enter a heading of *Remove Users* into this new cell – apply the *h1* style to it

- Leave row 2 empty; we'll just use it for spacing out our form

- In row 3, column 1, insert a checkbox and name it UserID

- Leave row 4 empty; we'll just use it for spacing out our form

- In row 5, column 1, insert a hidden field with a name of Submitted and a value of True

- In row 5, column 2, insert a submit button and give it a label of *Remove Selected Users*

Displaying Our Users On the Page

We now need to create a recordset that contains all of our users so we can display them on this page. Launch the *Recordset (Query)* builder in simple mode – fill it in as follows (then click *OK* to create the recordset):

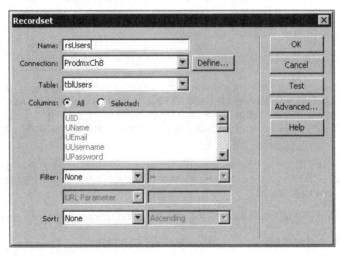

This recordset will simply select all users from our `tblUsers` table, which is exactly what we want. Now we need to bind `UName` and `UUsername` onto the page, and `UID` to the checkbox. To do this, drag and drop `UName` from the *Bindings* tab onto the cell at row 3, column 2, and drag and drop `UUsername` into row 3, column 3. Finally, click the checkbox to select it, then click the `UID` column in the *Bindings* panel and click *Bind*.

Now we need apply a repeat region to the whole of row three in order to show all the user records on the page, rather than just one. To do this, select the whole of this row, and go to *Server Behaviors > + > Repeat Region*.

In this dialog box, the recordset is already selected for us, as there is only one recordset on this page. Click the radio button next to *All Records* to make this repeat region display all the records in the recordset on this page. *OK* out of this dialog box.

In order that we can delete multiple users (or just one!) we need to add a command to the page that will run when the page is submitted – click *Command* on the *Server Behaviors* menu, to bring up the following dialog box:

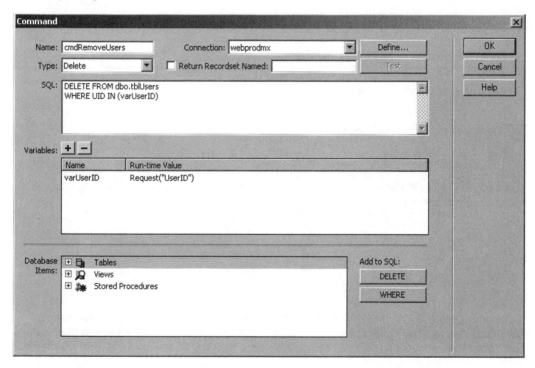

As seen above, call the command `cmdRemoveUsers` and select *Delete* from the *Type* drop-down list. Make sure *ProdmxCh8* is selected as your connection. Next, in the *Database Items* window select the `tblUsers` table and click *DELETE*, then select the `UID` column and click *WHERE*. To finish off our SQL statement, type `IN (varUserID)` after `WHERE UID`.

Lastly, create a new variable by clicking the + button next to *Variables*. For the variable *Name* enter `varUserID`, and for the *Run-time Value* column, type `Request("UserID")`. Click *OK* to apply the command and to close the dialog.

Running the Command

Now we need to add a little code to ensure that the command will only run when this page is submitted. (This page submits to itself, as will any page unless you specify otherwise.)

Click `cmdRemoveUsers` in the *Server Behaviors* panel, and then click the *Show Code View* button to switch from design view to Code View – your command code should be highlighted.

Remember the hidden field we added to our form called `Submitted`, with a value of `True`? Our code snippet is going to check the value of this field, and if it exists and contains the value "True" it will allow the command code to run.

We need to add some code to the command code – just after the opening delimiter, `<%`, add the following code:

```
IF Request("Submitted") <> "" THEN
  IF (Request("UserID") <> "") THEN
```

Just before the closing delimiter, `%>`, add the following code:

```
  END IF
  Response.Redirect("removeusers.asp")
END IF
```

The final code block should look like this:

```
<%
IF Request("Submitted") <> "" THEN
  IF (Request("UserID") <> "") THEN
    set cmdRemoveUsers = Server.CreateObject("ADODB.Command")
    cmdRemoveUsers.ActiveConnection = MM_ProdmxCh8_STRING
    cmdRemoveUsers.CommandText = "DELETE FROM tblUsers  WHERE UID IN (" +
Replace(cmdRemoveUsers__varUserID, "'", "''") + ")"
    cmdRemoveUsers.CommandType = 1
    cmdRemoveUsers.CommandTimeout = 0
    cmdRemoveUsers.Prepared = true
    cmdRemoveUsers.Execute()
  END IF
  Response.Redirect("removeusers.asp")
END IF

%>
```

What this code says is – "If the value of `Submitted` exists and there is a value in the `UserID` parameter then we can run the command. We then set up a redirect to come back to this page again. The reason we redirect back to this page afterwards is so it will display up-to-date information on the page."

One thing you should bear in mind is that in some cases, any extra code you add in to Dreamweaver MX-generated code may be lost if you edit the command or behavior that originally wrote the code. If the changes you make to Dreamweaver MX generated code are sufficient, a red exclamation mark will appear to the left of the behavior name. This doesn't mean that something is wrong, it just means that Dreamweaver thinks the code pattern for a behavior that it created is no longer on the page, but it can still see most of that pattern so it is a little confused.

Restricting Page Access

The final thing to add to this page is the server behavior to restrict access based on the user's access level. When the user logs in, their access level is stored in a session variable called MM_UserAuthorization, which we can now check to make sure they are authorized to access this page. We only want Administrators to access this page – we can do this using the *Restrict Access To Page* Server Behavior.

Select *Server Behaviors > + > User Authentication > Restrict Access To Page* – you should be presented with the following dialog box:

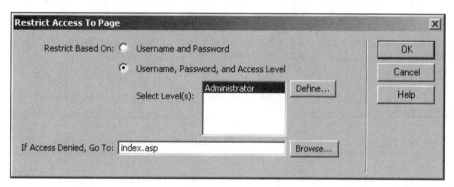

As seen above, select the *Username, Password, and Access Level* radio button. Next, click the *Define...* button to define our access level – in the second dialog box, type *Administrator* in the *Name* field and click *OK*. Back in the *Restrict Access To Page* dialog box, click *Browse...* to select the page to redirect unauthorized users to – we've chosen index.asp. Click *OK*, then *OK* again to apply the server behavior and close the dialog.

Now, when you log in and access this page with an access level of *Administrator*, you will be able to view the page contents. Without this access level, you will be redirected back to the home page. The final RemoveUsers.asp page looks like this:

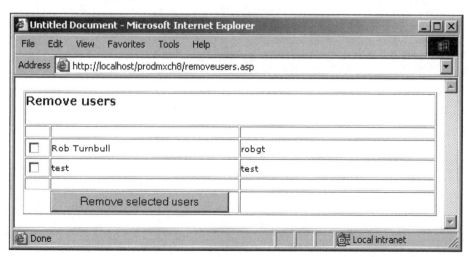

Open up the home page again; add a link to this page from the *Remove users* text and save the page again.

This page is not complex, but it deals with some complex issues that most developers today need to understand when building their web applications. The ability to restrict user access to any particular web page is vital – you don't want just anyone deleting records out of your database!

You might find the need to restrict only certain parts of a page from general access rather than the entire page, as this server behavior also allows you to do. You would need to hand code some of the details, but the component parts are already in place to make it easy for you. All you would need to do is to add a line of code to check that the user's access level (held in the `MM_UserAuthorization` session variable) matches the value you set.

For example, if you have a button on a page that you only want an administrator to see, you could accomplish it by surrounding the button code with some ASP, like this:

```
<% IF Session("MM_UserAuthorization") = "Administrator" THEN %>
  <input type="submit" name="Submit" value="Remove selected users" />
<% END IF %>
```

This button would only be visible to users who have *Administrator* as their access level.

Summary

The few pages that we have built here demonstrate some of the more common tasks that your web applications may be called on to perform. They cover the basics of user registration and login along with a page for registered users to edit their details, and an administration page to remove users.

We have also constructed a home page to link them all together and display different content dependent upon whether the user is logged in or not – individually, these pages are quite simple but together they provide powerful functionality that make a great starting point for many web applications.

More and more, we find ourselves needing to be informed about actions that have been performed on our web site – such as when a new user registers. In the next chapter, among other things, we will look at some dynamic e-mail interactions that enable this kind of information to be sent to us automatically.

9

- SMTP servers

- Static and dynamic e-mail

- Sample applications:

  - Forgotten password retrieval system

  - User messaging system

Author: Omar Elbaga

Dynamic E-mail Interaction

E-mail can add new levels of functionality to our dynamic web site. We all normally think of e-mails as in the context of sending our friends and family messages using Hotmail, Yahoo!, or by using an e-mail client such as Outlook Express, Netscape, or Eudora, but how would you feel about sending e-mail from your own ASP pages! What about allowing users to send e-mail from our own ASP pages? With the knowledge we have gained from the previous chapters, we can also send e-mail when particular events occur, such as when a user enters a record into a database for example. E-mail gives our dynamic web site that extra edge, through it we can send e-mail to our users, allow users to send e-mail to us, and allow users to send e-mail to each other. E-mail can even be used to help us keep track of what is going on at our site. Let's take a closer look.

SMTP Servers

E-mail is handled by a Simple Mail Transfer Protocol (SMTP) Server. Two SMTP servers connect to each other; one server sends the e-mail while the other accepts the e-mail. You need to have your SMTP server up and running locally before it executes mail. PWS does not have an SMTP server, but IIS comes with its own SMTP server. You can shut it down or start it as you like.

To make sure your SMTP server is configured properly follow these instructions. Open the **Internet Services Manager** from Administrative Tools in Control Panel. Collapse the plus sign next to the computer icon and the machine name of your PC. Right-click your Default SMTP Virtual Server and select *Properties*.

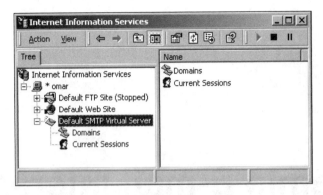

From the *General* tab, select your IP Address from the IP Address menu. If it is not listed, click the *Advanced* button beside the menu and add your IP Address. (You can get your IP Address by typing `ipconfig` at an MS DOS prompt in Windows 95/98 or the Command prompt in Windows 2000.)

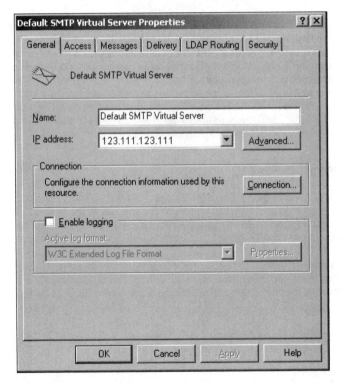

Select the **Access** tab. Click the **Authentication** button. Tick the checkbox to grant Anonymous access.

Click the **Connection** button. Tick the radio button beside the option labeled *Only the list below:*

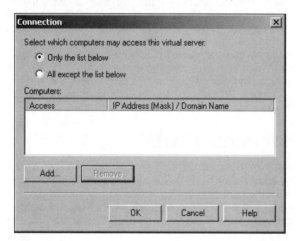

Add your IP Address to the list and hit *OK.* We've now allowed only our own IP address to connect to the SMTP server. This way no other machine can connect to our SMTP server without our permission. You can change this as you like, by adding more IP addresses or rejecting certain IP addresses. There only remains one more important step to secure the SMTP server.

Click the **Relay** button. Follow the same steps as you did for the Connection control. Tick the radio button beside the text "*Only the list below*". Add your IP address to the list and hit *OK.*

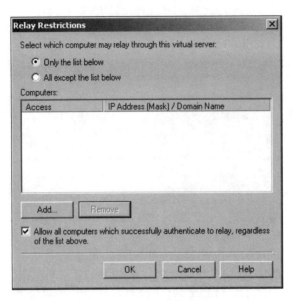

The SMTP server can relay e-mail messages by forwarding mail addressed to any e-mail domain. If this feature is accessible to Internet users besides you, then abusive users can use your SMTP server to forward unsolicited e-mail to thousands of people. With this option completed we've prevented computers besides our own IP address to relay messages through our SMTP server.

Your SMTP server should now be configured to send e-mail. Currently, your IP address will be the only one allowed to connect to and relay messages from your SMTP server. Feel free to change these options later on by adding more IP addresses or restricting specific ones under the Connection and Relay Restrictions options. When adding or restricting IP addresses, please be sure to complete both options to fully secure your SMTP server. We will test the SMTP server shortly.

ASP Mail Components (COM)

A component is an object containing code for a specific function for an application, and which provides access to that code through a well-specified set of methods and properties. They are installed on the server that will execute the component from an ASP page, and can be written in a variety of programming languages. For our purposes, we are particularly interested in the ASP mail components that enable us to send mail through our SMTP server, some of which are free.

> *Developing ASP components is a huge topic in itself. If you are interested in developing your own ASP components you may be interested in reading a book such as* Beginning Components for ASP *(Richard Anderson et al, Wrox Press, ISBN 1861002882).*

We will use three of the most popular free versions throughout our examples. Before we begin using the mail components though, there is something very important to note. Mail components have to be installed and configured on a server like any other ASP component. If you test your pages on your own local IIS, you can download, install, and begin using all of the mail components. On the other hand, hosting companies usually offer access to one particular mail COM to their clients, while others provide none, and others provide more than one. This should be mentioned in the hosting package details. Before signing up with a hosting company, make sure that you will have access to the mail component of your choice. If not you will not be able to trigger mail from your ASP pages.

Static E-mail

If you recall the difference between the terms static and dynamic from *Chapter 5,* you know that static means "unchanging" while dynamic means "changing". Before we explore dynamic e-mail interaction we will get used to sending simple static e-mail with hard-coded values.

Sending Mail

In order to send an e-mail of course there are certain values that are required: sender, receiver, subject, and body. When using a mail component, we usually need to specify the IP address of the SMTP server. Beyond these values, there are other syntactical requirements such as those for creating, executing, and closing the object. So we create the object, provide the values required for the content of the e-mail, execute the object, and finally close the object. Each component has its own syntax but, for the most part, they are used in similar ways. Additionally, each component has many properties and methods, but we will restrict ourselves to those that are essential for sending the e-mail. If you would like to explore the other properties of the particular mail component you're using has to offer, read through the manual at the company's web site.

There is an important point to mention before we jump right into using mail components. If you will be testing the mail component examples on a server on which you don't have access to administrative options, you may find that your web host will not allow you to send e-mails that are not hosted by that particular SMTP server. In other words, if within the syntax of your mail component you try to send e-mail from `omar@udnewbie.com` while the server you are sending it from does not host `udnewbie.com`, it will reject the e-mail and not send anything. This might drive you crazy, especially when we get to dynamic e-mail, because you are likely to want to allow your users to send e-mails using their own e-mail addresses (whose domains will probably not be hosted by the server you'll be using), but will be rejected if your host disallows anonymous domains. You will be stuck with using your own e-mail address with a domain that is local to the server.

This is inconvenient because you won't know the e-mail address of the sender since you will have had to resend every e-mail from your own e-mail address. There are some not-so-slick ways around this and we will get to it later, but we need to take this into account. Although this is an annoying inconvenience at times, there are valid reasons why a hosting company will disallow anonymous domains. Some malicious clients can use the server to send junk mail using an anonymous e-mail address from their web host's very own server. Web hosts disallow anonymous domains access to their SMTP server to protect themselves and others from these crude cyber e-mail tactics that can occur, which is why we specified the IP address of the relay host earlier.

> If you will be testing the examples from your local IIS, you will be good to go, and can use any e-mail address as the sender, so long that you adjust some administrative options for your SMTP server as shown in the SMPT server section above. However, if you will be testing the examples from a server hosted by a web hosting company who disallows anonymous domains to send e-mail from their SMTP server, you either need to contact the host or use a local e-mail address before wondering why the e-mail is not being sent. We are sorry, but there is no other way around this.

CDONTS

CDONTS is one of the most popular ASP mail components because it comes with IIS, and is installed by default. As a result, the IP address of the SMTP server need not be identified. Let's take a look at CDONTS syntax. To reiterate, these are components, or server objects, and have properties that we can set and methods that we can pass parameters to. Create a new page and save it as execute_cdonts.asp. In Code View type the following above the <html> tag, specifying your own e-mail addresses for the From and To properties. You can also create your own Subject and Body content:

```
<%
Set objCDO = Server.CreateObject("CDONTS.NewMail")
' Create Object

objCDO.From = "omar@udnewbie.com"
objCDO.To = "omar@udnewbie.com"

objCDO.Subject = "Test CDONTS"
objCDO.Body = "Hi, I was sent because the page execute_cdonts.asp on my server was
accessed."

objCDO.Send
' Send Email

Set objCDO = Nothing
' Destroy Object
%>
```

The code is quite straightforward. The following creates an instance of the CDONTS object within our ASP page:

```
Set objCDO = Server.CreateObject("CDONTS.NewMail")
```

I named the CDONTS object **objCDO**, you could name it whatever you like: objSendMail, Mail, CDOmail, and so on. Each object property is referred to in the context of its object, that is, objCDO.PropertyName. If you named the object objSendMail, you would refer to a property as objSendMail.PropertyName.

We have used four properties and one method: the From, To, Subject, and Body properties, and the Send method. The properties are self-explanatory. From contains the e-mail address of the sender, and To contains the e-mail address of the receiver. Subject contains the subject of the e-mail, and Body contains the body of the e-mail. Lastly, Send actually sends the e-mail. Finally, after the object does its job, we clear it from the server by destroying the object with the following code:

```
Set objCDO = Nothing
```

Test the execute_cdonts.asp page live by loading the page once in your browser. Once the page loads, the CDONTS should've already executed. The HTML page itself will come up blank as we haven't done anything else to it. To be sure the e-mail was sent you must check the e-mail of whatever e-mail address you defined for the To property. (I hope you didn't specify mine!) You should see the following as the body of your e-mail:

Hi, I was sent because the page execute_cdonts.asp on my server was accessed.

> For this chapter, try to use an e-mail account that you can check easily because we will be sending a lot of e-mails. For example, it may be best to send to an e-mail that you receive in Outlook Express. You can then leave the Outlook Express program loaded so you can check the e-mail right away.

Text/HTML Format

The text defined for the e-mail is plain text by default, thus all text defined for the `Body` property will be translated as plain text and any HTML contained within it will not be parsed. For example, add an HTML tag to the body text, execute the page, and check the e-mail:

```
<%
Set objCDO = Server.CreateObject("CDONTS.NewMail")

objCDO.From = "email address"
objCDO.To = "email address"

objCDO.Subject = "Test CDONTS"
objCDO.Body = "Hi, I was sent because the page <b>execute_cdonts.asp</b> on my
server was accessed."

objCDO.Send
Set objCDO = Nothing
%>
```

Note: Please replace the text "email address" set for the `From` and `To` properties with your e-mail addresses of choice.

The content of the e-mail will be:

Hi, I was sent because the page execute_cdonts.asp on my server was accessed.

In order to make sure HTML in the `Body` property is parsed, you must change the mail format manually. We will have to use two more properties to do so: `MailFormat` and `BodyFormat`. `MailFormat` refers to whether or not the message is sent in MIME format and `BodyFormat` refers to the actual text format for the body of the e-mail.

MIME (Multipurpose Internet Mail Extensions) is an official Internet standard that specifies how messages must be formatted when exchanged between various e-mail systems.

Both of these properties take the values of either `1` or `0`. `1` sends the e-mail in plain text and format, which is the default value, and `0` sends the e-mail in HTML and MIME format. The properties have to be used together in order to change the format to HTML. We must manually change the values for these properties to 0 in order to send in HTML.

Change the code for the `execute_cdonts.asp` page to the following in order to send the e-mail in HTML:

```
<%
Set objCDO = Server.CreateObject("CDONTS.NewMail")

objCDO.From = "email address"
objCDO.To = "email address"

objCDO.Subject = "Test CDONTS"
objCDO.Body = "Hi, I was sent because the page <b>execute_cdonts.asp</b> on my
server was accessed."
objCDO.BodyFormat = 0
objCDO.MailFormat = 0

objCDO.Send
Set objCDO = Nothing
%>
```

Execute the page on your live server. Check the e-mail and the following should be in the body:

*Hi, I was sent because the page **execute_cdonts.asp** on my server was accessed.*

Once you have changed the e-mail format to HTML, the content can be formatted with any of the HTML tags. For example, you can change the font and even add images. Let's say your logo (or any other image) exists in a folder on your server, you can embed it with the `<img>` tag in your e-mail. I might have a logo on my server whose URL path would be:
`http://www.udnewbie.com/images/logos/main_logo_272x42.gif`.

I can embed this in the HTML:

```
<img src="http://www.udnewbie.com/images/logos/main_logo_272x42.gif">
```

You could place this anywhere in the body of the e-mail. Before we test it, I need to point out something. You notice that this particular line of HTML uses double quotes. As you know from *Chapter 5*, double quotes mark the start and end of a variable value, and so double quotes contained within the value of a variable can break it, causing erroneous results. We need to escape the double quotes in the HTML tags by adding additional set of double quotes beside each one. Type two double quotes wherever one double quotes character is needed. This goes for double quotes that may appear anywhere within the e-mail body.

Change the code for the `execute_cdonts.asp` page to the following in order to add an image in the body:

```
<%
Set objCDO = Server.CreateObject("CDONTS.NewMail")

objCDO.From = "email address"
objCDO.To = "email address"

objCDO.Subject = "Test CDONTS"
objCDO.Body = "<img
src=""http://www.udnewbie.com/images/logos/main_logo_272x42.gif""> <p> Hi, I was
sent because the page <b>execute_cdonts.asp</b> on my server was accessed."
objCDO.BodyFormat = 0
```

```
objCDO.MailFormat = 0

objCDO.Send
Set objCDO = Nothing
%>
```

When you check the e-mail you should see your image in the body. You can see how many of the big web sites send those huge web page-looking newsletters to your inbox; you can add any HTML you like to produce a web page as the body of an e-mail. You can even use CSS in an HTML e-mail; you would either need to call an external stylesheet from your own server (in which case the person reading the e-mail would need to be online) or use inline or embedded CSS with all the CSS markup within the e-mail <head> element.

Before you decide to send all your e-mails in HTML, consider that some of your recipients' e-mail programs may not view HTML. Since HTML tags will not be parsed in an e-mail program that rejects HTML, sometimes an HTML e-mail can be completely unreadable. Plain text e-mails will work fine and probably be the format for the majority of your e-mails unless it becomes absolutely necessary to send the e-mail in HTML.

Carbon Copies (CC) and Blind Carbon Copies

You may be wondering how to send an e-mail to several e-mail addresses. To do this, you can simply repeat the objCDO.To property inputting a different e-mail address. For example this is how we would change the code for the execute_cdonts.asp page to send our e-mail to two different addresses:

```
<%
Set objCDO = Server.CreateObject("CDONTS.NewMail")

objCDO.From = "email address"
objCDO.To = "email address"
objCDO.To = "email address"
objCDO.Subject = "Test CDONTS"
objCDO.Body = "Hi, I was sent because the page <b>execute_cdonts.asp</b> on my
server was accessed."

objCDO.Send
Set objCDO = Nothing
%>
```

Alternatively, to send a carbon copy of the e-mail to another address, use the Cc property, objCDO.Cc:

```
objCDO.To = "email address"
objCDO.Cc = "email address"
```

But both methods will send a copy to the two e-mail addresses, where both recipients will see the other e-mail address unlike the blind carbon copies, where the main recipient will not be able to see who else received the mail.

To send a blind carbon copy, CDONTS has another property, unsurprisingly called Bcc which you can use:

```
objCDO.From = "email address"
objCDO.To = "email address"
objCDO.Bcc = "email address"
```

Execute the page on a live server and check both e-mail addresses. A copy of the e-mail should've been sent to both e-mail addresses.

Once you know the syntax of the properties of your mail component, you will be able to increase the power of your e-mail. We've covered a lot of the main features web developers are interested in while using mail components. In the next couple of sections I want to demonstrate the syntax of two other popular mail components: ASPEmail and Jmail, but we won't go into as much depth as we have in this section. It isn't that one is better than the other; you can do the same things with each component once you know its syntax, especially the properties.

> *For more on* CDONTS *properties and methods please see:*
> http://msdn.microsoft.com/library/default.asp?url=/library/en-
> us/cdo/html/_denali_newmail_object_cdonts_library_.asp.

ASPEmail

This mail component is another popular ASP mail component, although unlike CDONTS it doesn't come with IIS. It is proprietary software from Persits Software, Inc. (*http://www.Persits.com*). They offer a free version of this mail component on their site and some commercial premium features. When you download the free version, the commercial premium features will be available for 30 days, but the generic features will always be available. The commercial version comes with a few more useful properties that you can use, but the free version contains all that we need for these examples, and probably for most of your own examples down the road. You can download the ASPEmail 4.5 component from: *http://www.aspemail.com/download.html*. Once you download it, install it by double-clicking the file. Make sure you register the component when asked during installation.

Back in Dreamweaver MX, create a new dynamic ASP web page and save it as `execute_aspemail.asp`. Add the following code above the `<html>` tag:

```
<%
Set objASPEmail = Server.CreateObject("Persits.MailSender")

objASPEmail.Host = "123.111.123.111"
objASPEmail.From = "email address"
objASPEmail.AddAddress "email address"

objASPEmail.Subject = "Test ASPEMAIL"
objASPEmail.Body = "Hi, this is an ASPEmail component test."

objASPEmail.Send
Set objASPEmail = Nothing
%>
```

> *Please replace the text* "email address" *set for the* From *and* AddAddress *properties with your own e-mail* addresses.

As with the CDONTS object, we have to create an instance of the object:

```
Set objASPEmail = Server.CreateObject("Persits.MailSender")
```

For the ASPEmail component we have to specify the SMTP server address in a property called Host, something we didn't have to do with CDONTS. If you are testing locally you should input your IP Address. (You can get your IP Address by typing ipconfig at the command prompt.) If you are executing the page on a page hosted by a web host, you need to contact them for the correct SMTP server address.

The other properties are not new to you. The only differences are the property names, but they all have the same functionality as the CDONTS properties. You may be confused by the AddAddress method above. This is where you specify the recipient's e-mail address and is no different than the To property of CDONTS. OK, I lied. It does one other thing that the To property of CDONTS cannot do, which is specify a display name for the e-mail address. You can do so by adding a comma after the e-mail address and put the name within double quotes:

```
objASPEmail.AddAddress "email address", "omar"
```

Also, notice that to define a value for the AddAddress method in ASPEmail you don't have to use an equal sign. This is because where CDONTS uses the To **property**, ASPEmail uses the AddAddress **method**; while we **set** properties (using the = sign), we **pass** parameters to methods. These are some of the differences that occur in the syntax between the mail components. It's a good idea to keep a reference example for each mail component on your PC for quick reference.

> The AddAddress *does not use an equal sign because the e-mail address is being passed to a method. Properties will always be set using the = sign whereas methods will not.*

Execute the page on a live server and check the e-mail for the recipient e-mail address you specified. You should see the following in the body of your e-mail:

Hi, this is an ASPEmail component text.

Text/HTML Format

By default, ASPEmail sends mail in plain text format. You can send e-mail in HTML format by defining the following property as true: IsHTML = True. (If defined as False, it sends in plain text.) Change the code for the execute_aspemail.asp page to the following to send the e-mail in HTML format:

```
<%
Set objASPEmail = Server.CreateObject("Persits.MailSender")

objASPEmail.Host = "123.111.123.111"
objASPEmail.From = "email address"
objASPEmail.AddAddress "email address"

objASPEmail.Subject = "Test ASPEMAIL"
objASPEmail.Body = "Hi, this is an <b>ASPEmail</b> component test."
objASPEmail.IsHTML = True
```

```
objASPEmail.Send
Set objASPEmail = Nothing
%>
```

Execute the page on a live server and check the e-mail for the recipient e-mail address you specified. You should see the following in the body of your e-mail:

*Hi, this is an **ASPEmail** component text.*

Carbon Copies (CC) and Blind Carbon Copies (BCC)

ASPEmail also has a method for sending carbon copies, called `AddCc`. Make the following changes to the `execute_aspemail.asp` page:

```
<%
Set objASPEmail = Server.CreateObject("Persits.MailSender")

objASPEmail.Host = "123.111.123.111"
objASPEmail.From = "email address"
objASPEmail.AddAddress "email address"
objASPEmail.AddAddress "email address"
objASPEmail.AddCcc "email address"
objASPEmail.Subject = "Test ASPEMAIL"
objASPEmail.Body = "Hi, this is an <b>ASPEmail</b> component test."
objASPEmail.IsHTML = True

objASPEmail.Send
Set objASPEmail = Nothing
%>
```

Since `AddCc` is a method and not a property, you don't use an equal sign when passing a parameter to it. Execute the page on a live server and check both e-mail addresses. A copy of the e-mail should've been sent to both e-mail addresses.

You can also do the same thing by repeating the `AddAddress` method:

```
objASPEmail.AddAddress "email address"
objASPEmail.AddAddress "email address"
```

For blind carbon copies, you use the `AddBcc` method:

```
objASPEmail.AddBcc "email address"
```

Extras

Here are a couple of neat ASPEmail properties and methods you can use. You can define a display name for the sender e-mail address by using the `FromName` property. By using a method called `AddReplyTo` you can specify a different e-mail address to be used when the recipient clicks reply to the e-mail. Here are some examples:

```
objASPEmail.From = "email address"
objASPEmail.FromName = "omar"
objASPEmail.AddReplyTo "different email address"
```

For more properties see the online ASPEmail **manual** at: *http://www.aspemail.com/manual.html.*

Jmail

Jmail is another proprietary mail component from Dimac (*http://www.Dimac.net*). You can download the W3Jmail free version 4.3 at their official web site along with many other commercial products. You can find w3Jmail under the Products category, download the free version, and install by double-clicking the file.

Back in Dreamweaver MX, create a new dynamic ASP web page and save it as `execute_jmail.asp`. Add the following code above the `<html>` tag:

```
<%
Set JMail = Server.CreateObject("JMail.SMTPMail")

JMail.ServerAddress = "123.111.123.111"
JMail.Sender = "email address"
JMail.AddRecipient "email address"

JMail.Subject = "Test JMAIL"
JMail.Body = "Hi, this is a Jmail component test."

JMail.Execute
Set JMail = Nothing
%>
```

Please replace the text "email address" set for the Sender and AddRecipient properties with your e-mail addresses of choice.

Similar to the two previous mail components the properties and methods are self-explanatory. As with ASPEmail, you have to specify an IP Address in Jmail also.

Execute the page on your live server. Check the e-mail and the following should be in the body:

Hi, this is a Jmail component test.

Text/HTML Format

You can change the e-mail from plain text format to HTML by defining the `ContentType` property as `"text/html"`. Change the code for the `execute_aspemail.asp` page to the following in order to send the e-mail in HTML format:

```
<%
Set JMail = Server.CreateObject("JMail.SMTPMail")

JMail.ServerAddress = "123.111.123.111"
JMail.Sender = "email address"
JMail.AddRecipient "email address"

JMail.Subject = "Test JMAIL"
JMail.Body = "Hi, this is a <b>Jmail</b> component test."
Jmail.ContentType = "text/html"

JMail.Execute
Set JMail = Nothing
%>
```

Execute the page on a live server and check the e-mail for the recipient e-mail address you specified. You should see the following in the body of your e-mail:

*Hi, this is a **Jmail** component text.*

Carbon Copies (CC) and Blind Carbon Copies (BCC)

You can also send mail to several different e-mail accounts using the `AddRecipientCc` method, or by simply repeating the `AddRecipient` method. Here are two examples:

```
JMail.AddRecipient "email address"
JMail.AddRecipientcc "email address"
```

and

```
JMail.AddRecipient "email address"
JMail.AddRecipient "email address"
```

For more specific information about Jmail and other properties please log on to *http://dimac.net*. The Jmail **manual** can be found at: *http://www.dimac.net/files/pdf/w3_JMail.pdf*.

Sending a blind copy to another e-mail address is also easy. You need to add the following method: `AddRecipientBcc`. Here is an example:

```
JMail.AddRecipient "email address"
JMail.AddRecipientBcc "email address"
```

Dynamic E-mail

Time for some action! Since everyone is moving from static to dynamic web pages, let's take that attitude with our e-mail also. We now know how to send e-mail through our ASP pages, but only how to send it once a page loads and with pre-defined values. What about sending it after a specific action occurs or allowing the user to define the values for the properties? This is what I will call "dynamic" e-mail because property values are not hard coded, but ever-changing. Once we set up the web application, users of our web site will be able to alter the property values. How much control we want the user to have is up to us. We can allow the user to specify the sender e-mail address and pre-define the recipient. This is usually the case with feedback or contact forms. We can also allow the user to define the sender, subject, and body. The properties will act as regular variables. It's up to us which properties of the mail component we want the user to define.

In the above section we learned how to use three different mail components: CDONTS, ASPEmail, and Jmail. For the rest of the chapter examples we will restrict ourselves to CDONTS because it is more accessible since it comes with IIS. Now that you have been exposed to the syntax of all three, you can easily replace the code to use the mail component of your choice.

Send Mail By Hyperlink

We can trigger an e-mail based on many different conditions. Let's start by triggering an e-mail based on the clicking of a hyperlink. In Dreamweaver MX open a new document and enter the following script, saving it as `email_link.asp`:

```
<% If Request.QueryString("link") = "true" Then %>

<%
Set objCDO = Server.CreateObject("CDONTS.NewMail")

objCDO.From = "email address"
objCDO.To = "email address"

objCDO.Subject = "Hyperlink clicked"
objCDO.Body = "The link on email_link.asp was clicked."

objCDO.Send
Set objCDO = Nothing
%>
<% Response.Redirect "email_link.asp?email=true" %>

<% End If %>

<html>
<head><title>Email Link</title></head>
<body>

<a href="email_link.asp?link=true">send email</a>

</body>
</html>
```

Once the page is loaded, nothing happens except that the hyperlink is displayed:

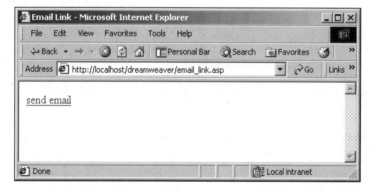

The e-mail is not triggered automatically because it is embedded in a conditional statement which tells it to execute on condition that a URL parameter named link exists and equals true. When the page is first loaded there won't be any URL parameters. Clicking the hyperlink takes you back to the same page, but this time passing the appropriate URL parameter which triggers CDONTS to send the e-mail. After CDONTS is executed, it redirects you back to the same page with a new URL parameter letting me know that the CDONTS was executed:

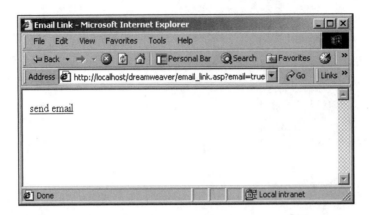

One of the cool things about this method is that everything is on a single page, yet it behaves as though two pages were used. The ASP script is not executed consecutively if the page is refreshed, it only executes if that particular hyperlink is clicked or the correct URL parameter is passed. The e-mail is only executed when a QueryString named `link` is `true`. After the QueryString is passed from the hyperlink the e-mail is executed and the user is redirected to the same page using `Response.Redirect` and the QueryString is cleared. For this reason, the e-mail can only execute if the hyperlink is clicked. Another way to do this would be to have the ASP script on a separate page. You could link to that page and redirect back or to another page, but in this case, the e-mail will be sent whenever the page with the `CDONTS` is accessed, whether intentionally or not. At any rate, you could always wrap conditional statements around your ASP script, making sure it is only executed if certain criteria are fulfilled. You could even allow the code to execute only if the page was accessed from a particular page.

Send E-mail by Form Button

Sending e-mail based on the click of a form button is just as easy. Create a new dynamic ASP web page and save it as `email_button.asp`. Select *Insert > Form*. Place your cursor inside the form and select *Insert > Form Objects > Button*. Rename the button to `email_submit` and change the label to "*Send Mail*". Have the action of the form submit to the same page. The form's method should be `POST` not `get`. (`get` will send the form values as URL Parameters.) Add the following code above the `<html>` tag:

```
<% If Request.Form("email_submit") <> "" Then %>

<%
Set objCDO = Server.CreateObject("CDONTS.NewMail")

objCDO.From = "email address"
objCDO.To = "email address"

objCDO.Subject = "Form button clicked"
objCDO.Body = "The form button on email_button.asp was clicked."

objCDO.Send
Set objCDO = Nothing
%>
<% Response.Redirect "email_button.asp?email=true" %>

<% End If %>
```

The conditional statement surrounding the ASP script checks to see if the form field named `email_submit` is empty. Once the form is submitted, this form field (the submit button) will have a value so the ASP script executes. (Please see *Chapter 5* for a review of VBScript syntax.)

> Checking whether a form button value is empty is a frequently used method for finding out if a form was submitted to the page.

Test the page live and click the form button to send the e-mail.

Sending e-mail based on our conditions is the first step in sending dynamic e-mail. We can also send e-mail based on other conditions such as an event that might occur within our ASP page. You may like to send yourself an e-mail whenever someone accesses a particular page on your web site, for example. Once you understand the concept you will find many scenarios in which you can apply it.

The next step in adding more dynamic behavior to our e-mail applications is making the property values themselves dynamic, not just the execution. An example where this is useful is when we want to add dynamic information that exists on the page, like URL parameters, into our e-mail. This could be used to collect dynamic values from the page. We might also simply want to collect dynamic values from the user, we could add dynamic variables into the subject and body or we can replace entire property values with those variables. We will look at both methods in the next sections.

Sending E-mail with Dynamic Values

Let's add some dynamic values on the page to our e-mails. We will collect the IP Address of the sender and the page he or she sent the e-mail from in the body of our e-mail. Create a new dynamic ASP web page and save it as `dynamic_values_in_email.asp`. Create the same form as in the previous example. Select *Insert > Form*. Place your cursor inside the form and select *Insert > Form Objects > Button*. Rename the button to `email_submit` and change the label to "*Send Mail*". Have the action of the form submit to the same page. The form's method should be `Post`. Add the following code above the `<html>` tag:

```
<% If Request.Form("email_submit") <> "" Then %>

<%
Set objCDO = Server.CreateObject("CDONTS.NewMail")

objCDO.From = "email address"
objCDO.To = "email address"

objCDO.Subject = "Form button clicked"
objCDO.Body = "Here is the IP Address of the sender: " &
Request.ServerVariables("REMOTE_HOST") & vbcrlf & "This is the page the sender
sent the page from: " & Request.ServerVariables("URL")

objCDO.Send
Set objCDO = Nothing
%>
<% Response.Redirect "dynamic_values_in_email.asp?email=true" %>

<% End If %>
```

Test the page live and click the form button to send the e-mail.

The code is basically the same as the previous example except that we've added some dynamic variables into the body of our e-mail. We also changed the value of the redirection page to the new page. In order to create the body of the e-mail with strings and dynamic variables we have to concatenate them together. (If you need a refresher on concatenation, see *Chapter 5*.)

> *If you leave out a concatenation character you may break the value so take care to concatenate the strings and variables together properly.*

We collected two environment variables: the IP address and the URL to the current page. The only new code in the body is: vbcrlf: this is simply a built in VBScript string constant that creates a carriage return and line feed. If you want to use HTML tags such as <br> instead we have to change the e-mail format to HTML using the properties described earlier in this chapter. We have now added dynamic variables inside the body of our e-mail. We could add the variables into the subject or you could also retrieve other environment variables.

Sending E-mail with Form Field Values

Now let's replace entire property values with dynamic variables instead of hard coding them. Create a new dynamic ASP web page and save it as send_email_form.asp. Insert an empty form and insert four textfields into it, to parallel the properties of the CDONTS properties. Rename the textfields and add labels and properties as presented in the table below:

Textfield	Label	Properties
sender	*Sender Email:*	
recipient	*Recipient Email:*	
subject	*Subject:*	
body	*Body:*	Multi line

Also insert a submit button and label it "*Send Email*". Highlight the form and from *Properties* change the action of the form to be sent back to the same page, making sure the method is set to Post. The user will insert the CDONTS property values through this form.

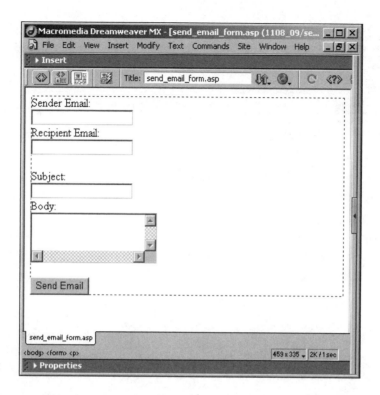

Note that some developers use a naming convention where textfield names are prefixed with txt so that they can be easily recognized when retrieved. In these examples, we are not following this convention.

Switch to Code View and type the following ASP script above the `<html>` tag. Leave the values of the From, To, Subject, and Body properties empty:

```
<% If Trim(Request.Form("submit")) <> "" Then %>
<%
Set objCDO = Server.CreateObject("CDONTS.NewMail")

objCDO.From =
objCDO.To =

objCDO.Subject =
objCDO.Body =

objCDO.Send
Set objCDO = Nothing
%>
<% End If %>
```

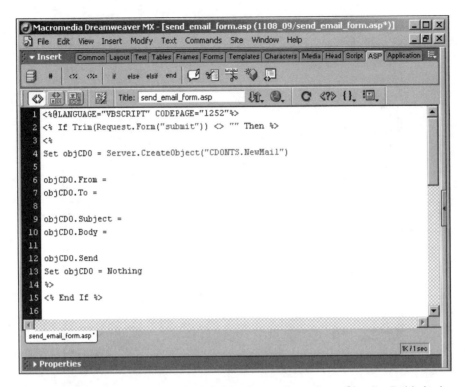

We need to retrieve the values of the form fields. As you know from *Chapter 5,* this is done with `Request.Form("textfield_name")`. We also know that in order to trim variables from extra spaces left to the right of the value we can use the VBScript function `Trim`, like this:

```
Trim(Request.Form("textfield_name")).
```

We could simply enter this using the appropriate form field name as the value for each property. However, Dreamweaver MX makes this even easier for us. Place your cursor to the right of the equal sign of the `From` property. Choose the ASP tab from the *Insert* panel, and click the *Trimmed Form Element* icon. It is the icon with scissors beside a form.

You can change the insert panel so that this displays icons only, text only, or both from Edit > Preferences > General > Editing Options > Insert Panel.

Dreamweaver MX will insert the following code for you: `Trim(Request.Form(""))` and place the cursor in between the double quotes so that you can type the name of the form field you want to retrieve. For the `From` property we want to retrieve the textfield named `sender`, so type `sender` between the double quotes. Follow the same procedure for the rest of the properties. Change the name of the form field to reflect the particular one we want to retrieve for the property value you are defining. Here's what your code should look like:

```
<% If Trim(Request.Form("submit")) <> "" Then %>
<%
Set objCDO = Server.CreateObject("CDONTS.NewMail")
```

```
objCDO.From = Trim(Request.Form("sender"))
objCDO.To = Trim(Request.Form("recipient"))

objCDO.Subject = Trim(Request.Form("subject"))
objCDO.Body = Trim(Request.Form("body"))

objCDO.Send
Set objCDO = Nothing
%>
<% End If %>
```

Test the page live, enter appropriate values for each form field, and submit the form. The CDONTS will have executed once your page reloads. Finally, check the e-mail you entered for the recipient e-mail account.

We mentioned earlier that your web host might have disallowed anonymous domains access to the SMTP server. Therefore, if your user enters his or her own e-mail address as the sender, the e-mail will not be sent unless the e-mail address's domain is hosted by the server, which is highly unlikely! So, to allow the user to submit an e-mail, we have to hard code the From property with our own e-mail address which is associated with the domain being hosted by the web host.

I mentioned earlier that there is a workaround. Mail headers include details about the e-mail and we can set mail headers from our CDONTS code. We still have to hard code the From property with our own e-mail address, there is no way around this, but we can collect the user's e-mail address from the Sender form field and set it in the From mail headers. This will be invisible to the sender.

Let's see the code. Open the send_email_form.asp page we just created. You can leave the form as it is. The user will enter his or her own e-mail address thinking the e-mail is being sent from it. In Code View, remove the Trim(Request.Form("sender")) code from the value of the From property and enter your own e-mail address within double quotes. Add the following two lines of code to the script:

```
objCDO.Value("From") = Trim(Request.Form("sender"))
```

These two lines set the From mail header with the e-mail inputted in the sender form field. When the mail is received the From mail header will display this e-mail, and not the one hard coded in the From property.

Here's a look at the full code:

```
<% If Trim(Request.Form("submit")) <> "" Then %>
<%
Set objCDO = Server.CreateObject("CDONTS.NewMail")

objCDO.From = "email address"
objCDO.Value("From") = Trim(Request.Form("sender"))
objCDO.To = Trim(Request.Form("recipient"))

objCDO.Subject = Trim(Request.Form("subject"))
objCDO.Body = Trim(Request.Form("body"))

objCDO.Send
Set objCDO = Nothing
%>
<% End If %>
```

The value of the `From` mail header will serve as the `Reply-To` mail header by default, but you may also find it useful to utilize the `Reply-To` mail header using the following line:

```
objCDO.Value("Reply-To") = Trim(Request.Form("sender"))
```

This is the e-mail that will be used for the *Reply To* field when a user clicks reply from his e-mail tool.

You can also set the value of the `Sender` form field to the value of the `Body` property so that the recipient knows who sent the e-mail from within the e-mail body. You can reconfigure the `Body` property value to the following:

```
objCDO.Body = Trim(Request.Form("body")) & vbcrlf & vbcrlf & "This page was sent
by: " & Trim(Request.Form("sender"))
```

The body will now be defined as whatever the user inputs in the `body` textfield, but will be followed by two line breaks, and then some text saying, "*This page was sent by:* ", followed by the e-mail address entered in the `sender` textfield.

Test the page live and check the recipient e-mail. This workaround is nice because you can also stop users from using someone else's e-mail address to send e-mail. Even though a user can still put any e-mail address in the `sender` textfield, the e-mail will not be sent from that e-mail address. It will be sent from yours, which will make it easier for you to deal with any problems that occur. You can also append the sender's IP address to the body and have every e-mail sent to you so you can identify the sender in a more dependable manner.

These issues are always debated amongst web developers, but honestly in all my years of web development I have rarely encountered malicious users, especially if you use the right approach. The majority of your users are not interested in using your web application for malicious reasons, but there is that minority that can come along and do so. If you use a few simple tactics such as checking the e-mails and retrieving the IP address of senders, you can usually stop that minority without having to go through drastic measures to protect your web application. I am not saying don't bother taking protective measures, instead you should use appropriate measures, taking into account the context of the web application and the audience of your web site.

With the examples above, you have enough knowledge to do a lot of different tricks. It's just a matter of applying the various concepts to create the web application. Let's take a look at a complete "send page to friend" application, in which we will apply the techniques outlined previously. We will hard code some of the property values, and allow users to define other property values. We will also use HTML in the body this time.

Create a new dynamic ASP web page and save it as `send_page_form.asp`. Create a form with four textfields and a submit button:

- Rename the first textfield "`sender_email`"

- Rename the second textfield "`sender_name`"

- Rename the third textfield "`recipient_email`"

- Rename the fourth textfield "`recipient_name`"

- Change the label of the submit button to "Send"

Format your form however you like. Here is my `send_page_form.asp` page:

The HTML has been styled with CSS, for a refresher on CSS see Chapter 3.

Load this page in Dreamweaver MX and switch to Code View. Enter the following ASP script above the `<html>` tag:

```asp
<% If Trim(Request.Form("submit")) <> "" Then %>
<%
Set objCDO = Server.CreateObject("CDONTS.NewMail")

objCDO.From = Trim(Request.Form("sender_email"))
objCDO.To = Trim(Request.Form("recipient_email"))

objCDO.Subject = "A friend has sent you a udnewbie.com page"
objCDO.Body = "Hi " & Trim(Request.Form("recipient_name")) & "!" & "<br>" &
Trim(Request.Form("sender_name")) & " thought you might like to check out this
page:<p>" &  "<a href=" & """http://localhost" & Request.ServerVariables("URL") &
""">" & "http://localhost" & Request.ServerVariables("URL") & "</a>"

objCDO.MailFormat = 0
objCDO.BodyFormat = 0

objCDO.Send
Set objCDO = Nothing
%>
<% Response.Redirect "send_page_form.asp?email=true" %>
<% End If %>
```

We simply assign the value of the `sender_email` textfield to the `From` property, and the value of the `recipient_email` textfield to the `To` property, and add the properties that change the text format to HTML. Now for the `Body` property, don't let this code confuse you. We concatenated some pre-defined strings with form fields to produce the statement in the e-mail:

```
Hi <recipient_name>!
<sender_name> though you might like to check out this page:

<url>
```

The only confusing code may be how we put together the URL link. We need to produce the markup for the anchor element:

```
<a href="url">url</a>
```

The URL appears twice in the element, and is put together with a hard-coded string and an environment variable called URL. Because this environment variable does not retrieve the domain name, we have to pre-pend it with the domain name, like this:

```
"http://localhost" & Request.ServerVariables("URL")
```

This code will give us the complete URL, which we can then insert into both places within the HTML anchor element.

> Since we are testing locally we used the domain `http://localhost` in the `href` attribute. If you were testing on a remote server, you would replace this with `http://` plus your domain, for instance, `http://www.domain_name.com`.

Now let's consider the double quotes. Because each double quote has to be escaped with another double quote we end up with many double quotes. Not only does this call for two double quotes, we have to add a double quote to surround the two to define it as a string. It's up to you how you want to break apart the final HTML code for the anchor element, I broke it up in the following blocks:

```
<a href="http://localhost Request.ServerVariables("URL")">
  http://localhost Request.ServerVariables("URL") </a>
```

Each double quote that resides inside a string has to be changed into two double quotes. (There are two altogether in the above blocks; the two double quotes surrounding the URL in the `a` tag). Then each string block itself has to be surrounded with double quotes. We then have to concatenate string blocks and the dynamic variables to put together the following code:

```
"<a href=" & """http://localhost" & Request.ServerVariables("URL") & """>" &
"http://localhost" & Request.ServerVariables("URL") & "</a>"
```

For a refresher on concatenation, see Chapter 5.

After the CDONTS executes we redirect to the same page, adding a URL parameter to inform us that the action has occurred. Test the page live, add some vales in the form fields, submit the form, and check the e-mail.

Let's make this web application even cooler. We can display a message after the e-mail has been sent informing the sender. We already have a way of letting the user know that the CDONTS executed, which is the fact that we pass a URL parameter along with the redirection underneath the ASP script. Add the following code to your Dreamweaver MX document:

```
<% If Request.QueryString("email") = "sent" Then %>
Thank you, the page has been sent to.
<% End If %>
```

We will not be able to display one or all of the form fields using Request.Form in this message because the values are lost once we Response.Redirect to another page, even though, in this case, we are redirecting to the same page. But if we really want to display one of them we can pass the values in the URL, or even create sessions out of them. For example, you can change the Response.Redirect value in the example above to pass the recipient_email textfield as a URL parameter to:

```
<% Response.Redirect "send_page_form.asp?email=true&recipientemail=" &
Request.Form("recipient_email") %>
```

You can then retrieve the e-mail from the QueryString to display it. Let's change the If statement above that displays the message to also display the recipient e-mail:

```
<% If Request.QueryString("email") = "sent" Then %>
Thank you, the page has been sent to <%=Request.QueryString("recipientemail") %>.
<% End If %>
```

Sending E-mail with Session Values

We can also assign values of session variables to CdONTS properties, just like we did with form elements. You know from *Chapter 7* that the Log In server behavior creates a session variable called MM_Username out of the Username field. You can use these session variables as the entire property value or inside a property value.

Create a new dynamic ASP web page and save it as send_email_sessions.asp. Add an empty form and insert two textfields and a submit button. Call the first textfield recipient_email and the second textfield message. From *Properties* change the message textfield from Single line to Multi line. Change the label of the button to "*Send*". Highlight the form and, from *Properties*, change the action of the form to be sent back to itself (send_email_sessions.asp), and make sure the method is set to Post. Format the form as you like.

Add the following code above the <html> tag:

```
<%
Session("MM_Username") = "cooldude"
Session("OE_Email") = "email address"
%>
```

```asp
<% If Trim(Request.Form("submit")) <> "" Then %>
<%
Set objCDO = Server.CreateObject("CDONTS.NewMail")

objCDO.From = Trim(Session("OE_Email"))
objCDO.To = Trim(Request.Form("recipient_email"))

objCDO.Subject = "User " & Trim(Session("MM_Username"))  & " has sent you a
message"
objCDO.Body = Trim(Request.Form("message"))

objCDO.Send
Set objCDO = Nothing
%>
<% Response.Redirect "send_email_sessions.asp?email=true" %>

<% End If %>
```

Test the page live and check the recipient e-mail. The subject of the e-mail will be:

User cooldude has sent you a message

You can use any dynamic variables in your ASP script, not only form elements, but also sessions, URL parameters, and others. Feel free to use them whenever appropriate, when sending e-mail from your ASP pages.

Sending E-mail with Recordset Values

We can also send mail with values that come from a database. We can filter a recordset to retrieve a user's information and use that information in the e-mail. Create a new dynamic ASP web page and save it as send_email_recordset.asp. Add an empty form and insert two textfields and a submit button. Call the first textfield recipient_email and the second textfield message. Once again, from *Properties*, change this textfield from Single line to Multi line. Change the label of the button to "*Send*". Highlight the form and from *Properties* change the action of the form to be sent back to itself, and make sure the method is set to *Post*. Format the form as you like.

Create a new recordset called rsGetUser, select the conn_webprodmx connection, and use the following SQL:

```sql
SELECT username, first_name, last_name, email
FROM users
WHERE username = 'MMColParam'
```

Add the following **variable** directly below:

```
MMColParam        x      Session("MM_Username")
```

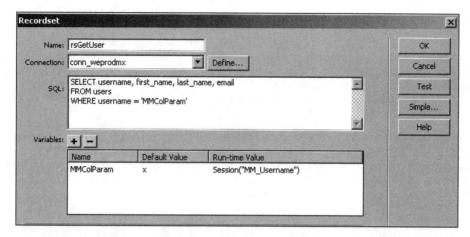

Hit *OK*, switch to Code View, and add the following code to create a Session **above** the recordset code:

```
<% Session("MM_Username") = "omar" %>
```

Next, add the following ASP script **below** the recordset code:

```
<% If Trim(Request.Form("submit")) <> "" Then %>
<%
Set objCDO = Server.CreateObject("CDONTS.NewMail")

objCDO.From = rsGetUser.Fields.Item("email").Value
objCDO.To = Trim(Request.Form("recipient_email"))

objCDO.Subject = rsGetUser.Fields.Item("email").Value & " has sent you a message"
objCDO.Body = Trim(Request.Form("message")) & vbcrlf & vbcrlf & "This message was
sent by " & rsGetUser.Fields.Item("first_name").Value & " " &
rsGetUser.Fields.Item("last_name").Value

objCDO.Send
Set objCDO = Nothing
%>
<% End If %>
```

When the page is loaded, the session will be created and a recordset will be opened filtering the users table to retrieve Omar's record. Once the record is retrieved, we have the columns at our disposal. Just as we can display them in Dreamweaver MX by dragging and dropping them from Bindings, we can also use them in our ASP script. The following is the code that retrieves the value of a database column:

```
RecordsetName.Fields.Item("ColumnName").Value
```

So we can retrieve the e-mail column from our recordset with the following code:

```
rsGetUser.Fields.Item("email").Value
```

The From property is automatically filled with Omar's e-mail. We also used other columns for the Subject and Body properties. Test the page live before you move on to the next section.

Sending E-mail After Insert Record

Now we will send ourselves an e-mail after an insert record. This can come in tremendously handy as we build our web site. We can send ourselves an e-mail every time a record is inserted at our web site, we can even add the values that the user sent in the e-mail into a record. This has many applications, for example you may opt to do this for a mailing list application to save all the e-mails you send in the database, or for user registers at your site by inserting the registration details and sending them in an e-mail back to the user.

Create a new dynamic ASP web page and save it as `insert_and_email.asp`. Insert a Record Insertion Form from *Insert > Application Objects > Record Insertion Form*. Select the `conn_webprodmx` connection and insert into the `users` table. After inserting, redirect to the same page. Delete all the form fields except the following: `username`, `user_pwd`, `first_name`, `last_name`, and `e-mail`.

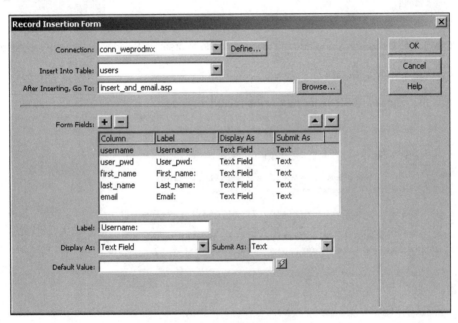

Take a look at the form, Dreamweaver MX adds a hidden field named `MM_insert`. It uses the form name as its value. When the form is submitted, this hidden field is submitted and the insert record executes. If we want to execute the e-mail once the insert record occurs we can simply check for the submission of this hidden field also. Switch to Code View and above the insert record code add the following code:

```
<% If Request.Form("MM_insert") <> "" Then %>
<%
Set objCDO = Server.CreateObject("CDONTS.NewMail")

objCDO.From = "email address"
objCDO.To = "email address"
```

```
objCDO.Subject = "An Insert Record has just occurred"
objCDO.Body = "Hi Omar," & vbcrlf & "An Insert Record has just occurred." & vbcrlf
& "username: " & Trim(Request.Form("username")) & vbcrlf & "password: " &
Trim(Request.Form("user_pwd")) & vbcrlf & "first name: " &
Trim(Request.Form("first_name")) & vbcrlf & "last name: " &
Trim(Request.Form("last_name")) & vbcrlf & "email: " & Trim(Request.Form("email"))

objCDO.Send
Set objCDO = Nothing
%>
<% End If %>
```

The body will display all the form field values. As a note you can also send the e-mail to whatever e-mail inputted in the e-mail textfield:

```
objCDO.To = Trim(Request.Form("email"))
```

Test the page live. Insert a record and check your e-mail.

The ASP script can actually go anywhere in your page because it is wrapped with a conditional statement that allows it to execute once the MM_insert hidden field is submitted to the page. It doesn't matter what happens first, the e-mail or the actual insert, since both get their values from the form fields. But if you want to make sure the CDONTS executes only after the insert record is successful, you can place it in the appropriate place within the Insert Record code. In Code View, scroll through the insert code until you find the following towards the end of the code:

```
' execute the insert
    Set MM_editCmd = Server.CreateObject("ADODB.Command")
    MM_editCmd.ActiveConnection = MM_editConnection
    MM_editCmd.CommandText = MM_editQuery
    MM_editCmd.Execute
    MM_editCmd.ActiveConnection.Close
```

This is when the actual insert executes. You can place the ASP script directly below this code block. Since this entire code is already surrounded by delimiters, you should add the ASP script without them, also you don't need to check for the MM_insert code because we're placing it within the insert code itself, which is already configured to execute when the MM_insert hidden field is submitted:

```
Set objCDO = Server.CreateObject("CDONTS.NewMail")

objCDO.From = "email address"
objCDO.To = "email address"

objCDO.Subject = "An Insert Record has just occurred"
objCDO.Body = "Hi Omar," & vbcrlf & "An Insert Record has just occurred." & vbcrlf
& "username: " & Trim(Request.Form("username")) & vbcrlf & "password: " &
Trim(Request.Form("user_pwd")) & vbcrlf & "first name: " &
Trim(Request.Form("first_name")) & vbcrlf & "last name: " &
```

```
Trim(Request.Form("last_name")) & vbcrlf & "email: " & Trim(Request.Form("email"))

objCDO.Send
Set objCDO = Nothing
```

The ASP script will now execute only when the Insert is successfully inserted.

Sending E-mail After an Update or Delete Record

We can do similar things with Update records and Delete records as well. Whenever Dreamweaver MX adds one of the behaviors to a document (Insert, Update, Delete) it adds a hidden field named MM_insert, MM_update, or MM_delete whose value is the name of the form (which is named form1 by default) so that once the form is submitted the action executes. All we have to do is check for the existence of this form field.

In order to send an e-mail after an Update form is submitted you could use the following conditional statement:

```
<% If Request.Form("MM_update") <> "" Then %>
<%
Set objCDO = Server.CreateObject("CDONTS.NewMail")

objCDO.From = "email address"
objCDO.To = "email address"

objCDO.Subject = "An Update Record has just occurred"
objCDO.Body = "Hi Omar," & vbcrlf & "An Update Record has just occurred."

objCDO.Send
Set objCDO = Nothing
%>
<% End If %>
```

The e-mail code above is only a sample e-mail. You should manipulate the e-mail to reflect your own Update record form.

You can also make sure the e-mail is sent only after the Update record is successful by adding the ASP script **after** the following Dreamweaver MX code from the Update Record Behavior, which usually resides at the end of the code:

```
' execute the update
Set MM_editCmd = Server.CreateObject("ADODB.Command")
MM_editCmd.ActiveConnection = MM_editConnection
MM_editCmd.CommandText = MM_editQuery
MM_editCmd.Execute
MM_editCmd.ActiveConnection.Close
```

To achieve the same effect with Delete records, simply use the same code, but checking for an **MM_delete** form field instead:

```
<% If Request.Form("MM_delete") <> "" Then %>
```

Forgotten Password Web Application

We have gained a lot of knowledge in this chapter about sending e-mail from our ASP web pages. Let's create a final real-world example. With all this e-mailing going on, you may be curious to find out about e-mailing users their passwords when they forget. Let's allow users to be e-mailed their passwords by simply submitting their usernames. The concept is very simple and you have all the knowledge necessary to implement it. It's done using the same concept as in the *Send E-mail with Recordset Values* section previously. All we need to do is create a form with which the user will submit his or her username. The username will be submitted to a page that filters a recordset retrieving the record that corresponds to the username submitted. We then simply send an e-mail, putting any of the recordset values in the e-mail.

Create a new dynamic ASP web page and save it as `forgotten_pwd.asp`. Insert a form with one textfield and one submit button. Call the textfield `username` and change the label of the button to *"E-mail password"*. Change the action of the form to submit back to itself, `forgotten_pwd.asp`, and make sure the method is set to `Post`. Add a new recordset named `rsGetUser`, select the `conn_webprodmx` connection, and add the following SQL:

```
SELECT email, first_name, user_pwd
FROM users
WHERE username = 'MMColParam'
```

Add the following **variable** directly below:

```
MMColParam        x        Request.Form("username")
```

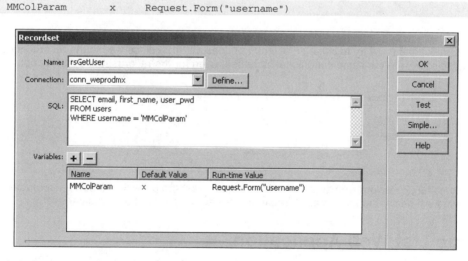

Hit *OK*. The recordset will retrieve the `email`, `first_name`, and `user_pwd` columns for the username submitted in the form. We will add a conditional statement around both the recordset and the ASP script. Since we haven't added the ASP script yet, type the following part of the `If` statement code **above** the recordset code:

```
<% If Trim(Request.Form("submit")) <> "" Then %>
```

Add the following ASP script directly **below** the recordset code:

```
<%
Set objCDO = Server.CreateObject("CDONTS.NewMail")

objCDO.From = "email address"
objCDO.To = rsGetUser.Fields.Item("email").Value

objCDO.Subject = "Here is your password"
objCDO.Body = "Your password is: " & rsGetUser.Fields.Item("user_pwd").Value

objCDO.Send
Set objCDO = Nothing
%>
<% Response.Redirect "forgotten_pwd.asp?email=true" %>
<% End If %>
```

The `To` property is set to the e-mail retrieved from the record. We then add the password to the body of the e-mail. Finally, we redirect and close the `If` statement with `End If`. The web application is basically complete. There is one last thing to do. In Code View, scroll to the bottom of the page. You will find the code that destroys the recordset object:

```
<%
rsGetUser.Close()
Set rsGetUser = Nothing
%>
```

We also have to keep this code from executing until the form is submitted. If not, the page will throw an error because it will try to close an object that does not exist since we hid the recordset object. Wrap the code with the same conditional statement used for the recordset and ASP script:

```
<% If Trim(Request.Form("submit")) <> "" Then %>
<%
rsGetUser.Close()
Set rsGetUser = Nothing
%>
<% End If %>
```

Our Forgotten Password web application is complete. Test the page live, insert a username, and the password will be sent to the e-mail stored in the e-mail column for that particular user.

Mailing List Web Application

Before we end this chapter, let's try one more web application that involves, sending e-mail to our users. With this page you can send e-mails to your users whenever you need to. The e-mail addresses will be pulled from a recordset and then we will add the mail component code and have it repeat itself to send the e-mail to each e-mail address in the recordset. In our database we have stored the e-mail addresses of each user in a column in the `users` table. For our example we will pull e-mail addresses from this table and send the same e-mail message to each one in one shot.

Create a new dynamic ASP web page and save it as `mailing_list.asp`. Create a recordset called `rsMailingListEmails`. Select the `conn_webprodmx` connection from the *Connections* menu and add the following SQL:

```
SELECT email
FROM users
```

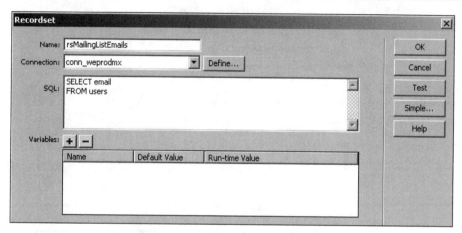

Hit *OK*. Add a form to your page with two textfields and a button. Call the first textfield `subject` and the second one `body`. From *Properties,* change both textfields to `Multi-line`. Change the name of the submit button to `email_submit` and the label to "*Send Mail*".

Now we need to add the ASP script to our page. We've been hand coding so much this chapter; let's utilize the Snippets panel to save a sample of our ASP script. Right-click on an empty space in your document and select *Create New Snippet* from the shortcut menu. When the dialog box opens, name the snippet `CDONTS` and change the Snippet Type to *Insert Block*. Insert the following code in the box:

```asp
<%
Set objCDO = Server.CreateObject("CDONTS.NewMail")

objCDO.From = "email address"
objCDO.To = "email address"

objCDO.Subject = Trim(Request.Form("subject"))
objCDO.Body = Trim(Request.Form("body"))

objCDO.Send
Set objCDO = Nothing
%>
```

Change the Preview Type to Code. Hit *OK*:

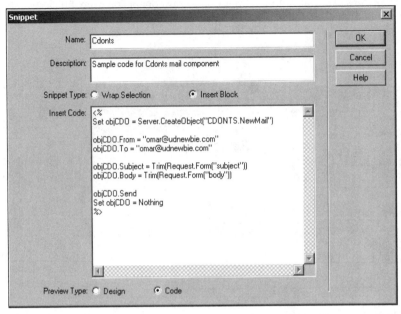

In the snippet code, feel free to use e-mail addresses that you frequently use for the From *and* To *properties so they are set once you insert the snippet.*

This snippet will now be available at any time in your CDONTS Snippets Panel. Of course, you may need to change the property values of the ASP script according to different circumstances, but it will provide the bulk of your code and you can manually change what you need to as you work. Select *Window > Snippets*. You should see your CDONTS snippet at the end of the list. In Design View, drag and drop this snippet underneath the form you just created. You should then see an ASP placeholder which will represent the ASP script. Take a look at the ASP script in Code View. We need to manually change the To property to take the e-mail from the rsMailingListEmails recordset as its value. Change the value of this property to the following:

```
objCDO.To = rsMailingListEmails.Fields.Item("email").Value
```

Go back to Design View, highlight the ASP placeholder that represents the CDONTS code and select *Server Behaviors > Repeat Region*. Select the rsMailingListEmails recordset from the menu and show all records. Hit *OK*. Finally we need to make sure the ASP script along with the repeat region only executes when the form is submitted. In Code View, find this code which is the beginning of the repeat region code block:

```
<%
While ((Repeat1__numRows <> 0) AND (NOT rsMailingListEmails.EOF))
%>
```

Add the following code **above** the start of the repeat region:

```
<%
If Request.Form("email_submit") <> "" Then
%>
```

Next, in Code View find the end of the repeat region code:

```
<%
    Repeat1__index=Repeat1__index+1
    Repeat1__numRows=Repeat1__numRows-1
    rsMailingListEmails.MoveNext()

Wend
%>
```

Add the following code directly **after** the end of the repeat region code:

```
<%
Response.Redirect "mailing_list.asp?email=true"
End If
%>
```

Here is the block you should've just created in Code View:

That's it. When the page is tested live, the Recordset will have retrieved all the e-mails from the `users` table. Once the form is submitted the ASP script will execute to send the e-mail message to each e-mail account. Finally it will redirect to the same page adding a URL parameter informing you that the e-mail was sent.

Summary

In this chapter we looked at most of what we need to know to send e-mails from within our own ASP pages. We looked at how to configure your SMTP server. We then looked at the syntax of three of the most popular ASP mail components: CDONTS, ASPEmail and Jmail and how each can be used to send static e-mails from an ASP page. Then we moved on to sending dynamic e-mails, based on conditions, changing the values of the mail component properties on the fly and even allowing users to change them. Finally we looked at two full e-mail applications: forgotten password and a mailing list. You should now be able to create your own custom e-mail web applications for your web site.

10

- Advanced sample applications:

  - User wish list application

  - Two way messaging application

Author: Omar Elbaga

Advanced Techniques

In previous chapters we learned how to use Dreamweaver MX server behaviors to add a lot of functionality to our web site. Most of the web applications we've built so far were set up using a database and a few built-in server behaviors and did not require too much manual manipulation.

Dreamweaver users often feel limited because they don't understand the scope it has. For example, a user might know how to create logins and how to use the *Insert Record* feature, but if asked to create, say, a user registration, they would get stumped because there isn't a server behavior explicitly called "*User Registration*". And yet, it is the familiar *Insert Record* feature that is used to create user registrations. To develop advanced applications in Dreamweaver it is important to understand the flexibility of server behaviors such as the *Insert Record* which can be used for a multitude of tasks: user registrations, forgotten passwords, administrative inserts, and much more.

In this chapter we will be creating two web applications:

- A user wish list

- A user messaging application

The first web application will allow users to enter book titles into their own personal wish list that can be accessed by logging in. The second web application will allow users to send messages to each other from your web site. You will shortly see how even the simplest Dreamweaver MX server behaviors can be used to help you build very advanced web applications.

User Wish List

The web application we are about to build will allow users to save book titles in their own personal wish list that can be accessed through a login. The concept can be applied to many other applications. For example, say we had a page displaying database-driven news or articles; we could give users the ability to save news stories or articles in personal lists that can be accessed through a login. In our case, since we have book details stored in a database, we will allow users to save a list containing titles they might want to purchase at some point that will act as a wish list, similar to the ones found at *www.bn.com* or *www.amazon.com*.

In order to do this we need to store the `username` and `book_id` of the book in a separate table. The user should be able to insert records into this table. Since the `username` is unique, we can query that table to retrieve all books for a particular user, which will serve as his or her wish list. Hence, we need to create a new table that will store that info. Open the database we created in *Chapter 7* named `webprodmx_data.mdb` and create a new table named `wishlist` with the following columns and data types:

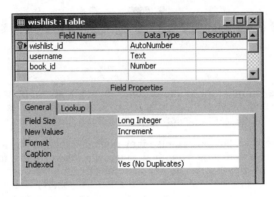

```
Table: wishlist
wishlist_id          Autonumber (primary key)
username             Text
book_id              Number
```

Here is the table design in Access:

We can leave the default values for the field properties as they are. Now that we have created the table in our database we need to create three pages to realize our application:

- A page that will list the books from our table

- A page that will act as a "Details" page, displaying additional information about a selected book and allow the user to perform an insert into the `wishlist` table by adding his or her `username` and the `book_id` of the selected book

- A third page that will query the `wishlist` table and display all books stored in it that are associated with the particular `username` of the logged-in user

Before continuing, please ensure you have created a virtual directory named `webprodmx` on your server. We should also have a site defined named `webprodmx` and created a connection to the `webprodmx_data.mdb` database in Dreamweaver MX. These steps were described in Chapter 7. Please refer back to it if you need more information.

Books_display.asp

This web application needs to utilize a login system, because we want to make sure the user logs in to see his or her wish list. For sake of time, I would rather not have you build a login page; hopefully you should have the login pages that were used in *Chapters 7* and *8*.

If you do have one handy, open it in Dreamweaver MX and reload the *Log In* behavior, changing it so that the user is redirected to the `books_display.asp` page after logging in. This is the page that will display the books that we will create below.

If you don't have a login page handy, we will do the next best thing. The *Log In* behavior simply authenticates a username and password and sets the username in a session. Since we, the administrators, don't need the login for testing, we can manually create a session called `MM_Username` for one of the users and treat the actual login process as a "given" until we actually go live with the application. We will use the first username in the table, `omar`, and create a session out of it. So long as this session exists, we can continue building the application as if a login has already occurred. We will create this session on the first page.

This first page will simply display all the book details from the `books` table, and also serve as a master page for a detail page we will create afterwards. Create a new dynamic ASP web page and save it as `books_display.asp`. Before anything, if you are using a completed login page you need to make sure the username session is created once the page loads. In Code View, add the following code at the top of the page:

```
<% Session("MM_Username") = "omar" %>
```

This will create the session called `MM_Username`, which will store the username `"omar"` as its value.

> *Bear in mind that setting this session manually is serving as a sort of "dummy" login. Anyone accessing this page will be assumed to be logged in as Omar. Please be sure to remove this line and create a separate login page before these pages go into a production environment.*

Create a new recordset called `rsGetBooks`, choose the `conn_webprodmx` connection and insert the following SQL:

```sql
SELECT book_id, book_image_path, book_author_fname, book_author_lname, book_title,
book_price
FROM books
ORDER BY book_title ASC
```

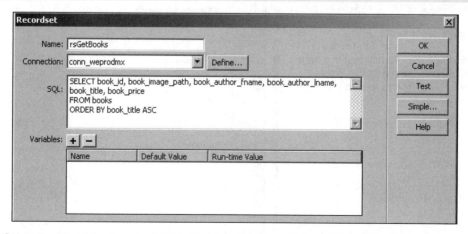

Hit *OK*. In Design View, insert a table with one row, two columns, 50% width. Place your cursor in the left-hand column of the table and select *Insert > Image*. Choose *Data Sources* from the top of the dialog box. Select the *book_image_path* column from the `rsGetBooks` recordset.

Add the following URL details **before** the recordset column variable that was just added in the URL field:

http://localhost/webprodmx/

In Code View, the final URL should be:

```
http://localhost/webprodmx/<%=(rsGetBooks.Fields.Item("book_image_path").Value)%>
```

Hit *OK* to close the dialog box. Place your cursor in the right column of your table. Drag and drop the following columns into it:

```
book_title
book_author_fname
book_author_lname
book_price
```

Feel free to format the text as you like. Highlight the dynamic text for the price and select the drop-down arrow beside the book_price column under *Bindings*. Select *Currency > Default* to format the price with dollar signs. Select the dynamic text for the book_title and link it to a page called book_details.asp. Pass a URL parameter named book_id whose value should come from the book_id column in the rsGetBooks recordset. You can do so from *Properties*; click the folder beside the Link field. Hit the *Parameters* button and add the parameter.

The link should now look like this:

```
book_details.asp?book_id=<%=(rsGetBooks.Fields.Item("book_id").Value)%>
```

Place your cursor inside the table and select the <tr> code from the document's status bar. Select *Server Behaviors > Repeat Region*. When the dialog box opens check the show all records option and hit *OK*.

Our page is complete. Add a link to a wishlist.asp page wherever you like on the page. Finally test the page live to make sure the books display properly. Feel free to format the page how you like.

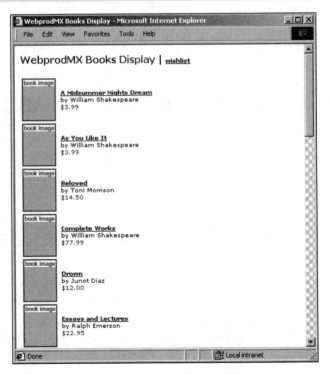

Book_details.asp

The second page will display the details of a book selected from the `books_display.asp` page. Create a new dynamic ASP web page and save it as `book_details.asp`. Create a new recordset named `rsGetBook`, choose the `conn_webprodmx` connection and add the following SQL:

```
SELECT *
FROM books
WHERE book_id = MMColParam
```

Add the following variable directly below:

```
MMColParam          0         Request.QueryString("book_id")
```

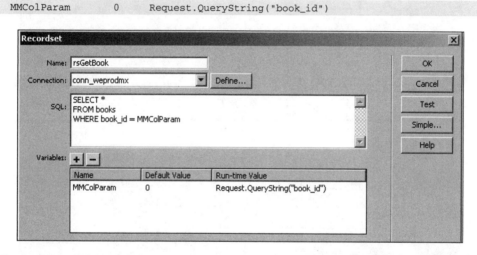

In Design View, insert a table with two rows, two columns, and 50% width. Place your cursor in the left column of the first row of the table and insert an image whose path should come from the `book_image_path` column from the `rsGetBook` recordset as it did in the previous example. In Code View, the source URL that will display the image should be:

```
http://localhost/webprodmx/<%=(rsGetBooks.Fields.Item("book_image_path").Value)%>
```

Place your cursor in the right column of the first row and drag and drop the following columns from your `rsGetBook` recordset in *Bindings*:

```
book_title
book_author_fname
book_author_lname
book_price
page_count
book_isbn
```

Place your cursor in the right column of the second row and select *Insert > Application Objects >
Record Insertion Form*. Choose the `conn_weprodmx` connection. Insert into the `wishlist` table we
created earlier. After inserting, redirect to a `wishlist.asp` page. Delete the `wishlist_id` from the
form fields list because we don't want the user to be able to insert a value into this column. We need
to use default values for both the `book_id` and `username` columns. The `book_id` column should
use the value from the `book_id` URL parameter. The `username` column should use the value stored
in the session `MM_Username`. Highlight the `book_id` column from the form fields list. Select *Hidden
Field* from the *Display As* option and then add the following code as its default value:

```
<%=Request.QueryString("book_id") %>
```

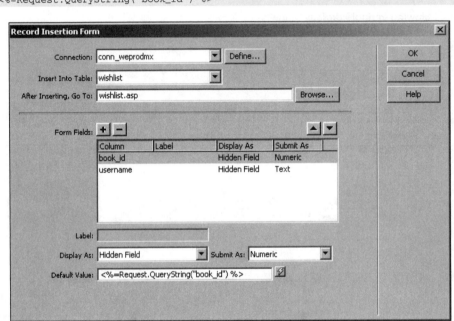

Highlight the `username` column from the form fields list. Select *Hidden Field* from the *Display As*
option and then add the following code as its default value:

```
<%=Session("MM_Username") %>
```

After inputting all the information hit *OK*. An insert record form should be created in your document
with two textfields for both the `book_id` and `username` columns. We really don't want the user to
have to manually add the `book_id` since he or she would have already selected it from the previous
page. And we certainly don't want the user to manually add the username, because not only is it an
inconvenience, but the user could add any username he or she wants, therefore adding books to
other users' wishlists, which is why we need to display these fields as hidden fields. When you go
back to Design View, change the label of the insert button to "*Add to Wish List*".

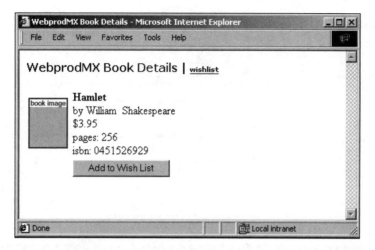

The page is now complete. The user will be able to add a particular book to a wish list that will be associated only with his or her username. If you test this page live, make sure you load the `books_display.asp` page first to set the `MM_Username` session before going to the `book_details.asp` page, otherwise the username in the insert record will be empty, and the book inserted into the `wishlist` table will not be associated with the user who inserted the record! Whenever you create a web application like this for a real web site, make sure that whenever the user has the opportunity to add something to the `wishlist` the session that holds the unique identifier for the user actually exists.

Wishlist.asp

Let's create our last web page, the page that actually displays the wishlist. This page will simply query the `wishlist` table to pull the books associated with the `username` of the logged-in user. Since the `wishlist` table only stores the `username` and `book id`, our query must be run against both the `wishlist` table and the `books` table, so that we can also display the book title of the books retrieved. (For a refresher on SQL, see *Chapter 6*.)

Create a new dynamic ASP web page and save it as `wishlist.asp`. Create a recordset named `rsGetWishList`, select the `conn_webprodmx` connection and add the following SQL:

```
SELECT wishlist.book_id, books.book_image_path, books.book_title
FROM wishlist, books
WHERE wishlist.book_id = books.book_id AND wishlist.username = 'MMColParam'
```

Add the following variable directly below:

```
MMColParam       x       Session("MM_Username")
```

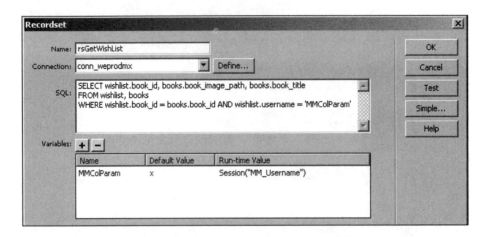

You may be wondering why the default value is x here, while we used 1 elsewhere. In this case, the dynamic variable has a `string` data type so we used a string default. When we used 1 in other recordsets this was because the dynamic variable had a number data type.

Hit *OK*. The SQL query above selects three sets of data from the `books` table:

- The `book_id` column from the `wishlist` table

- The `book_image_path`

- And the `book_title`

where the `username` stored in the `username` column of the `wishlist` table is the same as the `username` stored in the `MM_Username` session.

Insert a table with two rows, two columns, and 50% width. Place your cursor in the left column of the first row. Insert the book image whose source should come from the `book_image_path` column of the `rsGetWishList` recordset as you've inserted it on the two previous pages. Place your cursor in the right column of the first row and drag and drop the `book_title` from the `rsGetWishList` recordset in *Bindings*. You can link the book to the `book_details.asp` page, but if you do, be sure to pass the `book_id` from the recordset in a URL parameter named `book_id` since this is how the `book_details.asp` filters the recordset for the book selected.

We need to make the page display all the books contained in the wishlist, so place the cursor somewhere in the first row and select the `<tr>` code from the document's status bar. Select *Server Behaviors > Repeat Region*. When the dialog box opens check the *Show All Records* option and hit *OK*.

In case the returned recordset has no records in it, display a message informing the user that his or her wishlist is empty. Place your cursor in the right column of the second row and type the text "*You have not added any books to your Wish List*". We need to show this text only if the recordset comes up empty, so highlight the entire text and select *Server Behaviors > Show Region > Show Region If Recordset Is Empty*.

The bulk of our wishlist is done. When a user accesses the page it will display the books (or lack thereof) stored in the wishlist for the logged-in user.

Delete Book from Wishlist

Finally we need to give the user the ability to delete books from his or her wishlist. We will simply add a Delete Record server behavior to our page. Add an additional column by placing your cursor in the right column of the first row, right-clicking and selecting *Table > Split Cell* and splitting the cell into two columns, see the screenshot below:

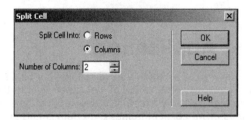

In the new column insert an empty form with a submit button inside it. Make sure the delete form is within the Repeat Region. Change the label of this button to "*Delete from Wish List*". Select *Server Behaviors > Delete Record*. Select the `conn_webprodmx` connection. Delete from the `wishlist` table. Select the record from the `rsGetWishList` recordset. Select the `book_id` from the *Unique Key Column*. Delete by submitting the form you just created. After deleting, go to `wishlist.asp`.

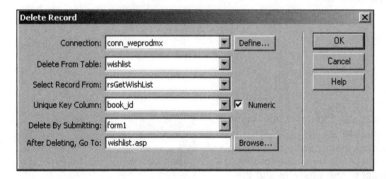

Hit *OK*. Our `wishlist.asp` page is complete. Here is a look at my wishlist after adding two books.

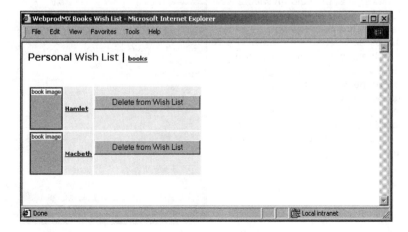

Always make sure the session is created before adding a book . Remember that the session is created on the `books_display.asp` page. If the session is not created, the username hidden field in the insertion form on the `book_details.asp` page that inserts into the wishlist table will be empty, therefore the book will not be associated with any user.

Test your page live. Feel free to play with the application by adding and deleting books to your wishlist.

User Messaging Application

We will now create a fabulous web application that will allow your users to leave messages for each other on your site. Users will have a personal list of messages sent to them, be able to view them and reply to them. This web application will require a new table to be added to our database, which will store the message details. If we collect the message details and two usernames (sender, receiver) associated with the message we can then query the database to display messages associated with those usernames on our ASP pages. We must create a new table that will store that info. Open the `webprodmx_data.mdb` database and create a new table named `usermessages` with the following columns and data types:

```
Table: usermessages
message_id           Autonumber (primary key)
from_username        Text
to_username          Text
subject              Text
message              Memo
viewed_status        Yes/No
dtstamp              Date/Time
```

The `from_username` column should store the username of the sender. The `to_username` column will store the username of the receiver. Of course the `subject` column will store the subject of the message and the `message` column will store the message text itself. The `viewed_status` column will be a Boolean data type, which will store whether or not the message has been viewed. The Boolean value of the `viewed_status` will be `False` by default and set to `True` when the message is first viewed. The `dtstamp` column will store the date and time the message was sent. Give this column a default value to generate the date and time when the record is created, using `Now()` for Access, or `GetDate()` for SQL Server. Here is a look at the table design in Access:

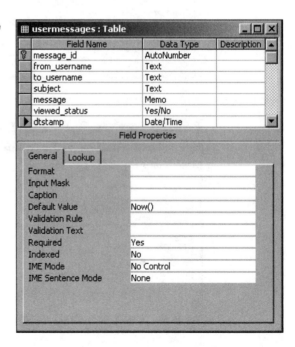

This web application will also consist of 4 dynamic ASP pages.

- The first page will allow a user to select another user to send a message to

- The second page will allow the user to submit a message to a database table that will store the message including the submitting and receiving of usernames

- The third page will display the received messages for the logged-in user

- The fourth page will display all the details of the message selected from the list on the third page

Just like the Wish List application this one will require users to login so that we can save the username in the table. If we don't save the username in the table we will not be able to associate users with their messages. Again, instead of creating a Log In application at this stage, we will simply create a session named MM_Username for one of the users, to mimic the results of a Dreamweaver MX Log In. However, in this case we also want to do one other thing that we didn't do when creating the session for the Wish List application. To help us in testing we need the ability to switch from user to user to check our system.

So let's create a small form to give us the ability to change the value of the MM_Username session to mimic the login of a different user.

display_users.asp

The first page we will create will be a list of the users from which we can select a particular user to send a message to. We will create hyperlinks, passing the username as a URL parameter to the next page, where we will actually send the message.

Create a new dynamic ASP web page and save it as display_users.asp. On your page, right below the <body> tag add the following navigation code in Code View or create it in Design View:

```
Welcome <%= Session("MM_Username") %> | <a href="display_users.asp">Home</a> | <a href="my_messages.asp"> My Messages</a>
```

> It's a good idea to place this set of navigation links at the top of all your pages for better organization. This helps you navigate through the web pages easily when testing pages. Make sure the MM_Username session is set to see which username you are logged in with.

Create a new recordset named rsGetUsers, select the conn_webprodmx connection and add the following SQL:

```
SELECT username
FROM users
```

This recordset will retrieve all the usernames. Underneath the navigation bar we created, insert a table with a single row, three columns, and 50% width. From *Bindings*, drag and drop the `username` column into the first column. In the second column, type the text "*Send Message*". Link this text to a `send_message.asp` page that we'll be making next. Pass a URL parameter named `username` whose value should come from the `username` column of the `rsGetUser` recordset. The final link should look like this:

```
send_message.asp?username=<%=(rsGetUsers.Fields.Item("username").Value)%>
```

You should now repeat the records. Place your cursor in the first row of the table, select the `<tr>` tag from the document status bar and select *Server Behaviors > Repeat Region*. When the dialog box opens, check the option to show all records and hit *OK*.

Finally we want to be able to test our web application with various usernames, so we need to create the dummy login I referred to earlier. Again, all it does is mimic the Dreamweaver MX Log In server behavior by setting a session called `MM_Username`. In our case, we will be allowed to change the logged-in `username` form this page. Of course, this is only for testing purposes.

Place your cursor in the third column and type the text "*Log In*". Link the text back to the same page and pass a URL parameter named `dummy_login` whose value should come from the `username` column of the `rsGetUser` recordset. The final link should look like this in Code View:

```
display_users.asp?dummy_login=<%=(rsGetUsers.Fields.Item("username").Value)%>
```

Switch to Code View and add the following code at the top of your page; above the connections include:

```
<% if Request.QueryString("dummy_login") <> "" Then %>
<% Session("MM_Username") = Request.QueryString("dummy_login") %>
<% End If %>
```

What this code does, is check if a URL parameter named `dummy_login` is passed. If it is, it sets a session called `MM_Username`, which will contain whatever username is passed in the URL parameter. Finish formatting your page and then view it live. Log in as your desired user: I logged in with the username *omar*. As we complete other pages you will want to log in as different users to send and view messages between users. You could test it now by logging in with different usernames. The username beside the welcome messages should reflect the logged-in username.

send_message.asp

This page will allow the user to actually send the message. The message will be stored in the `usermessages` table to be retrieved by the user later. Before we begin building the page, take a look back at the most important columns of the `usermessages` database table:

```
from_username      Text
to_username        Text
subject            Text
message            Memo
```

We will be inserting values into these columns from this page. We will collect the username passed in the `username` URL parameter, and insert it into the `to_username` column; this is the `username` selected on the previous page, which represents the recipient username. The sender's username is the username of the logged-in user. Fortunately we always have this at our fingertips as the value of the `MM_Username` session, which we insert into the `from_username` column. Both these values will be inserted into their appropriate columns from hidden fields in the form. The `subject` and `message` will be collected normally through form textfields and inserted respectively. Now we need to create the insert form that will collect the message details.

Create a new dynamic ASP web page and save it as `send_message.asp`. Add the navigation bar that we created in `display_users.asp`, to the top of this page. Below the navigation bar, insert a table with four rows, one column, and 25% width. Insert an empty form inside the table. Place your cursor **inside** the empty form and insert another table with four rows, one column, and 100% width. Place your cursor in the first row, switch to Code View, and add the following code:

```
Send a message to <%= Trim(Request.QueryString("username")) %>
```

This column will inform the sender which user he or she is sending the message to. The recipient username will come from the URL parameter passed from the previous page. Back in Design View, place your cursor in the second row, type the text "*Subject:*", enter a line break and insert a textfield. Rename the textfield "`subject`". Place your cursor in the third row, type the text "*Message:*", enter a line break and insert a textfield. Rename the textfield "`message`". From *Properties* change the type from *Single line* to *Multi line*. Change the character width to 22 and number of lines to 9. Place your cursor in the fourth row and insert a submit button. Change the label of the button to "*Send*".

The subject and message will be created by the user. We need to add the sender and recipient usernames to hidden fields, which will be inserted into the table along with the subject and message. So, after the submit button insert two hidden fields. Make sure the hidden fields are still inside the form, otherwise they will not be submitted and the insert record will throw an error. Rename the first hidden field to "`from_username`" and give it the following value:

```
<%=Session("MM_Username") %>
```

Rename the second hidden field "`to_username`" and give it the following value:

```
<%=Request.QueryString("username") %>
```

Our form is now complete.

Select *Server Behaviors > Insert Record*. When the dialog box opens, select the `conn_webprodmx` connection. Insert into the `usermessages` table. After inserting, redirect to `display_users.asp`. Submit the form fields to the appropriate columns and hit *OK*.

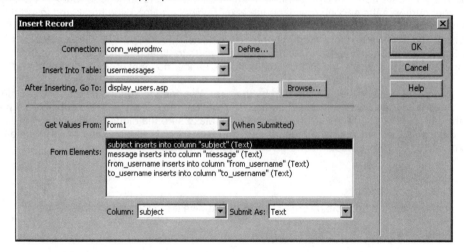

Our page is complete for now, although we will do a couple of more things to the page later such as creating the page that will display a list of messages, and another page to display the details of any selected message. You may test the page live by trying to send a message to another user, and you can check that the messages are getting saved, if you like, by opening the database. Before you do so, make sure the MM_Username session is set (if you see the username you selected from the dummy login by the welcome message then you are ok).

We can now send messages but we still need to create the page that retrieves the messages for our users. Now let's create the page that actually displays a list of messages sent to the user.

my_messages.asp

This page will act in a similar way to an inbox for our users. They will go to this page to view a list of messages sent to them. This is one of the easiest pages to create! All we have to do is retrieve records from the usermessages table where the to_username column equals the username stored in the MM_Username session.

Create a new dynamic ASP web page and save it as my_messages.asp. Don't forget to add the navigation bar we used for the other pages at the top of this page. Create a new recordset named rsGetMessages. Select the conn_webprodmx connection and add the following SQL:

```
SELECT *
FROM usermessages
WHERE to_username = 'MMColParam'
ORDER BY viewed_status DESC
```

Add the following variable directly below:

```
MMColParam        x        Session("MM_Username")
```

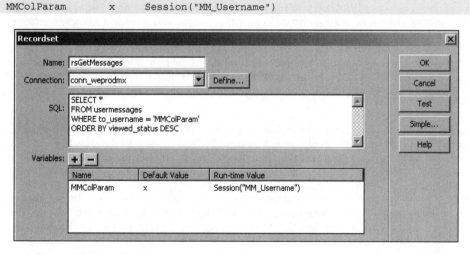

The SQL query will retrieve the entire record stored in the usermessages table, where the value of the to_username column is the same as the value of the MM_Username session. We ordered the query to display records that haven't been viewed by the user yet, first.

In Design View, just below the navigation bar, insert a table with four rows, three columns and 80% width. In the first column type the text "*INBOX*". Now for the second row: in the first column type the text "*From*", in the middle column type the text "*Subject*", in the last column type the text "*Date*". In my own example, I changed the background color of the columns that had text in them at this stage to an orange color (*#FF3300*).

Take a look at your recordset in the *Bindings* window. You should see all the columns in your `rsGetMessages` recordset. Drag and drop the `from_username` column to the first column of the third row of your table. Drag and drop the `subject` column to the middle column of the third row. Drag and drop the `dtstamp` column **twice** to the last column of the third row. We need these two because we want to display both the date and the time of the message separately.

In Design View highlight the first `dtstamp` dynamic text and then from *Bindings* format it from the *Date/Time* formatting to display the date only in a style of your choice. Highlight the second `dtstamp` dynamic text and then from *Bindings* format it to display the time only in a style of your choice. At this point, I changed the background for the rows with the dynamic text to a yellowish color (*#FFFF99*).

Place your cursor in the third row, select the `<tr>` code in the document's status bar and select *Server Behaviors > Repeat Region*. When the dialog box opens check the option to show all records and hit *OK*.

We want the user to be able to select a message to view more details. Highlight the *subject* dynamic text in Design View and link it to a `view_message.asp` passing a URL parameter named `message_id` whose value should come from the `message_id` column of the `rsGetMessages` recordset. The final link for the subject dynamic text should look like this in Code View:

```
view_message.asp?message_id=<%=(rsGetMessages.Fields.Item("message_id").Value)%>
```

The user can now select the subject of the message to view it on the next page, which we will be creating shortly. Before we do that, however, we should probably display a friendly message to let them know if they have no messages. If there are no messages for this user it means that no records will be retrieved in the recordset `rsGetMessages` because the `username` of the logged-in user won't be in the `to_username` column of any records. In the first column of the last row of your table in Design View, type the text "*You have no messages*". Highlight this text and select *Server Behaviors | Show Region | Show Region If Recordset Is Empty*. It will now be displayed if the recordset comes up empty.

This page is complete now. You should test the pages we've produced so far by sending messages to different users and then checking them. You wont be able to view all the details of a particular message yet because we haven't created that page, but you will see the messages sent to a particular user listed by logging in with his or her name and accessing `my_messages.asp`.

Remember when you test the pages out that the `MM_Username` session has to be set, otherwise no records will display on the `my_messages.asp` page. Log in with a user from the `display_users.asp` page and click the *send message* text beside another user to send him or her a message...

...send your message...

...and then go back to the `display_users.asp` page to log in with the `username` you just sent a message to. Check the `my_messages.asp` page and the message should be listed.

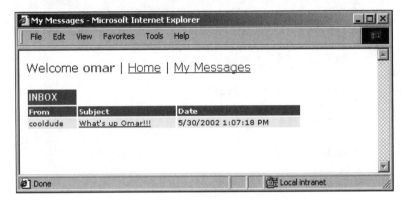

view_message.asp

There only remains one last page to complete our application. This will display the full subject and body of a message selected from the `my_messages.asp` page. It will also have to change the value of the `viewed_status` column to `True`, which will be done using the *Command* behavior without the user's intervention.

Create a new dynamic ASP web page and save it as `view_message.asp`. Before we do anything add the navigation bar to the top of the page in Design View.

Now create the recordset that will retrieve the message that was selected from the previous page. The `message_id` was passed to this page as a URL parameter. We need to retrieve the record from the `usermessages` table where the value of the `message_id` column equals the value of the `message_id` URL parameter. Create a new recordset named `rsGetMessage`. Select the `conn_webprodmx` connection and add the following SQL:

```
SELECT *
FROM usermessages
WHERE message_id = MMColParam
```

Add the following variable directly below:

```
MMColParam        0        Request.QueryString("message_id")
```

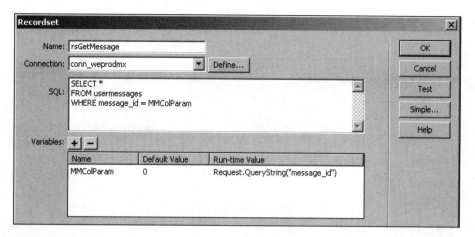

Underneath the navigation bar, insert a table with seven rows, one column, and 35% width in Design View. In the first row type the text "*Subject:*". In the second column drag and drop the `subject` column from *Bindings*. In the third row type the text "*Message:*". In the fourth column drag and drop the `message` column from *Bindings*. In the fifth row type the text "*From:*". Enter a space to the right of this text and drag and drop the `from_username` column beside it. The user will now be able to view the contents of the message sent to them. Leave the last two rows empty for now. This page will display the subject, message, and the sender username.

As it stands, the message may contain carriage returns but they will not be preserved when the page is displayed, that is the message will appear as one paragraph even if the sender used carriage returns to space out his or her message. This is because the page will be generated in HTML which employs (`<br>`) or paragraph breaks (`<p></p>`) instead of carriage returns, however, we can replace ASCII carriage returns with HTML line breaks. Highlight the message dynamic text in Design View and then switch to Code View and change the code for the message dynamic text to the following:

```
<%=Replace(rsGetMessage.Fields.Item("message").Value, chr(13),"<br>")%>
```

This code will find and replace all carriage returns represented by the `chr(13)` ASCII characters from the sender's input with HTML line breaks.

Now that the message has been viewed, we change the `viewed_status` by changing its value from `False` to `True`. In Access we have to check off the `Yes/No` column for this record. Since we want the user to be oblivious to this process, we will create a *Command* to automatically update the record once the page loads. Remember that we have the ID of the message stored in the URL parameter.

Select *Server Behaviors > Command*. Name the command `cmdViewedStatus`, select the `conn_webprodmx` connection, and select `Update` from the *Type* menu. Dreamweaver MX should generate the basic SQL for an `Update` statement. Add the following values:

```
UPDATE usermessages
SET viewed_status = True
WHERE message_id = MMColParam
```

Add the following variable directly below:

```
MMColParam          Request.QueryString("message_id")
```

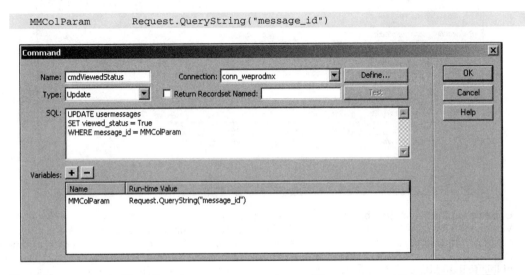

The SQL command will set the `viewed_status` column of the `message_id` stored in the URL parameter named `message_id` to `True`. This command will be executed once the page loads.

You should now test your pages live.

Extras

If you are content with the way the web application works so far, then you don't have to go any further. If you want to add a few more special features then keep reading! We will add a few more things to our pages to make them even more user-friendly.

Deleting Unwanted Messages

We will add a couple more features to our `view_message.asp` page, but before we do so I want you to make a copy of this page as it is currently because it will be used later for one of the other extra features. Reload the `view_message.asp` page in Dreamweaver MX and save it as `view_sent_message.asp`. Before you close it change the text "*From*" to "*To*" in the fifth row of the HTML table and change the `from_username` dynamic text alongside it to the `to_username` dynamic text. Put this page away for now.

It would be nice to give the users the ability to delete unwanted messages after viewing them. Reload the `view_message.asp` page in Dreamweaver MX. Insert a horizontal rule below the HTML table that displays the message. Insert a table with one row and 35% width. Insert an empty form inside the table and insert a button inside the form. Rename the form `frm_delete` and change the label of the button to "*Delete*". Select *Server Behaviors / Delete Record*. When the dialog box opens select the `conn_webprodmx` connection. Delete from the `usermessages` table. Select the record from the `rsGetMessage` recordset. Select the `message_id` as the *Unique Key Column*. Choose to submit the "*frm_delete*" form and redirect to the `my_messages.asp` page after the delete action takes place.

The users will now be able to delete the message after viewing it.

Reply to Messages

Let's do something even nicer for our users. Now that they can view a message it would be more useful if we give them the opportunity to reply to that particular message rather than send a new message. Instead of creating a new page we can use the same `send_message.asp` page for the reply.

Remember, our HTML table in `view_message.asp` has seven rows, and we left the last two blank. Leave the sixth row blank, for now, but place your cursor in the seventh row and insert an empty form. Set the `Action` of the form to submit to "`send_message.asp`" and make sure the `Method` is set to `Post`. Insert two buttons and three hidden fields inside the form. Rename the first submit button "`submit_reply`" and change the label to "*Reply*". Highlight the second submit button and from *Properties* change its `Action` to `None` and change the label to "*Cancel*". While the button is highlighted go to *Window > Behaviors* and select *Go To URL* from the behaviors list:

Input `my_messages.asp` for the URL field and hit *OK* to close the dialog box. This button will simply redirect without submitting the form to the `my_messages.asp` if the user decides not to reply.

Rename the first hidden field "`username`" and from *Bindings* bind the `from_username` column as its value. Although this is the sender's username for this message, it will submit back to the `send_message.asp` to become the recipient's username. If you remember we passed the recipient username in a URL parameter named `username` from the `display_users.asp` page to the `send_message.asp` page. Now we will send it as a form post using the same name. Rename the second hidden field "`subject`" and from *Bindings* bind the `subject` column as its value. The value should look like this:

```
<%=(rsGetMessage.Fields.Item("subject").Value)%>
```

Rename the third hidden field "*message*" and from *Bindings* bind the `message` column as its value. The value should look like this:

```
<%=(rsGetMessage.Fields.Item("message").Value)%>
```

We will send the subject, message, and recipient usernames back to the `send_message.asp` page, which will be used on the send message form if the user chooses to reply.

The sender username will be coming from the `MM_Username` session. In order for this to work properly we need to adjust the form on our `send_message.asp` page to accept form fields submitted from the form on this page.

Reload the `send_message.asp` page and take a good look at the form on this page. There are four fields that insert into the `usermessages` table. Now we have values that can come to this page from two different pages. We have a `username` that can come from the `display_users.asp` page and a `username`, `subject`, and `message` values that can come from a form submitted through a form on the `view_message.asp` page. The `display_users.asp` page submits a URL parameter named `username` that takes the value of the hidden field in the form called `to_username`. We want to make sure that this field gets a value from the username either in the URL parameter or through the reply form. The default value for this field is currently:

```
<%=Request.QueryString("username") %>
```

which forces it to accept a parameter called `username` only from the `QueryString`. Change it to the following:

```
<%=Request("username") %>
```

It will now accept a parameter named `username` from either a query string or form post. Do the same for `username` dynamic text in the first row of the table. It should now read:

```
Send a message to <%=Request("username") %>
```

That takes care of the username. The recipient's username will either come from the URL parameter when the user is sending a new message or from a form post when the user is replying. The sender username will always come from the `MM_Username` session whether the user is sending a new message or replying to an existing one.

Utilizing the Original Subject and Message in Reply

There is one thing left to do: when a user uses this form to reply to the message viewed on the `view_message.asp` page, we want to populate the subject textfield with the original subject of the message adding *Re:* in front of the subject, so the recipient knows it's a reply. Fortunately, we have submitted the subject and message values to this page from the reply form on `view_message.asp` page. If that form is submitted we want to populate the subject textfield on this page to the value of the original subject. Highlight the subject textfield and add the following code as its value:

```
<% If Request.Form("submit_reply") <> "" Then %>Re: <%=Request.Form("subject")%><%
End If %>
```

The `<input>` tag should now look like this in Code View:

```
<input name="subject" type="text" id="subject" size="29" value="<% If
Request.Form("submit_reply") <> "" Then %><%=Request.Form("subject")%><% End If %>">
```

The conditional statement will check to see if the reply form was submitted to this page. If so, it populates the subject value with the original subject submitted from the reply form on the `view_message.asp` page.

Another nice feature would be to populate the message textfield with the original message. We will use the > character to precede lines of the original message which will separate the original message from the reply message. Add the following code as the initial value for the textarea:

```
<% If Request.Form("submit_reply") <> "" Then %>
<%=Replace(Request.Form("message"),chr(10), "> ")%><% End If %>
```

> *The code above should be written as one line. Please leave an empty space after the > character in the line* < *%=Replace(Request.Form("message"),chr(10), "> ")%* > *so that some distance appears between the character and the beginning of the original message lines.*

The <textarea> tag should now look like this in Code View:

```
<textarea name="message" cols="22" rows="9" id="message"><% If
Request.Form("submit_reply") <> "" Then %>
<%=Replace(Request.Form("message"),chr(10), "> ")%><% End If %></textarea>
```

The conditional statement will check to see if the reply form was submitted to this page. If so, it populates the message value with the original message submitted from the reply form on the view_message.asp page. It also places a > character at the beginning of every new line so that both the sender and recipient users can differentiate between the original message and the new message.

Differentiating Between Read and Unread Messages

It would be friendlier if the user could know, just by looking, which messages have already been viewed on the `my_messages.asp` page. Well, now that we have created the command to update the `viewed_status` column on the `view_message.asp`, we will have a way of knowing whether or not the user has read a given message. If it is, the column will equal `True` and if not it will equal `False`.

Reload the `my_messages.asp` page in Dreamweaver MX. Place your cursor in the first column of the third row of your table. We will show a different background color for messages that have been read. Switch to Code View and the code for the background color of the column should look like this: `bgcolor="#FFFF99"` Change the value of the `bgcolor` to the following:

```
bgcolor="<% If rsGetMessages.Fields.Item("viewed_status").Value <> True Then
%>#FFFF99<%Else%>#FFFFCC<% End If %>"
```

Feel free to do this for the `bgcolor` of the next two columns in the third row. This way the color of the entire row that displays message details will be more obvious.

This code will use the color `#FFFF99` if the `viewed_status` column is `False` which means the message has not been read and `#FFFFCC` if the `viewed_status` column is `True` which means the message has been read. Feel free to test the page by sending new messages and viewing them. When you click a subject to view a message on the `my_messages.asp` page you will then be taken to the `view_message.asp` page. When you go back to the `my_messages.asp` page make sure you reload the page to see the updated background color.

Displaying Sent Messages

Finally, how about allowing the user to view not only the messages he or she received but sent messages also? The idea behind this is simple, and is the same concept behind our `my_messages.asp` page. The recordset on that page retrieves records where the `to_username` column equals the value of the `MM_Username` session. This will retrieve messages that were sent to the logged-in user, but in order to display messages that the logged-in user sent, the recordset must retrieve records where the `from_username` column equals the value of the `MM_Username` session. The `rsGetMessages` recordset on this page should be changed to the following in order to retrieve sent messages:

```
SELECT *
FROM usermessages
WHERE from_username = 'MMColParam'
ORDER BY viewed_status DESC
```

We could simply create a new page with this recordset, but let's use the same page. You might be wondering how we could possible use the same page as the SQL is hard coded to filter for a specific column. Well we can make even the SQL dynamic, so that it changes depending on a dynamic variable passed to the page. We will allow the user to change the column name from a URL parameter. It will switch from `to_username` to `from_username` depending on what the user wants.

First reload the `my_messages.asp` page in Dreamweaver MX. Link the "*INBOX*" text in the first column of the HTML table back to itself with no URL parameters. Add the text "*SENT*" to the second column of the first row. Link the text back to the same page also but pass a URL parameter named `OEusername` with the value `from_username`. The final link should look like this:

```
my_messages.asp?OEusername=from_username
```

This link will pass the `from_username` column to the SQL. We need to adjust the SQL to accept this parameter. Currently the SQL for this page looks like this:

```
SELECT *
FROM usermessages
WHERE to_username = 'MMColParam'
ORDER BY viewed_status DESC
```

Variables:

```
MMColParam        x        Session("MM_Username")
```

Reload the `rsGetMessages` recordset and change this SQL to the following:

```
SELECT *
FROM usermessages
WHERE OEusername = 'MMColParam'
ORDER BY viewed_status DESC
```

Add the following variables directly below:

```
MMColParam        x              Session("MM_Username")
OEusername        to_username    Request.QueryString("OEusername")
```

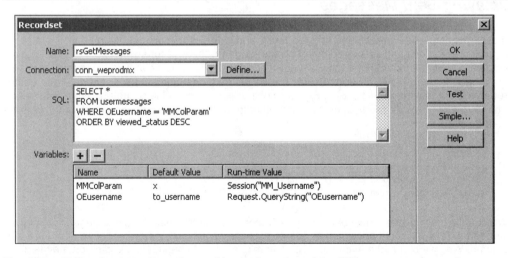

The SQL will filter for the column that resides in the value of the URL parameter named `OEusername`. Since this URL parameter won't be passed until the user selects the *SENT* link, we made the default column `to_username` so that the SQL displays messages sent to the logged-in user by default until the user chooses otherwise. If we don't add a default value the SQL may break, because it won't know which column to filter for when the page loads.

You may test the page live and everything should work fine. There is one problem, when the user selects to view a message it will go to the `view_message.asp`. You might see nothing wrong with this, but the problem is that this page allows the user to reply or even delete the message, but we don't want to allow users to delete or reply to Sent messages otherwise it would disappear from the inbox of the recipient user as well.

So, if the user selects a Sent message then we need to redirect to a page that displays the message without the ability to delete or reply. This is why I asked you earlier to save a copy of the original `view_message.asp` page named `view_sent_message.asp` before adding the reply and delete features. We should link to this page if the user is viewing Sent messages. Well, how do we know if the user is viewing Sent messages? We know by the existence of a URL parameter named `OEusername`. If it exists that means the user has selected the *SENT* link. We need to use a conditional statement to link the subject to `view_message.asp`, if the user is viewing the *INBOX* and `view_sent_message.asp` if the user is viewing the *SENT* messages. In Design View highlight the subject dynamic text that does the linking. Switch to Code View and the full link should look like this:

```
<a
href="view_message.asp?message_id=<%=(rsGetMessages.Fields.Item("message_id").Valu
e)%>"><%=(rsGetMessages.Fields.Item("subject").Value)%></a>
```

Change this entire code to the following:

```
<% If Request.QueryString("OEusername") = "" Then %>
    <a
href="view_message.asp?message_id=<%=(rsGetMessages.Fields.Item("message_id").Valu
e)%>"><%=(rsGetMessages.Fields.Item("subject").Value)%></a>
    <% Else %>
    <a
href="view_message_x.asp?message_id=<%=(rsGetMessages.Fields.Item("message_id").Va
lue)%>"><%=(rsGetMessages.Fields.Item("subject").Value)%></a>
    <% End If %>
```

The link will change depending on the existence of the `OEusername` URL parameter.

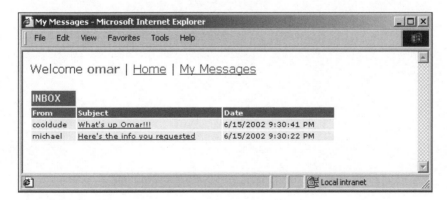

Summary

These web applications can be created in various ways and the concepts behind them can be used for other types of web applications. We have created two fabulous web applications that are often used by web developers. The concept behind the wishlist web application can be used for any other things you want to personalize for your members. It is the same concept behind many web sites like those that allow you to remember your bookmarks, articles, and so on. We added some very useful features to our e-mail message web application. With some thought you can add a lot more. By utilizing the knowledge you have gained from this chapter, explore this web application further to build your own custom features.

Index

A Guide to the Index

The index is arranged hierarchically, in alphabetical order, with symbols preceding the letter A. Most second-level entries and many third-level entries also occur as first-level entries. This is to ensure that users will find the information they require however they choose to search for it.

Notes

Notes

Notes

Notes

Notes